PSYCHOTHERAPY RESEARCH

PROCEEDINGS OF THE AMERICAN PSYCHOPATHOLOGICAL ASSOCIATION

Vol. I (33rd Meeting): *Trends of mental disease.* Joseph Zubin (Introduction), 1945.*

Vol. II (34th Meeting): *Current therapies of personality disorders.* Bernard Glueck (Ed.), 1946.

Vol. III (36th Meeting): *Epilepsy.* Paul H. Hoch and Robert P. Knight (Eds.), 1947.

Vol. IV (37th Meeting): *Failures in psychiatric treatment.* Paul H. Hoch (Ed.), 1948.

Vol. V (38th Meeting): *Psychosexual development in health and disease.* Paul H. Hoch and Joseph Zubin (Eds.), 1949.

Vol. VI (39th Meeting): *Anxiety.* Paul H. Hoch and Joseph Zubin (Eds.), 1950.

Vol. VII (40th Meeting): *Relation of psychological tests to psychiatry.* Paul H. Hoch and Joseph Zubin (Eds.), 1951.

Vol. VIII (41st Meeting): *Current problems in psychiatric diagnosis.* Paul H. Hoch and Joseph Zubin (Eds.), 1953.

Vol. IX (42nd Meeting): *Depression.* Paul H. Hoch and Joseph Zubin (Eds.), 1954.

Vol. X (43rd Meeting): *Psychiatry and the law.* Paul H. Hoch and Joseph Zubin (Eds.), 1955.

Vol. XI (44th Meeting): *Psychopathology of childhood.* Paul H. Hoch and Joseph Zubin (Eds.), 1955.

Vol. XII (45th Meeting): *Experimental psychopathology.* Paul H. Hoch and Joseph Zubin (Eds.), 1957.

Vol. XIII (46th Meeting): *Psychopathology of communication.* Paul H. Hoch and Joseph Zubin (Eds.), 1958.

Vol. XIV (47th Meeting): *Problems of addiction and habituation.* Paul H. Hoch and Joseph Zubin (Eds.), 1958.

Vol. XV (48th Meeting): *Current approaches to psychoanalysis.* Paul H. Hoch and Joseph Zubin (Eds.), 1960.

Vol. XVI (49th Meeting): *Comparative epidemiology of the mental disorders.* Paul H. Hoch and Joseph Zubin (Eds.), 1961.

Vol. XVII (50th Meeting): *Psychopathology of aging.* Paul H. Hoch and Joseph Zubin (Eds.), 1961.

Vol. XVIII (51st Meeting): *The future of psychiatry.* Paul H. Hoch and Joseph Zubin (Eds.), 1962.

Vol. XIX (52nd Meeting): *The evaluation of psychiatric treatment.* Paul H. Hoch and Joseph Zubin (Eds.), 1964.

*This volume was published by King's Crown Press (Columbia University). Volumes II through XXVI were published by Grune & Stratton. Volumes XXVII through XXXI were published by The Johns Hopkins University Press. Volumes XXX through XXXIX were published by Raven Press.

Psychotherapy Research:
Where Are We and Where Should We Go?

Edited by Janet B. W. Williams and
Robert L. Spitzer

PROCEEDINGS OF THE 73RD ANNUAL
MEETING OF THE AMERICAN
PSYCHOPATHOLOGICAL ASSOCIATION,
NEW YORK CITY, MARCH 3–5, 1983

THE GUILFORD PRESS
New York   London

Printed in the United States of America

LIBRARY OF CONGRESS CATALOGING IN PUBLICATION DATA
American Psychopathological Association. Meeting
  (73rd : 1983 : New York, N.Y.)
  Psychotherapy research.

  Includes indexes.
    1. Psychotherapy—Congresses.   2. Psychotherapy—
Research—Congresses.   I. Williams, Janet B. W.,
1947–   . II. Spitzer, Robert L.   III. Title.
[DNLM: 1. Psychotherapy—Congresses.   2. Research—
Congresses. W3 AM 632 73rd 1983p / WM 420 A512 1983p]
RC475.5.A49   1984   616.89′14   83-26660
ISBN 0-89862-635-8

Preface

This book reflects the excitement and sense of urgency that now characterize the field of psychotherapy research. The excitement results from recent methodological advances in the standardization of psychotherapy techniques and in the diagnostic characterization of patient samples, and from the findings of controlled studies that demonstrate the efficacy of certain forms of psychotherapy for certain patient groups. The sense of urgency stems from pressure from government and private reimbursement agencies for evidence of the efficacy of the psychotherapies whose increasing costs they are asked to pay.

The chapters of this volume, originally presented at the Seventy-third Annual Meeting of the American Psychopathological Association, are divided into five sections. The first section reviews the evidence for the efficacy of psychotherapy for several mental disorder categories that have been the focus of much recent psychotherapy research: conduct disorder, anxiety disorder, depression, and schizophrenia. This section concludes with a chapter by Dr. Aaron T. Beck, the recipient of the Paul Hoch Award, in which he discusses the integration of cognitive therapy, behavior therapy, psychoanalysis, and pharmacotherapy.

In Section II, participants in the NIMH Treatment of Depression Collaborative Research Program describe how the treatment variables (cognitive therapy, interpersonal therapy, and pharmacotherapy) have been standardized and monitored. Section III includes chapters from the principal investigators of five major psychotherapy studies of the past. They each summarize the findings from their studies and the implications for designing future psychotherapy research. This section concludes with Dr. Robert L. Spitzer's Presidential Address in which he suggests that, despite new developments in standardized diagnostic interviews that allow lay interviewers to conduct such interviews, the clinical approach to diagnostic assessment is still optimal.

In Section IV contrasting viewpoints about the adequacy of the evidence for the efficacy and specificity of psychotherapy are presented, as well as a discussion of the advantages and limitations of meta-analysis for providing data to answer the relevant questions. The final section consists of a panel in which the participants each present a position paper about public policy toward reimbursement for psychotherapy.

We hope the reader will, by reading edited portions of the audience discussion that followed each paper and each session, have a greater appreciation for the complex issues addressed at this meeting.

J. B. W. W.
R. L. S.

Contents

SECTION III. "IF ONLY WE KNEW THEN WHAT WE KNOW NOW": STRATEGIES OF
PSYCHOTHERAPY RESEARCH—LESSONS FROM THE PAST FOR THE FUTURE

SECTION IV. "THE BOTTOM LINE": INTEGRATING PSYCHOTHERAPY RESEARCH
FINDINGS—HOW GOOD IS THE EVIDENCE FOR EFFICACY AND SPECIFICITY?

SECTION V. "THE BUCK STOPS HERE": PSYCHOTHERAPY AND PUBLIC POLICY WHEN THE EVIDENCE IS NOT ALL IN

PSYCHOTHERAPY RESEARCH

"WHAT WORKS WITH WHAT?": PSYCHOTHERAPY EFFICACY FOR SPECIFIC DISORDERS— AN OVERVIEW OF THE RESEARCH

1

Treatment of Conduct Disorders

ALAN E. KAZDIN
Western Psychiatric Institute and Clinic,
University of Pittsburgh School of Medicine

INTRODUCTION

Definition and Diagnosis

Antisocial behavior among children and adolescents is a well-recognized clinical phenomenon. Several labels have been used such as acting-out behaviors, conduct problems, externalizing behavior, and others to denote the problem. They encompass a variety of behaviors such as aggression against persons or property, truancy, stealing, lying, disobedience, and so on. The severity of the dysfunction can vary markedly as a function of the specific behaviors and their combination, their duration and severity, and the problems of social adjustment that they may cause (e.g., expulsion from school or one's home). Considering any one of these dimensions reveals the range of dysfunction that may be evident.

There is general agreement over the constellation of symptoms defining antisocial behavior. Both descriptive and multivariate approaches to childhood taxonomy reveal a syndrome including aggression, defiance, and oppositionalism (Achenbach & Edelbrock, 1978; American Psychiatric Association [APA], 1980; Quay, 1979; Rutter, Shaffer, & Shepherd, 1975). In the *Diagnostic and Statistical Manual of Mental Disorders* (DSM-III) (APA, 1980), the constellation is defined as conduct disorder and refers to a repetitive and persistent pattern of conduct (of at least 6 months' duration) in which either the basic rights of others or major age-appropriate societal norms or rules are violated. Four subtypes are delineated: aggressive or nonaggressive behavior, and socialized or undersocialized behavior. Aggressive subtypes include children whose problems include physical violence against other persons or properties or aggressive confrontations (e.g., in a robbery); nonaggressive include other behaviors such as persistent stealing, running away, fire setting, lying, and truancy. Socialized subtypes refer to

3

children who have peer-group friendships, exhibit concern for others, and show remorse, as distinguished from children who do not have these characteristics (undersocialized).[1]

Significance of the Problem

Several areas of research attest to the significance of conduct disorder as a clinical and social problem. To begin with, epidemiological research has shown that among childhood problems, the prevalence of antisocial behaviors is relatively high. The prevalence of conduct disorder is difficult to pinpoint exactly because of the multiple terms and criteria used over the years in identifying persons with antisocial behavior and also because of variations in child ages and geographical locales. In the Isle of Wight study of rural children ages 10–11 years, 4% of the children were found to show symptoms of conduct disorder. However, the rate was approximately twice that high in the study of an urban area (London) (Rutter, Cox, Tupling, Berger, & Yule, 1975). Boys have been consistently found to be more likely than girls to engage in antisocial behavior. The precise ratio has varied across studies in part because of different criteria to delineate children as antisocial. Also, the ratio of antisocial boys to antisocial girls may vary as a function of age, since the onset of the behaviors tends to be later in girls than in boys (Robins, 1966). Nevertheless, antisocial behavior is at least three times more common among boys (Graham, 1979).

Aggressiveness, conduct disorder, and antisocial behavior represent the most frequent referral problems for outpatient clinics; they encompass from one-third to one-half of referrals (Gilbert, 1957; Herbert, 1978; Robins, 1981). Even so, the number of cases identified for treatment probably grossly underestimates the extent of the problem (Robins, 1974). Many children with antisocial behavior come into contact with the police and courts rather than with psychiatric facilities. In schools these children initially may be identified as underachievers with learning disabilities because of their problems in academic areas, and some of them are diagnosed as merely hyper-

---

1. The diagnosis of conduct disorder depends on several other conditions. As already noted, the diagnosis requires that severe problems of conduct be evident for at least 6 months. Isolated acts of antisocial behavior that are not persistent are delineated as childhood or adolescent antisocial behavior (*V* code). With conduct disorder, the pattern is not only persistent but is also associated with impairment in social and school functioning. The diagnosis usually is reserved for children and adolescents (18 years old or younger). If the pattern of conduct disorder begins in childhood (before age 15 years) but continues into adolescence and adulthood, the diagnosis of antisocial personality disorder is made. The latter diagnosis is reserved for persons over 18 years old whose conduct disorder has continued. The diagnosis of conduct disorder is also important to distinguish from oppositional disorder in which less severe acting-out behaviors appear (e.g., disobedience, negativism, provocation). In oppositional disorder, the child does not evince serious norm violation to the extent required for conduct disorder.

active. Of course, not all children who are diagnosed as hyperactive or who have academic problems in school would be considered as having conduct disorders. Yet the overlap is sufficiently great to obscure the rates of children who would be diagnosed as antisocial.

The significance of conduct disorder is attested by several factors other than its relatively high prevalence. Among the many childhood disorders, antisocial behaviors tend to be relatively stable over time (Graham & Rutter, 1973; Olweus, 1979; Robins, 1966). The stability of conduct problems departs from other disorders that often are age-specific (e.g., many fears). Second, antisocial behaviors portend other problems of adulthood including psychoses, alcoholism, and criminal behavior (e.g., Robins, 1979; Wolfgang, Figlio, & Sellin, 1972). Apart from specific psychiatric or legal complications in adulthood, personal maladjustment and dissatisfaction in everyday interpersonal situations are more likely among persons with a history of conduct disorder. Third, the long-term effects of severe antisocial behavior have untoward consequences not only for the persons themselves but also for their children (Robins, 1981). Males with conduct problems father as many children as other men (despite their higher rates of marital disruption), and their children have increased risks for childhood deviance and antisocial behavior. Finally, and perhaps obviously, many of the problems encompassed by conduct disorder can have serious untoward consequences for innocent victims. Serious aggressive behavior and antisocial acts against persons and/or property (e.g., fire setting) can result directly in injury and fatalities to others.

From a clinical perspective, the prevalence, persistence, and prognosis of conduct problems make identification of effective treatment an especially important area for investigation. From a social perspective, treatment for conduct problems is also critical because antisocial behavior may be the most costly of childhood disorders to society (Robins, 1981). Because a significant proportion of severely aggressive children eventually come into contact with adult mental and criminal justice systems, the monetary costs of managing or containing the persons as adults are high.

ALTERNATIVE TREATMENTS

Overview

Given the prevalence of children with antisocial behavior and their frequent referral to clinics, they are prime candidates for treatment research. In fact, there is a paucity of treatment studies with conduct disorder children. In clinical lore, it is widely acknowledged that antisocial children and their families are not the most rewarding group to work with. Also, insight-

oriented therapy, to which most clinics are devoted, is not readily administered to this group. Nevertheless, the paucity of data in child treatment is not
restricted to conduct disorder children. Outcome research with disorders of
childhood and adolescence is sparse in general (Barrett, Hampe, & Miller,
1978; Hartmann, Roper, & Gelfand, 1977).

Several treatments have been proposed and implemented for antisocial behavior including diverse forms of individual and group counseling,
psychotherapy and behavior therapy, pharmacotherapy, residential treatment, and psychosurgery (for recent reviews see Campbell, Cohen, &
Small, 1982; Kazdin & Frame, 1983; Morrison, 1981). It is fair to state
that no treatment has been clearly shown to ameliorate the disorder and
to circumvent the untoward consequences to which it often leads. Yet it
is important to note that a few techniques have been carefully investigated
in controlled trials. Among psychosocial interventions, two promising techniques have recently emerged. These techniques, referred to as parent management training and cognitive therapy, warrant elaboration because they
point to the types of advances that are being made in the treatment of
conduct problem children, the limitations of current treatment, and issues
for future research.

Parent Management Training

Background and Underlying Rationale. Parent management training
refers to procedures in which parents are trained to alter their child's
behavior in the home. The parents meet with a therapist or trainer who
teaches them to use a variety of specific procedures to alter their interaction
with their child, to promote prosocial behavior, and to decrease deviant
behavior. Training is based on the general view that conduct problem behaviors is inadvertently developed and sustained in the home by maladaptive child–parent interactions. Altering these interaction patterns can
decrease antisocial child behavior.

Patterson (1976, 1980, 1982) has developed a theoretical framework
based on supporting research to explain specific interaction patterns that lead
to the development of antisocial behavior in the home. Patterson refers to
his view as *coercion theory.* Coercion is defined as a type of interpersonal
interaction in which deviant behavior of one person (e.g., the child) is
supported or directly reinforced by the other person (e.g., the parent). The
notion of coercion is designed to explain a particular type of interaction
pattern often referred to as a "reinforcement trap." Deviant behavior performed by a child directed toward his or her parent—usually the mother—
may be reinforced (rewarded) when the parent gives in or complies. The
"trap" is that the parent may yield to end the child's aversive behavior (e.g.,

tantrum) in the short run but inadvertently increases the likelihood that the behavior will recur in the future.

From the standpoint of the child, *positive reinforcement*—compliance on the part of the parent—has been provided for aversive behavior. Thus, the aversive behavior is likely to increase in the future. From the standpoint of the parent, *negative reinforcement* is operative. The aversive behavior of the child is terminated when the parent complies with the request. Termination of the aversive event increases the likelihood that the parent will comply in the future. The fact that aversive child behavior will increase in the long run has little or no impact on the parent because of the immediate effects that compliance has on terminating the child's aversive behavior.

A critical issue of coercion theory is how coercive child behaviors emerge to begin with and how they escalate to the level of severity seen in antisocial children. Apart from any heredity influences, children have many opportunities to learn aggressive interpersonal behaviors in the home. Parents of antisocial children tend to use harsh and inconsistent discipline and have a relatively high proportion of child abuse (Farrington, 1978; Hetherington & Martin, 1979; Reid, Taplin, & Loeber, 1981). Thus, the child witnesses the use of physical aggression and its effects on the victim. Perhaps as important, research has shown that parents directly reinforce deviant child behavior by their attention to aggression and their compliance with increasingly severe child coercive behaviors, and fail to reinforce prosocial behavior (Patterson, 1982).

Coercion theory and its supporting research cannot be developed fully here. Suffice it to say that the characteristics of family interaction that directly promote antisocial behavior have been reasonably well documented (see Patterson, 1982). For present purposes, the critical feature to note is that the findings have served as the basis for developing effective treatment— namely, parent management training. The general purpose of parent management training is to alter the pattern of interchanges between parent and child so that prosocial rather than coercive behavior is directly reinforced and supported within the family. Parents of aggressive children are less effective in their parenting skills than are parents of normal children. Family interaction can serve as the vehicle for altering child behavior. The key agent is the mother, given her frequent interaction with the child and her likely role as a victim in the coercive interchanges (Patterson, 1980). Also, the coercive interchanges need to be focused on directly in training because of their tendency to escalate until the child's deviant behavior is reinforced. The mother's use of punishment despite (or because of) its relatively high frequency is usually ineffective in suppressing behavior. Consequently, a pivotal feature of treatment is to train parents how to punish more effectively. This does *not* amount to punishing more often or more severely. Punishment needs to stop deviant child behavior quickly to avoid the escalation of coercive behavior. The consistent application of nonviolent forms of punishment occupies an important role in parent management training.

Punishment is by no means the only focus. Effective child rearing requires a more general restructuring of the interaction between parent and child to support prosocial behavior and to suppress antisocial behavior. This requires the development of several different parenting behaviors such as establishing rules for the child to follow, providing positive reinforcement for appropriate behavior, delivering nonviolent punishment when called for, solving problems, and negotiating compromises.

Characteristics of Treatment. Parent management training programs train parents to implement specific procedures in the home. Among the many different programs that exist, several commonalities can be identified. First, and certainly the most obvious, the contact between the therapist and the child is minimal. Treatment is achieved primarily through the parents, who directly implement several procedures they learn in therapy. The child may be seen as part of an initial interview or observed while interacting with the parents at the clinic or in the home. However, there is usually no direct intervention of the therapist with the child.

Second, training usually includes didactic instruction in social learning principles. These principles include concepts from operant conditioning such as reinforcement, punishment, and extinction as they apply to social interaction in the home and everyday situations.

Third, parents are trained to identify, define, and observe problem behavior in new ways. The identification and definition of problem behavior focus on careful descriptions of behavioral problems in terms as objective and descriptive as possible. The careful specification of the problem is essential for the delivery of reinforcing or punishing consequences for specific behaviors and for evaluating if the program is working. Once behaviors are well specified, they are observed for a portion of the day in the home by the parents daily or almost daily. The evaluation of problem behavior in the home is central to most training programs and precedes implementing special intervention techniques.

Fourth, the treatment sessions cover the concepts and procedures of several content areas. Considerable time is devoted to positive reinforcement in which the use of praise, attention, and tokens or points is incorporated in a program to follow prosocial behavior. Punishment is also covered, especially the use of time out from reinforcement, loss of privileges, and loss of tokens. Contingency contracting is often covered and includes the identification of behaviors the child and parents agree to perform in the home and the rewards and sanctions that follow performance or nonperformance of the behaviors. With each of these procedures, the focus is on training parents how to apply procedures in the home.

Fifth, the sessions provide opportunities for parents to see how the techniques are implemented and to practice using the techniques. To develop the skills in the parents, the therapist uses instructions, modeling, role playing, and rehearsal. Also, treatment sessions usually review the behavior change program that is implemented in the home over the course of the previous week. Problems, changes, and refinements in the program are discussed.

The immediate goal of the program is to develop specific skills in the parents. This is usually achieved by having parents apply their skills to relatively simple behaviors that can be easily observed and that are not enmeshed with more provoking interactions (e.g., punishment, battles of the will, coercive interchanges). Also, an initial purpose is to help parents reestablish control over child behavior in the home. As the parents become more proficient, the focus of the program can address the child's most problematic behaviors and encompass other problem areas, such as behavior in school.

Overview of the Outcome Evidence. Parent management training has been evaluated in hundreds of studies with behavior problem children varying in age and degree of severity of dysfunction (Conger, 1981; Forehand & Atkeson, 1977; Patterson & Fleischman, 1979). The work of Patterson and his colleagues, which has spanned almost two decades, exemplifies the outcome research on parent training. Over 200 families have been seen that include primarily aggressive children (ages 3 to 12 years) referred for outpatient treatment (see Patterson, 1982). Approximately 50% of the children also engage in truancy, stealing, and fire setting. The effectiveness of treatment has been evaluated in parental and teacher reports of deviant behavior and by direct observation of the child's behavior at home and at school. Several studies have revealed marked changes over the course of treatment and have indicated that the changes surpass those achieved with variations of family-based psychotherapy, attention placebo (discussion), and no-treatment conditions (Patterson, 1974; Patterson, Chamberlain, & Reid, 1982; Walters & Gilmore, 1973; Wiltz & Patterson, 1974). Follow-up assessment has shown that the gains are often maintained 1 year after treatment, a finding that has been replicated (Fleischman, 1981; Fleischman & Szykula, 1981). Other programs of research have also demonstrated the effectiveness of parent management training in controlled studies (e.g., Forehand & McMahon, 1981; Wahler, Leske, & Rogers, 1979), with follow-up data showing the continued benefits of treatment up to 4.5 years (Baum & Forehand, 1981).

Outcome studies, naturally, have focused on the impact of treatment on the specific behaviors of the child referred for treatment. However, research has suggested that the impact of treatment is relatively broad. To begin with, the effects of treatment are evident for behaviors that have not been focused on directly as part of training (e.g., Patterson, 1974; Wells, Forehand, & Griest, 1980). Also, the deviant behaviors of siblings, who are at risk for conduct disorder, improves even though they are not directly focused on in treatment (Humphreys, Forehand, McMahon, & Roberts, 1978; Lavigueur, Peterson, Sheese, & Peterson, 1973). Improvements in the siblings are also maintained over the course of follow-up (Arnold, Levine, & Patterson, 1975). In addition, maternal psychopathology, particularly depression, has been shown to decrease systematically following present management training (Eyberg & Robinson, 1982; Forehand, Wells, & Griest, 1980; Patterson & Fleischman, 1979). These changes suggest that the focus on family interaction patterns can affect multiple aspects of dysfunctional families.

Factors That Contribute to Outcome. Parent management training has been very effective in some treatment applications but has exerted little or no impact in others. The reasons are difficult to identify because of the heterogeneity of training programs. For example, programs vary widely in their duration (e.g., from 5 to over 50 hours of treatment), in whether home and school behaviors are incorporated into the program, in the severity of child and family dysfunction, and in other factors. Time-limited programs that provide prespecified but limited treatment regimens have frequently failed to show the benefits of treatment (e.g., Bernal, Klinnert, & Schultz, 1980; Eyberg & Johnson, 1974; Ferber, Keeley, & Shemberg, 1974).

Parent and family characteristics that relate to treatment outcome have been studied. As might be expected, families characterized by many risk factors associated with childhood dysfunction (e.g., father absent, low socioeconomic status, marital discord, parent psychopathology) tend to show fewer gains in treatment than families without these risk factors (Patterson, 1974; Reisinger, Frangia, & Hoffman, 1976; Strain, Young, & Horowitz, 1981). Moreover, gains achieved in treatment are unlikely to be maintained in families with socioeconomic disadvantage (Dumas & Wahler, 1983).

Wahler and his colleagues (Dumas & Wahler, 1983; Wahler & Afton, 1980; Wahler et al., 1979) have shown that the mother's social support system outside of the home contributes to the efficacy of parent management training. Mothers who are insulated from social supports outside the home, those who have few positive social contacts with relatives and friends, fail to profit from treatment. Moreover, the nature of the social contacts mothers experience outside the home on a daily basis has direct impact on parent–child interactions and deviant child behavior. This work has suggested that variables beyond the specific parent–child interactions need to be incorporated into treatment. Indeed, recent work indicates that parent management training that addresses many of the problems of families (e.g., parental adjustment, marital adjustment, and extrafamilial relations) surpasses the effects of parent management training alone (Griest, Forehand, Rogers, Breiner, Furey, & Williams, 1982).

Issues and Limitations. Parent management training makes several demands on the parents that raise important issues. Parents may be required to master educational materials that convey major principles underlying the program, conduct observations of deviant child behavior at home, and implement several specific procedures at home with their child. Also, parents need to attend individual sessions, usually on a weekly basis that may extend to several months, and respond to frequent telephone contacts made by the therapist or other persons from the clinic who make requests for specific information about the child's behavior or to check on how the program is going. In some programs, an additional demand may include sending observers to the home for several consecutive days before and immediately after treatment and over the course of follow-up to assess child behavior directly. In short, among alternative treatments for antisocial behavior, the demands made on the parents are relatively great.

The demands may influence who agrees to participate in the program to begin with and who remains in the treatment once the program starts. Parent attrition has varied across treatment reports but typically falls somewhere between 17% and 32% (Eyberg & Johnson, 1974; McMahon, Forehand, Griest, & Wells, 1981; Patterson & Fleischman, 1979). Parents who are likely to drop out of treatment tend to be relatively low in socioeconomic status and relatively high in depression, and tend to have been referred to treatment from external sources rather than self-referred (McMahon *et al.*, 1981; Worland, Carney, Weinberg, & Milich, 1982).

Even if parents do not drop out, they may differ greatly in the extent to which they comply with the demands of treatment such as completing the reading assignments or conducting the observations of the child's behavior at home. Applying rewarding consequences or making further progress in treatment contingent on specific parent behaviors has been shown to improve parent adherence to the program. For example, in one investigation, returning portions of a refundable deposit, engaging in phone calls with parents, and conducting a treatment session depended on the parents' completing their assigned tasks (e.g., conducting observations at home and bringing in the information) (Eyberg & Johnson, 1974). Parents exposed to this regimen, when compared to those who completed training without these contingencies, completed more of their assigned tasks, were rated by their therapists as more cooperative, and were able to treat a larger number of problem child behaviors over the course of treatment. Thus, it is possible to increase parent adherence to the requirements of the program, and increased adherence may have important clinical implications.

For some families, the demands of treatment may be too great to make parent management training a viable option. In other cases, parents may express unwillingness to participate in treatment in behalf of their child or decline the option given the many other stressors (e.g., marital discord), demands (e.g., employment, care of a sick relative), or personal dysfunction (e.g., parent psychopathology). Consequently, in instances in which the child might be a candidate for this form of treatment, a parent may be unavailable. The proportion of cases of conduct disorder children in which parents are not available for treatment has not been systematically investigated.

Outcome of parent management training usually involves several different measures including direct observation of child and parent behavior in the home, parent and/or teacher reports of deviant child behaviors, and global ratings. Emphasis is placed on direct observations of behavior in the home, because these reflect most clearly the effects of treatment. In many ways, the measurement of treatment outcome in parent management training has surpassed the evaluation standards of other techniques because of the multiple assessment methods and use of multiple perspectives (teachers, parents, clinicians). Moreover, in several investigations the impact of treatment is evaluated by assessing whether deviant behavior of the treated children falls within normative levels of their peers who are functioning adequately (Eyberg & Johnson, 1974; Patterson, 1974; Wells *et al.*, 1980).

Despite the positive assessment features, important outcome issues remain to be addressed. First, the assessment methods have been directed to relatively high frequency problem behaviors such as noncompliance and verbal and physical aggression in the home. Many behaviors of conduct disorder children are of high intensity but low frequency (e.g., stealing, acts of cruelty, fire setting). Evaluation of the treatment effects on these behaviors is difficult. Occasionally children may fail to show improvements from parent management training in part because the actual frequency of their deviant behaviors was low to begin with (see Patterson, 1982). Many of the measures of direct behavior used to evaluate parent management are composite scores of several deviant behaviors. So the problem of low frequency of individual behaviors may be circumvented for purposes of evaluation by being combined with other behaviors. Yet the difficulties of evaluating parent management training or other treatments with low frequency problems warrants mention.

A second issue pertains to the type of measures that need to be included in parent management training programs. Parent and teacher ratings and direct observations are important but leave many questions unanswered. The effects of treatment on measures of social functioning need to be incorporated into the programs. For example, contacts with the police or courts or other mental health services, school attendance, grades, graduation from high school, and similar measures need to be added to evaluate if treatment is to have an impact on measures of social functioning over the course of childhood, adolescence, and adulthood. It is possible that dramatic changes are achieved in overt behaviors and parent ratings but that other measures of social impact do not reflect these changes (see Kirigin, Braukmann, Atwater, & Wolf, 1982). The social impact of treatment needs to be assessed more fully in parent management training.

Overall Evaluation. Several features of parent management training make it one of the more promising treatments for conduct disorders. First, the treatment has been shown to be effective with conduct problem children varying in severity of clinical dysfunction. Treatment effects have been demonstrated on behavior changes in the home and at school, and these effects have been shown to be maintained up to 1 year and occasionally longer. Moreover, changes at home and at school have been shown to bring deviant behavior of treated children within the range of that of children functioning normally. In many cases, the effects of training have varied as a function of parent and family characteristics. Little or no change has been evident in families with severe dysfunction and socioeconomic disadvantage. However, the findings have not shown that treatment is invariably ineffective with such families.

Second, the benefits of treatment are often broad and extend beyond the target child. For example, siblings of the target child have been shown to profit from parent management training. This may be a unique advantage of parent management training among alternative treatments for conduct problem children. Since siblings are also likely to be at risk for antisocial behavior, this benefit of treatment should not be looked upon lightly.

Third, along with outcome investigations, basic research has been conducted on family interaction patterns and influences outside of the home that may affect treatment outcome. Basic research of this sort is likely not only to contribute directly to improved treatment outcomes, but also to yield greater understanding of the emergence of antisocial behavior. Thus, parent management training has developed a research base for developing and improving treatment.

Fourth, a major advantage is the availability of treatment manuals and training materials for parents and professional therapists (see Ollendick & Cerny, 1981, for a list). These materials encompass programs for antisocial, mentally retarded, physically handicapped, and autistic children as well as normal children whose problems are relatively minor by comparison. The extensive materials make this modality of treatment potentially widely available.

Several limitations of parent management training can be identified as well. As already noted, some families may not respond to parent management training as currently practiced. Explicit procedures may need to be included in treatment that address family and parent problems that influence the outcome of parent management training. Perhaps even more significant, for many antisocial children, parent management training is simply not a viable option. Some parents cannot participate because of their own dysfunction; others will not participate because they feel they have reached their limits in trying to help their child or because they cannot meet the many demands of treatment. Finally, for some antisocial children, there is no parent available because the child has to be removed from the home owing to neglect or abuse.

Many questions about the effects of parent management training remain to be addressed. In particular, the child, parent, and family characteristics that influence outcome warrant much further elaboration. For example, few reports have included antisocial adolescents. This population may be less readily influenced by the consequences of reward and punishment that parents can apply in the home. Also, different types of antisocial children may not respond equally well to treatment. For example, preliminary evidence suggests that aggressive children respond better than do children whose problems are primarily nonaggressive (e.g., stealing, truancy) (Patterson, 1982). The interaction of treatment with child and family characteristics needs to be investigated more systematically.

On balance, parent management training is one of the most promising treatment modalities investigated to date. No other intervention for antisocial children has been investigated so thoroughly as parent management training and has shown as favorable results. Few comparative investigations have examined the efficacy of parent management relative to other viable alternatives. The difficulty at this point is that few viable alternatives with demonstrated efficacy have been established to the point of parent management training.

Cognitive (Problem-Solving) Therapy

Background and Underlying Rationale. Cognitive therapy focuses on the child's cognitive processes that are presumed to underlie maladaptive behavior. The cognitive processes that serve as the focus of change may include perceptions, self-statements, attributions, expectations, strategies, and problem-solving skills. The assumption of cognitive therapy is that children with deviant behavior suffer a deficiency in particular processes, or an inability to use or apply cognitive skills.

At present it is premature to provide a complete account of cognitive processes that emerge as part of normal development and their aberrations that result in deviant behavior. However, research has progressed by showing that maladjusted children vary in diverse processes including perceptions of social situations, thought processes, and problem-solving skills. For illustrative purposes, selected findings can be only highlighted here.

Cognitive processes have been frequently accorded a major role in conduct problems such as aggressive behavior (Berkowitz, 1977; Novaco, 1978). Aggression is not merely triggered by environmental events but is the result of how these events are perceived and processed. The processing refers to the child's appraisals of the situation, anticipated reactions of others, and statements in response to particular environmental events. Psychiatric inpatient children and school children identified as aggressive have shown a predisposition to attribute hostile intent to others, especially in social situations where the cues of actual intent are ambiguous (Dodge, 1980; Nasby, Hayden, & DePaulo, 1980). Understandably, when situations are initially perceived as hostile, children are more likely to react aggressively (Deluty, 1981).

The ability to take the perspective of, or to empathize with, other persons has also been shown to relate to aggressive behavior. Among delinquents, for example, those who are aggressive (i.e., have committed acts against other persons or property) are less empathic than nonaggressive delinquents (Aleksic, 1976; Ellis, 1982). The ability to take the perspective of others appears to increase with age among normal children and adolescents and to be inversely related to the expression of aggression (Feshbach, 1975).

Reflection–impulsivity (Kagan, 1966) is a general cognitive style that has been associated with maladaptive behavior including aggression. Impulsive children tend to respond quickly and to make many errors on tasks; reflective children tend to delay responding, to consider alternatives, and to make fewer errors. A relationship has been found between impulsivity and diverse childhood problems including acting out, aggressive behavior, inattentiveness, overactivity, brain damage, and learning problems (Messer, 1976; Messer & Brodzinsky, 1979). Impulsive children also tend to utilize more self-stimulatory speech in play situations (e.g., word play, repetitive use of words), whereas reflective children tend to use speech that regulates performance (e.g., self-instructions that guide behavior) (Meichenbaum, 1977). More specific tests with aggressive children (6–8 years old) have shown that they respond impulsively and use self-guiding verbalizations less frequently and their self-verbalizations are less likely to control their overt behavior than nonaggressive children (Camp, 1977). Thus, reflection–impulsivity is related to other cognitive processes such as self-regulatory speech.

The relationship between cognitive processes and behavioral adjustment has been evaluated extensively by Spivack, Shure, and their colleagues (Shure & Spivack, 1978; Spivack, Platt, & Shure, 1976; Spivack & Shure, 1974). These investigators have identified different cognitive processes or interpersonal cognitive problem-solving skills that underlie social behavior. These processes include:

1. Alternative Solution Thinking—the ability to generate different operations (solutions) that can solve problems in interpersonal situations.

2. Means–Ends Thinking—awareness of the intermediate steps required to achieve a particular goal.

3. Consequential Thinking—the ability to identify what might happen as a direct result of acting in a particular way or choosing a particular solution.

4. Causal Thinking—the ability to relate one event to another over time and to understand why one event led to a particular action of other persons.

5. Sensitivity to Interpersonal Problems—the ability to perceive a problem when it exists and to identify the interpersonal aspects of the confrontation that may emerge.

These processes are assessed by presenting the child with hypothetical interpersonal problems (e.g., getting one's toy back from a sibling, entering a game that one's peers are already playing) and asking the child how many different ways the goal could be achieved, the consequences of particular actions, and so on (see Kendall, Pellegrini, & Urbain, 1981).

Ability to engage in the above problem-solving steps is related to behavioral adjustment, as measured in teacher ratings of acting out behavior and social withdrawal in children. Disturbed children tend to generate fewer alternative solutions to interpersonal problems, to focus on ends or goals rather than the intermediate steps to obtain them, to see fewer consequences associated with their behavior, to fail to recognize the causes of other people's behavior, and to be less sensitive to interpersonal conflict arising in the behaviors of others (Spivack et al., 1976). Several studies have shown that deficits in problem-solving skills and the relation of these deficits to maladaptive behavior cannot be accounted for by such other variables as socioeconomic class, intelligence, gender, or ability to comprehend social situations.

Overall, the research has shown that children with behavioral problems suffer deficits in problem-solving skills. This research, by itself, does not show that maladaptive cognitions are causally related to deviant behaviors. However, several studies have shown that training children to engage in specific problem-solving skills improves classroom performance and social behavior (Spivack et al., 1976).

Characteristics of Treatment. Many variations of cognitive therapy have emerged for conduct problem children (Camp & Bash, 1978; Meichenbaum, 1977; Spivack et al., 1976; Urbain & Kendall, 1980). The variations share many characteristics. First, the emphasis is on *how* the child approaches situations. Although it is obviously important that the child ultimately select appropriate means of behaving in everyday life, the primary focus is on the thought *processes* rather than the *outcome* or specific behavioral acts that result. Therapy can never anticipate all of the situations to which the child will be exposed. Yet, if the child masters the process of problem solving, he or she is likely to be equipped to handle new situations that arise.

Second, the treatment attempts to teach the child to engage in a step-by-step approach to solve problems. The method is usually achieved by having the child make statements (self-instructions) to himself or herself that direct attention to certain aspects of the problem or tasks that lead to effective solutions. Thus, the approach tends to be very methodical both in the means that are used in training and the ends toward which they are directed.

Third, treatment utilizes structured tasks involving games, academic activities, stories, or, for young children, even puppets. The tasks provide the opportunity to apply the particular processes or steps. Over the course of treatment, specific tasks continue to be used but are more likely to consist of vignettes involving interpersonal situations. By the end of treatment, the cognitive problem-solving skills are applied to real-life situations.

Fourth, the therapist usually plays an active role in treatment. He or she models the cognitive processes by making verbal self-statements, applies the sequence of statements to particular problems, provides cues to the child to prompt use of the skills, and delivers feedback and praise to develop correct use of the skills. Finally, treatment usually involves the combination of several different procedures. Modeling the use of problem-solving skills or self-instructions on the part of the therapist was already mentioned. Modeling is likely to be followed with practice and role playing on the part of the child, the application of reinforcement and mild punishment (loss of points or tokens) by the therapist, and so on. The various techniques that are used in treatment are all directed to the aim of developing use of the problem-solving and self-instructional steps rather than to alter the clinically relevant behaviors directly.

The training program developed by Spivack and Shure (Shure & Spivack, 1978; Spivack *et al.*, 1976) nicely illustrates the thrust and focus of cognitive therapy. Treatment is designed to overcome deficits in specific problem-solving skills, outlined earlier. The child is instructed to think outloud and to ask himself or herself such questions as: (1) What is my problem? (2) What am I supposed to do? (3) What is my plan? and (4) How do I do it? After each question, the child states the answers to himself or herself and thus approaches the particular task or problem in a systematic step-by-step fashion. The child is encouraged to engage in a self-dialogue while actually doing the task. Early tasks are impersonal in nature (e.g., drawing lines, completing mazes) in that they do not identify situations where interpersonal problems may arise. Over the course of treatment, interpersonal situations are presented. The child is prompted to generate solutions, to identify consequences of what would happen if different courses of action were selected, to characterize the feelings of others, and so on. The emphasis is on the process such as generating many different alternative ways of responding and their consequences rather than merely selecting particular ways of responding.

Outcome Evidence. Several outcome studies have examined variations of cognitively based therapies with children. Most of the investigations have evaluated the impact of training on cognitive processes and laboratory-task performance (e.g., to measure impulsivity) rather than deviant child behavior (see Abikoff, 1979; Cole & Kazdin, 1980; Kazdin, 1982; Urbain & Kendall, 1980). As a conspicuous exception, Spivack and Shure have demonstrated with different age groups that developing interpersonal problem-solving skills leads to improved ratings of behavioral adjustment in the classroom as well as increased interpersonal attributes such as popularity and likability (see Spivack *et al.*, 1976). For example, in one of the early studies, preschool children were exposed to 46 daily sessions (20–30 minutes in length) of problem-solving training in class that involved various activities and games conducted by the teacher (Spivack & Shure, 1974). The program emphasized generating solutions to interpersonal problems, enumerating consequences, and pairing solutions with consequences. Trained children improved relative to no-treatment control children on problem-solving skills but also in teacher ratings of behavioral adjustment. Improvements in ratings of adjustment were also evident 1 year later when new teachers rated the children.

In other studies emerging from this research program, training has improved problem-solving skills and ratings of classroom adjustment (Spivack *et al.*, 1976). Typically, these studies have involved normal children who display varying degrees of behavioral problems. The significance of the research has been the repeated demonstration of the relationship between deficits in specific problem-solving skills and behavioral adjustment at different ages and the degree of change in these skills and improvement in adjustment.

Relatively few studies have evaluated cognitive therapy with clinical child populations. In some cases where clinical populations are used, the focus is on impulsivity rather than on the problems that precipitated treatment or hospitalization (e.g., Kendall & Finch, 1978). When clinical populations are studied, measures of cognitive function often reflect change but measures of overt behavior (e.g., the classroom) yield equivocal results (e.g., Camp, Blom, Hebert, & van Doorninck, 1977; Douglas, Parry, Marton, & Garson, 1976. Thus, the clinical efficacy of treatment has not been clearly demonstrated.

Factors That Contribute to Outcome. Few studies have elaborated the factors that contribute to treatment outcome. Tentative factors can be identified even though they have not been directly tested. To begin with, the amount of treatment may be important. As already noted, many investigations suggest that laboratory but not real-life performance improves with cognitive therapy. Yet, these investigations usually provide a relatively small dose of treatment (2–6 sessions) (Kendall & Wilcox, 1980; Moore & Cole, 1978; Palkes, Stewart, & Friedman, 1972). Programs that have been shown to affect performance in the classroom often extend over several weeks or months of treatment and up to 40 or 50 sessions (Spivack *et al.*, 1976; Weissberg & Gesten, 1982).

The specific focus of treatment sessions also may influence what is altered. Most studies focus on specific cognitive processes that are assessed on laboratory tasks. Perhaps changes in real-life performance should not be expected unless this is the explicit focus of treatment. For example, in one investigation, cognitive therapy focused on the application of problem-solving skills to classroom behaviors (e.g., talking out, not attending) rather than on cognitive task performance (Drummond, 1974). Treatment gains were evident on classroom behavior but not on a cognitive measure of impulsivity. These results stand in sharp contrast to the overwhelming majority of findings that show treatment effects on measures of cognitive performance but not on teacher ratings. Even though no study has directly tested the proposition, it appears that the content of the sessions may dictate the areas of performance affected by treatment (Kendall & Wilcox, 1980). To date, little evidence exists that shows that acting out behaviors such as aggression are altered significantly with cognitive therapy, yet no studies have taken this as the primary focus with a group of children whose behavior has been identified as antisocial.

Age and level of cognitive development would also be expected to influence treatment. Different problem-solving skills and the impact of particular skills on behavior vary as a function of age (Spivack *et al.*, 1976). Both laboratory and treatment studies have suggested that the extent to which behavior is mediated by self-statements and the specific types of statements that influence behavior vary as a function of the child's age and stage of cognitive development (Cole & Kazdin, 1980; Meichenbaum & Asarnow, 1979).

Issues and Limitations. Research to date has generally adopted the view that children with problems of adjustment, broadly conceived, have cognitive deficits. There has been little attempt to relate specific cognitive deficits to particular types of clinical dysfunction. For example, much of the literature has focused on cognitive style (reflection–impulsivity) of normal school children and psychiatric patients of diverse diagnoses. Little attempt has been made to show that this style uniquely relates to a particular childhood disorder. Spivack *et al.* (1976) have found similar cognitive deficits of children who are socially withdrawn or who act out. Their work with adolescents and adults has also shown that drug addicts, delinquents, and schizophrenics evince cognitive deficits compared to normals matched on various demographic variables. Finer distinctions need to be explored to delineate the cognitive correlates or underpinnings of specific clinical problems. There would be value in attempting to delineate cognitive processes specific to clinical disorders and then designing treatment to alter these processes.

Evaluating the clinical efficacy of cognitive therapy is impeded by the frequent failure of outcome studies to delineate the population that is treated (Abikoff, 1979). Most of the outcome studies have focused on school children identified as impulsive. In some cases, when clinical samples are used, they are still selected because of their impulsivity on laboratory tasks rather than because of the clinical dysfunction. Few studies have utilized stringent selection criteria or have described the sample well enough to instill confidence that the children were severely impaired and that the application of treatment was related to the nature of the impairment (e.g., Camp *et al.*, 1977; Douglas *et al.*, 1976). The relative paucity of studies with clinical populations has obvious implications for interpreting the evidence. Possibly, the changes consistently obtained with cognitive therapy result from the fact that the children usually are not seriously disturbed to begin with. Cognitive therapy, even if provided very briefly or in weak doses, might produce change in populations with little disturbance (e.g., Zahavi & Asher, 1978).

Existing studies show that various forms of cognitive therapy can produce relatively consistent changes on a variety of measures that reflect cognitive style, thought processes, perception, aspects of intelligence, and academic performance. Although impulsive cognitive style is associated with many different childhood disorders, its relationship to deviance outside of the laboratory is weak (Abikoff, 1979; Cole & Kazdin, 1980). Few studies attest to the efficacy of cognitive therapy in altering performance in everyday situations in the classroom, in the community, or at home. In many studies, changes in cognitive skills are altered, but similar changes are not reflected on the measures of everyday performance. The fact that some change is demonstrated indicates that treatment is having an effect. Perhaps the effects are not strong enough to alter deviant behavior.

Overall Evaluation. Cognitive therapy at this time has not been shown to be an effective treatment for antisocial behavior. Nevertheless, there are several features of the work in this area that make it one of the more promising psychosocial approaches to the problem. First, cognitive therapy is tied to theory and research in developmental psychology. Theory and research on the emergence and maturation of cognitive processes and the relationship of these processes to adjustment provide an important foundation for generating and testing treatment techniques. Also, research on the development of maladaptive cognitive processes has been shown to relate to other variables (e.g., parents' child-rearing practices) that are correlated with the development and maintenance of antisocial behavior (Shure & Spivack, 1978). A major problem in the development of treatment techniques is a sound basis in theory and basic research. Cognitive therapy, among alternative approaches, is relatively strong on this dimension.

Second, variations of cognitive therapy consider developmental differences that may need to be taken into account in designing effective treatments. For example, the investigations of Spivack and Shure have shown that different problem-solving skills relate to behavioral adjustment at different points in development. Processes highly significant at one age (e.g., means–ends thinking in adolescents) may not be critical at other ages (early childhood). Treatment directed to particular clinical problems may need to emphasize processes as a function of developmental level.

Third, rigorous evidence attests to the fact that cognitive therapies can produce change in children with mild adjustment problems or clinical impairment. The types of changes demonstrated to date leave a great deal to be desired. Yet that change is achieved at all and that these changes cannot be attributed to such influences as participation in training sessions, exposure to specific tasks or stimulus materials, and discussion of interpersonal situations, should not be treated lightly.

The literature cannot be dismissed as being incapable of producing clinically relevant change. Different characteristics of outcome research have made it difficult to evaluate the clinical potential of cognitive therapy. Often, few treatment sessions are provided and the focus is not directed at the children's clinical problems (e.g., peer interaction, antisocial behavior). Significant changes on clinically important behavior have been evident (Chandler, 1973), but the attempt to study such changes is rare. Additional attempts to alter specific clinical problems are needed before the efficacy of cognitive therapies for childhood disorders can be evaluated.

Fourth, a major feature of cognitive therapy for purposes of clinical application and research is that the techniques are often available in manual form (e.g., Camp & Bash, 1978; Padawer, Zupan, & Kendall, 1980; Spivack *et al.*, 1976; Weissberg, Gesten, Leibenstein, Doherty-Schmid, & Hutton, 1980). The advantage is that treatment can be disseminated systematically. Specification of treatment procedures in manual form helps promote further research on the efficacy of treatment and the components of treatment that are necessary, sufficient, or facilitative of therapeutic change.

On balance, several features suggest that cognitive therapy is promising as a treatment approach. The background of theory and research and the rigorous empirical research that much of the outcome investigations reflect may generate effective intervention techniques. Nevertheless, after all is said and done, at this time cognitive therapy cannot be regarded as an empirically demonstrated treatment for antisocial behavior.

CURRENT STATUS OF TREATMENTS FOR CONDUCT DISORDERS

Parent management training and cognitive therapy have been highlighted in lieu of reviewing all available treatment modalities, because they reflect highly promising treatment approaches. The features that make each of these techniques promising are manifold. Both treatments (1) are based on underlying conceptual models about the nature and emergence of deviant child behavior, (2) have provided direct evidence that specific (family or cognitive) processes in fact are related to child adjustment, (3) have specified concrete procedures (in treatment manual form) that can be applied clinically, and (4) have been subjected to clinical research. These features are essential for the identification of effective and empirically based treatment techniques.

Yet there are limitations with these treatments as well. At the present time, neither can be said to have demonstrated unequivocally that treatment gains are invariably produced among antisocial children and that these gains affect the poor prognosis that has been frequently documented (e.g., Robins, 1966). The evidence is greater for parent management training than for cognitive therapy at present, but major questions about treatment and the child and family factors that interact with outcome remain.

Any particular form of treatment and the conceptual position on which it is based tends to ignore the complexity of the clinical phenomena to which it is addressed. Conduct disorders are not simply the result of misguided child-rearing practices or devastating family interaction patterns or faulty cognitive processes. Extensive evidence from epidemiological research and adoption studies indicates that antisocial behavior cannot be attributed to isolated factors and single determinants (Farrington, 1978; Hutchings & Mednick, 1975; Robins, West, & Herjanic, 1975; Twito & Stewart, 1982). Yet, effective treatment techniques may emerge without a full understanding of the causes of conduct disorder and a clear understanding of the many different variations, subtypes, and constituent disorders encompassed by the diagnosis. The issue for treatment research is identifying the point of intervention that can be made to produce therapeutic change. Family interaction and cognitive processes are two promising points of intervention given the current status of outcome research.

An important issue in the treatment of conduct disorder children in general, and reflected in the two specific treatments highlighted above, is the optimal focus of treatment. Parent management training focuses on family interaction and cognitive therapy focuses on the child, yet the child's presenting problem often does not reveal the areas that many need to be addressed in treatment. Many of the risk factors for antisocial behavior (e.g., parent psychopathology, marital discord) are not merely correlates or antecedents of the problem. They often reflect current dimensions that directly affect clinical management and the implementation and feasibility of treatment. Thus, if parent management training is shown to be an effective treatment for conduct disorders, it may not be applicable in a large proportion of cases because of the chaotic family conditions in which the child is enmeshed. Families often are not interested in or in a position to engage in the sort of treatment regimen required by parent management training. Analogously, cognitive therapy may prove to be effective as well. Yet for many children severe cognitive deficits and maladaptive cognitive problem solving of parents in the home may make the treatment difficult to apply or simply ineffective.

Questions about the efficacy of treatments, factors that moderate treatment, therapeutic change, and feasibility of implementing the procedures clinically are obviously important but not discouraging. The unique features of contemporary research is that viable treatments have been identified, and they are being subjected to rigorous outcome research. The state of the art has made a small but clearly detectable step in identifying empirically based clinical interventions for children and adolescents.

ACKNOWLEDGMENTS

Completion of this chapter was facilitated by a Research Scientist Development Award (MH00353) and Grant (MH35408) from the National Institute of Mental Health.

REFERENCES

Abikoff, H. Cognitive training interventions in children: Review of a new approach. *Journal of Learning Disabilities*, 1979, *12*, 65–77.

Achenbach, T. M., & Edelbrock, C. S. The classification of child psychopathology: A review and analysis of empirical efforts. *Psychological Bulletin*, 1978, *85*, 1275–1301.

Aleksic, P. A study of empathic inhibition of aggression in juvenile delinquents (Doctoral dissertation, Miami University, 1975). *Dissertation Abstracts International*, 1976, *36*, 4675B–4676B.

American Psychiatric Association, *Diagnostic and statistical manual of mental disorders* (3rd ed.). Washington, D.C.: American Psychiatric Association, 1980.

Arnold, J. E., Levine, A. G., & Patterson, G. R. Changes in sibling behavior following family intervention. *Journal of Consulting and Clinical Psychology*, 1975, *43*, 683–688.

Barrett, C. L., Hampe, I. E., & Miller, L. C. Research on child psychotherapy. In S. L. Garfield & A. E. Bergin (Eds.), *Handbook of psychotherapy and behavior change: An empirical analysis* (2nd ed.). New York: Wiley, 1978.

Baum, C. G., & Forehand, R. Long term follow-up assessment of parent training by use of multiple outcome measures. *Behavior Therapy*, 1981, *12*, 643–652.

Berkowitz, L. Situational and personal conditions governing reactions to aggressive cues. In D. Magnusson & N. S. Endler (Eds.), *Personality at the crossroads: Current issues in interactional psychology*. Hillsdale, N.J.: Erlbaum, 1977.

Bernal, M. E., Klinnert, M. D., & Schultz, L. A. Outcome evaluation of behavioral parent training and client-centered parent counseling for children with conduct problems. *Journal of Applied Behavior Analysis*, 1980, *13*, 677–691.

Camp, B. Verbal mediation in young aggressive boys. *Journal of Abnormal Psychology*, 1977, *86*, 145–153.

Camp, B., Blom, G., Hebert, F., & van Doorninck, W. "Think aloud": A program for developing self-control in young aggressive boys. *Journal of Abnormal Child Psychology*, 1977, *5*, 157–169.

Camp, B. W., & Bash, M. S. *Think aloud program: Group manual*. Denver: University of Colorado Medical Center, 1978.

Campbell, M., Cohen, I. L., & Small, A. M. Drugs in aggressive behavior. *Journal of the American Academy of Child Psychiatry*, 1982, *21*, 107–117.

Chandler, M. J. Egocentrism and antisocial behavior: The assessment and training of social perspective-taking skills. *Developmental Psychology*, 1973, *9*, 326–332.

Cole, P. M., & Kazdin, A. E. Critical issues in self-instruction training with children. *Child Behavior Therapy*, 1980, *2*, 1–23.

Conger, R. D. The assessment of dysfunctional family systems. In B. B. Lahey & A. E. Kazdin (Eds.), *Advances in clinical child psychology* (Vol. 4). New York: Plenum, 1981.

Deluty, R. H. Alternative-thinking ability of aggressive, assertive, and submissive children. *Cognitive Therapy and Research*, 1981, *5*, 309–312.

Dodge, K. A. Social cognition and children's aggressive behavior. *Child Development*, 1980, *51*, 162–170.

Douglas, V. I., Parry, P., Marton, P., & Garson, C. Assessment of a cognitive training program for hyperactive children. *Journal of Abnormal Child Psychology*, 1976, *4*, 389–410.

Drummond, D. Self-instructional training: An approach to disruptive classroom behavior. Unpublished doctoral dissertation, University of Oregon, 1974.

Dumas, J. E., & Wahler, R. G. Predictors of treatment outcome in parent training: Mother insularity and socioeconomic disadvantage. *Behavioral Assessment*, 1983, *5*, 301–313.

Ellis, P. L. Empathy: A factor in antisocial behavior. *Journal of Abnormal Child Psychology*, 1982, *10*, 123–134.

Eyberg, S. M., & Johnson, S. M. Multiple assessment of behavior modification with families: Effects of contingency contracting and order of treated problems. *Journal of Consulting and Clinical Psychology*, 1974, *42*, 594–606.

Eyberg, S. M., & Robinson, E. A. Parent–child interaction training: Effects on family functioning. *Journal of Clinical Child Psychology*, 1982, *11*, 130–137.

Farrington, D. P. The family backgrounds of aggressive youths. In L. A. Hersov, M. Berger, & D. Shaffer (Eds.), *Aggression and anti-social behaviour in childhood and adolescence*. Oxford: Pergamon, 1978.

Ferber, H., Keeley, S. M., & Shemberg, K. M. Training parents in behavior modification: Outcome of and problems encountered in a program after Patterson's work. *Behavior Therapy*, 1974, *5*, 415–419.

Feshbach, N. Empathy in children: Some theoretical and empirical considerations. *Counseling Psychologist*, 1975, *5*, 25–30.

Fleischman, M. J. A replication of Patterson's "Intervention for boys with conduct problems." *Journal of Consulting and Clinical Psychology*, 1981, *49*, 343–351.

Fleischman, M. J., & Szykula, S. A. A community setting replication of a social learning treatment for aggressive children. *Behavior Therapy*, 1981, *12*, 115–122.

Forehand, R., & Atkeson, B. M. Generality of treatment effects with parents as therapist: A review of assessment and implementation procedures. *Behavior Therapy*, 1977, *8*, 575–593.

Forehand, R., & McMahon, R. J. *Helping the noncompliant child: A clinician's guide to parent training*. New York: Guilford, 1981.

Forehand, R., Wells, K. C., & Griest, D. L. An examination of the social validity of a parent training program. *Behavior Therapy*, 1980, *11*, 488–502.

Gilbert, G. M. A survey of "referral problems" in metropolitan child guidance centers. *Journal of Clinical Psychology*, 1957, *13*, 37–42.

Graham, P., & Rutter, M. Psychiatric disorder in the young adolescent: A follow-up study. *Proceedings of the Royal Society of Medicine*, 1973, *66*, 1226–1229.

Graham, P. J. Epidemiological studies. In H. C. Quay & J. S. Werry (Eds.), *Psychopathological disorders of childhood* (2nd ed.). New York: Wiley, 1979.

Griest, D. L., Forehand, R., Rogers, T., Breiner, J., Furey, W., & Williams, C. A. Effects of parent enhancement therapy on the treatment outcome and generalization of a parent training program. *Behaviour Research and Therapy*, 1982, *20*, 429–436.

Hartmann, D. P., Roper, B. L., & Gelfand, D. M. An evaluation of alternative modes of child psychotherapy. In B. B. Lahey & A. E. Kazdin (Eds.), *Advances in clinical child psychology* (Vol. 1). New York: Plenum, 1977.

Herbert, M. *Conduct disorders of childhood and adolescence: A behavioural approach to assessment and treatment.* Chichester, England: Wiley, 1978.

Hetherington, E. M., & Martin, B. Family interaction. In H. C. Quay & J. S. Werry (Eds.), *Psychopathological disorders of childhood* (2nd ed.). New York: Wiley, 1979.

Humphreys, L., Forehand, R., McMahon, R., & Roberts, M. Parent behavior training to modify child noncompliance: Effects on untreated siblings. *Journal of Behavior Therapy and Experimental Psychiatry*, 1978, *9*, 235–238.

Hutchings, B., & Mednick, S. A. Registered criminality in the adoptive and biological parents of registered male criminal adoptees. In R. Fieve, D. Rosenthal, & H. Brill (Eds.), *Genetic research in psychiatry*. Baltimore: Johns Hopkins University Press, 1975.

Kagan, J. Reflection–impulsivity: The generality and dynamics of conceptual tempo. *Journal of Educational Psychology*, 1966, *71*, 17–24.

Kazdin, A. E. Current developments and research issues in cognitive–behavioral interventions: A commentary. *School Psychology Review*, 1982, *11*, 75–82.

Kazdin, A. E., & Frame, C. Treatment of aggressive behavior and conduct disorder. In R. J. Morris & T. R. Kratochwill (Eds.), *The practice of child therapy*. New York: Pergamon, 1983.

Kendall, P. C., & Finch, A. J. A cognitive–behavioral treatment for impulsivity: A group comparison study. *Journal of Consulting and Clinical Psychology*, 1978, *46*, 110–118.

Kendall, P. C., Pellegrini, D. S., & Urbain, E. S. Approaches to assessment of cognitive–behavioral interventions with children. In P. C. Kendall, & S. D. Hollon (Eds.), *Assessment strategies for cognitive–behavioral interventions*. New York: Academic, 1981.

Kendall, P. C., & Wilcox, L. E. Cognitive–behavioral treatment for impulsivity: Concrete versus conceptual training in non-self-controlled problem children. *Journal of Consulting and Clinical Psychology*, 1980, *48*, 80–91.

Kirigin, K. A., Braukmann, C. J., Atwater, J. D., & Wolf, M. M. An evaluation of teaching-family (Achievement Place) group homes for juvenile offenders. *Journal of Applied Behavior Analysis*, 1982, *15*, 1–16.

Lavigueur, H., Peterson, R. F., Sheese, J. G., & Peterson, L. W. Behavioral treatment in the home: Effects on an untreated sibling and long-term follow-up. *Behavior Therapy*, 1973, *4*, 431–441.

McMahon, R. J., Forehand, R., Griest, D. L., & Wells, K. C. Who drops out of treatment during parent behavioral training? *Behavioral Counseling Quarterly*, 1981, *1*, 79–85.

Meichenbaum, D. H. *Cognitive-behavior modification: An integrative approach.* New York: Plenum, 1977.

Meichenbaum, D. H., & Asarnow, J. Cognitive–behavioral modification and metacognitive development: Implications for the classroom. In P. C. Kendall & S. D. Hollon (Eds.), *Cognitive–behavioral interventions: Theory, research, and procedures.* New York: Academic, 1979.

Messer, S. B. Reflection–impulsivity: A review. *Psychological Bulletin*, 1976, *83*, 1026–1052.

Messer, S. B., & Brodzinsky, D. M. The relation of conceptual tempo to aggression and its control. *Child Development*, 1979, *50*, 758–766.

Moore, S. F., & Cole, S. O. Cognitive self-mediation training with hyperkinetic children. *Bulletin of the Psychonomic Society*, 1978, *12*, 18–20.

Morrison, H. L. The asocial child: A destiny of sociopathy? In W. H. Reid (Ed.), *The psychopath: A comprehensive study of antisocial disorders and behaviors.* New York: Brunner/Mazel, 1981.

Nasby, W., Hayden, B., & DePaulo, B. M. Attributional bias among aggressive boys to interpret unambiguous social stimuli as displays of hostility. *Journal of Abnormal Psychology*, 1980, *89*, 459–468.

Novaco, R. W. Anger and coping with stress: Cognitive behavioral intervention. In J. P. Foreyt &
    D. P. Rathjen (Eds.), *Cognitive behavioral therapy: Research and application.* New
    York/London: Plenum, 1978.
Ollendick, T. H., & Cerny, J. A. *Clinical behavior therapy with children.* New York: Plenum,
    1981.
Olweus, D. Stability of aggressive reaction patterns in males: A review. *Psychological Bulletin,*
    1979, *86,* 852-875.
Padawer, W., Zupan, B. A., & Kendall, P. C. *Developing self-control in children: A manual of
    cognitive behavioral strategies.* Minneapolis: University of Minnesota, 1980.
Palkes, H., Stewart, M., & Freedman, J. Improvement in maze performance of hyperactive
    boys as a function of verbal training procedures. *Journal of Special Education,* 1972, *5,*
    337-342.
Patterson, G. R. Interventions for boys with conduct problems: Multiple settings, treatments,
    and criteria. *Journal of Consulting and Clinical Psychology,* 1974, *42,* 471-481.
Patterson, G. R. The aggressive child: Victim and architect of a coercive system. In E. J. Mash,
    L. A. Hamerlynck, & L. C. Handy (Eds.), *Behavior modification and families.* New
    York: Brunner/Mazel, 1976.
Patterson, G. R. Mothers: The unacknowledged victims. *Monographs of the Society for
    Research in Child Development,* 1980, *45* (Serial No. 186, Issue 5), 1-54.
Patterson, G. R. *Coercive family process.* Eugene, Ore.: Castalia, 1982.
Patterson, G. R., Chamberlain, P., & Reid, J. A comparative evaluation of a parent-training
    program. *Behavior Therapy,* 1982, *13,* 638-650.
Patterson, G. R., & Fleischman, M. J. Maintenance of treatment effects: Some considerations
    concerning family systems and follow-up data. *Behavior Therapy,* 1979, *10,* 168-185.
Quay, H. C. Classification. In H. C. Quay & J. S. Werry (Eds.), *Psychopathological disorders
    of childhood* (2nd ed.). New York: Wiley, 1979.
Reid, J. B., Taplin, P. S., & Loeber, R. A social interactional approach to the treatment of
    abusive families. In R. Stuart (Ed.), *Violent behavior: Social learning approaches to
    prediction, management and treatment.* New York: Brunner/Mazel, 1981.
Reisinger, J. J., Frangia, G. W., & Hoffman, E. H. Toddler management training: Generaliza-
    tion and marital status. *Journal of Behavior Therapy and Experimental Psychology,*
    1976, *7,* 335-340.
Robins, L. N. *Deviant children grown up.* Baltimore: Williams & Wilkins, 1966.
Robins, L. N. Antisocial behavior disturbances of childhood: Prevalence, prognosis, and
    prospects. In B. J. Anthony & C. Koupernik (Eds.), *The child and his family: Children at
    psychiatric risk.* New York: Wiley, 1974.
Robins, L. N. Follow-up studies. In H. C. Quay & J. S. Werry (Eds.), *Psychopathological
    disorders of childhood* (2nd ed.). New York: Wiley, 1979.
Robins, L. N. Epidemiological approaches to natural history research: Antisocial disorders in
    children. *Journal of the American Academy of Child Psychiatry,* 1981, *20,* 566-580.
Robins, L. N., West, P. A., & Herjanic, B. Arrest and delinquency in two generations: A study
    of black urban families and their children. *Journal of Child Psychology and Psychiatry,*
    1975, *16,* 125-140.
Rutter, M., Cox, A., Tupling, C., Berger, M., & Yule, W. Attainment and adjustment in two
    geographical areas: I—The prevalence of psychiatric disorder. *British Journal of Psy-
    chiatry,* 1975, *126,* 493-509.
Rutter, M., Shaffer, D., & Shepherd, M. *A multi-axial classification of child psychiatric dis-
    orders.* Geneva: World Health Organization, 1975.
Shure, M. B., & Spivack, G. *Problem-solving techniques in child-rearing.* San Francisco:
    Jossey-Bass, 1978.
Spivack, G., Platt, J. J., & Shure, M. B. *The problem solving approach to adjustment.*
    San Francisco: Jossey-Bass, 1976.

Spivack, G., & Shure, M. *Social adjustment of young children: A cognitive approach to solving real-life problems.* San Francisco: Jossey-Bass, 1974.

Strain, P. S., Young, C. C., & Horowitz, J. An examination of child and family demographic variables related to generalized behavior change during oppositional child training. *Behavior Modification,* 1981, *5,* 12–26.

Twito, T. J., & Stewart, M. A. A half-sibling study of aggressive conduct disorder: Prevalence of disorders in parents, brothers and sisters. *Neuropsychobiology,* 1982, *8,* 144–150.

Urbain, E. S., & Kendall, P. C. Review of social-cognitive problem-solving interventions with children. *Psychological Bulletin,* 1980, *88,* 109–143.

Wahler, R. G., & Afton, A. D. Attentional processes in insular and non-insular mothers: Some differences in their summary reports about child problem behavior. *Child Behavior Therapy,* 1980, *2,* 25–42.

Wahler, R. G., Leske, G., & Rogers, E. S. The insular family: A deviance support system for oppositional children. In L. A. Hamerlynck (Ed.), *Behvioral systems for the developmentally disabled: I. School and family environments.* New York: Brunner/Mazel, 1979.

Walters, H., & Gilmore, S. K. Placebo versus social learning effects in parent training procedures designed to alter the behavior of aggressive boys. *Behavior Therapy,* 1973, *4,* 361–377.

Wells, K. C., Forehand, R., & Griest, D. L. Generality of treatment effects from treated to untreated behaviors resulting from a parent training program. *Journal of Clinical Child Psychology,* 1980, *9,* 217–219.

Weissberg, R. P., & Gesten, E. L. Considerations for developing effective school-based social problem-solving (SPS) training programs. *School Psychology Review,* 1982, *11,* 56–63.

Weissberg, R. P., Gesten, E. L., Leibenstein, N. L., Doherty-Schmid, K., & Hutton, H. *The Rochester social problem-solving (SPS) program: A training manual for teachers of 2nd–4th grade children.* Rochester, N.Y.: University of Rochester, 1980.

Wiltz, N. A., & Patterson, G. R. An evaluation of parent training procedures designed to alter inappropriate aggressive behavior of boys. *Behavior Therapy,* 1974, *5,* 215–221.

Wolfgang, M. E., Figlio, R. M., & Sellin, T. *Delinquency in a birth cohort.* Chicago: University of Chicago Press, 1972.

Worland, J., Carney, R. M., Weinberg, H., & Milich, R. Dropping out of group behavioral parent training. *Behavioral Counseling Quarterly,* 1982, *2,* 37–41.

Zahavi, S., & Asher, S. R. The effect of verbal instructions on preschool children's aggressive behavior. *Journal of Psychology,* 1978, *16,* 146–163.

COMMENTARY

Dr. Donald F. Klein*: You mentioned that there are a number of different measures of effectiveness, including ratings from the parents and the teachers. In general, in psychotherapy research, and in particular this sort of research, there is a tremendous problem with the reactivity of the measures. In general, those people who are dispensing the reinforcements, such as the

---

*New York State Psychiatric Institute and College of Physicians and Surgeons, Columbia University.

parents and the teachers, are the ones who rate the biggest effects. Therefore, the utility of having an external independent evaluator, or objective measures such as being thrown out of school, are tremendously helpful.

In our own research using a contingency management program with hyperactive children, for instance, we found rather marked effects based on the reports of the teachers and parents. When we used a classroom observer, there was no effect whatsoever. This questions what you are finding.

Dr. Kazdin: I am glad you raised this point. I am certainly familiar with the well-known program and rating instruments that you used, and the development of such instruments is an area of research by itself. In fact, some of the best research on the reactivity of such measures, as I am sure you know, has been conducted in the context of research on parent management training.

In the research I presented, concern with reactivity has been a major issue. Observers are usually sent into the home, which in itself may be reactive, and into the school. To circumvent the problem of reactivity, randomly activated tape recorders have occasionally been placed in the home to provide data that are later evaluated. In the research I presented, less reactive non-parent- and non-teacher-completed measures do reflect the behavioral changes to some extent, in addition to totally nonreactive observational methods that have been used, such as random tape recordings.

Dr. Robert A. Neimeyer*: Do you know of any efforts that are currently taking place to integrate these two perspectives: the cognitive and the parent training models?

Dr. Kazdin: At Western Psychiatric Institute and Clinic we are trying to combine these techniques because they conceptually overlap. Ultimately, child-rearing practices seem to affect cognitive processes in children; we are trying to combine the two models to see if they have a synergistic or even additive effect. Unfortunately, we do not have any data on the effectiveness of a combined approach.

*Memphis State University.

2

The Psychosocial Treatment of Anxiety Disorders: Current Status, Future Directions

DAVID H. BARLOW AND J. GAYLE BECK
State University of New York at Albany

INTRODUCTION

Reports of being "anxious" or "nervous" are a part of everyday experience. Complaints of anxiety, in many cases reaching severe proportions, are among the most common problems presenting to health practitioners. One poll, using reliable sampling methodology and conservative definitions, revealed that 30–40% of the general population suffered from the presence of anxiety, with greater prevalence in females (Shepherd, Cooper, Brown, & Kalton, 1966). People do seek out treatment for anxiety in numbers that dwarf most emotional and behavioral problems. One study revealed anxiety as the fifth most common reason for visits to a primary care physician, ranking only behind preventive examination, hypertension, lacerations and trauma, and pharyngitis and tonsillitis (Marsland, Wood, & Mayo, 1976). It is also becoming apparent that severe anxiety often presents to health practitioners as any one of a number of other problems that may mask the primary anxiety disorder. For example, in a recent study over one-third of patients presenting to a clinic for problem drinking were found to be self-medicating an anxiety disorder (Mullaney & Trippett, 1979). Others have also noted a high rate of addictive behavior masking anxiety disorders (e.g., Quitkin, Rifkin, Kaplan, & Klein, 1972).

Despite the prevalence of these disorders, progress in the development of effective treatments has advanced in an uneven fashion. Over the past 20 years, seemingly effective psychosocial treatments have been devised for the phobic disorders, particularly agoraphobia, as well as obsessive–compulsive disorders. Much less progress has been made in the categories of anxiety disorders that would seem to be far more prevalent, such as generalized anxiety disorder. This chapter will review the state of the art of the current psychosocial treatment approaches to all of the anxiety disorders. While advances have been substantial in some areas, gaps in our knowledge remain

29

overwhelming and many important questions in treatment–assessment research remain unanswered. Recent advances in our knowledge of the psychopathology of anxiety disorders shed some light on these questions, and this new information will be integrated into this chapter at appropriate points. After a description of the most up-to-date information on classification, the status of psychosocial treatments for each category of anxiety disorders will be discussed in turn. A discussion of our rather limited knowledge of patient–treatment interactions will follow the review, and the chapter will close with a description of some deficits in basic knowledge that are retarding research efforts at this time.

THE CLASSIFICATION OF ANXIETY DISORDERS

The advent of DSM-III (American Psychiatric Association, 1980) signaled a shift of emphasis in classification; the anxiety disorders reflect the benefits of this trend most clearly. Unlike its predecessors, DSM-III presents a more descriptive, less theoretically based system. Within this system, the anxiety disorders are grouped into three major categories: (1) phobic disorders, which include agoraphobia, social phobia, and the simple or focal phobias such as claustrophobia; (2) anxiety states, involving panic disorder, generalized anxiety disorder, and obsessive–compulsive disorder; and (3) post-traumatic stress disorder, a new diagnostic category involving characteristic symptoms following an unusually traumatic event. It is notable that this diagnostic system excludes the more traditional concepts of "neuroses," focusing instead upon specific symptomatology which is characteristic within each diagnostic category. For example, what was formerly "phobic neurosis" in DSM-II has been redefined into the several categories of phobias listed above. This shift in approach is based on data suggesting that the "neuroses," as conceived by the theoretical stance employed in DSM-III, were not defined specifically enough to predict differential treatment response (e.g., Marks, Boulougouris, & Marset, 1971) or long-term course (e.g., Akiskal, Bitar, Puzantian, Rosenthal, & Walker, 1978). DSM-III would thus seem to represent a major advancement in classification, relying upon empirically derived categories which seem to offer considerable clarity and a solid base for subsequent research into treatment, natural history, prognosis, and phenomenology. (See Spitzer, Williams, & Skodol, 1980, for a more complete description.) Of course, the deletion of neuroses from our terminology is strictly in American phenomonon (e.g., Barlow, 1982; Marks, 1981) that will be accepted elsewhere only when data on the validity of this approach are forthcoming. In fact, recent research indicates that each subcategory listed in DSM-III can be reliably identified by clinicians using a structured interview designed for this purpose: the Anxiety Disorders Interview Schedule (ADIS)

(DiNardo, O'Brien, Barlow, Waddell, & Blanchard, 1983). In the original validation of this device, the one exception was the "residual" category of "generalized anxiety disorder," which could not be identified reliably. The category of "post-traumatic stress disorder" was not tested in this initial study. The fact that subcategories of anxiety disorders can be refined and reliably identified is a major advance in the study of the psychopathology of anxiety (Barlow & Maser, 1983). Unfortunately, these categories and their definitions are so new that there has been little opportunity for treatment outcome or psychopathology research to relate to this specific system.

A related advancement, conceptually relevant to classification, is Lang's (1968) phenomenological reconceptualization of "anxiety" as comprising at least three response systems: behavioral, physiological/affective, and cognitive/self-report. This conceptualization, which has received considerable experimental support, suggests the need for multisystem assessment and may have important treatment implications (e.g., Barlow & Mavissakalian, 1981). Within the categories of anxiety disorders described below, this conceptualization appears to fit well with the existing data supporting the grouping of these disorders.

Phobic Disorders

The essential feature of this group of disorders is a persistent, irrational fear of a specific object, activity, or situation that leads the individual to avoid the phobic stimulus. Thus, "anxiety" is demonstrated through behavioral avoidance, heightened physiological responding, and reports of "cognitive fear," often involving catastrophizing self-statements.

Agoraphobia. Agoraphobia, the most severe subtype of this category, is characterized by a fear of being alone or being in public situations from which escape or help is not available. This phobia often comes to dominate the individual's life, frequently leading to severe constriction of daily activities, such as employment and social opportunities. This disorder may occur with or without panic attacks, characterized as periods of intense fear and marked physiological responding (e.g., dyspnea, palpitations, choking sensations, trembling, vertigo, sweating). Data from a number of clinical and research settings indicate that agoraphobia without panic is rare. In a recent study described above (DiNardo *et al.*, 1983), none of a series of 23 consecutive agoraphobics presented without panic. These data may have important implications for classification.

The course of this disorder is chronic (Agras, Chapin, & Oliveau, 1972), and severity fluctuates with periods of relative freedom, occasionally with time-limited, spontaneous remission of the fears (Mavissakalian & Barlow, 1981). Unlike other phobics, the majority of agoraphobics tend to be women and the disorder frequently begins in late adolescence or early adulthood (e.g., Agras *et al.*, 1972; Marks & Herst, 1970; Snaith, 1968). The prevalence of this disorder has been estimated by Agras, Sylvester, and Oliveau (1969) to be approximately 6/1,000 (8%), on the basis of data collected in interviews conducted in a probability sample of the household population in a small city in Vermont. Another recent estimate places the prevalence at 12/1,000 (Uhlenhuth, Balter, Mellinger, Cisin, & Clinthorne, 1981). While agoraphobia is not the most prevalent of the phobic disorders in the community, it does rank first of all phobias seen in a hospital setting, comprising 50% of a clinical series derived from the Agras *et al.* (1969) survey. A number of authors have commented upon the somewhat unusual marital and familial relationships that are seen clinically in agoraphobics (e.g., Agulnik, 1970; Andrews, 1966; Webster, 1953). Goldstein and Chambless (1978) have observed that agoraphobia most often develops in a climate of interpersonal conflict. They label agoraphobia with this etiology "complex agoraphobia," whereas agoraphobia arising out of traumatic or drug related situations is termed "simple agoraphobia." Whether this particular distinction is valid is an empirical question.

The presence of "spontaneous" panic attacks in agoraphobia—that is, panics not associated with any specific phobic stimuli—is actually the phenomenological highlight of this particular phobia. Indeed, patients are often unable to distinguish spontaneous and stimulus-bound panics. This feature has led several investigators to conclude that "fear of fear" is the central phobic component in this disorder. Thus, what agoraphobics are avoiding is the occurrence of panic—that is, anxiety in anticipation of panic accounts for the behavioral disruption (Goldstein & Chambless, 1978; Klein, 1981; Mavissakalian & Barlow, 1981). This conceptualization has important treatment implications, as it suggests a complex interplay of cognitive and physiological responding.

Social Phobia. Social phobia is defined diagnostically as a persistent fear of and desire to avoid social situations in which the individual is exposed to possible scrutiny by others and may risk embarrassment. This category comprises a new diagnostic label, and, as such, a large body of literature is yet to develop concerning its relevant parameters. One report from the United Kingdom (Marks, 1969) estimates that social phobias comprise 8% of clinical phobias seen in a major treatment center. Other work suggests that social anxiety occurs in one out of three psychiatric outpatients (Bryant, Trower, Yardley, Urbieta, & Letemendia, 1976) and 7% of inpatients (Curran, Miller, Zwick, Monti, & Stout, 1980). The disorder frequently begins in late childhood and is usually chronic, occasionally interfering with occupational advancement in its manifestation as fear and avoidance of public speaking or performing in public.

Simple Phobia. Simple or specific phobias are defined as an irrational fear and avoidance of an object or situation other than being alone or embarrassment in social situations; as such, it constitutes the residual category of the phobic disorders. Examples include claustrophobia (fear of enclosed spaces), acrophobia (fear of heights), and phobias of specific objects such as small animals. These phobias usually begin in childhood and often have a chronic course without spontaneous remission. Prevalence estimates hold that animal phobias occur in 14% of the population, acrophobia in 5%, and phobias of storms in 18% (Agras *et al.*, 1969). The prevalence in a clinical sample was much lower (e.g., 4% of a clinical series reported animal phobias) (Agras *et al.*, 1969). Thus, these disorders do not create so severe a level of impairment as some of the other anxiety disorders.

A recent examination supports the validity of distinguishing fearful from phobic individuals. Last and Blanchard (1982) examined nonphobic, fearful individuals (subclinical) and phobics, employing a semistructured interview, several self-report inventories, and a heartrate measure. These data provide some validation for this diagnostic distinction, indicating that catastrophic thinking, which was correlated with intense anxiety, occurred only within the clinical population. Such data may have important implications for unraveling the mechanism by which treatment effects change, as well as suggesting important qualitative differences between fearful and phobic symptomatology.

Anxiety States

Unlike the phobic disorders, these syndromes do not involve behavioral avoidance of a specific nature, but rather are characterized by heightened autonomic responding and cognitive events involving fear-related thoughts, feelings of tension or apprehension, or recurrent, ego-alien images or ideas.

Panic Disorder. Panic disorder is characterized by the frequent occurrence of panic attacks involving the sudden onset of feelings of intense terror or fear and a number of physiological and cognitive symptoms (e.g., palpitations, vertigo, feelings of unreality, faintness, trembling, fear of loss of control). This disorder appears to be prevalent and is diagnosed more often in women than in men. The disorder frequently begins during periods of interpersonal stress or change in the patient's life-style (e.g., Marks, 1970). The course is variable, ranging from a single episode to chronicity. Some authors view panic disorder as a precursor to the development of agoraphobia, dependent upon coping and attributional styles (Mathews, Gelder, & Johnston, 1981). Thus, panic disorder and agoraphobia may really be variants of the same disorder with differences only in coping styles or environmental contingencies determining whether avoidance develops (Barlow & Maser, 1983).

Generalized Anxiety Disorder. A distinct diagnostic category is generalized anxiety disorder (GAD), defined as continuous, persistent, generalized anxiety involving autonomic hyperactivity, motor tension, apprehensive expectation, and vigilance. The rationale for differentiating these two diagnostic categories is based, in part, upon Klein's work testing imipramine and MAO inhibitors (Klein, 1981; Klein & Fink, 1962; Zitrin, Woerner, & Klein, 1981). Data from these series suggest a differential response to certain treatments of panic and more generalized or background anxiety. In fact, some recent evidence does support this differentiation (Raskin, Peeke, Dickman, & Pinkster, 1982; Waddell, Barlow, & O'Brien, 1983). But other work does not (Marks, 1981), and it is not yet clear if panic is qualitatively different from GAD or simply quantitatively different (Barlow & Maser, 1983). In any case, GAD seems to be a very heterogeneous category which fits with its residual nature. Problems with reliable identification were mentioned above. To date little information has accumulated concerning prevalence or prognosis of this syndrome, although DiNardo *et al.* (1983) report a base rate of 10% for GAD within a total sample of 60 outpatients presenting at an anxiety disorders clinic. Other, less systematized data collected by the Gallup organization, and mentioned above, suggest that as much as 30–40% of the general population experience marked anxiety, with greater prevalence in females than males.

  Obsessive-Compulsive Disorder. Obsessive–compulsive disorder also falls within this subcategory and is defined by recurrent obsessions (persistent, unwanted, ego-alien ideas or thoughts, often involving repugnant, obscene, or blasphemous content; see Akhtar, Wig, Verma, Pershod, & Verma, 1975) and/or compulsions (repetitive, stereotyped acts which are regarded as excessive and generally produce distress). Black (1974) has summarized the existing studies concerning incidence of this disorder, estimating that 3–6% of all psychiatric outpatients were diagnosed as such, whereas obsessionals constitute a larger percentage of the inpatient population, approximating 2% (Rachman & Hodgson, 1980). The degree of impairment is generally severe, and mean age of onset is late adolescence to early adulthood (Black, 1974). Prognosis is frequently poor; one report has revealed that patients with less severe obsessions were more likely to have a gradual onset, although this was not related to therapeutic outcome (deSilva, Rachman, & Seligman, 1977). It is interesting to note that one report has examined the phenomenology of normal versus clinical obsessions, revealing that normal obsessions are a common experience and are similar in form and content to clinical obsessions. Clinical obsessions, in contrast, were more frequent, more intense, and of longer duration. They tended to be more ego-alien, more resisted, and more difficult to resist (Rachman & deSilva, 1978). This finding has important treatment implications in terms of both providing patients with a therapeutic rationale and increasing the conceptual understanding of this disorder. It is relevant to note that obsessions and compulsions may occur in isolation (although this is rare) or may be present simultaneously. This distinction implies differential treatment approaches, as will be outlined below.

Post-Traumatic Stress Disorder (PTSD)

This new category consists of a range of symptomatology following an unusually traumatic event; these maladaptive reactions include reexperiencing the trauma (e.g., recurrent nightmares), numbing of responsiveness to the external environment, and a range of autonomic and cognitive impairments (e.g., exaggerated startle response, memory impairment). Recent work (e.g., Horowitz, Wilner, Kaltreider, & Alvarez, 1980) suggests that some of the characteristic symptomatology may comprise attempts at control aimed at reducing the intrusive thoughts and feelings of repetitive aspects of the traumatic experience. This is the characteristic most commonly reported in these patients. As such, this disorder would appear to have some functional similarity to obsessive–compulsive disorder. Others have noted the similarity to simple phobia and the apparent role of a process analogous to classical conditioning in etiology similar to theories of the development of phobia in general (Barlow & Maser, 1983). To date, exact prevalance data do not exist and prognosis remains unknown. Preliminary support for the validity of this diagnosis is provided by Malloy, Fairbank, and Keane (1983) and Blanchard, Kolb, Pallmeyer, and Gerardi (1982). These authors examined psychophysiological responding in Vietnam veterans suffering PTSD to combat-related stimuli and neutral stimuli. Both reports reveal that patients with PTSD demonstrated heightened autonomic responsivity to combat scenes, relative to veterans with non-PTSD psychiatric disorders, well-adjusted veterans, and nonveteran controls. These data support the DSM-III diagnostic contention that PTSD, at its core, consists of a maladaptive stress response characterized, in part, by extreme autonomic reactivity to trauma-related cues. However, as discussed by Hough and Gongla (1982), the range of symptomatology included in DSM-III is not always clearly related to central features of the diagnosis itself other than in a descriptive sense. For example, features such as memory impairment, mentioned in DSM-III, do not appear directly related to the stress response to trauma-related cues (the central clinical concern of this disorder). Empirical examination appears warranted, exploring the clustering of symptoms as well as related concerns such as severity of symptoms and length of episode.

Conclusions

Although there is little question that this new classification system is a major advance, particularly in view of data on reliability (DiNardo *et al.*, 1983), the validity of these diagnostic distinctions has not yet been established. For example, there is a marked similarity in the phenomenological nature of the anxiety disorders (Barlow & Maser, 1983). All of the anxiety disorders are characterized by some variation of the autonomic stress response, highlighted in PTSD. Recent psychophysiological studies demonstrate that heightened autonomic arousal characterizes agoraphobia, obsessive–compulsive disorder, and "anxiety neurosis" (Kelly, 1980; Lader, 1978). Such similarities have led some authors to suggest that agoraphobia could be considered a variant of GAD (Hallam, 1978). Other writers have construed these similarities to indicate that GAD and panic disorder should be grouped hierarchically under agoraphobia (Mavissakalian, 1982). The presence of the equivalent of compulsive rituals in agoraphobia has also been noted by several investigators (e.g., Borkovec, 1981; Mavissakalian, 1982). Finally, many leading investigators conclude that anxiety disorders are dimensional rather than categorical, and may take many forms, depending on environmental contingencies, personality variables, levels of stress, and so on (Barlow & Maser, 1983). In this sense, the variety of anxiety disorders may be simply variations on a theme, with the particular form (e.g., obsessions, panic) changing over time. Clinically, this seems to happen (Barlow & Maser, 1983). The similarity of this notion to the concept of "neurosis" has not escaped us. Nevertheless, increased and more intensive research into the psychopathology of anxiety may reveal that it is more useful for treatment purposes to assess core components of anxiety, such as the three-response system analysis would suggest. In this sense, assessing the patterning of somatic, cognitive, and behavioral responses may have more important implications for treatment and change processes than the particular form that the anxiety disorder happens to be taking at that moment.

Finally, the complex and important relationship between anxiety and depression needs mention in any discussion of classification. Differential diagnosis of these two categories has been characterized by muddled conceptualization, since most standardized instruments for assessing depression contain a number of "anxiety" items and *vice versa* (Foa & Foa, 1982). In some cases the two conditions respond differentially to the same treatment; in other cases the response is the same. Similarly, progress in determining the biological features and substrates of these disorders reveals some differences and some intriguing similarities (Barlow & Maser, 1983). Recent ethological speculations suggest some interesting connections between anxiety and depression (Klein, 1981). Psychopathological studies will have to unravel this complex relationship, but no review of studies of treatment outcome can ignore the role of depression as a potential predictor or moderating factor in outcome.

TREATMENT OF THE ANXIETY DISORDERS: STATE OF THE ART

A large number of treatment strategies have been applied to the anxiety disorders; in view of the fuzziness of classification before DSM-III, however, it is not always clear what was being treated. Nevertheless, it is possible to make definitive treatment recommendations for some of these clinical syndromes, and these recommendations will be outlined below. In addition, the current state of this work suggests a number of complex clinical issues that deserve empirical attention (e.g., Barlow & Wolfe, 1981). These will be discussed in the context of the various DSM-III categories discussed above.

Phobic Disorders

Within the phobic disorders, the bulk of existing evidence points to the necessity of reducing phobic anxiety and avoidance through exposure to the feared situation or object; this approach, in its many forms, is considered the treatment of choice (Barlow & Wolfe, 1981). This exposure can occur in a variety of ways that take the form of different techniques, as outlined below.

Agoraphobia. Agoraphobia, the most complex of the phobic disorders, can be treated successfully by one of the following formats: direct exposure, also termed "flooding *in vivo*" or "reinforced practice," which involves arranging for the patient to be exposed to feared situations such as walking or driving away from a safe place or safe person, or being in a crowded shopping center. In the most usual form, this procedure is termed prolonged *in vivo* exposure and involves a therapist accompanying the patient during a difficult situation on activity until anxiety diminishes. One example would be remaining in a shopping mall for as long as 4 hours or more. The primary therapist can accompany the patient, but often the therapist is an assistant or an ex-phobic who is trained in facilitating this type of activity (Marks, 1981). Direct exposure, however, can also occur on a graduated basis and its "mildest" form need not require the presence of a therapist or a therapy aide. For example, the patient can be requested to move up a hierarchy of fear-producing situations very gradually, in a self-paced manner. This would be done on the instructions of the therapist, with the patient reporting back to the therapist each week to discuss progress (e.g., Mathews, Johnston, Lancashire, Munby, Shaw, & Gelder, 1976).

A second type of exposure can be labeled "indirect exposure." In this procedure the patient is not directly exposed to the phobic situation, but rather is presented in imagination or symbolically (such as through the use of film) with fear-arousing cues. Systematic desensitization is included in this category since this procedure is characterized by gradual, imaginal presentation of a hierarchy of feared stimuli paired with relaxation. Other imaginal procedures, such as imaginal flooding, could be included here (Mavissakalian & Barlow, 1981).

A number of early studies demonstrated quite clearly the superiority of direct exposure to indirect exposure (Barlow, Leitenberg, Agras, & Wincze, 1969; Emmelkamp & Wessels, 1975; see Mavissakalian & Barlow, 1981). Furthermore, early studies looking at outcome immediately after the conclusion of alternative treatments concluded that prolonged *in vivo* exposure or "intensive" exposure was more efficacious than gradual or spaced exposure (Foa, Jameson, Turner, & Payne, 1980; Rachman & Wilson, 1980; Stern & Marks, 1973).

However, the picture changes considerably if one looks at the outcome of treatment at follow-up points of 3 to 6 months. At this point, any differences disappear since either more graduated, self-paced direct exposure, or even indirect exposure techniques, produce therapeutic gains that "catch up" to those produced by prolonged *in vivo* exposure (Mathews *et al.*, 1976; Mathews, Teasdale, Munby, Johnston, & Shaw, 1977; Munby & Johnston, 1980). Klein, Zitrin, Woerner, and Ross (1983) found that self-paced exposure taking place in the context of supportive therapy delivered within a phobia clinic was as effective as imaginal exposure (systematic desensitization) at follow-up. Klein *et al.* (1983) point out—correctly, we think—that almost any treatment delivered within the context of a phobia clinic will "instigate" graduated self-paced exposure *in vivo*, and therefore lead to improvement.

The outcome of exposure-based treatments is fairly consistent when one examines a number of different studies conducted by clinicians in various parts of the world. If dropouts are excluded, the best estimates of outcome indicate that from 60% to 70% of those agoraphobics completing treatment will show some clinical benefit and that these effects will be maintained, on the average, for periods of 4 years or more (Emmelkamp & Kuipers, 1979; Jansson & Öst, 1982; McPherson, Brougham, & McLaren, 1980; Munby & Johnston, 1980). In view of the consistency of this outcome and the fact that the effectiveness of this approach has been demonstrated repeatedly in controlled experimentation when compared to no treatment or some good placebo (e.g., Mathews, 1978; Mavissakalian & Barlow, 1981; O'Brien & Barlow, in press), this development represents one of the success stories of psychotherapy. Nevertheless, having demonstrated that this approach is successful, investigators are beginning to examine its limitations. It is now becoming increasingly apparent that the outcome of these treatments is characterized by many examples of failure, relapse, and limited clinical improvement. For example, one major problem most often overlooked in the treatment of agoraphobia is dropouts. An updated review of a large number of studies indicates that the median dropout rate from exposure-based treatments is 12%, with rates from 25% to 40% recorded when drugs are added to exposure-based treatments (Jansson & Öst, 1982; Zitrin, Klein, & Woerner, 1978, 1980). Furthermore, data reflecting success rates of 60–70% are also reflecting the fact that 30–40% of all agoraphobics who complete treatment fail to benefit. And of the remaining 60–70%, a substantial percentage may not reach clinically meaningful levels of functioning. For example, Marks (1971) reported that only three of 65 clients (4.6%) were completely symptom-free at follow-up, as determined by assessors' clinical ratings. McPherson *et al.* (1980) reported that among clients who showed some improvement following behavioral treatment, only 18% who were reached at follow-up rated themselves as being completely free of symptoms. Finally, Munby and Johnston (1980) observed relapses occurring in as many as 50% of clients who had benefited clinically, although in most cases these clients were evidently able to return to a level of clinical improvement previously reached in treatment.

Furthermore, it now seems possible that prolonged *in vivo* exposure, carried out in an intensive fashion, may be less effective than previously assumed and might even be detrimental if viewed in a broader context. For example, returning to the issue of dropouts, intensive *in vivo* exposure, administered over a short period of time, seems to produce a dropout rate considerably higher than the median 12% (e.g., Emmelkamp & Ultee, 1974; Emmelkamp & Wessels, 1975). On the other hand, a more gradual self-initiated exposure program, carried out over a longer period of time with a cooperative partner in the environment, produces a very low dropout rate (Jannoun, Munby, Catalan, & Gelder, 1980; Mathews *et al.*, 1977). Another disadvantage is the sometimes deleterious effect of dramatic behavioral changes following *in vivo* exposure on the interpersonal system of the client, particularly the spouse (e.g., Hafner, 1977; O'Brien, Barlow, & Last, 1982). Since at least 75% of agoraphobics are women, the majority of whom are married, these effects most often show up in the husband (Mavissakalian & Barlow, 1981). In addition, it has been consistently observed that continued progress, after treatment is terminated, does not occur with intensive, therapist-assisted, *in vivo* exposure. This is a serious problem since we have already noted that improvement is often far less than desired. Other investigators suggest that therapist-assisted, *in vivo* exposure may produce a dependence on the therapist which in and of itself precludes further improvement once the therapist is absent (e.g., Mathews *et al.*, 1977). Finally, this approach is associated with a higher relapse rate than less intensive treatments (Hafner, 1976; Jansson & Öst, 1982).

In view of these clinical results, there have been a number of attempts to improve the effectiveness of exposure-based treatments by additions to or alterations in the therapeutic package. One addition that does not seem successful, at least on the basis of evidence to date, is the use of cognitive therapy or cognitive restructuring (e.g., Mahoney, 1974; Meichenbaum, 1977). Whether cognitive therapy is attempted in isolation for the treatment of phobia (e.g., Biran & Wilson, 1981; Emmelkamp, Kuipers, & Eggeraat, 1978) or whether cognitive therapy is added to exposure-based treatment (e.g., Emmelkamp & Mersch, 1982; Williams & Rappaport, 1983), no major benefit is obvious from cognitive therapy. This is an interesting finding because clinically these procedures seem useful and patients often attribute their therapeutic gains to the use of cognitive procedures (e.g.,

Ascher, 1980; O'Brien & Barlow, in press). It is still possible, for example, that these procedures may prove effective in subsequent studies or may be useful in the long term to prevent relapse (e.g., Last, Barlow, & O'Brien, in press). Nevertheless, there is no evidence for their usefulness at this time.

There are two therapeutic approaches, however, that do seem to enhance the results of exposure-based treatments. The first is the use of antidepressants such as tricyclics and MAO inhibitors, which target the reduction of panic (Zitrin, 1981). In one of the best studies to date, Zitrin *et al.* (1980) report that some clinical improvement was noted in approximately 70% of a group receiving exposure *in vivo*, which is typical of results found around the world, but that this improvement, as rated by the therapist, increased to 92% with the addition of imipramine. However, both dropouts and relapses were very high in this study. At 6-month follow-up, approximately 65% of each group remained clinically improved according to therapist ratings. If one subtracts dropouts, then the percentage of those showing some clinical improvement drops to 49% for each group at 6-month follow-up, somewhat below the typical outcome of exposure-based treatment calculated in a similar fashion. Zitrin, Klein, Woerner, and Ross (1983) report a similar comparison between imaginal exposure (systematic desensitization) with and without imipramine (other groups were also involved in this comparison). Once again, results from completers at post-treatment measurement revealed an advantage to imipramine, but, at follow-up, when one subtracts dropouts, 54% of the imaginal exposure group improved compared to 52% of the imaginal exposure plus imipramine group. However, the pharmacological approach to treatment is not the subject of this chapter, and further research is needed with particular attention paid to dropouts and relapses to document the potential promise of this therapeutic approach.

Another approach that seems to enhance treatment, without some of the disadvantages of the pharmacological approaches noted above, is the addition of a spouse or other concerned family member or friend to a more gradual self-paced treatment protocol. For example, Hand, Lamontagne, and Marks (1974) noted that agoraphobics treated in what became a cohesive group stayed in touch with one another and supported each other after treatment, evidently resulting in further improvement. Mathews *et al.* (1977), in the uncontrolled clinical trial mentioned above, included spouses of agoraphobics as co-therapists and noted that over 90% were much improved at the end of treatment, with improvement continuing at follow-up. Munby and Johnston (1980) conducted follow-ups of a series of studies carried out by the same group of investigators and noted that the treatment in which spouses were directly included produced continuing improvement and results that were superior at a 4- to 9-year follow-up to those from agoraphobics treated in separate clinical trials, but more intensively and without spouses. Sinnott, Jones, Scott-Fordham, and Woodward (1981) also noted that agoraphobics treated as a group, who were all taken from the same neighborhood, were superior on many outcome measures to a group composed of agoraphobics from diverse geographical regions who presumably did not meet, socialize, or generally support each other during or after therapy. In view of the fact that agoraphobia often arises during stressful situations, such as periods of marital disruption, including the spouse in treatment may produce a particular advantage. This advantage was recently demonstrated in a controlled trial of couples in treatment for agoraphobia (Barlow, O'Brien, & Last, in press) in which agoraphobics who engaged in a self-paced, exposure-based treatment that was graduated in nature and without the direct participation of a therapist, did significantly better if their spouses were included than did a group treated identically without their spouses. In this study, 86%, or 12 of a group of 14 patients treated in this manner, responded clinically, closely replicating the results of the Mathews *et al.* (1977) study.

Finally, more graduated, home-based treatments where patients proceed at their own pace within the context of a structured treatment program produce significantly fewer dropouts than the more intensive, prolonged, exposure *in vivo* or the pharmacological treatments. For example, Mathews *et al.* (1977), Jannoun *et al.* (1980), and Barlow *et al.*, (in press) all recorded dropout rates of under 5%. This type of outcome statistic is often overlooked when one considers treatment efficacy, but is receiving increased attention from psychotherapy researchers (Barlow & Wolfe, 1981).

Thus, exposure-based techniques are the psychosocial treatment of choice for agoraphobia, but we're learning more about the important conditions that must obtain to deliver these techniques in their most effective manner. Futhermore, at the end of this chapter, the critical lack of knowledge on mechanisms of action of these approaches which must be discovered if we are to improve their efficacy will be outlined as well as other major deficiencies in our knowledge of treatment at this point in time.

Social Phobia. Despite its (presumably) greater prevalence, research into the clinical treatment of social phobia is not nearly as advanced as in agoraphobia. To date, four studies have appeared which treat a homogeneous group of clinical social phobics. This does not include, of course, numerous studies involving volunteers, usually college students with test anxiety, fears of public speaking, or heterosocial anxiety. These studies have focused on the techniques of systematic desensitization and social-skills training (a structured treatment approach designed to shape more appropriate social behavior through the use of reinforcement, rehearsal, feedback, and homework). Marzillier, Lambert, and Kellet (1976) compared these two treatments to a waiting-list control, reporting that both approaches led to improvement in social functioning, with outpatients reporting anxiety in a range of social situations. Only patients receiving social-skills training maintained these gains at 6-months follow-up. Neither treatment produced clinically or statistically significant reductions in self-reported anxiety. However, Trower, Yardley, Bryant, and Shaw (1978) examined the effects of these two treatments with social phobics and patients demonstrating social inadequacy. On self-report measures, the socially phobic patients fared equally well with both treatments, although change was not seen on the behavioral measures. Shaw (1979) compared the two treatment groups from the Trower *et al.* study with a third group treated with imaginal flooding. No treatment differences emerged, although all patients showed improvement. In the absence of a controlled investigation, these findings are difficult to interpret.

What seems to be the best study to date is that of Öst, Jerremalm, and Johansson (1981). Subjects were outpatients with a major presenting complaint of anxiety in social situations. Patients were assessed on self-report, behavioral, and physiological measures prior to treatment. On the basis of these measures, they were classified as "behavioral reactors" or "physiological reactors," depending on which response pattern was prominent. Two treatment approaches were applied: social-skills training and applied relaxation. Among behavioral reactors, social-skills training produced maximal results; among physiological reactors, relaxation was superior. These data suggest that clinically meaningful results can be obtained with these two treatment approaches, given careful patient–treatment matching. This finding deserves replication. In addition, there are a number of research needs in this area, not the least of which includes an examination of the role of exposure with this disorder (Barlow & Wolfe, 1981). It is possible, for example, that exposure alone has contributed to the results achieved with social-skills training and relaxation, since patients are presented *in vivo* and imaginally with their feared stimuli. This hypothesis suggests a more easily implemented treatment, relative to those which have been examined to date.

It is also possible that cognitive procedures will play a more important role in social phobias which, once again, are essentially a fear of scrutiny or evaluation. For example, in a detailed examination of test anxiety, which is a form of social phobia, Sarason (1982) found that somatic components of anxiety (e.g., trembling, increased heartrate, perspiration, rapid breathing) did not interfere with performance, but that task-irrelevant thoughts ("I'm going to fail," "What will my parents think?" "What will I do?") were responsible for decrements in performance. The area of sexual dysfunction, in fact, also resembles a social phobia, with fear of performance and subsequent evaluation prominent features. Barlow, Sakheim, and Beck (1983) demonstrated that increasing somatic or physiological aspects of anxiety in normals, through a fear-producing paradigm concurrent with viewing an erotic stimulus, actually increased sexual arousal. These data suggest that "anxiety" as originally conceptualized may not diminish arousal. Presumably, subjects "attributed" their increased autonomic arousal to the sexual context in a "transfer of emotion" fashion common in the laboratories of social psychology (e.g., Schachter, 1966). Other research has demonstrated, however, that task-irrelevant cognitive distractions reliably lower sexual arousal (Farkas, Sine, & Evans, 1979; Geer & Fuhr, 1976). In sexual dysfunction, as in other social phobias, research is needed to examine the role of cognitions involving fear of negative evaluation with a focus on treatment implications. These basic psychopathological studies suggest a role for cognitive focusing strategies in the treatment of fear of social evaluation, and also underline the potential usefulness of a three-response system analysis of fears.

Simple Phobia. Treatment of the simple or specific phobias has followed a similar development, with respect to the type of techniques employed, to the treatment of agoraphobia. The several variants of exposure treatment outlined earlier have been employed. In the review of this literature, several conflicting opinions have emerged. Morganstern (1973) concluded that indirect exposure (systematic desensitization) was more effective than *in vivo* exposure, whereas Levis and Hare (1977) have drawn the opposite conclusion. In a more refined review, Mathews (1978) notes that *in vivo* techniques proved more effective with analogue populations (e.g., college students presenting with fearful, nonphobic symptomatology) but not with clinical populations. In light of the qualitative differences in symptoms between these two groups, this distinction appears important. Linden (1981) examined this literature, taking into account methodological quality of the studies involved, and concluded that direct comparison of these two forms of exposure has been insufficiently investigated with clinical populations. The outcome of these various reviews overall is that some form of exposure therapy is effective in treating the simple phobias, although there is debate as to specific therapeutic format. This treatment area, more than any other, has been subjected to rigorous methodological examination with analogue populations. The development of a body of literature on systematic desensitization, summarized by Rachman and Wilson (1980), has included much attention to internal and external validity of this treatment. Although there is some debate as to whether this approach has shown itself as more effective than the most rigorous control for nonspecific treatment effects, particularly with volunteers (e.g., Kazdin & Wilcoxon, 1976), its efficacy is well established. A number of cognitive–behavioral approaches have been employed as well, based primarily on self-statement training, a technique devised to modify a patient's maladaptive thoughts and expectancies. To date, a large body of literature has not appeared analyzing these approaches, although some authors feel that they may be useful, either in conjunction with an exposure-based technique or by themselves (e.g., Barlow & Wolfe, 1981; O'Brien, 1981).

Anxiety States

Overall, treatments for the disorders in this subcategory have followed a slightly different course, although the theoretical explanation for their effectiveness is similar to that provided for the public disorders. Given that the anxiety states are not characterized by behavioral avoidance in the same sense as phobias, the psychosocial treatments and pharmacological approaches tested to date have targeted cognitive and physiological aspects of the disorder.

Panic Disorder. As discussed previously, research suggests that imipramine and MAO inhibitors alleviate panic attacks in the anxiety disorders. These agents target the somatic symptoms involving heightened autonomic responding, but of course do not deal directly with the more cognitive experiential aspects of nonphobic anxiety. Feelings of unreality, fear, and apprehension concerning dying or "going crazy," for example, comprise the subjective element of fear. A recent investigation has explored the application of cognitive–behavioral techniques and relaxation procedures in the treatment of panic disorder (Waddell *et al.*, 1983). Utilizing a single case experimental design (e.g., Hersen & Barlow, 1976), three adult males were treated initially with self-statement training, followed by relaxation procedures. All three patients showed decreases in frequency and duration of panic-related intense anxiety during the cognitive intervention, but little change was noted in general "background" anxiety level for two of them during either treatment phase. This suggests the effectiveness of psychosocial treatments for nonphobic panic, but requires replication and extension. The possible advantage of this approach is the targeting of both somatic and cognitive aspects of panic with relaxation and cognitive procedures. Of course, panic is a significant component of agoraphobia, and 60–70% of agoraphobics respond to psychosocial treatments. This suggests that "panic" must also respond to these treatments, even though the focus is on the avoidance behavior through the use of exposure-based procedures (e.g., Barlow *et al.*, in press). But it is interesting that few, if any, studies have actually monitored or measured the occurrence of panic, and it is therefore difficult to draw conclusions. Furthermore, the treatments for panic that do not include exposure in cases where there is no "feared situation" and therefore no avoidance, are quite different than the treatments for agoraphobia. The Waddell *et al.* (1983) study described above appears to be the first test of psychosocial treatments for panic disorder. It is also noteworthy, from the point of view of psychopathology, that generalized or background anxiety responded differently from intense anxiety or panic, replicating with psychological treatments the pharmacological dissection work first described by Klein and his associates (Klein, 1981).

Generalized Anxiety Disorder. The treatment of generalized anxiety disorder is in its infancy, as well, with respect to empirically based treatment approaches. This, of course, is not true of the clinical treatment of generalized anxiety which, as noted at the outset, is one of the most common problems presenting to health professionals. Treatment with minor tranquilizers or psychotherapy goes on daily in the office of clinicians. Nemiah (1981), for example, discusses treatment of generalized anxiety from a psychoanalytic perspective, employing relevant case material to illustrate the role of ego defenses in creating various symptomatology. But, from the point of view of diagnosis, the components of GAD are unclear and not reliably recognized, and there has been surprisingly little research into treatment effectiveness (Barlow & Wolfe, 1981). Generally, two types of therapeutic approaches have been applied, much as in panic disorders. One group targets the heightened physiological arousal, and the other focuses on the cognitive symptomatology. Given that no behavioral avoidance exists in this disorder, these two response systems comprise the crux of this disorder once again, as in panic disorder.

Within the somatic treatments, several pharmacological approaches have been employed, including benzodiazepines and beta blockers. The most popular of this latter drug group, propranalol, has the effect of reducing heart palpitations and is used increasingly, especially given the questionable effectiveness of the benzodiazepines (Solomon & Hart, 1978). However, its clinical effectiveness in treating generalized anxiety has yet to be empirically demonstrated. A second form of somatic treatment involves the use of biofeedback. Rice and Blanchard (1982) reviewed this literature and conclude that frontal EMG feedback offers the most promising results of this approach. There is little support to suggest that EMG alpha and heartrate feedback is helpful in facilitating anxiety reduction. Within this literature, two studies have demonstrated specific EMG reduction associated with clinical improvements in anxiety disorders (Arnarson & Sheffield, 1980; Townsend, House, & Addario, 1975), and work by Canter, Kondo, and Knott (1975) has shown that EMG feedback has a clinical advantage over drug treatments, since there are no risks or side effects associated with this psychophysiological treatment. There is a clear need to test this technique in applied settings, as the bulk of research to date has been conducted with analogue populations in laboratory settings.

A related form of somatic treatment is relaxation training. Although the evidence for the effectiveness of these procedures is fairly strong, often showing equal or greater magnitude of change relative to EMG feedback (e.g., Beiman, Isreal, & Johnson, 1978) and clear superiority over no treatment or placebo controls (e.g., Borkovec, Grayson, & Cooper, 1978; Lewis, Biglan, & Steinblock, 1978), most of this work has been conducted with college students. The studies that have employed this technique with actual patient populations (e.g., Borkovec & Sides, 1979; Lehrer, 1978) have demonstrated its effectiveness, especially in treating individuals with specific physiological symptoms. In light of the ease of implementation of this treatment strategy, its use in applied practice appears warranted.

The cognitive treatment approach also has been applied to chronic, generalized anxiety and appears to hold some promise as an effective approach. Beck, Laude, and Bohnert (1974) outlined specific cognitions associated with elevated levels of anxiety, based upon clinical contacts with this population, and state that a cognitive approach can be highly effective. The content of these thoughts centers around themes of physical harm or of psychosocial trauma; this content is the substance to which cognitive behavioral techniques are applied. Woodward and Jones (1980) compared a combination cognitive approach–systematic desensitization package with each treatment alone, reporting that the combination proved more effective than either approach in isolation for treatment of clinical anxiety. It will be recalled that the cognitive–behavioral treatment component was somewhat effective at reducing "background" (or generalized) anxiety when applied to individuals with panic disorder (Waddell *et al.*, 1983). Further research is needed on the treatment approaches to GAD. To date, the somatic treatments seem to offer promise for reducing the autonomic symptomatology which are present frequently, whereas cognitive approaches may target the cognitive phenomena involved (apprehension, vigilance). Possibly, these two treatment approaches affect specific, differential types of change; a research strategy like that employed by Öst *et al.* (1981) in the treatment of social phobia could help in exploring this hypothesis, as could a carefully designed single case approach, employing well-chosen measures across both response domains. Research to date has also left us with little information on the extent of clinical effectiveness or the percentage of patients reaching clinically important levels of functioning, since the few studies reported have relied in statistical rather than clinical significance.

Obsessive–Compulsive Disorder. Obsessive–compulsive disorder has received the most empirical attention of the syndromes in this subcategory. Possibly because of its recalcitrant nature, a number of treatment investigations have been conducted, and consensus has been reached that the treatment of choice is *in vivo* exposure combined with response prevention (e.g., Foa & Tillmanns, 1980; Marks, 1977; Rachman & Hodgson, 1980). (For a detailed clinical description of these procedures, see Foa & Tillmanns, 1980.) For example, Foa, Steketee, and Milby (1980) examined the separate treatment effects of these two techniques in a clinical trial involving eight obsessive–compulsives with washing rituals. In this examination, exposure was designed to produce prolonged, continuous exposure to discomfort-eliciting stimuli (defined for each patient), while response prevention involved prohibiting the washing rituals to take place. Half the patients initially were given 10 days of exposure treatment alone, followed by 10 days of combined treatment; the remaining patients received response prevention alone for 10 days, followed by the combined treatment. Results indicate that exposure alone reduced self-reported anxiety significantly, and that response prevention reduced self-recorded duration of hand washing. The combined treatment equalized the two groups on both measures. It would thus appear that within this treatment approach, exposure effects change in subjective anxiety levels, whereas preventing the ritualizing behavior produces specific behavioral change, although these authors are careful to call for replication in light of the small sample size and use of patients' self-recording as the primary data source. Several authors report relatively high failure and relapse rates following this treatment approach (Marks, Hodgson, & Rachman, 1975, report a 25% failure rate; Steketee, Foa, & Grayson, 1982, report a 20% relapse rate). Across studies, 60–85% of these patients are improved at follow-up, a rate similar to that achieved with agoraphobia and with some of the same limitations regarding extent of clinical improvement.

Marks (1981) is quick to provide some important qualifications for this treatment approach, accurately noting that this form of treatment requires extensive cooperation on the part of the patient. Toward this end, the therapeutic rationale provided by the therapist seems to be an important aspect of utilizing this approach. One potential rationale relies on the data provided by Rachman and deSilva (1978) described earlier; in essence, it is explained to the patient that obsessions are not an atypical occurrence, that what is problematic is his or her response to them (e.g., more resistance is attempted by the patient and the obsessions are felt to be more alien). Treatment is offered as a strategy by which to reduce emotional responding to the thoughts, as well as to eliminate the consequences following such thoughts which help to maintain them (compulsions). Although no data exist concerning the potency of various therapeutic rationales in determining patient cooperation and compliance, our clinical experience suggests that this may be an important ingredient of treatment. Given that exposure (flooding) may produce more dropouts from treatment, and often is the least readily accepted of available therapeutic alternatives (Rachman & Hodgson, 1980), the therapeutic context seems to be an important treatment consideration.

Emmelkamp (1982) has reported preliminary data that suggest that including spouses in the treatment of this disorder may strengthen therapeutic effects; in this case, spouses were employed as "coaches," encouraging exposure although not providing reassurance when asked (since this can reduce the anxiety-eliciting effects of exposure treatment). This approach may prove useful in increasing compliance and preventing treatment dropout, factors which deserve empirical attention.

A variety of treatment strategies have been applied to pure obsessions (in the absence of existing ritualistic compulsions; see Salzman, 1966), but the effectiveness of these approaches is not supported by research. Recently, two empirically based strategies have been tested that are somewhat similar to those treatments that have proved successful with compulsive behavior. Both of these approaches rely on Rachman's (1976) conceptualization that obsessions are often followed by anxiety-reducing cognitive compulsions. This would suggest that exposure to the anxiety-producing obsessions, coupled with cognitive response prevention, should be employed. To date, the two forms of treatments that have been examined are variants of exposure (e.g., satiation, desensitization) and techniques oriented toward suppression of thoughts (e.g., thought stopping, aversion relief). Though data are scarce for both, exposure has not produced impressive results. Solyom, Garza-Perez, Ledwidge, and Solyom (1972) employed paradoxical intension aimed at obsessive thoughts, reporting that five of ten patients improved, three remained unchanged, and two failed to comply with therapeutic instructions.

With respect to thought suppression strategies, data are mixed. Stern, Lipsedge, and Marks (1975) examined relaxation procedures alone and in combination with thought stopping, reporting that 4 of 11 patients showed clinical improvement with thought stopping. A subsequent replication attempt (Stern, 1978) produced even less impressive results. Several authors have reported successful treatment of obsessions using aversive techniques (e.g., Bass, 1973; Kenny, Mowbray, & Lalani, 1978). Overall, this approach has not been employed widely. Current treatment recommendations include habituation treatment and evocation of the thoughts by instruction, with cognitive response prevention where necessary (Rachman & Hodgson, 1980).

Pharmacological approaches have also been employed in the treatment of obsessive–compulsive disorder, with the tricyclic antidepressants showing the greatest promise (Marks, 1981). The most advanced work to date has been conducted by Marks, Stern, Mawson, Cobb, and McDonald (1980) and Rachman, Cobb, Grey, McDonald, Mawson, Sartory, and Stern (1979). Since these large studies also involved psychosocial components, they will be included in this section. These investigators examined the effects of clomipramine and behavioral treatments (relaxation training, *in vivo* exposure, and self-imposed response prevention) with 40 severe obsessive–compulsives. During the first 4 weeks of the study, patients received either clomipramine (oral dosage) or a placebo; following this, all were admitted to inpatient status, where each group was further subdivided, half receiving relaxation and half receiving *in vivo* exposure and response prevention for 3 weeks. In the final 3 weeks of treatment, all patients received exposure and response prevention, plus additional therapy as needed. A 2-year follow-up was conducted, with psychological treatment administered only when necessary.

Results indicate that, consistent with previous data, response prevention and exposure were superior to relaxation procedures at reducing ritualizing behavior. No differential effect on mood was found for these treatments. However, clomipramine showed an effect on both rituals and mood, but *only* for patients displaying significant depression. There did not appear to be any interactive effects of drug and behavioral treatments, either during treatment itself or afterward. A 1-year follow-up revealed that the effects of clomipramine peaked at 18 weeks, with relapse often seen when the drug was discontinued. Interestingly, these authors report that clomipramine increased compliance with behavioral treatment. These reports are extremely important, as they delineate specific effects of behavioral and pharmacological treatment upon separate areas of functioning. Additionally, there is the suggestion that pharmacological treatment of obsessive–compulsive disorder is warranted only when significant depression coexists, a topic to be discussed in more detail in a later section of this chapter.

Post-Traumatic Stress Disorder

As with other disorders that are relative newcomers within DSM-III, there is not much information on the treatment of PTSD. Keane and Kaloupek (1982) report the use of imaginal flooding in the single-case treatment of a Vietnam veteran; on the basis of self-monitoring, standardized psychological test results, and physiological responding, these authors demonstrated the efficacy of this approach. This report exemplifies the creative use of single-case methodology in exploring potential treatments for this new disorder, and illustrates the clinical change in a relatively severe case. A similar case treatment is described by Fairbank and Keane (1982). Other reports, employing systematic desensitization (e.g., Kipper, 1977; Schinder, 1980) have demonstrated the efficacy of this treatment strategy, targeting both recurrent nightmares and intense anxiety. The accumulated effect of these preliminary reports suggests that, as with the other anxiety disorders, exposure may be the critical treatment ingredient, although this remains speculative pending controlled research employing multiple measures and rigorous methodology. Horowitz (1976) has presented an information-processing account to explain the mechanism by which exposure effects anxiety reduction in PTSD. According to this account, traumatic events that are not easily assimilated within the individual's cognitive schemata will continue to evoke emotional responding, owing to "active" memory representation. The individual seeks cognitively to avoid assimilation, with each confrontation (forced or accidental) of the traumatic recollection forcing processing to occur. Ultimately, aberrant stress responses are reduced when the recollection is processed within existing cognitive schemes. This account suggests that flooding may achieve therapeutic effects by producing rapid assimilative processing, whereas systematic desensitization results in more gradual resolution. This approach provides one account of the mechanism through which exposure produces decrements in anxiety. Pending treatment efficacy data, however, it remains speculative.

Conclusions

The state of the art in treatment of the anxiety disorders is advanced for some disorders and preliminary for others. For the phobic disorders and obsessive–compulsive disorders, specific therapeutic approaches exist that seem superior to available alternatives. For the "newer" diagnoses of generalized anxiety disorder, panic disorder, and post-traumatic stress syndrome, emerging developments are promising. It is important to note that although considerable advances have been made in the treatment of these disorders, many if not most patients are far from symptom-free at the end of successful treatment. Many require adjunct therapy, often targeting marital and social functioning. As has been seen, the effective treatments for these disorders appear to effect specific types of changes, with somatic therapies reducing physiological arousal, behavioral treatments producing behavior and some subjective change, and, to a lesser extent, cognitive interventions targeting the specific cognitive symptomatology. This specificity of effect supports current conceptualizations of behavior change, but seems to imply that greater attention must be paid to producing more generalized, meaningful clinical effects. Perhaps, greater understanding of the mechanisms by which these interventions produce change will assist in this endeavor. These questions appear to be relevant to applied practice, in that current approaches, though relatively efficacious, do not appear maximally, or even moderately, effective in many cases. This large variability in treatment response, with some patients "cured," others moderately better, and some who show no improvement or even deteriorate, is masked by our usual between-group comparison approach with the emphasis on statistical rather than clinical significance. Needless to say, the issue of which individual patients respond to which treatment or aspect of treatment is crucial to the practicing therapist. A number of patient–treatment interactions appear to exist that have clear implications for clinical practice.

PATIENT-TREATMENT INTERACTIONS

As interventions for the anxiety disorders have evolved, a number of important patient–treatment interactions have emerged. These findings may in time help to guide our understanding of the nature of these disturbances and to improve our treatments. Many of these interactions were first noted in clinical and clinical-research settings. But these observations were often not the primary goal of the clinical or clinical-research efforts in which they were ultimately discovered. This is due to the preeminence of a research methodology that deemphasizes the response of the individual patient and makes the search for patient–treatment interactions difficult if not impossible (Barlow, 1981; Barlow, Hayes, & Nelson, 1983). Nevertheless, some interactions have been discovered; these will be discussed in the context of the disorders in which they have been examined.

Phobic Disorders

One issue receiving a great deal of attention in research on agoraphobia concerns the relationship of a patient's marital satisfaction to the outcome of treatment. It was first suggested by Webster (1953) and then by a number of other investigators (e.g., Agulnik, 1970; Andrews, 1966; Goldstein & Chambless, 1978) that the origins and maintenance of agoraphobia might be intimately wrapped up in the patient's interpersonal situation. This was outlined in the beginning of this chapter. Subsequent studies have demonstrated, in fact, that marital satisfaction prior to treatment does predict outcome (Hafner, 1977, 1979; Milton & Hafner, 1979). For example, Milton and Hafner (1979) reported that agoraphobics with unsatisfactory marriages, defined as those couples in the lower half of a median split on a measure of overall marital adjustment, were less likely than patients with satisfactory marriages to improve following intensive, prolonged *in vivo* exposure. Patients with unsatisfactory marriages were also more likely to relapse during the 6-month follow-up period. Similar results were reported by Bland and Hallam (1981). The implication here, of course, as noted by Bland and Hallam (1981), is that poor marriages may be associated with less favorable outcome since spouses may be less likely to provide spontaneous support and encouragement to their partners during treatment and follow-up, and that patients may be less likely to accept such support even if offered.

Recent research from our laboratory (Barlow, O'Brien, Last, & Holden, 1983; Barlow *et al.*, in press) have elaborated on these initial findings. In this clinical trial, 28 agoraphobics were treated by means of a self-paced instructional program in which they came to the clinic once a week and met in small groups of five or six patients where they received cognitive therapy and detailed instructions on practicing and coping with feared situations between sessions. These feared situations were arranged in hierarchical order so that patients would progress to more difficult situations over a period of 12 weeks. For half of these patients, their husbands attended all group sessions and were included in treatment as co-therapists. The other half were treated without their husbands. Data from this clinical trial replicated earlier results in that patients in initially unsatisfactory marriages did more poorly than patients with satisfactory marriages. However, this effect was overcome if the husbands of patients with unsatisfactory marriages attended treatment. This subgroup ended up doing as well as those patients with satisfactory marriages. More intensive analysis of the behavior of patients from poor marriages treated with and without their spouses may reveal exactly what it is that happens within these marriages that accounts for greater or less improvement. Discovery of the reasons for this and other patient–treatment interactions will, of course, greatly improve the efficacy of our treatments.

In addition, a detailed examination of treatment failures in this clinical trial, identifying several factors that may be associated with this lack of clinical response, was performed. One of the patients reported a fear that anxiety or panic would cause her to lose control and "go insane." This patient, who was brought up with a brother, later diagnosed schizophrenic, believed in the rationality of this fear and limited her verbal participation in groups for fear that the therapist would diagnose her psychotic. However, Emmelkamp and Van der Hout (1982) did not find "overvalued ideation" (which is Foa's [1979] term for irrational ideas held strongly) in their agoraphobics who failed to benefit from exposure therapy. Thus, this observation that overvalued ideation may contribute to failure is not confirmed. However, the similarity of what Foa (1979) has termed overvalued ideation to obsessional thinking is striking. Three additional patients in the Barlow *et al.* (in press) series reported heightened somatic complaints, and were unresponsive to reassurances from the therapist that these were benign. Perhaps one of the existing strategies for reducing physiological arousal, such as relaxation training, may have facilitated exposure therapy. Finally, one patient reported feeling uncomfortable in her treatment group, stating that since she was considerably older, her presenting problems were different from those of the other members. This, combined with an early report by Hand *et al.* (1974) concerning the role of social support in motivating continuing progress during and after group therapy, seems to imply the importance of therapeutic context within which these procedures are implemented. These hypotheses, derived from clinical reports, deserve empirical attention.

Another factor with some evidence of predicting treatment outcome with exposure-based procedures is level of depression. Zitrin *et al.* (1980) report that more depressed patients fared less well as a result of exposure therapy, regardless of whether imipramine was included in treatment. However, this relationship was not observed in our clinical trial (Barlow *et al.*, in press). In view of the considerable overlap in classification criteria between depression and the anxiety disorders noted in the first section of this chapter, this prognostic factor must be examined in considerably more detail. For example, a number of authors (e.g., Gardos, 1981; Marks, 1981) have speculated that certain of the anxiety disorders are psychosomatic variants of affective disorder and that the therapeutic effects of antidepressants are, in fact, mediated by reducing depression rather than by targeting anxiety directly. It is notable, in this regard, that Zitrin (1981) reported a substantial number of patients with both agoraphobia and mixed phobias, who demonstrated sensitivity to imipramine, displaying excitatory symptoms, including insomnia, jitteriness, irritability, and unusual energy (reminiscent of drug-induced hypomania). This finding would argue against the contention that agoraphobia and mixed phobias are variants of depression, as imipramine sensitivity is not common in the latter diagnostic category. Sharper definitions and basic psychopathological research into the relationship of anxiety and depression are needed before the prognostic value of presence and level of depression is clear.

Another relevant patient–treatment interaction is termed "desynchrony," defined as a low degree of covariance in change among the various response systems (Rachman & Hodgson, 1974). There are preliminary data to suggest that desynchrony (or lack of generalization among response systems) following treatment may indicate high potential for relapse (e.g., Barlow, Mavissakalian, & Schofield, 1980; Grey, Rachman, & Sartory, 1981). In other words, someone with reduced anxiety in subjective and behavioral response systems following treatment but continued high autonomic responding might be a greater risk for relapse than a patient showing "synchronous" decrease in all three response systems. If this notion were confirmed, then clinicians would want to administer careful pre- and post-treatment assessments, with individually tailored treatments applied to those response systems that show problematic functioning. However, this approach is premature at this time since a minority of treatment studies to date have employed measures in all three response systems, which would allow study of the predictive validity of desynchrony. The study of related phenomena, including what Rachman (1978) has termed "courageous" or "fearless" individuals (those persons who show no signs of anxiety on any dimension during an objectively dangerous situation), may also prove fruitful in understanding the nature of anxiety and the treatment implications of desynchrony (Barlow & Maser, 1983). For example, it seems that some who are skillful at performing well under objectively dangerous conditions, such as the astronauts, produce high autonomic responding, coupled with a subjective sense of mastery of the task. In this case, desynchrony does not seem a problem. Of course, there may be considerable dfferences between rational and irrational fears, differences that may have important implications for the study of desynchrony and behavior change.

Anxiety States

Several important patient–treatment interactions have emerged in the treatment of obsessive–compulsive disorder. As discussed previously, based upon the clinical series conducted by Rachman *et al.* (1979) and Marks *et al.* (1980), tricyclic antidepressants appear to affect both rituals and mood, but only with patients displaying significant levels of depression. Other investigators have suggested that severely depressed patients with this diagnosis are less likely to benefit from exposure therapy (Foa, 1979; Foa, Grayson, Steketee, Doppelt, Turner, & Latimer, 1983; Marks, 1973; Rachman & Hodgson, 1980). Boulougouris (1977) has reported a negative relationship between depression and interference scores on the Leyton Obsessional Inventory, following treatment. Foa (1979) has speculated that depression interferes with the habituation of anxiety displayed during exposure sessions, the treatment element postulated to be the critical ingredient for effective exposure. Data presented by Lader and Wing (1969) support this contention, demonstrating the absence of GSR habituation to neutral auditory stimuli in patients with primary depression. However, more recent evidence suggests that this notion is too simplistic. Foa, Grayson, and Steketee (1982) examined three levels of depression (high, moderate, and low) in obsessive–compulsive patients treated with *in vivo* exposure. Highly depressed patients improved less than patients demonstrating low and moderate levels of depression on both obsessions and compulsions at post-treatment and follow-up. In examining patterns of habituation, the least depressed group habituated more within and between sessions, relative to the group demonstrating high levels of depression. The moderately depressed group surprisingly demonstrated habituation patterns similar to those of the highly depressed group. From more refined analyses, these authors conclude that the failure to respond to treatment shown by severely depressed patients could not be accounted for solely as a failure to habituate. Degree of habituation was related to treatment outcome only when it occurred between sessions, not just within a treatment session—a finding that supports the contention that improvement in this disorder is produced in part by long-term habituation to fear.

Further findings from this research team have revealed other prognostic factors (Foa *et al.*, 1982). Patients with earlier onset of symptomatology maintained the gains accrued by treatment at follow-up more than those with later onset. This factor proved significant in a path analytic model, constructed with data collected from 50 severe obsessive–compulsives. Level of anxiety was predictive of outcome, in part; that is, low initial anxiety predicted successful outcome, though high anxiety did not necessarily predict outcome either way. No relationship was found between severity of obsessive–compulsive symptoms and treatment outcome, a finding that runs counter to clinical observation and may be due to the restricted sample employed. Level of depression affected treatment outcome, mediated by reactivity; that is, level of autonomic reactivity to feared stimuli was correlated .46 with presenting level of depression and, in the path analysis, predicted within- and between-session habituation, consistent with previous data. It thus appears that depression may affect the benefits of exposure therapy by dampening reactivity to feared stimuli; this would suggest a slightly different mechanism for exposure than previously outlined, implying that "anxious" responding may play a role in creating therapeutic change with this procedure. Pre-treatment levels of anxiety and depression were related significantly. In addition, these authors report that patients showing immediate gains after treatment had a high risk of relapse at follow-up. Though the reasons for this are unknown, this relationship suggests the need for maintenance strategies, as well as exploration of factors predicting relapse in this population.

Foa (1979) has provided one other observation concerning patient-treatment interactions in the area of obsessive–compulsive disorder that was also described above in the section on agoraphobia. In examining the reasons for treatment failure in patients who complied with the therapeutic regime, Foa reported that patients who believed their obsessions and fears to be justified (or realistic) showed within-session habituation during exposure treatment but failed to show between-session habituation. This observation concerning "overvalued ideation" highlights, once again, the importance of long-term habituation to fear in exposure therapy. In addition, it suggests that interventions oriented toward changing the patient's belief concerning the realistic nature of their obsessions may be necessary prior to initiating exposure therapy with this subset of individuals who display strong irrational belief systems. But this observation is speculative and retrospective at present, and needs well-controlled prospective testing before this variable can be considered important.

As noted above, treatment in the area of panic disorder is relatively underdeveloped, owing to its status as a new diagnostic category. Of course, several physical abnormalities such as hypoglycemia, thyroid conditions, and, a condition that has received a great deal of attention of late, mitral-valve prolapse (MVP, also called Barlow syndrome). MVP is characterized by attacks of chest pain, palpitations, headache, and "giddiness," accompanied by an unusual and difficult-to-characterize systolic murmur. As such, this syndrome mirrors the diagnostic criteria for panic disorder and would appear to be an important differential diagnosis. However, Gorman, Fyer, Glicklich, King, and Klein (1981) report that response to imipramine is independent of the presence of MVP in individuals with panic disorder, and family studies (e.g., Crowe, Paul, Slymen, & Noyes, 1980) have also pointed out the independence of these disorders. Recently, some investigators have not found a greater prevalence of MVP in panic-disorder or agoraphobia patients than in normals (Mavissakalian, 1983), and others have suggested that the high prevalence of MVP in anxiety disorders is due to biased screening (Hartmann, Kramer, Brown, & Devereux, 1982).

Conclusions

To date, there is little in the way of conclusive evidence to suggest possible patient–treatment interactions with PTSD, generalized anxiety disorder, and social phobias. Given the relatively high prevalence of secondary depression that has been reported in generalized anxiety and panic disorders (e.g., Dealy, Ishik, Avery, Wilson, & Dunner, 1981), one can speculate that high levels of depression may complicate treatment with these individuals, possibly by diminishing reactivity and habituation, in line with Foa's work in the area of obsessive–compulsive disorder. A strategy like that employed by Öst *et al.* (1981) in the area of social phobia might prove fruitful in exploring patient–treatment interactions. As described above, these authors matched patient response characteristics to treatment approach, demonstrating that individuals presenting with high levels of physiological arousal showed maximal therapeutic gains with a treatment focusing upon somatic responding, whereas patients displaying behavioral symptoms responded best to a treatment shaping more socially appropriate behaviors. This demonstration is encouraging and suggests the importance of careful understanding of the nature of these disorders, understanding that will be needed before truly effective interventions can emerge.

LIMITATIONS OF EXISTING KNOWLEDGE

We pointed out in the introduction to this chapter that the anxiety disorders are a relatively understudied set of problems relative to other behavioral and emotional problems. Thus, there is a great deal to be accomplished by clinicians and clinical researchers to answer some of the major questions remaining if we are to devise efficient and effective treatments for these disorders. We have made reference to many of these issues throughout the review of treatment outcome data and patient–treatment interactions. Additional research needs have been outlined in recent papers on both treatment and psychopathology of the anxiety disorders (Barlow & Maser, 1983; Barlow & Wolfe, 1981).

Primary among these needs is greater knowledge on basic issues involving classification and psychopathology of the anxiety disorders. While the DSM-III has provided much-needed improvement in precision and conceptual clarity of classification, further research on the reliability and validity of these categories will be necessary before we can proceed with confidence in devising treatments specifically tailored to each of these disorders. This is particularly true of some of the newer categories, such as panic disorder, generalized anxiety disorder, and post-traumatic stress disorder. As reviewed above, treatments are further along for the more traditional problems of agoraphobia and obsessive–compulsive disorder as well as the specific phobias. The area of social phobia presents a special case, since this has long been recognized as a common problem. Given that the salient characteristics of this particular phobia reaction have been reconceptualized by DSM-III, new approaches are likely in both the study of the psychopathology of this disorder and treatment–assessment research.

A second gap in our knowledge regarding treatment effectiveness for these disorders is shared with the whole field of treatment–assessment research. This has to do with our basic style of research, reflecting as it does an emphasis on between-group experimental comparisons and analyses of statistical rather than clinical significance. What is lost in this experimental approach, so typical of psychotherapy outcome studies, is an analysis of the individual response to treatment and the relevant patient–treatment interactions: specifically, who benefits from therapy, who benefits perhaps only marginally, and who does not benefit or possibly deteriorates as a function of therapy. The basic issue, then, is one of generalization of therapeutic change to each individual entering a clinician's office, and we do not now have the answers to these important questions of generalization (Barlow, 1981; Barlow, Hayes, & Nelson, 1983). This would seem to be the reason that so few of our research findings seem to influence clinical practice in the area of psychotherapy. A strategy that would begin to redress this deficit in our knowledge has been termed clinical replication (Barlow, 1980, 1981). In this strategy, a therapeutic technique or procedure with some evidence for its effectiveness, based on experimentally sound investigation, would be administered to a series of patients in a clinical setting. These clinicians or clinical researchers, using a procedure that Cronbach (1975) has termed "intensive local observation," would observe both successes and failures, defined clinically rather than statistically in this series of individual patients. An attempt can then be made to identify not only the overall percentage of patients who improve, but, more importantly, reasons that might be associated with failures or minimal improvement. Using the procedure of logical generalization, clinicians could then "infer" the probability of success or failure of any patient walking into their office based on similarities to patients who succeeded or failed in the clinical replication series. If enough of these series accumulated, we would have a great deal of information on the generality of effectiveness of any psychotherapeutic procedure with given individuals. That is, we would learn much more about patient–treatment interactions than we would from our grand factorial studies. In the case of agoraphobia, for example, we are as sure as science will allow that exposure-based treatments are effective in treating phobic disorders. Furthermore, we have a rough idea that from 60% to 70% of people receiving these treatments will benefit. But we know almost nothing, other than what has been described in the previous section, about which individual will benefit, which individual will fail, and what characteristics would be associated with success or failure. This does not then allow clinicians, who presumably should be consuming research findings, to do anything more than gamble that the next agoraphobic walking into their office will benefit from an exposure-based treatment. Clinical replication series have enormous potential to contribute to the clinical science of psychotherapy research.

Yet another area, a large deficit in even the most advanced areas of treatment–outcome research, is the specification of mechanisms of action of change. For example, we have no idea why exposure-based treatments work, although theories abound (Barlow & Mavissakalian, 1981). Basic theories regarding habituation, cognitive change involving modification of personal constructs of fear, and sophisticated information processing analyses have all been offered of late as an explanation for the success of exposure-based treatments (Barlow & Mavissakalian, 1981). What all these theories have in common is a realization that "exposure," whether applied to agoraphobia or obsessive–compulsive disorder, is simply an empirical description of what is happening and not an explanation for why therapeutic benefits result. The three-response system analysis of anxiety described above seems to have produced some theoretical headway in analyzing and understanding the effects of our treatments. For example, it was noted in the section on the treatment of obsessive–compulsive disorders that exposure seems to reduce subjective experience of fear in obsessionals whereas response prevention for rituals has a direct and specific effect on the ritualistic behavior itself. Pharmacological intervention, in contrast, affects the depressed mood so often found in obsessives compulsives. Exposure-based treatment for phobia, in particular agoraphobia, however, combines the exposure and response prevention roles that are separate in obsessive–compulsive disorder. That is, when an agoraphobic confronts a feared situation, he or she is also preventing the ritual of escape as well as, perhaps, subjectively habituating to the feared situation or, more accurately, the fear of physiological manifestations of panic. However, there seem to be many other "rituals" in phobic reactions besides simply escaping the feared situation. These involve cognitive rituals wherein a patient will think certain thoughts, dress in a certain way, carry an empty bottle of pills in a pocket, hum certain songs, or sit in the back of a church or the movie theater, all of which represent, at the very least, a "cognitive avoidance" equivalent to rituals in obsessive–compulsive disorder (Borkovec, 1981; Mavissakalian, 1982). An exploration into the mechanisms of action of treatment is perhaps the single most important task confronting psychotherapy researchers in the anxiety disorders.

Finally, the problem of measuring change is increasingly confronting psychotherapy researchers as we devise and develop procedures that seem to be more effective in producing this change. For example, taking again one of the more advanced areas of treatment–outcome research, it is not yet clear how best to represent change in agoraphobia. Questionnaires and global, clinical ratings alone seem unsatisfactory since they often ignore important behavioral and physiological dimensions of fear. The role of physiological responsivity, as noted in the beginning of this chapter, is unclear as it relates to outcome, although there are intriguing hints concerning its importance. To take one example from our clinic that illustrates the difficulty in determining appropriate measures, one agoraphobic male at a year's follow-up responded very positively to all questionnaires and during a clinical interview reported that he was doing everything with considerable ease and only minimal anxiety, thus receiving a much improved clinical rating. Physiological indexes also revealed some improvement. However, careful monitoring of a behavior diary, taken for a period of several weeks at the 1-year follow-up, which was confirmed by his wife, revealed an almost total behavioral relapse (Last *et al.*, in press). Recent investigations in several clinical centers, including ours, have reported change in terms of a composite index sampling change in all relevant response systems, including global clinical ratings (e.g., Barlow *et al.*, in press). Whether this will be an improvement awaits studies on validity of this index of change in conjunction with other clinical research centers working in the area of anxiety disorders.

Conclusions

Studies in psychopathology and treatment outcome within the anxiety disorders represent one of the more exciting areas of clinical research at this time. Advances in the conceptualization and classification of these disorders have a great deal to do with the increased interest in studies of psychopathology. Furthermore, some of the most exciting developments in psychotherapy research concern the development of effective treatments for phobia and obsessive–compulsive disorders over a period of the last 10–20 years. Although this chapter makes it clear that we have a long way to go before we can truly say we have efficient and effective treatments for these problems, the progression of our research to date should instill confidence that effective psychosocial treatments in existence can be improved and new interventions can be developed. Though the obstacles to advancing our knowledge remain formidable, the growing interaction and cooperation of biological and psychological investigators increases our optimism concerning further advances, to the ultimate benefit of the field and patients suffering from these problems.

REFERENCES

Agras, W. S., Chapin, H. N., & Oliveau, D. C. The natural history of phobia. *Archives of General Psychiatry*, 1972, *26*, 315–317.

Agras, W. S., Sylvester, D., & Oliveau, D. The epidemiology of common fear and phobia. *Comprehensive Psychiatry*, 1969, *10*, 151–156.

Agulnik, P. L. The spouse of the phobic patient. *British Journal of Psychiatry*, 1970, *117*, 58–67.

Akhtar, S., Wig, N. H., Verma, V. K., Pershod, D., & Verma, S. K. A phenomenological analysis of symptoms in obsessive–compulsive neuroses. *British Journal of Psychiatry*, 1975, *127*, 342–348.

Akiskal, H. S., Bitar, A. H., Puzantian, V. R., Rosenthal, T. L., & Walker, P. W. The nosological status of neurotic depression. *Archives of General Psychiatry*, 1978, *35*, 756–766.

American Psychiatric Association. *Diagnostic and statistical manual of mental disorders* (3rd ed.). Washington, D.C.: American Psychiatric Association, 1980.

Andrews, J. D. W. Psychotherapy of phobias. *Pyschological Bulletin*, 1966, *66*, 455–480.

Arnarson, E. O., & Sheffield, B. The generalization of the effects of EMG and temperature biofeedback procedures in patients suffering from anxiety states. In *Proceedings of the Biofeedback Society of America eleventh annual meeting*. Denver: Biofeedback Society of America, 1980.

Ascher, L. M. Paradoxical intention. In A. Goldstein & E. B. Foa (Eds.), *Handbook of behavioral interventions: A clinical guide*. New York: Wiley, 1980.

Barlow, D. H. Behavior therapy: The next decade. *Behavior Therapy*, 1980, *11*, 315–328.

Barlow, D. H. On the relation of clinical research to practice: Current issues, new directions. *Journal of Consulting and Clinical Psychology*, 1981, *49*, 147–156.

Barlow, D. H. The death of neurosis: Review of Marks, I. *Cure and care of neuroses: Theory and practice of behavioral psychology*. *Contemporary Psychology*, 1982, *27*, 512–514.

Barlow, D. H., Hayes, S. C., & Nelson, R. O. *The scientist-professional: Research and accountability in mental health and education*. New York: Pergamon, 1983.

Barlow, D. H., Leitenberg, H., Agras, W. S., & Wincze, J. P. The transfer gap in systematic desensitization: An analog study. *Behaviour Research and Therapy*, 1969, *7*, 191–196.

Barlow, D. H., & Maser, J. D. The psychopathology of anxiety disorders: A report on the NIMH research workshop. Submitted for publication, 1983.

Barlow, D. H., & Mavissakalian, M. Directions in the assessment and treatment of phobia: The next decade. In M. Mavissakalian & D. H. Barlow (Eds.), *Phobia: Psychological and pharmacological treatment*. New York: Guilford, 1981.

Barlow, D. H., Mavissakalian, M., & Schofield, L. D. Patterns of desynchrony in agoraphobia: A preliminary report. *Behaviour Research and Therapy*, 1980, *18*, 441–448.

Barlow, D. H., O'Brien, G. T., & Last, C. G. Couples treatment of agoraphobia. *Behavior Therapy*, in press.

Barlow, D. H., O'Brien, G. T., Last, C. G., & Holden, A. E. Couples treatment of agoraphobia. In K. D. Craig & R. J. McMahon (Eds.), *Advances in clinical behavior therapy*. New York: Brunner/Mazel, 1983.

Barlow, D. H., Sakheim, D. K., & Beck, J. G. Anxiety increases sexual arousal. *Journal of Abnormal Psychology*, 1983, *92*, 49–54.

Barlow, D. H., & Wolfe, B. E. Behavioral approaches to anxiety disorders: A report on the NIMH–SUNY, Albany research conference. *Journal of Consulting and Clinical Psychology*, 1981, *49*, 448–454.

Bass, B. An unusual behavioral technique for treating obsessive ruminations. *Psychotherapy: Theory and Practice*, 1973, *10*, 191–192.

Beck, A. T., Laude, R., & Bohnert, M. Ideational components of anxiety neurosis. *Archives of General Psychiatry*, 1974, *31*, 319–325.

Beiman, I., Isreal, E., & Johnson, S. A. During training and posttraining effects of live and taped extended progressive relaxation, self-relaxation, and electromyogram biofeedback. *Journal of Consulting and Clinical Psychology*, 1978, *46*, 314–321.

Biran, M., & Wilson, G. T. Treatment of phobic disorders using cognitive and exposure methods: A self-efficacy analysis. *Journal of Consulting and Clinical Psychology*, 1981, *49*, 886–899.

Black, A. The natural history of obsessional neurosis. In H. R. Beech (Ed.), *Obsessional states*. London: Methuen, 1974.

Blanchard, E. B., Kolb, L. C., Pallmeyer, T. P., & Gerardi, R. J. The development of a psychophysiological assessment procedure for post-traumatic stress disorder in Vietnam veterans. *Psychiatric Quarterly*, 1982, *54*, 220–229.

Bland, K., & Hallam, R. S. Relationship between response to graded exposure and marital satisfaction in agoraphobics. *Behaviour Research and Therapy*, 1981, *19*, 335–338.

Borkovec, T. Facilitation and inhibition of functional CS exposure in the treatment of phobias. In J. C. Boulougouris (Ed.), *Learning theory approaches to psychiatry*. Chichester, England: Wiley, 1981.

Borkovec, T. D., Grayson, J. B., & Cooper, K. M. Treatment of general tension: Subjective and physiological effects of progressive relaxation. *Journal of Consulting and Clinical Psychology*, 1978, *46*, 518–528.

Borkovec, T. D., & Sides, J. K. Critical procedural variables related to the physiological effects of progressive relaxation: A review. *Behaviour Research and Therapy*, 1979, *17*, 119–126.

Boulougouris, J. C. Variables affecting the behavior modification of obsessive–compulsive patients treated by flooding. In J. C. Boulougouris & A. D. Rabavilas (Eds.), *The treatment of phobic and obsessive–compulsive disorders*. Oxford, England: Pergamon, 1977.

Bryant, B., Trower, P., Yardley, K., Urbieta, H., & Letemendia, F. J. J. A survey of social inadequacy among psychiatric patients. *Psychological Medicine*, 1976, *6*, 101–112.

Canter, A., Kondo, C. Y., & Knott, J. R. A comparison of EMG feedback and progressive muscle relaxation training in anxiety neurosis. *British Journal of Psychiatry*, 1975, *127*, 470–477.

Cronbach, L. J. Beyond the two disciplines of scientific psychology. *American Psychologist*, 1975, *30*, 116–127.

Crowe, R. R., Paul, G. L., Slymen, D. J., & Noyes, R. A family study of anxiety neurosis. *Archives of General Psychiatry*, 1980, *37*, 77–79.

Curran, J. P., Miller, I. E., Zwick, W. R., Monti, P. M., & Stout, R. L. The socially inadequate patient: Incidence rate, demographic and clinical features, and hospital and posthospital functioning. *Journal of Consulting and Clinical Psychology*, 1980, *48*, 375–382.

Dealy, R. S., Ishik, D. M., Avery, D. H., Wilson, L. G., & Dunner, D. L. Secondary depression in anxiety disorders. *Comprehensive Psychiatry*, 1981, *22*, 612–618.

deSilva, P., Rachman, S., & Seligman, M. Prepared phobias and obsessions: Therapeutic outcome. *Behaviour Research and Therapy*, 1977, *15*, 54–77.

DiNardo, P. A., O'Brien, G. T., Barlow, D. H., Waddell, M. T., & Blanchard, E. B. Reliability of DSM-III anxiety disorder categories using a new structured interview. *Archives of General Psychiatry*, 1983, *40*, 1070–1074.

Emmelkamp, P. M. G. *Phobic and obsessive–compulsive disorders: Theory, research and practice*. New York: Plenum, 1982.

Emmelkamp, P. M. G., & Kuipers, A. C. M. Agoraphobia: A follow-up study of four years after treatment. *British Journal of Psychiatry*, 1979, *134*, 352–355.

Emmelkamp, P. M. G., Kuipers, A., & Eggeraat, J. Cognitive modification versus prolonged exposure *in vivo*: A comparison with agoraphobics. *Behaviour Research and Therapy*, 1978, *16*, 33–41.

Emmelkamp, P. M. G., & Mersch, P. P. Cognition and exposure *in vivo* in the treatment of agoraphobia: Short-term and delayed effects. *Cognitive Research and Therapy*, 1982, *6*, 77–90.

Emmelkamp, P. M. G., & Ultee, K. A. A comparison of "successive approximation" and "self-observation" in the treatment of agoraphobia. *Behavior Therapy*, 1974, *5*, 606–613.

Emmelkamp, P. M. G., & Van der Hout, A. Failure in treating agoraphobia. In E. B. Foa & P. M. G. Emmelkamp (Eds.), *Failures in behavior therapy*. New York: Wiley, 1982.

Emmelkamp, P. M. G., & Wessels, H. Flooding in imagination vs. flooding *in vivo*: A comparison with agoraphobics. *Behaviour Research and Therapy*, 1975, *13*, 7–15.

Fairbank, J. A., & Keane, T. M. Flooding for combat-related stress disorders: Assessment of anxiety reduction across traumatic memories. *Behavior Therapy*, 1982, *13*, 499–510.

Farkas, G. M., Sine, L. F., & Evans, I. M. The effects of distraction, performance demand, stimulus explicitness and personality on objective and subjective measures of male sexual arousal. *Behaviour Research and Therapy*, 1979, *17*, 25–32.

Foa, E. B. Failure in treating obsessive–compulsives. *Behaviour Research and Therapy*, 1979, *17*, 169–179.

Foa, E. B., & Foa, U. G. Differentiating anxiety and depression: Is it possible? Is it useful? *Psychopharmacology Bulletin*, 1982, *18*, 62–68.

Foa, E., Grayson, J., & Steketee, G. Depression, habituation, and treatment outcome in obsessive–compulsives. In J. C. Boulougouris (Ed.), *Learning theory approaches to psychiatry*. Chichester, England: Wiley, 1982.

Foa, E. B., Grayson, J. B., Steketee, G. S., Doppelt, H. S., Turner, R. M., & Latimer, P. R. Success and failure in the behavioral treatment of obsessive–compulsives. *Journal of Consulting and Clinical Psychology*, 1983, *51*, 287–298.

Foa, E. B., Jameson, J. S., Turner, R. M., & Payne, L. L. Massed vs. spaced exposure sessions in the treatment of agoraphobia. *Behaviour Research and Therapy*, 1980, *18*, 333–338. (a)

Foa, E., Steketee, G. S., & Milby, M. B. Differential effects of exposure and response prevention in obsessive–compulsive washers. *Journal of Consulting and Clinical Psychology*, 1980, *48*, 71–79. (b)

Foa, E., & Tillmanns, A. The treatment of obsessive–compulsive neurosis. In A. Goldstein & E. Foa (Eds.), *Handbook of behavioral interventions*. New York: Wiley, 1979.

Gardos, G. Is agoraphobia a psychosomatic form of depression? In D. F. Klein & J. Rabkin (Eds.), *Anxiety: New research and changing concepts*. New York: Raven, 1981.

Geer, J., & Fuhr, R. Cognitive factors in sexual arousal: The role of distraction. *Journal of Consulting and Clinical Psychology*, 1976, *44*, 238–243.

Goldstein, A. J., & Chambless, D. L. A reanalysis of agoraphobia. *Behavior Therapy*, 1978, *9*, 47–59.

Gorman, J. M., Fyer, A. F., Glicklich, J., King, D. L., & Klein, D. F. Mitral valve prolapse and panic disorders: Effect of imipramine. In D. F. Klein & J. Rabkin (Eds.), *Anxiety: New research and changing concepts*. New York: Raven, 1981.

Grey, S. J., Rachman, S., & Sartory, G. Return of fear: The role of inhibition. *Behaviour Research and Therapy*, 1981, *19*, 135–143.

Hafner, R. J. Fresh symptom emergence after intensive behaviour therapy. *British Journal of Psychiatry*, 1976, *129*, 378–383.

Hafner, R. J. The husbands of agoraphobic women and their influence on treatment outcome. *British Journal of Psychiatry*, 1977, *131*, 289–294.

Hafner, R. J. Agoraphobic women married to abnormally jealous men. *British Journal of Medical Psychology*, 1979, *52*, 99–104.

Hallam, R. S. Agoraphobia: A critical review of the concept. *British Journal of Psychiatry*, 1978, *133*, 314–319.

Hand, I., Lamontagne, Y., & Marks, I. M. Group exposure (flooding) *in vivo* for agoraphobics. *British Journal of Psychiatry*, 1974, *124*, 588–602.

Hartmann, N., Kramer, R., Brown, W. T., & Devereux, R. B. Panic disorder in patients with mitral valve prolapse. *American Journal of Psychiatry*, 1982, *139*, 669–671.

Hersen, M., & Barlow, D. H. *Single-case experimental designs: Strategies for studying behavior change*. New York: Pergamon, 1976.

Horowitz, M. *Stress response syndromes*. New York: Aronson, 1976.

Horowitz, M. J., Wilner, N., Kaltreider, N., & Alvarez, W. Signs and symptoms of post-traumatic stress disorder. *Archives of General Psychiatry*, 1980, *37*, 85–92.

Hough, R. L., & Gongla, P. A. *Research problems in relation to post-traumatic stress disorders in Vietnam veterans.* Prepared for presentation at the Workshop on Anxiety Disorders, National Institute of Mental Health, Rockville, Md., May 1982.

Jannoun, L., Munby, M., Catalan, J., & Gelder, M. A home-based treatment program for agoraphobia: Replication and controlled evaluation. *Behavior Therapy*, 1980, *11*, 294–305.

Jansson, L., & Öst, L. G. Behavioral treatments for agoraphobia: An evaluative review. *Clinical Psychology Review*, 1982, *2*, 311–336.

Kazdin, A. E., & Wilcoxon, L. A. Systematic desensitization and non-specific treatment effects: A methodological evaluation. *Psychological Bulletin*, 1976, *83*, 729–758.

Keane, T. M., & Kaloupek, D. G. Imaginal flooding in the treatment of a post-traumatic stress disorder. *Journal of Consulting and Clinical Psychology*, 1982, *50*, 138–140.

Kelly, D. *Anxiety and emotions: Physiological basis and treatment.* Springfield, Ill.: Thomas, 1980.

Kenny, F. T., Mowbray, R. M., & Lalani, S. Faradic disruption of obsessive ideation in the treatment of obsessive neurosis. *Behavior Therapy*, 1978, *9*, 209–221.

Kipper, D. A. Behavior therapy for fears brought on by war experiences. *Journal of Consulting and Clinical Psychology*, 1977, *45*, 216–221.

Klein, D. F. Anxiety reconceptualized. In D. F. Klein & J. Rabkin (Eds.), *Anxiety: New research and changing concepts.* New York: Raven, 1981.

Klein, D. F., & Fink, M. Psychiatric reaction patterns to imipramine. *American Journal of Psychotherapy*, 1962, *119*, 432–438.

Klein, D. F., Zitrin, C. M., Woerner, M. G., & Ross, D. C. II. Behavior therapy and supportive psychotherapy: Are there any specific ingredients? *Archives of General Psychiatry*, 1983, *40*, 139–153.

Lader, M. H. Physiological research in anxiety. In H. M. van Praag (Ed.), *Research in neurosis.* New York: SP Medical and Scientific, 1978.

Lader, M. H., & Wing, L. Physiological measures in agitated and retarded depressed patients. *Journal of Psychiatric Research*, 1969, *7*, 89–100.

Lang, P. J. Fear reduction and fear behavior: Problems in treating a construct. In J. M. Shlien (Ed.), *Research in psychotherapy* (Vol. 3). Washington, D.C.: American Psychological Association, 1968.

Last, C. G., Barlow, D. H., & O'Brien, G. T. Cognitive changes during *in vivo* exposure in an agoraphobic. *Behavior Modification*, in press.

Last, C. G., & Blanchard, E. B. Classification of phobics versus fearful nonphobics: Procedural and theoretical issues. *Behavioral Assessment*, 1982, *4*, 195–210.

Lehrer, P. M. Psychophysiological effects of progressive relaxation in anxiety neurotic patients and of progressive relaxation and alpha feedback in nonpatients. *Journal of Consulting and Clinical Psychology*, 1978, *46*, 389–404.

Levis, D. J., & Hare, N. A review of the theoretical rationale and empirical support for the extinction approach of implosive (flooding) therapy. In R. M. Eisler & P. M. Miller (Eds.), *Progress in behavior modification* (Vol. 4). New York: Academic, 1977.

Lewis, C. E., Biglan, A., & Steinblock, E. Self-administered relaxation training and money deposits in the treatment of recurrent anxiety. *Journal of Consulting and Clinical Psychology*, 1978, *46*, 1274–1283.

Linden, W. Exposure treatments for focal phobias: A review. *Archives of General Psychiatry*, 1981, *38*, 769–775.

Mahoney, M. *Cognition and behavior modification.* Cambridge, Mass.: Ballinger, 1974.

Malloy, P. F., Fairbank, J. A., & Keane, T. M. Validation of a multimethod assessment approach to post-traumatic stress disorders in Vietnam veterans. *Journal of Consulting and Clinical Psychology*, 1983, *51*, 488–495.

Marks, I. M. *Fears and phobias.* London: Heineman Medical, 1969.

Marks, I. M. Agoraphobia syndrome (phobic anxiety state). *Archives of General Psychiatry,* 1970, *23,* 538–553.

Marks, I. M. Phobic disorders four years after treatment: A prospective follow-up. *British Journal of Psychiatry,* 1971, *118,* 683–688.

Marks, I. M. New approaches to the treatment of obsessive–compulsive disorders. *Journal of Nervous and Mental Disease,* 1973, *156,* 420–426.

Marks, I. M. Recent results of behavioral treatments of phobias and obsessions. *Journal of Internal Medicine Research,* 1977, *5,* 16–21.

Marks, I. M. Review of behavioral psychotherapy: I. Obsessive–compulsive disorders. *American Journal of Psychiatry,* 1981, *138,* 584–592.

Marks, I. M. *Cure and care of neuroses.* New York: Wiley, 1981.

Marks, I. M., Boulougouris, J. C., & Marset, P. Flooding versus desensitization in the treatment of phobic patients: A crossover study. *British Journal of Psychiatry,* 1971, *119,* 353–375.

Marks, I. M., & Herst, E. R. A survey of 1,200 agoraphobics in Britain. *Social Psychiatry,* 1970, *5,* 16–24.

Marks, I. M., Hodgson, R., & Rachman, S. Treatment of chronic obsessive–compulsive neuroses by *in vivo* exposure: A two-year follow-up and issues in treatment. *British Journal of Psychiatry,* 1975, *127,* 349–364.

Marks, I. M., Stern, R., Mawson, D., Cobb, J., & McDonald, B. Clomipramine and exposure for obsessive–compulsive rituals: I. *British Journal of Psychiatry,* 1980, *136,* 1–25.

Marsland, D. W., Wood, M., & Mayo, F. Content of family practice: A data bank for patient care, curriculum, and research in family practice—526, 196 patient problems. *Journal of Family Practice,* 1976, *3,* 25–68.

Marzillier, J. S., Lambert, C., & Kellet, J. A controlled evaluation of systematic desensitization and social skills training for socially inadequate psychiatric patients. *Behaviour Research and Therapy,* 1976, *14,* 225–238.

Mathews, A. M. Fear reduction research and clinical phobias. *Psychological Bulletin,* 1978, *83,* 390–404.

Mathews, A. M., Gelder, M. G., & Johnston, D. W. *Agoraphobia: Nature and treatment.* New York: Guilford, 1981.

Mathews, A. M., Johnston, D. W., Lancashire, M., Munby, M., Shaw, P. M., & Gelder, M. G. Imaginal flooding and exposure to real phobic situations: Treatment outcome with agoraphobic patients. *British Journal of Psychiatry,* 1976, *129,* 362–371.

Mathews, A. M., Teasdale, J., Munby, M., Johnston, D., & Shaw, P. A home based treatment program for agoraphobia. *Behavior Therapy,* 1977, *8,* 914–924.

Mavissakalian, M. Agoraphobia: The problem of treatment. *Behavior Therapist,* 1982, *5,* 173–175.

Mavissakalian, M. Personal communication. January 1983.

Mavissakalian, M., & Barlow, D. H. Phobia: An overview. In M. Mavissakalian & D. H. Barlow (Eds.), *Phobia: Psychological and pharmacological treatment.* New York: Guilford, 1981.

McPherson, F. M., Brougham, L., & McLaren, S. Maintenance of improvement in agoraphobic patients treated by behavioural methods—A four-year follow-up. *Behaviour Research and Therapy,* 1980, *18,* 150–152.

Meichenbaum, D. *Cognitive-behavior modification: An integrative approach.* New York: Plenum, 1977.

Milton, F., & Hafner, J. The outcome of behavior therapy for agoraphobia in relation to marital adjustment. *Archives of General Psychiatry,* 1979, *36,* 807–811.

Morganstern, K. P. Implosive therapy and flooding procedures: A critical review. *Psychological Bulletin,* 1973, *79,* 318–334.

Mullaney, J. A., & Trippett, C. J. Alcohol dependency and phobias: Clinical description and relevance. *British Journal of Psychiatry*, 1979, *135*, 565–573.

Munby, M., & Johnston, D. W. Agoraphobia: The long-term follow-up of behavioral treatment. *British Journal of Psychiatry*, 1980, *137*, 418–427.

Nemiah, J. C. The psychoanalytic view of anxiety. In D. F. Klein & J. Rabkin (Eds.), *Anxiety: New research and changing concepts*. New York: Raven, 1981.

O'Brien, G. T. Clinical treatment of specific phobias. In M. Mavissakalian & D. H. Barlow (Eds.), *Phobia: Psychological and pharmacological treatment*. New York: Guilford, 1981.

O'Brien, G. T., & Barlow, D. H. Agoraphobia. In S. M. Turner (Ed.), *Behavioral treatment of anxiety disorders*. New York: Plenum, in press.

O'Brien, G. T., Barlow, D. H., & Last, C. G. Changing marriage patterns of agoraphobics as a result of treatment. In R. DuPont (Ed.), *Phobia: A comprehensive summary of modern treatments*. New York: Brunner/Mazel, 1982.

Öst, L. G., Jerremalm, A., & Johansson, J. Individual response patterns and the effects of different behavioral methods in the treatment of social phobia. *Behaviour Research and Therapy*, 1981, *19*, 1–16.

Quitkin, F. M., Rifkin, A., Kaplan, J., & Klein, D. F. Phobic anxiety syndrome complicated by drug dependence and addiction: A treatable form of drug abuse. *Archives of General Psychiatry*, 1972, *27*, 159–162.

Rachman, S. The modification of obsessions: A new formulation. *Behaviour Research and Therapy*, 1976, *14*, 437–443.

Rachman, S. *Fear and courage*. San Francisco: Freeman, 1978.

Rachman, S., Cobb, J., Grey, S., McDonald, B., Mawson, D., Sartory, G., & Stern, R. The behavioural treatment of obsessional-compulsive disorders with and without clomipramine. *Behaviour Research and Therapy*, 1979, *17*, 467–478.

Rachman, S., & deSilva, P. Abnormal and normal obsessions. *Behaviour Research and Therapy*, 1978, *16*, 233–248.

Rachman, S., & Hodgson, R. J. Synchrony and desynchrony in fear and avoidance. *Behaviour Research and Therapy*, 1974, *12*, 311–318.

Rachman, S. J., & Hodgson, R. J. *Obsessions and compulsions*. Englewood Cliffs, N.J.: Prentice-Hall, 1980.

Rachman, S. J., & Wilson, G. T. *The effects of psychological therapy* (2nd ed.). Oxford, England: Pergamon, 1980.

Raskin, M., Peeke, H. V. S., Dickman, W., & Pinkster, H. Panic and generalized anxiety disorders: Developmental antecedents and precipitants. *Archives of General Psychiatry*, 1982, *29*, 687–689.

Rice, K. M., & Blanchard, E. B. Biofeedback in the treatment of anxiety disorders. *Clinical Psychology Review*, 1982, *2*, 557–577.

Salzman, L. Therapy of obsessional states. *American Journal of Psychiatry*, 1966, *122*, 1139–1146.

Sarason, I. G. *Stress, anxiety, and cognitive interference: Reactions to tests*. Arlington, Va.: Office of Naval Research, 1982.

Schachter, S. The interaction of cognitive and physiological determinants of emotional state. In C. D. Spielberger (Ed.), *Anxiety and behavior*. New York: Academic, 1966.

Schinder, F. E. Treatment by systematic desensitization of a recurring nightmare of a real life trauma. *Journal of Behavior Therapy and Experimental Psychiatry*, 1980, *11*, 53–54.

Shaw, P. A comparison of three behaviour therapies in the treatment of social phobias. *British Journal of Psychiatry*, 1979, *134*, 620–623.

Shepherd, M., Cooper, B., Brown, A. C., & Kalton, G. W. *Psychiatric illness in general practice*. London: Oxford University Press, 1966.

Sinnott, A., Jones, R. B., Scott-Fordham, A., & Woodward, R. Augmentation of *in vivo* exposure treatment for agoraphobia by the formation of neighborhood self-help groups. *Behaviour Research and Therapy*, 1981, *19*, 339–347.

Snaith, R. P. A clinical investigation of phobias. *British Journal of Psychiatry*, 1968, *114*, 673–679.

Solomon, K., & Hart, P. Pitfalls and prospects in clinical research on antianxiety drugs: Benzodiazepines and placebo—A research review. *Journal of Clinical Psychiatry*, 1978, *39*, 823–831.

Solyom, L., Garza-Perez, J., Ledwidge, B. L., & Solyom, C. Paradoxical intention in the treatment of obsessive thoughts: A pilot study. *Comprehensive Psychiatry*, 1972, *13*, 291–297.

Spitzer, R. L., Williams, J. B. W., & Skodol, A. E. DSM-III: The major achievements and an overview. *American Journal of Psychiatry*, 1980, *137*, 151–164.

Steketee, G., Foa, E. B., & Grayson, J. B. Recent advances in the behavioral treatment of obsessive–compulsives. *Archives of General Psychiatry*, 1982, *39*, 1365–1371.

Stern, R. S. Obsessive thoughts: The problem of therapy. *British Journal of Psychiatry*, 1978, *132*, 200–205.

Stern, R. S., Lipsedge, M., & Marks, I. Obsessive ruminations: A controlled trial of thought-stopping technique. *Behaviour Research and Therapy*, 1975, *11*, 659–662.

Stern, R., & Marks, I. M. Brief and prolonged flooding: A comparison in agoraphobic patients. *Archives of General Psychiatry*, 1973, *28*, 270–276.

Townsend, R. E., House, J. F., & Addario, D. A comparison of biofeedback-mediated relaxation and group therapy in the treatment of chronic anxiety. *American Journal of Psychiatry*, 1975, *132*, 598–601.

Trower, P., Yardley, K., Bryant, B., & Shaw, P. The treatment of social failure: A comparison of anxiety-reduction and skills-acquisition procedures on two social problems. *Behavior Modification*, 1978, *2*, 41–60.

Uhlenhuth, E. H., Balter, M. B., Mellinger, G. D., Cisin, I. H., & Clinthorne, J. *Quasi-diagnostic symptom clusters: Correlates and relations to drug use*. Paper presented at the 20th annual meeting of the American College of Neuropsychopharmacology, San Diego, Calif., December 1981.

Waddell, M. T., Barlow, D. H., & O'Brien, G. T. Cognitive and relaxation treatment for panic disorders: Effects on panic versus "background" anxiety. Submitted for publication, 1983.

Webster, A. The development of phobias in married women. *Psychological Monographs*, 1953, *67*, 1–18.

Williams, S. L., & Rappaport, A. Cognitive treatment in the natural environment for agoraphobics. *Behavior Therapy*, 1983, *2*, 299–314.

Woodward, R., & Jones, R. B. Cognitive restructuring treatment: A controlled trial with anxious patients. *Behaviour Research and Therapy*, 1980, *18*, 401–407.

Zitrin, C. M. Combined pharmacological and psychological treatment of phobias. In M. Mavissakalian & D. H. Barlow (Eds.), *Phobia: Psychological and pharmacological treatment*. New York: Guilford, 1981.

Zitrin, C. M., Klein, D. F., & Woerner, M. G. Behavior therapy, supportive psychotherapy, imipramine, and phobias. *Archives of General Psychiatry*, 1978, *35*, 307–321.

Zitrin, C. M., Klein, D. F., & Woerner, M. G. Treatment of agoraphobia with group exposure *in vivo* and imipramine. *Archives of General Psychiatry*, 1980, *37*, 63–72.

Zitrin, C. M., Klein, D. F., Woerner, M. G., & Ross, D. C. I. Comparison of imipramine hydrochloride and placebo. *Archives of General Psychiatry*, 1983, *40*, 125–139.

Zitrin, C. M., Woerner, M. G., & Klein, D. F. Differentiation of panic anxiety from anticipatory anxiety and avoidance behavior. In D. F. Klein & J. Rabkin (Eds.), *Anxiety: New research and changing concepts*. New York: Raven, 1981.

COMMENTARY

Dr. Aaron T. Beck*: You mentioned that radical 6- to 10-hour exposure treatments do not in the long run pay off as well as some of the more traditional therapies. What are some of these other types of treatment?

Dr. Barlow: I was referring to the more gradual self-paced kinds of approaches in which, perhaps, you gather a group of agoraphobics, get them to support each other, and simply give them homework assignments. They carry them out at their own pace, perhaps with the support of the people in the group or with friends. This is different from the "drag 'em to the mall" approach. Other treatments are more imaginal, even desensitization type of therapies. The latest Zitrin, Klein, and Woerner study showed the same relative efficacy of supportive therapy. But within that treatment, as within the context of a phobia clinic, I am sure there is an implicit demand that the work that needs to be done is to get out and begin to face some of the feared situations.

Dr. Beck: Do you have any figures on the psychodynamic therapies? As you know, Freud mentioned that without exposure, no psychodynamic therapy could work with phobias.

Dr. Barlow: I am not aware of any clinical series that looks at percentage of successes, or phobic remissions, with psychodynamic therapy.

Dr. John Clancy†: Do you know what proportion of nonresponder anxiety cases would be rediagnosed as having generalized anxiety disorder?

Dr. Barlow: Although we looked at the nonresponders in our particular study fairly closely, we could not find any one distinguishing feature, such as having generalized anxiety, among them. If there *were* any one feature that might be clear in these nonresponders, it is that they were more obsessional than the responders. The fears became, it seemed, more "obsessionalized," and therefore were much more difficult to deal with cognitively, in terms of working with them on what was rational and what was irrational.

Dr. Donald F. Klein§: I would like to raise a question about the difficulties in measuring improvement, particularly in the area of agoraphobia with panic attacks. I think this is a very clear-cut and discrete syndrome, and I don't think measuring improvement in it is difficult at all. As a matter of fact, in our work we have essentially ended up with a nice three-point scale which I think has clinical face validity.

*University of Pennsylvania.
†Washington University School of Medicine.
§New York State Pychiatric Institute and College of Physicians and Surgeons, Columbia University.

At the top of the scale is a patient with no panic attacks and no avoidance behavior, and at the very worst some slight anticipatory anxiety about going into some situations, but nevertheless the patient goes into them. That patient, by my definition, is a cure. At the bottom of the scale is a patient who says, "You haven't helped me at all; I can't do anything; I'm getting panic attacks; I'm in terrible shape." That is not a cure. In between, is everybody else. Now, I don't think that scale is difficult to use, and I think it is extremely reliable.

The use of such scales is conspicuously absent in the behavior therapy literature in the area of agoraphobia. There is no way to find out, over the entire literature, what proportion of the patients are cured. What are presented are statistically significant differences on rating scales, and this just doesn't speak to the clinical issues.

On another point, in our own studies, using both systematic hierarchical desensitization, and group *in vivo* techniques, I would say that roughly 30% of the patients end up as "cures" without the use of medication. So there clearly seems to be some benefit in these techniques. However, I would point out that with the use of antidepressant medication as an adjunct to these techniques, the cure rate goes up to 60%. Therefore, to discuss the psychotherapy of agoraphobia with panic attacks, in particular, without discussing the very clear evidence that medication produces tremendous improvements in the cure rate over and above the psychotherapy, seems to me to be missing the boat.

Dr. Barlow: I don't think anyone in this room is unaware of the importance of the pharmacologic treatment of agoraphobia; however, since I was asked to talk about psychotherapy and not pharmacology, I only touched on it briefly.

Let me say one thing about the improvement measures, because that is a very important issue. For the last 3 years we have been doing systematic observations in the home, which we call home visits. We put the agoraphobics through a series of exercises around their homes in a somewhat structured fashion, such as going to the drug store, to their local grocery store, etc. As everyone who has worked with agoraphobics knows, they are under a certain demand during these behavioral tasks, and will usually do a bit better than they and their family will report they usually do. Therefore, it becomes a pretty good measure of functioning, since if they can't do it, you're pretty sure it is a real deficit.

What I didn't have time to show today were data from a couple of patients who reported that they were fine after our treatment. But when, in fact, we did the behavioral measures in the home, we found out that even though the ratings on their questionnaires were improved, and they reported doing well, there was no improvement whatsoever. So while I think rating scales are important, they should be supplemented by direct behavioral observation.

We don't yet know what the predictive validity of physiological measures will be. We are just finishing up a 3-year trial looking at heart rate measures as a function of treatment and as a predictor of outcome. There is reason to believe, however, that behavioral and subjective improvement in the absence of basic physiological improvement might predict relapse.

3

Schizophrenia: A Review of Psychosocial Treatment Strategies[1]

SAMUEL J. KEITH AND SUSAN M. MATTHEWS
National Institute of Mental Health

In discussing any therapeutic approach to the person suffering from schizophrenia, it is important to establish a conceptual framework for the disorder which has relevance toward our clinical armamentarium. To do otherwise is to invite inappropriate treatment assignments or the withholding of potentially useful approaches. From the time of Kraepelin and Bleuler, many have struggled with various components of schizophrenia in an attempt to unify the clinical description, etiologic discrimination, and treatment implication. No completely satisfactory system has been developed. The past decade has seen remarkable progress in establishing the reliability of the diagnosis of schizophrenia, through the clinical application of DSM-III (American Psychiatric Association [APA], 1980), but even the very best reliability has failed to bring validity to the diagnosis. To date, no single, multiple, or cluster of biologic, psychophysiologic, psychologic, or social variables can be found in all schizophrenics. Additionally, the deterioration in course and the 6-month chronicity requirement of DSM-III have the unfortunate tendency to create a therapeutic pessimism that may not be entirely warranted.

There are available to us, however, a number of ways of reorganizing our descriptive understanding of schizophrenia which present possible interfaces with our current treatment armamentarium. The approach we found most useful was first presented by Strauss, Carpenter, and Bartko, (1974). Drawing from the work of Hughlings Jackson on the evolution–dissolution theory, they have presented a rather compelling argument based on precursors and prognosis for there being three groupings of problems associated with schizophrenic symptoms: positive symptoms, negative symptoms, and disorders of personal relationships. By positive symptoms they refer to symptoms of schizophrenia which characterize it by their presence, such as

---

1. The opinions expressed in this chapter are those of the authors and do not necessarily reflect the official position of the National Institute of Mental Health.

hallucinations and delusions; by negative symptoms they refer to those symptoms which characterize it by their absence—lack of goal directed behavior, blunting of affect, verbal paucity, and so forth; by disordered personal relationships they refer to patterns of asociality, withdrawal, and lack of close personal ties. Their data supported the following conclusions:

1. Positive Symptoms
   a. Develop over short period of time
   b. A reaction to biologic or socioenvironmental causes
   c. Minimal prognostic importance
2. Negative Symptoms
   a. Develop over an extended period of time
   b. Conceptualized as either the source of chronicity or the result of it
   c. Prognostically important
3. Disordered Personal Relationships
   a. Develop over long term
   b. Conceptualized as interactive process of uncertain etiology
   c. Prognostically important for productive functioning in its own area as well as in negative symptomatology and positive symptomatology

Applying our current treatment modalities to this nosologic conceptual framework offers us the possibility of achieving realistic treatment expectations from both pharmacologic and psychosocial approaches. Although advances in psychopharmacology and psychosocial treatments combined to produce a major revolution in the treatment of schizophrenia in the 1950s, the ensuing two decades have seen a parallel but, until recently, separate development of knowledge about these two elements of treatment.

The well-designed, rigorous clinical trials of neuroleptics have produced an imposing body of data pointing to their efficacy in the control of the positive symptoms of schizophrenia. Almost no one would question that positive symptomatology is profoundly affected by pharmacologic treatments. Furthermore, controlled studies of maintenance chemotherapy demonstrate a decided advantage to those assigned to receive drugs as compared with those assigned to placebo (Davis, Janicak, Chang, & Klerman, 1982). The distinct advantage of neuroleptic treatment is in controlling the flagrant, psychotic symptoms of schizophrenia. For those patients for whom neuroleptic medication is effective (and there is unfortunately a small but significant group who are nonresponders) this approach establishes a psychosis-free state. At this point in our understanding of schizophrenia and its effective treatment, this freedom from positive symptoms approaches a *sine qua non* status for psychosocial treatments. We say this even though we fully acknowledge the point made earlier: Positive symptoms are the least enduring and least prognostic aspect of schizophrenia. They are its most characteristic, most dramatic, and most frightening aspect. Although, there are indeed a few dedicated and talented clinicians working in settings where regressed behavior and florid symptomatology are accepted as relevant to therapeutic recovery (e.g., Mosher, 1972), most of us find it difficult to address issues of the negative symptoms and social competence in the presence of florid psychosis.

What must be borne in mind, however, is that recovery from schizophrenia is not synonymous with recovery from positive symptoms. Unless new drugs are found that have a more direct impact on negative symptoms and disordered interpersonal relationships—and not just creating the possibility for improvement in these areas—we shall apparently have to rely on other interventions to bring improvement in these areas. Furthermore, the benefits gained through pharmacologic treatment are not without a price. The various short-term side effects, while uncomfortable and potentially contributing to noncompliance, are generally tolerable or treatable. The *long*-term risk of tardive dyskinesia, however, is not easily dismissed. Currently, there is no effective treatment for it, and its manifestation may contribute negatively to social recovery.

PSYCHOSOCIAL TREATMENT

Given the long and rich history of psychosocial treatment including individual, group, and family therapies for schizophrenia going back well before the advent of neuroleptics, the availability of reported studies evaluating the utility is seriously lacking. Searching for explanations for this, we have come up with two thoughts. The first was eloquently expressed by Carpenter and Heinrichs (1980):

> Psychotherapy was the most prestigious form of psychiatric treatment, and the need for testing the therapeutic efficacy was not readily appreciated by those who presumed a treatment effect. We looked to the philosopher, the essayist, the metapsychologist, and the indoctrinated clinicians for new knowledge. Many leading psychiatrists came from the ranks of those who had a prolonged educational experience which stressed inculcation of beliefs, with neglect of scientific principles of hypothesis testing and theory disproof. Arrogance is no friend of science and we now face the consequences of having failed to establish a data base suitable for testing therapeutic efficacy of social treatments in general, and psychotherapy of schizophrenia in particular. (p. 242)

The second reason we must consider is that perhaps we have not defined our expectations from psychotherapy adequately. If we try to define psychotherapy as a panacea for schizophrenia, we are almost certain to be profoundly disappointed. The impact of psychotherapy in the absence of neuro-leptic medication has been repeatedly shown to be minimal (Klein, 1980). Indeed, there is an expanding literature which suggests the possibility of a "toxic" effect of psychosocial treatments when these are given to patients not taking medication or if the treatment itself is too intrusive or overstimulating.

It becomes rather obvious that the panacea rationale for psychosocial treatments is not one that can be substantiated by research evidence. What we would like to suggest, however, is that if the more modest target of improving negative symptoms and interpersonal relationships is set, there can be a reasonable expectation of success. What should also be borne in mind is that, unlike the neuroleptic-sensitive positive symptoms, the negative symptoms and disordered interpersonal relationships are all pervasive, fre-quently developmental in origin, and not likely to remit spontaneously. It becomes less likely, therefore, that a treatment which is time-limited (treat-ment for X weeks) or circumscribed (Y therapy for 1 hour per week) can be expected to contribute to reversing this process except in a rather ancillary manner. Furthermore, any psychosocial intervention that does not take into account the environment in which the patient is attempting to recover is inviting treatment failure—just as a noxious environment can overwhelm a biological treatment that is present 24 hours a day, so it can most certainly overwhelm the impact of a treatment that is present for an hour and a half each week. The interaction between the treatment modality, the predominant symptom pattern (positive or negative) and the environment in which the treatment is being given are all significant aspects to consider in the evalua-tion of any treatment approach.

For the purpose of this review, we would like to divide the relevant studies into two subgroups—psychotherapy and psychosocial treatment. Under the heading of psychotherapy, we are including those interpersonal interventions in which the primary focus is on the patient—in general, individual and group psychotherapy. Under psychosocial intervention, we are including those studies in which the patient's *environment* becomes the primary focus—in general, family management strategies. We are proposing this separation because we are sensing that there are not only major philosophical differences between the approaches, but also drug interaction and outcome differences.

INPATIENT INDIVIDUAL PSYCHOTHERAPY

Four major studies of individual psychotherapy have been completed (Grinspoon, Ewalt, & Shader, 1972; Karon & VandenBos, 1981; May, 1968; Rogers, Gendlin, Kiesler, & Truax, 1967) and one is nearing completion (Stanton, Knapp, & Gunderson, in preparation). Although many characteristics of these studies varied—type of individual psychotherapy, type of milieu, experience of therapists, premorbid adjustment status of the patients, level of chronicity—a common feature for each was that the therapy began while patients were in an actively psychotic phase of their illness requiring inpatient hospitalization. We emphasize this aspect of the clinical status because we feel that a critical variable to be considered in the evaluation of psychotherapeutic approaches is at what point in what could become a lifelong therapeutic process do the anticipated benefits of a specific treatment justify the commitment of precious and expensive resources.

Of the five studies of individual psychotherapy begun in an inpatient setting, three are mentioned for the sake of historical completeness and will not be interpreted. The Stanton *et al.* (in preparation) study of intensive, insight-oriented therapy has not reported results to date. The Karon and VandenBos study (1981) has generated many questions relative to its design and thus the investigators' positive interpretation of benefits achieved with experienced therapists working with schizophrenic patients becomes difficult to put into a proper perspective. The reader is referred to May and Tuma (1970) and Klein (1980) for a discussion of major criticisms which can be summarized as follows: The assignment to experienced and inexperienced therapists was not done randomly; many of the patients in the drug treatment group were transferred to what appeared to be a chronic unit early in the study; outcome assessment, as evaluated by length of hospital stay, was confounded by the involvement of the treating therapist in discharge decision.

The Rogers *et al.* study (1967) presents minimal evidence of a positive benefit from individual psychotherapy in an inpatient setting. However, this interpretation becomes confounded by a lack of clarity regarding patient drug use in the study. In most standard inpatient settings of the current era, the central issue is the reduction of acute positive symptoms. The repeated demonstration of the effectiveness of neuroleptic treatment for these positive symptoms of schizophrenia makes a study in which drug usage is unstated difficult to interpret. For example, the Rogers study found that their psychotherapy had no effect on schizophrenic *symptoms*. We do not consider this to be totally unexpected, as the treatment which might have accounted for an outcome difference on this variable, neuroleptic medication, was left unstated.

The remaining two studies, Grinspoon *et al.* (1972) and May (1968), examining the impact of individual psychotherapy on schizophrenic inpatients, approached the topic with quite different questions in mind. The Grinspoon *et al.* (1972) study was designed at a time when many psychoanalytically oriented therapists questioned whether medication interfered with psychotherapy for schizophrenic patients. The results of this study have considerably reduced the number of therapists who would adhere to this position on an inpatient unit in the 1980s. This study selected (random selection was attempted, but not completely accomplished because of patient refusal) two small groups ($n = 10$) of chronic schizophrenic patients (single, male, mean age 27, poor premorbid adjustment) to enter a study of psychoanalytically oriented individual therapy with experienced therapists. All patients had been hospitalized at least 3 years prior to intake into the study. Group 1 entered the research ward in May 1962; group 2 in September 1964. There was an initial 13-week placebo period followed by assignment to one of two treatment conditions: psychoanalytically oriented individual psychotherapy plus thioridazine, or psychoanalytically oriented psychotherapy plus placebo. Both groups received psychotherapy at least twice a week for 2 years. Only the group receiving drugs showed improvement in psychopathology, and when this group was placed back on 3 months of placebo treatment at the end of the study, the improvement disappeared after 4–6 weeks on placebo. It is impossible to draw direct conclusions about the additive effect of the psychotherapy because the group which did not receive psychotherapy was not in the same hospital as the experimental treatment group. What can be safely concluded from this study, however, is that for severely ill schizophrenic patients in a hospital setting, individual psychotherapy without drugs finds little support.

The Camarillo State Hospital study by May (1968) was an intensive investigation of five standard treatment modalities given to a sample of 228 first-admission, midrange prognosis schizophrenics between the ages of 16 and 45 in an inpatient setting. This study attempted to evaluate treatment modalities as they could be provided in a good public treatment program. The five modalities were psychotherapy alone, milieu, electroconvulsive therapy, neuroleptics alone, and neuroleptics plus psychotherapy. Although the results of this study have been questioned because the therapists were relatively inexperienced and the psychotherapy was not intense, if the study is considered as an evaluation of treatment strategies as they are most likely to be employed in a standard treatment setting, then these criticisms become less potent. The investigation's frequently cited results showed that the two drug conditions (drug alone and drug plus psychotherapy) were associated with significantly higher measures of clinical improvement than were the two nondrug conditions (milieu and psychotherapy alone) with ECT in between. The follow-up studies of discharged patients raise an additional point for consideration: Does the withholding of neuroleptic medication during the actively psychotic phase of the disorder have long-term consequences? During their follow-up studies, no control was attempted over the frequency or the type of treatment received, making definitive conclusions impossible; yet they have reported that the patients who did not receive drugs initially spent twice as many days in the hospital after discharge as those who received drugs. It is therefore possible that in a standard treatment program, initially treating the positive symptoms without drugs may lead to a poorer long-term course of the disorder, a finding suggested earlier by Greenblatt, Solomon, Evans, and Brooks (1965).

INPATIENT GROUP PSYCHOTHERAPY

There is no shortage of review articles on the efficacy of group therapy in the treatment of schizophrenia (Keith & Matthews, 1982; Luborsky, Singer, & Luborsky, 1976; Meltzoff & Kornreich, 1970; Mosher & Keith, 1980; Parloff & Dies, 1977). Each of these reviewers has identified a positive rationale for the use of group therapy and each has reported rather meager positive results. As we pointed out in our earlier review (Keith & Matthews, 1982), the ubiquitous nature of group therapy programs in both inpatient and out-patient settings does not seem to be dependent on its demonstrated efficacy. Indeed, from what we have discussed under the general principles of psycho-social treatment, group therapy for schizophrenics in an inpatient setting may not be the optional treatment modality.

Inpatient treatment in most settings occurs at a time when positive symptomatology or social disorganization is at its highest point. As we have learned from studies examining inpatient milieus (Mosher & Keith, 1980), a stimulus-decreasing environment is most useful in the early stages of acute symptomatology. Because group therapy is, in fact, a multiple stimulus situation frequently high in intensity, it may be counterproductive early in treatment. Pattison, Brissenden, and Wohl (1967) suggest, in fact, that psychoanalytically oriented group psychotherapy, used in an inpatient setting, showed no advantages and at least one disadvantage as found on a measure of self-acceptance. Kanas, Rogers, Kreth, Patterson, and Campbell (1980) found that psychotic patients treated in insight-oriented group therapy scored worse on both an objective rating scale and on a behavioral measure when compared to a group of psychotic patients who did not receive this form of treatment. They suggest that insight-oriented group therapy is not effectually used during the first 3 weeks of inpatient treatment with psychotic patients. We feel that to be effective in an inpatient setting, group therapy should begin after the resolution of the most flagrant psychotic symptoms, be focused on current problems in a structured fashion, and follow the patient into the community as an available and ongoing treatment. From a practical standpoint in those settings where short-term hospitalization is the rule, it may be difficult if not impossible to begin group therapy with only inpatients. Thus, it may be best to introduce an inpatient into an ongoing outpatient therapy group after the florid symptoms have remitted but prior to discharge from the hospital.

In summary, it would appear that in a standard inpatient setting for the treatment of schizophrenic patients, there is little evidence to suggest that specific psychotherapies, individual or group, when used without medication, are beneficial. Indeed, there is some suggestion that without neuroleptics there may be potential short-term or long-term negative effects of these therapies. Furthermore, the evidence for an additive effect of these therapies when given in combination with drugs is only modest. At a time when patients characteristically display dramatic positive symptomatology on a standard inpatient unit, pharmacologic therapies are crucial in bringing about a reduction in symptoms. The amount of resources one would devote to psychotherapy at this point in the treatment program may vary with any individual patient, but for overall programmatic recommendation, it would seem fair to conclude that beyond good clinical management, intensive interpersonal therapy provides little advantage.

INDIVIDUAL OUTPATIENT PSYCHOTHERAPY

Although some may find the previous sections on *inpatient* psychotherapies for schizophrenic patients quite sobering, we feel that the results are not at all surprising. Psychotherapies, we have earlier stated, are better suited for approaching negative symptoms of schizophrenia and problems of socialization. At the time of hospitalization, these problems assume far less importance; positive symptoms become the crucial, dominant, targeted variables that must be reduced, or the treatment outcome will be judged a failure.

As we now turn to *outpatient* studies of psychotherapy, we find a different structure of patient needs. Positive symptoms, which have been brought under control, must be kept from reappearing. If this can be accomplished, the focus of attention then becomes those problems that prevent the schizophrenic patient from developing a meaningful, functioning role in life. In a series of studies of schizophrenics, Hogarty, Goldberg, and Schooler (1974) examined this issue from an individual therapist–individual patient basis. The particular therapy evaluated was called major role therapy (MRT) and meets criteria for being classified as an individual psychotherapy provided by an experienced social worker. Few studies have matched the elegance of this design in which 374 schizophrenic outpatients, stratified by sex, were randomly assigned to one of four groups: MRT plus drug; MRT plus placebo; no MRT plus drug; no MRT plus placebo. The results in terms of prevention of relapse were quite clear after 24 months of treatment— 80% of placebo-treated patients relapsed as compared with 48% of drug-treated patients (Goldberg, Schooler, Hogarty, & Roper, 1977). Over the entire 24-month period, the addition of MRT to the drug condition produced a modest improvement in relapse. Of those study patients who did not relapse in the first 6 months, however, MRT reduced relapse for the final 18 months of the study (44% of all MRT vs. 58% of non-MRT relapsed from 7 to 24 months if still in the study at 6 months; Hogarty, Goldberg, Schooler, Ulrich, & Collaborative Study Group, 1974). At 18 months for those still in the study, an MRT effect on social adjustment appeared which was stronger at 24 months. It should be noted that the frequency of the MRT was relatively low (2.04 face-to-face contacts per month). Even at this frequency, however, two points deserve noting: the appearance of a toxic effect *early* in the study of MRT on newly remitted patients not maintained on neuroleptics; and social improvement and protection late in the study for those patients who had not previously relapsed.

OUTPATIENT GROUP PSYCHOTHERAPY

A large number of outpatient studies have examined the efficacy of group therapy. In general, the results can be summarized as follows:

1. In studies comparing the relative efficacy of group therapy versus individual therapy in which drug utilization was similar under each condition (Donlon, Rada, & Knight, 1973; Herz, Spitzer, Gibbon, Greenspan, & Reibel, 1974; Levene, Patterson, Murphey, Overbeck, & Veach, 1970; O'Brien, Hamm, Ray, Pierce, Luborsky, & Mintz, 1972), a significant advantage favoring group therapy was found in two studies (O'Brien *et al.*, 1972; Donlon *et al.*, 1973); one reported little difference except for patient and therapist preference for group therapy (Herz *et al.*, 1974); and one found relatively poor results with either (Levene *et al.*, 1970). It should be noted that because a "no therapy" comparison group was not included in these studies, conclusions must rest on the relative rather than absolute demonstration of therapeutic efficacy.

2. Three outpatient studies of group therapy versus no therapy with drugs given to both conditions provide some evidence for a positive effect. Borowski and Tolwinski (1969) found an overall improvement in the group-treated patients, but confidence in this study is eroded somewhat by the use of nonblind therapists as raters; Claghorn, Johnston, Cook, and Itschner (1974) found some improvement in what could be called insight in the group-treated patients. Shattan, Dcamp, Fujii, Fross, and Wolff (1966) found less rehospitalization and a trend toward an increased number of months out of the hospital favoring the group therapy condition. Overall, we feel that the evidence from these studies of group therapy is modestly positive.

3. One recent study by Malm (1982) has attempted to evaluate the impact of group therapy when given in addition to a "treatment as usual" condition (neuroleptics and social-skills training). In this study, the effect of 1 year of communication-oriented group therapy when added to the standard

treatment program of depot neuroleptics and social-skills training was examined in newly admitted schizophrenic patients. As expected, for all measures of acute psychopathological manifestations of schizophrenia, there was dramatic improvement over the first 30 days of neuroleptic treatment for all subjects. Patients who had completely recovered over this initial month were excluded from the study. The remainder were randomly assigned to receive either treatment as usual—social-skills training and depot neuroleptics ($n = 40$)—or the standard treatment plus group therapy ($n = 40$). However, six patients in each group either did not start or did not complete the study, leaving a final 34 patients in each group. Outcome measures included signs and symptoms, social function, life events, course of illness variables such as relapse rate, and global measures of recovery.

Results of the study indicated that, overall, few differences in change scores for symptoms and signs were found for either the therapy or control groups from the start of therapy through 2 years. However, individual items on the Comprehensive Psychopathological Rating Scale (CPRS) that showed significant differences favored the therapy group. Measures of social functioning and life events significantly favored the therapy group in several areas: more free-time activities, entries and reentries into social field, and increase in new personal habits. Variables related to the course of illness revealed a 15% relapse rate in both groups.

The author noted potential sources of error in the study—the inclusion of 11 subjects (32%) in the therapy group despite the fact that they did not complete the therapy, which may have had the impact of reducing differences between the therapy and control groups. Also, the author had multiple roles in the study, including ratings upon which conclusions were based. However, interrater reliability checks between the author and independent raters showed no significant score differences.

The results of this study support those reported by Hogarty *et al.* (1974) in that several differences were not detected until 1 or 2 years after treatment, indicating that treatment is a long-term process. In addition, these results highlight the importance of the timing of the initiation of a psychotherapy study: If begun too early (at a time when positive symptoms predominate, and outcome is therefore appropriately measured in terms of symptom remission), most of the variability will be accounted for by the drug effect; if begun too late, there will be little variability left to account for in evaluating the outcome. The optimal time, according to this study, would appear to be in the outpatient stabilization period.

We feel that the design and results from the Malm (1982) study provide evidence for the efficacy of psychosocial treatment in the alleviation of the negative symptoms inherent in schizophrenia. By introducing the treatment (group therapy) at a time when the patient was less vulnerable to the toxic effects resultant from an overstimulating treatment approach, the combined treatment efficacy of drugs and psychosocial treatment in the areas of negative symptoms and socialization was demonstrated.

In a previous review (Keith & Matthews, 1982), we concluded that the results of research examining the efficacy of group therapy with persons diagnosed as schizophrenic could only be described as disappointing. And indeed, our current state of knowledge regarding this therapeutic approach provides little additional support. However, this lack of positive evidence may be an artifact of the limited number of recent controlled investigations examining the effectiveness of group therapy rather than a failure of the treatment itself. The Malm (1982) study is one of the few recent reports providing support for the utility of group therapy within the therapeutic context previously described as being conducive for demonstrating positive results (i.e., a balance of stimulus intensity and patient vulnerability) with appropriate outcome measures. It remains clear that additional studies are required to assess adequately the impact of group therapy in the areas of negative symptoms and socialization.

SUMMARY OF PSYCHOTHERAPY

Overall, the evidence thus far for a positive impact of psychotherapy on patient functioning would appear to be confined to outpatient settings with patients who are either receiving neuroleptic medication or who are being treated in a system capable of preventing relapse by other means such as the early detection of precursors of relapse. Not all the evidence has been reported, however, and therefore a caveat is in order. We are currently awaiting the results of one additional study (Stanton *et al.*, in preparation) of intensive individual psychotherapy begun with acutely psychotic inpatients, using experienced therapists, and carried over into the outpatient setting. The comparison group will receive good clinical management including supportive psychotherapy. Both groups of patients will receive medication in accordance with clinical judgment. If the value of intensive individual psychotherapy is to be demonstrated, the results of the study must indicate that patients receiving individual psychotherapy function at a better level than those receiving good clinical management. If this positive outcome can be seen across a number of their comprehensive outcome measures and across their large population of acutely psychotic patients, then our conclusions will have to be modified. If this study effect is not demonstrated, or if the effect is confined to a small number of outcome measures or only for certain subgroups of patients, then individual psychotherapy for schizophrenics in a standard inpatient setting will be relegated to the status of being given by a very few to a very few.

The outpatient therapy studies, on the other hand, present the beginning of a data base suggesting (1) an additive effect of drugs and psychotherapy on the prevention of relapse; and (2) an improvement in negative symptoms, especially socialization—an effect that would appear to be unique to psychosocial treatments. Without neuroleptics, however, these therapies would appear to be as likely to increase the risk of relapse as they are to reduce it.

There remains the possibility, however, of an unfortunate interaction between these targeted psychotherapies and neuroleptics. That is, although the combination of psychotherapy and drugs is additive in reducing relapse, the drug effect (and side effects) on negative symptoms and socialization may impede to some extent the full expression of the positive impact of the psychotherapies. Several studies are now under way exploring possible strategies to reduce the need for medication through early detection of relapse in drug-free patients. In addition, low-dose strategies, which are attempting to find the lowest optimal level of medication to prevent relapse, are also being investigated. The studies in the next section suggest a possible mechanism to approach this problem from the psychosocial perspective.

PSYCHOSOCIAL TREATMENT

The search for psychosocial factors that influence the cause and course of schizophrenia has been the calling of many mental health workers who feel that these factors are potentially more alterable than those biologic factors that are determined by genes. Unfortunately, many of the initial findings either fell victim to a lack of evidence (e.g., early familial causality theories) or proved difficult to alter (e.g., increased prevalence of schizophrenia in the urban, low-socioeconomic-status setting). Despite the problems associated with demonstrating a familial causality for schizophrenia, however, there has been a continuing interest in psychosocial treatment approaches delivered through the family. It is our opinion that it is unnecessary to establish a position on causality in order to consider the family as an appropriate vehicle for the delivery of treatment. We take this position because we, like many others, feel that the environment in which a schizophrenic lives is in constant interaction with the patient and plays a major role in accounting for course and outcome. Initial evidence for the impact of institutionalism (Goffman, 1961) and impoverished social environment (Wing, 1978) showed a dramatic impact of the nonstimulating milieus on the production of negative symptoms. Recently, interest in environmental impact has been stimulated by those looking to explain the substantial relapse rates found in patients for whom medication compliance could be guaranteed. The answer could relate to medication: rapid metabolism, clearance, or another as yet unspecified phenomenon which prevents medication from having its desired effect. On the other hand, it is possible to propose that environmental toxicity plays a role in the production of relapse. We feel that the following three studies, taken together, provide initial evidence for this phenomenon and present viable approaches to preventing relapse.

The first of these studies, by Goldstein, Rodnick, Evans, May, and Steinberg (1978), examined the interaction of moderate (1 ml) and low-dose (.25 ml) fluphenazine enanthate with family oriented crisis intervention or no psychosocial treatment in a 2 × 2 factorial design. The family treatment was given once a week for 2 hours for 6 weeks to 104 consecutively admitted patients diagnosed as schizophrenic with a score greater than 4 on the New Haven Schizophrenia Index. The sample was stratified by sex and premorbid adjustment and randomly assigned to one of the four treatment groups following a brief inpatient treatment phase (mean 14 days). The results of the study, while complex, highlight several issues:

At 6 weeks a significant difference ($p < .05$) in relapse rates was found between standard dose (family therapy group—no relapse) and the low dose (no family therapy—24% relapse). These figures became stronger at 6 months ($p < .01$) with the corresponding relapse figures remaining 0% in the standard dose (family therapy group) and rising to 48% in the low dose (no family therapy condition). Although the drug effect was stronger ($p < .01$) at 6 months, the family therapy effect was also significant ($p < .05$). When symptom levels at 6 weeks were examined, the most profound effect of family therapy was on withdrawal and a component of blunted affect (negative symptoms). This effect was maintained at the 6-month follow-up, but only under the condition of family therapy combined with standard dose neuroleptics. This study argues convincingly that a treatment that combines a psychosocial management strategy with neuroleptic medication over a remarkably brief period of time (6 weeks) produces results even in relatively unstable (discharged after 2 weeks of inpatient treatment) patients.

Since the completion of the Goldstein study, a specific familial interaction phenomenon, expressed emotion (EE), has captured the interest of psychosocial researchers (Vaughn & Leff, 1976). Expressed emotion is defined as a critical, overinvolved, hostile attitude on the part of family members (parental or spousal) which in the presence of 35 hours per week of face-to-face contact produces a startling increase in patient relapse even in the presence of active neuroleptic treatment. The question remains whether EE is capturing a specific toxicity or is only one dimension representative of a toxic environment. Wing (1982) reported that a critical overinvolved attitude may have been what he captured iatrogenically when he initiated his study of "total push" rehabilitation and was able to produce dramatic relapse rates in formerly remitted patients. Although the role of EE in causing or resulting from environmental toxicity remains unclear, two studies have now evaluated the impact of a family management strategy on modifying this toxic environment.

The first study of family management, by Leff, Kuipers, Berkowitz, Eberlein-Vries, and Sturgeon (1982), evaluated the impact of a combined psychoeducational, family group (high EE relatives with low EE relatives), and targeted family sessions (the total treatment is called social intervention) on schizophrenic patients from high EE families. The comparison condition received an energetic treatment as usual. Both groups received fluphenazine decanoate. Twenty-four patients were randomly assigned to treatment. The results showed a relapse rate of 9% in the social intervention group and 50% in the control condition over a 9-month study period ($p = .04$). In addition, this group examined whether their treatment was accomplishing the stated goals of reducing EE. They found that their social intervention had produced a significant ($p < .01$) reduction in critical comments and an improvement in overinvolvement which did not reach significance ($.10 > p > .05$). There were no relapses in families that showed these reductions. The control cases showed nonsignificant changes on both dimensions. It should be noted that independent raters were not used. The results of this study provide both evidence for the existence of an environmental toxicity and also a means to offset it. The specificity of the family environment's being the key factor, while certainly strengthened, could still represent a parallel process of the environment in general.

The second study of family management has been recently reported on by Falloon, Boyd, McGill, Razini, Moss, and Gilderman (1982). They studied 36 schizophrenic outpatients considered to be at high risk for relapse on the basis of high EE families or with a few patients residing in low-EE households but considered to be at high risk for relapse on the bases of poor premorbid adjustment, multiple recent psychiatric admissions, or evidence of extreme levels of family tension. The design called for "optimal" doses of neuroleptic medication with patients randomly assigned to either a home-based, structured, problem-solving family management strategy or a clinic-based, individual, supportive psychotherapy. Ratings were done blindly at monthly medication clinic visits. At the 9-month assessment on completion of the study, statistically significant advantages favoring the family management condition were found in each of the measurements of symptom severity. In addition, the family management approach found improved social functioning of patients and a reduced burden on parents. In terms of the various clinical trade-offs which frequently are made, this particular approach avoided a lowering of positive symptoms at the expense of lowered social functioning. Although this study also risks the criticism that there was not a comparison treatment which received no psychosocial treatment, and that therefore the improvement seen with family management is relative only to a deterioration in the individual group, this possibility is made less likely by the demonstration that, relative to their prior clinical course, the individual group also improved.

In general, these psychosocial management approaches emphasize the gains made in outpatient treatment by utilizing a significant aspect of the patient's environment as an agent for producing change. Although the current group of studies has focused on the family environment, there is evidence from such specialized environmental approaches as Soteria House (Mosher, 1972) and the Paul and Lentz (1977) study that the family need not be the only entry point for this strategy. Indeed, the findings from the community support systems literature, such as the Training in Community Living (Stein & Test, 1976), would support the idea of the benefits of approaching the treatment of the schizophrenic patient through the environment in which he or she lives.

SUMMARY

Our enthusiasm for psychosocial approaches to schizophrenia over the specific psychotherapies for the condition stems from the current positive results achieved with family management approaches and the generally modest findings from our review of psychotherapy studies, especially those that focused on inpatient settings. It is always difficult to make conclusions about a field that is subject to change with the next report in the literature. How timeless this particular review will be depends on the energy we are able to inject into a field that needs considerable expansion of its current data base. It is our hope, therefore, that this review will rapidly become outdated.

In conclusion, we would like to hope that attempts to replicate charisma or technologies that are so specialized that only a handful of highly trained professionals can implement them will occupy a less significant place in the future. We have no doubt that there is a difference in outcome based on personal charisma, skill, level of training, and technique, but if we cannot identify strategies that have general applicability, our contribution to the overall state of the schizophrenic condition will indeed be minimal.

REFERENCES

American Psychiatric Association. *Diagnostic and statistical manual of mental disorders* (3rd ed.). Washington, D.C.: American Psychiatric Association, 1980.

Borowski, T., & Tolwinski, T. Treatment of paranoid schizophrenics with chlorpromazine and group therapy. *Diseases of the Nervous System,* 1969, *30,* 201–202.

Carpenter, W. T., Jr., & Heinrichs, D. W. The role of psychodynamic psychiatry in the treatment of schizophrenic patients. In J. S. Strauss, M. Bowers, T. W. Downey, S. Fleck, S. Jackson, & I. Levine (Eds.), *The psychotherapy of schizophrenia.* New York: Plenum, 1980.

Claghorn, J. L., Johnston, E. D., Cook, T. H., & Itschner, L. Group therapy and maintenance treatment of schizophrenics. *Archives of General Psychiatry*, 1974, *31*, 361–365.

Davis, J. M., Janicak, P., Chang, S., & Klerman, K. Recent advances in the pharmacologic treatment of the schizophrenic disorders. In L. Grinspoon (Ed.), *Psychiatry 1982 annual review*. Washington, D.C.: American Psychiatric Association, 1982.

Donlon, P. T., Rada, R. T., & Knight, S. W. A therapeutic aftercare setting for "refractory" chronic schizophrenic patients. *American Journal of Psychiatry*, 1973, *130*, 682–684.

Falloon, I., Boyd, J., McGill, C. W., Razini, J., Moss, H. B., & Gilderman, A. M. Family management in the prevention of exacerbations of schizophrenia: A controlled study. *New England Journal of Medicine*, 1982, *306*, 1437–1440.

Goffman, E. *Asylums: Essays on the social situation of mental patients and other inmates.* New York: Doubleday-Anchor, 1961.

Goldberg, S. C., Schooler, N. R., Hogarty, G. E., & Roper, M. T. Predictions of relapse in schizophrenic outpatients treated by drug and sociotherapy. *Archives of General Psychiatry*, 1977, *34*, 171–184.

Goldstein, M. J., Rodnick, E. H., Evans, J. R., May, P. R. A., & Steinberg, M. R. Drug and family therapy in the aftercare of acute schizophrenics. *Archives of General Psychiatry*, 1978, *35*, 1169–1177.

Greenblatt, M., Solomon, M. H., Evans, A. S., & Brooks, G. W. *Drug and social therapy in chronic schizophrenia.* Springfield, Ill.: Thomas, 1965.

Grinspoon, L., Ewalt, J. R., & Shader, R. I. *Schizophrenia: Pharmacotherapy and psychotherapy.* Baltimore: Williams & Wilkins, 1972.

Herz, M. I., Spitzer, R. L., Gibbon, M., Greenspan, K., & Reibel, S. Individual versus group aftercare treatment. *American Journal of Psychiatry*, 1974, *131*, 808–812.

Hogarty, G. E., Goldberg, S. C., & Schooler, N. R. Drug and sociotherapy in the aftercare of schizophrenic patients: VII. Adjustment of nonrelapsed patients. *Archives of General Psychiatry*, 1974, *31*, 609–618.

Hogarty, G. E., Goldberg, S. C., Schooler, N. R., Ulrich, R. F., & Collaborative Study Group. Drug and sociotherapy in the aftercare of schizophrenic patients: II. Two-year relapse rates. *Archives of General Psychiatry*, 1974, *31*, 603–608.

Kanas, N., Rogers, M., Kreth, E., Patterson, L., & Campbell, R. The effectiveness of group psychotherapy during the first three weeks of hospitalization. A controlled study. *Journal of Nervous and Mental Disease*, 1980, *168*, 487–492.

Karon, B., & VandenBos, G. *Psychotherapy of schizophrenia.* New York: Jason Aronson, 1981.

Keith, S.J., & Matthews, S. M. Group, family, and milieu therapies and psychosocial rehabilitation in the treatment of the schizophrenic disorders. In L. Grinspoon (Ed.), *Psychiatry 1982 annual review*. Washington, D.C.: American Psychiatric Association, 1982.

Klein, D. F. Psychosocial treatment of schizophrenia, or psychosocial help for people with schizophrenia? *Schizophrenia Bulletin*, 1980, *6*, 122–130.

Leff, J., Kuipers, L., Berkowitz, R., Eberlein-Vries, R., & Sturgeon, D. A controlled trial of social intervention in the families of schizophrenic patients. *British Journal of Psychiatry*, 1982, *141*, 121–134.

Levene, H. L., Patterson, V., Murphey, B. G., Overbeck, A. L., & Veach, T. L. The aftercare of schizophrenics: An evaluation of group and individual approaches. *Psychiatric Quarterly*, 1970, *44*, 296–304.

Luborsky, L., Singer, B., & Luborsky, L. Comparative studies of psychotherapies: Is it true that "everybody has won and all must have prizes"? *Proceedings of the American Psychopathological Association*, 1976, *64*, 3–22.

Malm, U. The influence of group therapy on schizophrenia. *Acta Psychiatrica Scandinavica*, 1982, Supplement 297.

May, P. R. A. *Treatment of schizophrenia: A comparative study of five treatment methods.* New York: Science House, 1968.

May, P. R. A., & Tuma, A. H. Methodological problems in psychotherapy research: Observations on the Karon–VandenBos study of psychotherapy and drugs in schizophrenia. *British Journal of Psychiatry*, 1970, *117*, 569–570.

Meltzoff, J., & Kornreich, M. *Research in psychotherapy*. New York: Atherton, 1970.

Mosher, L. R. Research design to evaluate psychosocial treatments of schizophrenia. In D. Rubinstein & Y. O. Alanen (Eds.), *Psychotherapy of schizophrenia*. Amsterdam: Excerpta Medica, 1972.

Mosher, L. R., & Keith, S. J. Psychosocial treatment: Individual, group family, and community support approaches. *Schizophrenia Bulletin*, 1980, *6*, 10–41.

O'Brien, C., Hamm, K., Ray, B., Pierce, J., Luborsky, L., & Mintz, J. Group versus individual psychotherapy with schizophrenics. *Archives of General Psychiatry*, 1972, *27*, 474–478.

Parloff, M. B., & Dies, R. R. Group psychotherapy outcome research 1966–1975. *International Journal of Group Psychotherapy*, 1977, *27*, 281–319.

Pattison, E. M., Brissenden, A., & Wohl, T. Assessing specific effects of inpatient group psychotherapy. *International Journal of Group Psychotherapy*, 1967, *17*, 283–297.

Paul, G. L., & Lentz, R. J. *Psychosocial treatment of chronic mental patients: Milieu vs. social learning programs*. Cambridge, Mass.: Harvard University Press, 1977.

Rogers, C. R., Gendlin, E. G., Kiesler, D. J., & Truax, C. B. (Eds.). *The therapeutic relationship and its impact: A study of psychotherapy with schizophrenics*. Madison, Wisc.: University of Wisconsin Press, 1967.

Shattan, S. P., Dcamp, L., Fujii, E., Fross, G. G., & Wolff, R. J. Group treatment of conditionally discharged patients in a mental health clinic. *American Journal of Psychiatry*, 1966, *122*, 798–805.

Stanton, A., Knapp, P., & Gunderson, J. The effects of psychotherapy in schizophrenia. In preparation.

Stein, L. I., & Test, M. A. Training in community living: One year evaluation. *American Journal of Psychiatry*, 1976, *133*, 917–918.

Strauss, J. C., Carpenter, W. T., Jr., & Bartko, J. Part III. Speculations on the processes that underlie schizophrenic signs and symptoms. *Schizophrenia Bulletin*, 1974, *2*, 61–69.

Vaughn, E. C., & Leff, J. P. The influence of family and social factors in the course of psychiatric illness. *British Journal of Psychiatry*, 1976, *129*, 125–137.

Wing, J. K. (Ed.). *Schizophrenia: Towards a new synthesis*. London: Academic Press, 1978.

Wing, J. K. *Social factors in schizophrenia*. Paper presented at the Annual Meeting of the National Alliance for the Mentally Ill, Rosslyn, Va., 1982.

COMMENTARY

Dr. Loren R. Mosher*: I think it is worthwhile to point out that in the Falloon study, the family therapy variable, or family management, was conducted in the home. I think that is a very important part of that study that should not be overlooked.

Dr. Keith: There are very many interesting facts that obviously had to be omitted in this rather brief review. That, I think, is a very important one,

---

*Uniformed Services University of the Health Sciences.

and raises the issue of feasibility. It should be noted that the Falloon study was conducted in a less than thriving area of Los Angeles where many of the fears that would certainly come up in many people's minds about visiting homes did have to be overcome. The therapists in that study did find that in point of fact, the families were very supportive in guarding them and making sure that they had access to the home. Indeed, that approach *was* feasible, and may in some respect have been absolutely essential, especially since the families that do seem to have rather high rates of relapse even with neuroleptic medication are families in which you might suspect there is an uncooperative relative. Now relatives will be uncooperative in missing clinic visits, but most of them won't stay away from home just to miss you. So that is something that needs to be kept in mind.

Dr. John P. Docherty*: I want to expand a bit on a point you made that has to do with a very important development in the methodology and technology for carrying out psychotherapy research. Basically, the current work makes clear the necessity for defining specific therapeutic approaches; psychotherapy can no longer be studied as a generic entity. It is important, however, not to discard a generic approach without understanding exactly what it was. For example, in the family studies of schizophrenia, there are three relatively different types of treatments: the problem-solving type that Ian Falloon has carried out; Goldstein's work, which is more crisis-oriented; and Hogarty's work, which is more family-systems-oriented. These are three very different types of approaches.

You pointed out the importance of considering issues of timing when the therapy is employed. I would also suggest that we not discard the potential relevance of psychosocial or psychotherapeutic interventions in inpatient populations, as we develop specific treatments and begin to test them as definable entities.

Dr. Keith: I agree that it is very important to understand that, even though I have lumped these three studies together, they are in fact very different. Each is also considerably more elaborate than I was able to present in this paper. I do think this does represent at least a generic grouping of studies of ways to approach schizophrenia that are effective. And I agree that once a generic group of approaches has been deemed effective, it becomes very important to understand the specifics of what makes up that particular therapy. If it is ineffective, then the differentiation becomes less important.

Dr. Alan E. Kazdin†: I would like to make a related point, about a kind of research that I think you might be discouraging. You mentioned that there would be little interest in showing that a particular charismatic person

*National Institute of Mental Health.
†Western Psychiatric Institute and Clinic, University of Pittsburgh School of Medicine.

or a small group with a particular treatment is effective, with which I fully agree. However, I think there is an intermediate criterion with which you would agree. That is, we should look to find anyone, charismatic or otherwise, or any small group or program, that can produce change. If the treatment is replicable, one can then analyze it. A large number of advances in treatment—maybe not psychotherapy, but maybe medical advances—might be generated from some small group of special talents that later become technology that can then be passed on. So the issue might not be if a particular charismatic school or leader can produce it, but if it can ever be replicated. That is probably the only criterion one would want to invoke.

Dr. Keith: I would like to agree and disagree simultaneously with that point, which is the prerogative of the speaker. The issue of charisma and charismatic technologies in treating schizophrenia should be understood with a good deal of warning. The past 50 years of the treatment of schizophrenia are littered with charismatic—frequently biologic—treatments such as tooth removal, colonic irrigation, subarachnoid injection of horse serum, hemithyroidectomies, vasectomies, which were all initially reported to be effective. As we move into the current studies of hemodialysis and so forth, one should be aware that many "charismatic biologic treaments," for want of having a better term to characterize them, are effective initially, and do build up high expectations in people who have been disappointed throughout their lives. To face one more disappointing charismatic therapy is something that we must balance with the idea that we surely do need something that works better than what we have now.

4

The Psychological Treatment of Depression: An Update of Clinical Trials

MYRNA M. WEISSMAN
*Yale University School of Medicine
and Connecticut Mental Health Center*

INTRODUCTION

In 1979, stimulated by an ACNP request to review the previous decade of scientific progress in establishing the efficacy of psychotherapy, I presented a review of the available clinical trials testing the efficacy of various psychological treatments alone, in comparison with, and in combination with pharmacotherapy among homogeneous samples of depressed outpatients (Weissman, 1979). That was 5 years after Lieberman, in his scholarly report, "Survey and Evaluation of the Literature on Verbal Psychotherapy of Depressive Disorders," covered the 1967–1974 literature on the psychotherapy of depression and reached pessimistic conclusions about the quality of the research (Lieberman, 1975). It was also 4 years after the Parloff and Dies (1975) review of group psychotherapy outcome research, which was equally pessimistic about the quality of efficacy studies for depressive disorders. Although his review covered more than 200 articles, Lieberman (1975) found no completed controlled trials of psychotherapy among them that included homogeneous samples of depressed patients, used minimum scientific standards for clinical trials, and had more than ten patients in each treatment.

The Lieberman (1975) and the Parloff and Dies (1975) reviews had been preceded by the independent reviews of Cristol (1972) and Luborsky, Singer, and Luborsky (1975), who had expressed a similar view about the quality of the research. The pessimism was not about the benefits that might be achieved by psychotherapy in depression but about the lack of good studies. In 1974 there were no data that met reasonable scientific standards on the efficacy of psychotherapy specifically among depressed patients. Even though there had been numerous studies, diagnostically the populations were heterogeneous and inadequately defined, and the procedures for their selection and allocation to treatment were inadequately described.

When Lieberman (1975) arrived at his gloomy conclusions about the "state of psychotherapy" he did not anticipate the great increase in the availability of data that was to characterize the next 5 years. Between 1974 and 1979, 12 clinical trials had been completed that could provide efficacy data on the psychotherapeutic treatment of depression, and five studies were under way at that time (Weissman, 1979).

Lieberman's review represented part of the groundwork for developments then taking place or being planned which converged to improve the situation. Some of these developments follow.

Guidelines for Designing Clinical Trials of Psychotherapy

The classic papers laying the ground rules for efficacy studies in psychotherapy were published in 1969 by Strupp and Bergin and in 1970 by Fiske and associates. These reports provided the conceptual basis for psychotherapy outcome studies, defined the methodological issues, and compiled the empirical data on factors that might confound outcome and therefore needed to be considered in the design of psychotherapy outcome studies (Fiske, Hunt, Luborsky, Orne, Parloff, Reiser, & Tuma, 1970; Strupp & Bergin, 1969).

A Catalog of Outcome Measures

In 1974 Waskow and Parloff compiled a catalog of outcome measures suitable for measuring change in psychotherapy outcome studies, in which they emphasized the importance of using multiple outcome measures and the fact that psychotherapy may have its impact on domains of social functioning rather than on the reduction of symptoms. The main impact of their catalog was that it encouraged greater uniformity in the use of change measures and facilitated comparisons between studies.

Impact of the Therapist's Characteristics

In 1979 Parloff, Waskow, and Wolfe presented a review of studies on therapist variables such as experience, personality, and empathy, which could affect the patient's progress and outcome in psychotherapy and should therefore be an important consideration when planning outcome. This review followed the many observations of clinicians that some therapists consistently did better than others. However, the Parloff et al. (1979) review found that only a few therapist characteristics were promising as predictors of patient progress and outcome in psychotherapy. According to Luborsky (1983), there was moderate support for psychological similarities between patient and therapist, and for the therapist's psychological health–sickness, with healthier therapists providing a more positive experience for the patients.

Better Specification of the Patients

Between 1974 and 1979, Spitzer and associates developed and published the Research Diagnostic Criteria, which made available operationally defined diagnostic criteria (Spitzer, Endicott, & Robins, 1978). The positive results from the psychopharmacologic trials had increasingly focused attention on the importance of studying homogeneous diagnostic groups (Morris & Beck, 1974). Consequently, much more reliable methods for obtaining diagnoses became available.

Better Specification of the Treatments

Psychotherapy manuals began to appear which specified the main procedures of the psychotherapy being tested and enhanced consistency among the therapists engaged in that particular treatment. These treatment manuals specified the identifying characteristics of the psychotherapy, including the tasks and their sequence. The tasks were operationalized through definition and by case example, and often were supplemented by videotapes.

The first manuals were designed by the behavior therapists. It was the ability of the behaviorists to specify interventions (such as implosion, desensitization, etc.) with precision, which gave impetus to the field. The first nonbehaviorally oriented treatment manual (supportive–expressive psychoanalytically oriented psychotherapy) was developed by Luborsky (1976, 1977, in press).

The development of treatment manuals for outcome studies is now a burgeoning field. Several psychotherapies, both for depression (Beck, 1976; Klerman, Rounsaville, Chevron, Neu, & Weissman, 1982) and for other disorders (Luborsky, 1972; Strupp & Binder, 1982), have been developed and specified in manuals. In fact, treatment manuals are not just applicable to psychotherapy. Fawcett and Epstein, in Chicago, have developed comparable manuals for the administration of pharmacotherapy as it is being used in the NIMH Treatment of Depression Research Program (Waskow, Hadley, Autry, & Parloff, 1980). There are many psychotherapies that are amenable both to specification and testing but for which manuals are not available. While the availability of a manual did not necessarily imply an endorsement of the specific therapy for which it was developed, the manuals did enhance the procedural consistency and reliability of the treatments under study.

Better Training of the Therapists

Another important development was the use of standardized training programs based on manual-specified procedures of the psychotherapy being tested. The training programs developed for psychotherapy outcome studies were not designed to teach the inexperienced person how to become a therapist. They were not designed to teach fundamental skills such as empathy, handling of transference, and timing. The training programs for efficacy studies were designed to modify the practices of fully trained, experienced, and competent psychotherapists to conduct the psychotherapy under study as specified in the manual (Klerman & Weissman, 1982; Rush, 1983; Weissman, Rounsaville, & Chevron, 1982). The development of a shared language and specified procedures in an agreed sequence was a major focus.

Certification criteria for the psychotherapists were developed and utilized in these training programs and were based on the goals and tasks outlined in the treatment manual. Through the viewing of videotapes of the trainees' psychotherapy sessions, several independent evaluators could determine whether the therapists had met competence criteria and could be certified to participate in the clinical trials (Chevron & Rounsaville, 1983; Chevron, Rounsaville, Rothblum, & Weissman, 1983).

THE FIRST NIMH COLLABORATIVE STUDY OF PSYCHOTHERAPY

These technological advances in the study of psychotherapy efficacy, many of them developed by members of the NIMH staff, and the promising data on the efficacy of psychotherapy led NIMH, in 1978, to begin piloting and planning the first multisite collaborative study of the treatment of depression that would include psychotherapy. Based on the models used to test the efficacy of the new psychotropic drugs in the 1960s, this study was designed to test two psychotherapies, interpersonal psychotherapy (IPT) and cognitive behavior psychotherapy (CB), among depressed patients in three centers simultaneously, and to include standardized training for the psychotherapies and for the pharmacotherapy (imipramine) under testing (Waskow et al., 1980).

The purpose of this chapter is to summarize briefly the state of evidence between 1974 and 1979 as reported by Weissman (1979), and to focus on the state of evidence since then. This review will show that, in addition to the 12 studies completed between 1974 and 1979, six more studies have been completed since 1980, and seven additional ones are in progress. Thus 25 studies will contribute to understanding the efficacy of psychotherapy alone, in comparison and in combination with pharmacotherapy in the treatment of depressive disorders.

SUMMARY OF EVIDENCE

Criteria for Inclusion in Study

Only those studies are reviewed which included homogeneous samples of depressed patients (although the criteria for depression varied), used random assignment, and included at least eight patients per treatment cell (most studies included much larger numbers of patients per treatment cell). All of the studies included reasonable scientific standards; however, none is without flaws or reasonable alternative approaches. In this limited space no effort will be made to add a detailed critique of each study.

Status of Psychotherapy Studies

Table 1 shows that the progress of clinical trials between 1980 and 1983 has kept pace with those conducted between 1974 and 1979. Twelve clinical trials of psychotherapy were completed between 1974 and 1979; six studies have been completed since 1980, and seven more are under way, most of which will be completed within the next 2 years.

Type of Psychotherapy Studied

As can be seen in Table 2, CB is the type of psychotherapy most frequently included (59%) in the 25 available studies between 1974 and 1983. A drug condition is included in the majority (68%) of the studies, and often pharma-cotherapy in combination with a psychotherapy (45% of the studies) is included. Sixty-three percent of the psychotherapy studies include a nondrug control condition (e.g., low contact, waiting list).

Table 1. Status and Number of Psychotherapy Studies: 1974–1983

	1974–1979	1980–1983	Total
Completed	12	6	18
In process	—	7	7
Total	12	13	25

Table 2. Type of Treatment Studied: 1974–1983

	1974–1979 ($n = 12$) percentage	1980–1983 ($n = 13$) percentage	Total ($n = 25$) percentage
CB	42	73	59
IPT	17	36	27
Behavioral	33	27	32
Other psychotherapies	17	45	32
Any drug included	42	91	68
Drug and psychotherapy combination	33	55	45
Control for psychotherapy included	75	52	63

Note. Treatments are not mutually exclusive.

Since 1979 studies of CB, IPT, and psychotherapy in comparison with or in combination with drugs have increased. There has been a marked increase in studies including a drug condition, a slight increase in studies of psychotherapies other than IPT, CB, or behavioral treatment, and a decrease in the use of a nondrug control for psychotherapy. The latter probably reflects the availability of many studies showing the efficacy of psychotherapy against a control for depressive disorders (Weissman, 1979).

Description of Studies

Table 3 describes the six studies completed between 1980 and 1983, and Table 4 describes the seven studies still ongoing. A description of the studies completed between 1974 and 1979 can be found in the review by Weissman (1979). The following is a summary of the evidence for the efficacy of psychotherapy alone, in comparison and in combination with drugs based on the completed studies since 1974.

Psychotherapy Alone Compared with a Control Group (1974–1983)

In the review by Weissman (1979) there were nine studies testing the efficacy of psychotherapy compared with a low-contact, waiting-list, or no-active-treatment control group. All the studies supported the efficacy of psychotherapy alone as compared with a control group. Since 1980 there has been one additional study that supports the efficacy of social work intervention against no such intervention, but only in the treatment of acutely depressed patients with a superimposed chronic course (Corney, 1981).

Table 3. Completed Studies (1980–1983)

Treatment	Sample	Time (weeks)	Outcome	Investigators
CB, interpersonal skills, pleasant events	Depressed outpatients (MMPI interview) ($n = 70$)	4	All treatment equal and not specific in outcome; all patients improve	Zeiss, Lewinsohn, & Muñoz (1979)
Behavior, insight, amitriptyline, relaxation	Primary major depression (Feighner) ($n = 178$)	12	$B > A = R > I$	McLean & Hakstian (1979)
CB, CB + drug, drug alone	Primary major depression (RDC) ($n = 64$)	23	GP patients: CB, CB + drug > drug; Psychiatric outpatients: CB + drug > CB > drug	Blackburn, Bishop, Glen, Whalley, & Christie (1981)
Social skills + amitriptyline, social skills + placebo, insight psychotherapy + placebo, amitriptyline	Major depression (Feighner) ($n = 72$)	Weekly for 12 weeks, monthly for 6 months	Results vary; all treatments seem equal	Bellack, Hersen, & Himmelhoch (1981)
Social work, no social work	Acute depression (GHQ) ($n = 80$)	24	SW > no SW in acute + chronic depression; SW = no SW in acute depression	Corney (1981)
Parallel studies				
CB group, psychodynamic group	Major depression, elderly (DSM-III) ($n = 26$)	36	CB = psychodynamic	Jarvik, Mintz, Steuer, & Gerner (1982)
Doxepin, imipramine, placebo	($n = 58$)		D = I > placebo; Drugs had higher improvement rate then psychotherapy	

Table 4. Studies in Process (1980–1983)

Treatment	Sample	Time (weeks)	Investigators
CB group + imipramine, CB group, traditional group	Major depression (DSM-III) ($n = 70$)	12	Covi & Lipman
CB, IPT, imipramine + management, placebo + management	Major depression (RDC) ($n = 240$) (3 sites)	16	NIMH Collaborative Study
CB, CB + nortriptyline, nortriptyline, CB + placebo	Major depression (Feighner) ($n = 70$)	12	Murphy
CB, CB + imipramine, imipramine + management	Major depression (RDC) ($n = 113$)	12	Hollon
Acute Treatment IPT + imipramine	Recurrent major depression (DSM-III) ($n = 125$)	Weekly 12, biweekly 8	Kupfer & Frank
Maintenance treatment IPT, IPT + placebo, IPT + imipramine, management + imipramine, management + placebo		Monthly for 3 years	

| CB group with homework, CB group without homework, IPT, waiting list | Major depression (RDC) (n = 140) | 10 | Neimeyer, Twentyman, & Prezant |
| Nortriptyline, placebo, IPT | Hamilton score of 18, major depression or dysthymia, age 60 + (n = 60–90) | 16 | Staples & Sloane |

Addendum

Following the completion of this chapter we learned of two relevant studies now in process[a]:

Time-limited versus time-unlimited psychotherapy for depression

| TL (time limit), TUL (no time limit), treatment-on-demand | Major (nonpsychotic/ nonsuicidal) or minor depression (RDC) (n = 75) | 12 weeks | Klein, Greist, & Gurman |

Running as treatment for depression

| Jogging, meditation–relaxation, group CB | Major (nonpsychotic/ nonsuicidal) or minor depression (RDC) (n = 74) | 12 weeks | Greist, Klein, Gurman, & Neimeyer |

[a]This brings the total of clinical trials on the efficacy of psychological treatment for depression to 27, of which nine are still in process.

Psychotherapy in Comparison with Drugs

In 1979 there were five completed studies from which information on psychotherapy in comparison with a tricyclic antidepressant could be drawn: One study found CB superior to drugs (imipramine), one found IPT and drugs (amitriptyline) about equal for acute symptom reduction, and three studies were equivocal. Pharmacotherapy was superior to psychotherapy (IPT, marital, or group) for prevention of relapse. The psychotherapies were somewhat superior to drugs or minimal treatment in the enhancement of social and interpersonal functioning.

The superiority of cognitive therapy to drugs was the most unexpected and provocative finding and the one most in need of replication. Since 1979 three studies (Bellack, Hersen, & Himmelhoch, 1981; Blackburn, Bishop, Glen, Whalley, & Christie, 1981; McLean & Hakstian, 1979) have replicated these findings. Blackburn *et al.* (1981) found cognitive therapy to be superior to doctor's choice of tricyclic among depressed patients attending general practice, but not in patients attending psychiatric clinics. McLean and Hakstian (1979) found behavioral therapy, rather than insight therapy, to be more effective than amitriptyline on symptom reduction. While the initial results reported by Bellack *et al.* (1981) suggested that social-skills therapy and placebo had a significantly better treatment effect than amitriptyline alone, subsequent analyses of larger samples found no significant difference between social-skills therapy and amitriptyline (Hersen, 1983). Each of the treatments was effective to some degree.

Psychotherapy in Combination with Drugs

In the 1979 review, four studies tested psychotherapy in combination with drugs and all found the combination more effective than either treatment alone. Since then, those findings have been replicated by Blackburn *et al.* (1981), who found that cognitive therapy in combination with doctor's choice of tricyclic was superior to either treatment alone, but only among psychiatric outpatients, not among patients attending general practice. This finding was not replicated by Bellack *et al.* (1981) with social-skills therapy. Depressed patients receiving social-skills therapy and placebo did as well as patients receiving social-skills therapy and amitriptyline (Hersen, 1983). The complete results of the Bellack and Hersen studies are still in process and more information will be forthcoming.

Differential Outcome by Patient Type

Information emerging from the studies conducted since 1974 will begin to answer the question about the specificity of the treatments for particular patients. Prusoff, Weissman, Klerman, and Rounsaville (1980) found that endogenous nonsituational (RDC) depressed patients responded best to the combination of drugs and psychotherapy (IPT), equally well to drugs or IPT, and worse to IPT alone. The situational patients did equally well with drugs, IPT, or the combination, and better with any of these treatments than with a nonscheduled control treatment.

Blackburn *et al.* (1981) did not find a treatment difference between endogenous and nonendogenous patients but found that psychiatric clinic patients, as compared with patients in general practice, did best on the combination of cognitive therapy and drugs. As noted before, Blackburn *et al.* (1981) found cognitive therapy alone or in combination with drugs to be slightly better than drugs alone among general-practice patients.

Kovacs (1980) did not find a correlation between endogenous depression and poor response to cognitive therapy. The Blackburn *et al.* (1981) and Kovacs (1980) studies did not separate out endogenous patients who were also situational from the patients who were only endogenously depressed.

Differential Effects of Drugs and Psychotherapy

DiMascio, Weissman, Prusoff, Neu, Zwilling, and Klerman (1979) found a differential effect of drugs and IPT psychotherapy. IPT had its effect on social and interpersonal functioning, whereas amitriptyline had its effect on symptom reduction.

Rush, Kovacs, Beck, Weissenburger, and Hollon (1981) found that cognitive therapy had a more pervasive and significant impact on self-concept than did amitriptyline, and produced a greater reduction in hopelessness than did amitriptyline.

Specificity of the Psychotherapies

Zeiss, Lewinsohn, and Muñoz (1979), studying various behavioral approaches, found no differential outcome between three behavioral approaches. Findings were also similar for Jarvik, Mintz, Steuer, and Gerner (1982) studying CB group versus psychodynamic group therapy in elderly depressed patients. However, in the two studies (Bellack *et al.*, 1981; McLean & Hakstian, 1979) comparing behavioral approaches to insight psychotherapy, the behavioral approaches were found to be somewhat more efficacious.

A partial answer to the question of specificity of treatments awaits the results of the NIMH Collaborative Study, in which two different psychotherapies, CB and IPT, are compared. The most important features of the NIMH study are (1) that the treatments were not developed in the centers conducting the trials, (2) there is no ideological commitment to one or another form of treatment, and (3) the therapists have been well trained in both treatments.

Can the Psychotherapies Be Differentiated?

DeRubeis, Hollon, Evans, and Bemis (1982) undertook a study to determine whether it was possible to identify distinct and theoretically meaningful differences between two forms of therapy, cognitive and IPT, used in the treatment of depression. Blind ratings of videotapes enabled 12 raters to distinguish the treatments consistently in the direction of experts' predictions. Similar findings for different treatments were reported by Luborsky, Woody, McLellan, and O'Brien (1982). They found that independent judges were also able to distinguish three different forms of psychotherapy—cognitive-behavioral, supportive–expressive psychoanalytically oriented psychotherapy, and drug counseling.

Are Psychotherapy Effects Sustained?

In two studies (Weissman, Klerman, Prusoff, Sholomskas, & Padian, 1981; Kovacs, Rush, Beck & Hollon, 1981) it was found that acutely depressed patients who had received psychotherapy without drugs were doing better 1 year after treatment. The IPT effects were on social functioning, only after 16 weeks of treatment. However, patients were doing equally well 1 year after 8-month maintenance treatment with amitriptyline and IPT, alone or in combination, and compared with low contact and placebo. The studies are too few and too inconsistent in terms of degree of maintenance of psychotherapy effect to draw conclusions.

CONCLUSIONS

In summary, over the last decade a number of well-designed clinical trials of the efficacy of psychotherapy have been initiated and the pace of this research has been sustained. There has also been increased interest in the feasibility, methodology, and policy implications of psychotherapy outcome studies (American Psychiatric Association [APA], 1982; Greenspan & Sharfstein, 1981; Hine, Werman, & Simpson, 1982; Karasu, 1980, 1982; Kazdin & Wilson, 1978; London & Klerman, 1982; Parloff, 1980). The precision of these studies, particularly the efforts to specify the treatments, the patients, and the therapists, has shown vast improvement over the past 3 years. There continues to be considerable interest in the efficacy of psychotherapy (particularly CB) in comparison to drugs. Research efforts to determine the specificity of which treatment for which patient are beginning to yield findings. Several of the studies in process will be published shortly, so any definitive conclusions must await these results.

A considerable gap still remains, however, between clinical practice and research studies. Most depressed patients, if they receive any treatment at all, and if that treatment is psychotherapy, are more likely to receive a psychodynamic psychotherapy (however defined) than cognitive or behavioral treatments. To close the gap between research and clinical practice, the next wave of clinical trials should include psychodynamic psychotherapeutic treatments. If the results are to be useful, however, the studies should also include the technological advances in the specification of the treatments and the training procedures.

ACKNOWLEDGMENTS

This work was supported in part by Alcohol, Drug Abuse, and Mental Health Administration IPT Training Grant MH 33827 and IPT Marital Grant MH 34501, from the Psychosocial Treatments Research Branch, National Institute of Mental Health, Rockville, Md. Appreciation is expressed to the many investigators who provided us with updates of their work; to G. E. Woody, L. Luborsky, R. J. DeRubeis, M. Hersen, H. Strupp, and G. Murphy for their comments on the manuscript; to Amy Margolis, BS, for compiling the literature; and to Joan Smolka for editorial assistance.

REFERENCES

American Psychiatric Association, APA Commission on Psychotherapies. *Psychotherapy research: Methodological and efficacy issues.* Washington, D.C.: American Psychiatric Association, 1982.

Beck, A. *Cognitive therapy and the emotional disorders.* New York: International Universities Press, 1976.

Bellack, A. S., Hersen, M., & Himmelhoch, J. M. Social skills training compared with pharmacotherapy and psychotherapy in the treatment of unipolar depression. *American Journal of Psychiatry*, 1981, *138*, 1562–1567.

Blackburn, I. M., Bishop, S., Glen, A. I. M., Whalley, L. J., & Christie, J. E. The efficacy of cognitive therapy in depression: A treatment trial using cognitive therapy and pharmacotherapy, each alone and in combination. *British Journal of Psychiatry*, 1981, *139*, 181–189.

Chevron, E. S., Rounsaville, B. J., Rothblum, E. D., & Weissman, M. M. Selecting psychotherapists to participate in psychotherapy outcome studies: Relationship between psychotherapist characteristics and assessment of clinical skills. *Journal of Nervous and Mental Disease*, 1983, *171*, 348–353.

Chevron, E. S., & Rounsaville, B. J. Evaluating the clinical skills of psychotherapists: A comparison of techniques. *Archives of General Psychiatry*, 1983, *40*, 1129–1132.

Corney, R. H. Social work effectiveness in the management of depressed women: A clinical trial. *Psychological Medicine*, 1981, *11*, 417–423.

Cristol, A. H. Studies of outcome psychotherapy. *Comprehensive Psychiatry*, 1972, *13*, 189–200.

DeRubeis, R. J., Hollon, S. D., Evans, M. D., & Bemis, K. M. Can psychotherapies for depression be discriminated? A systematic investigation of cognitive therapy and interpersonal therapy. *Journal of Consulting and Clinical Psychology*, 1982, *50*, 744–756.

DiMascio, A., Weissman, M. M., Prusoff, B. A., Neu, C., Zwilling, M., & Klerman, G. L. Differential symptom reduction by drugs and psychotherapy in acute depression. *Archives of General Psychiatry*, 1979, *36*, 1450–1456.

Fiske, D. W., Hunt, H. F., Luborsky, L., Orne, M. T., Parloff, M. B., Reiser, M. F., & Tuma, A. H. Planning of research on effectiveness of psychotherapy. *Archives of General Psychiatry*, 1970, *22*, 22–32.

Greenspan, S. I., & Sharfstein, S. S. Efficacy of psychotherapy. *Archives of General Psychiatry*, 1981, *36*, 1213–1219.

Hersen, M. Personal communication, March 1, 1983.

Hine, F. R., Werman, D. S., & Simpson, D. M. Effectiveness of psychotherapy: Problems of research on complex phenomena. *American Journal of Psychiatry*, 1982, *139*, 204–208.

Jarvik, L. F., Mintz, J., Steuer, J., & Gerner, R. Treating geriatric depression: A 26-week interim analysis. *Journal of the American Geriatrics Society*, 1982, *30*, 713–717.

Karasu, T. B. The ethics of psychotherapy. *American Journal of Psychiatry*, 1980, *137*, 1502–1512.

Karasu, T. B. Psychotherapy and pharmacotherapy: Toward an integrative model. *American Journal of Psychiatry*, 1982, *139*, 1102–1113.

Kazdin, A. E., & Wilson, G. T. Criteria for evaluating psychotherapy. *Archives of General Psychiatry*, 1978, *35*, 407–416.

Klerman, G. L., & Weissman, M. M. Interpersonal psychotherapy: Theory and research. In A. J. Rush (Ed.), *Short-term psychotherapies for depression: Behavioral, interpersonal, cognitive, and psychodynamic approaches*. New York: Guilford, 1982.

Klerman, G. L., Rounsaville, B., Chevron, E., Neu, C., & Weissman, M. M. *Manual for short-term interpersonal psychotherapy (IPT) of depression*. New Haven–Boston Collaborative Depression Project. June, 1982, 5th draft.

Kovacs, M. The efficacy of cognitive and behavior therapies for depression. *American Journal of Psychiatry*, 1980, *137*, 1495–1501.

Kovacs, M., Rush, A. J., Beck, A. T., & Hollon, S. D. Depressed outpatients treated with cognitive therapy or pharmacotherapy: A one year follow-up. *Archives of General Psychiatry*, 1981, *38*, 33–39.

Lieberman, M. *Survey and evaluation of the literature on verbal psychotherapy of depressive disorders*. Clinical Research Branch, National Institute of Mental Health, March 7, 1975.

London, P., & Klerman, G. L. Evaluating psychotherapy. *American Journal of Psychiatry*, 1982, *139*, 709–717.

Luborsky, L. *A general manual for supportive-expressive psychoanalytically oriented psychotherapy*. Unpublished manuscript, 1976. (Available from L. Luborsky, Piersol Building, Room 207, Hospital of University of Pennsylvania, 36th and Spruce Streets, Philadelphia, Pa. 19104.)

Luborsky, L. *Individual treatment manual for supportive-expressive psychoanalytically oriented psychotherapy: Special adaptation for treatment of drug abuse*. Copyright, 1977. (Available from L. Luborsky.)

Luborsky, L. Personal communication, March 7, 1983.

Luborsky, L. *Principles of psychoanalytic psychotherapy: A manual for supportive-expressive treatment*. New York: Basic Books, in press.

Luborsky, L., Singer, B., & Luborsky, L. Comparative studies of psychotherapies. *Archives of General Psychiatry*, 1975, *32*, 995–1008.

Luborsky, L., Woody, G. E., McLellan, A. T., & O'Brien, C. P. Can independent judges recognize different psychotherapies? An experience with manual-guided therapies. *Journal of Consulting and Clinical Psychology*, 1982, *50*, 49–62.

McLean, P. D., & Hakstian, A. R. Clinical depression: Comparative efficacy of outpatient treatments. *Journal of Consulting and Clinical Psychology*, 1979, *47*, 818–836.

Morris, J. B., & Beck, A. T. The efficacy of antidepressant drugs. *Archives of General Psychiatry*, 1974, *30*, 667–674.

Parloff, M. B. Psychotherapy and research: An anaclitic depression. *Psychiatry*, 1980, *43*, 279–293.

Parloff, M. B., & Dies, R. R. Group psychotherapy outcome research 1966–1975. *International Journal of Group Psychotherapy*, 1975, *27*, 281–319.

Parloff, M. B., Waskow, I. E., & Wolfe, B. E. Research on therapist variables in relation to progress and outcome. In S. L. Garfield & A. E. Bergin (Eds.), *Handbook of psychotherapy and behavior change: An empirical analysis* (2nd ed.). New York: Wiley, 1979.

Prusoff, B. A., Weissman, M. M., Klerman, G. L., & Rounsaville, B. J. Research diagnostic criteria subtypes of depression: Their role as predictors of differential response to psychotherapy and drug treatment. *Archives of General Psychiatry*, 1980, *37*, 796–803.

Rush, A. J. Cognitive therapy of depression. *Psychiatric Clinics of North America*, 1983, *6*, 105–128.

Rush, A. J., Kovacs, M., Beck, A. T., Weissenburger, J., & Hollon, S. D. Differential effects of cognitive therapy and pharmacotherapy on depressive symptoms. *Journal of Affective Disorders*, 1981, *3*, 221–229.

Spitzer, R. L., Endicott, J., & Robins, E. Research diagnostic criteria: Rationale and reliability. *Archives of General Psychiatry*, 1978, *35*, 773–782.

Strupp, H., & Bergin, A. E. Some empirical and conceptual bases for coordinated research in psychotherapy: A critical review of issues, trends and evidence. *International Journal of Psychiatry*, 1969, *7*, 180–190.

Strupp, H., & Binder, J. *Time limited dynamic psychotherapy (TIDP)*—A treatment manual. Nashville, Tenn.: Center for Psychotherapy Research, 1982.

Waskow, I. E., Hadley, S. W., Autry, J. H., & Parloff, M. B. NIMH Treatment of Depression Research Program (Pilot Phase), Revised Research Plan, January, 1980. Psychosocial Treatment Research Branch, National Institute of Mental Health, Rockville, Md.

Waskow, I., & Parloff, M. B. (Eds.). *Psychotherapy change measures: Report of the Clinical Research Branch, N.I.M.H.* Washington, D.C.: U.S. Government Printing Office, 1974.

Weissman, M. M. The psychological treatment of depression: Evidence for the efficacy of psychotherapy alone, in comparison with, and in combination with pharmacotherapy. *Archives of General Psychiatry*, 1979, *36*, 1261–1269.

Weissman, M. M., Klerman, G. L., Prusoff, B. A., Sholomskas, D., & Padian, N. Depressed outpatients: Results one year after treatment with drugs and/or interpersonal psychotherapy. *Archives of General Psychiatry*, 1981, *38*, 51–55.

Weissman, M. M., Rounsaville, B. J., & Chevron, E. Training psychotherapists to participate in psychotherapy outcome studies: Identifying and dealing with the research requirements. *American Journal of Psychiatry*, 1982, *139*, 1442–1446.

Zeiss, A. M., Lewinsohn, P. M., & Muñoz, R. F. Nonspecific improvement effects in depression using interpersonal skills training, pleasant activity schedules, or cognitive training. *Journal of Consulting and Clinical Psychology*, 1979, *47*, 427–439.

COMMENTARY

Dr. Solomon C. Goldberg*: I wonder if you could comment on the difficulty of maintaining blindness in any study of psychotherapy. You could take pains to videotape interviews and delete anything that would give away the treatment before ratings are done, but that still doesn't eliminate the fact

*Medical College of Virginia.

that the patient is not blind and may have a particular bias in one direction or another. If you use self-report forms, in which the patient rates only his or her own status, that too has some effect, which is very difficult to eliminate, although it is different from the lack of blindness in a rater watching an interview. A related problem, of course, is the differential attention that might be given to someone in the experimental group as opposed to someone in the control group. Someone on a waiting list may only be given minimal attention, simply being evaluated, as opposed to someone getting some kind of therapy.

Dr. Weissman: One of the ways around the problem you mentioned is the use of blind evaluators, and the collaborative study, unlike many of the studies I reported on, has incorporated this. I think you have to get the patient's report, the clinician's report, a significant other's report if you can, and also a blind evaluator. In our studies, and this includes the collaborative study, the patient is told that "we want to get an outside opinion to see how you are doing, so that we can really tell whether the treatment is working." Also, an evaluator who is blind to the treatment comes in at regular intervals, usually once every 4 weeks, and does some of the assessments. This is a methodological improvement that has not been incorporated in many of these studies.

As to your question about the waiting list, or how does one control for psychotherapy, I think my Table 2 indicates a somewhat negative trend. There seems to be so much belief in the efficacy of psychotherapy for depression that many of these studies are not using control groups to control for time or attention. I think this is something that ought to be examined and perhaps even changed in future studies. We are not yet at the stage where we know these treatments are so good that we don't need to test them against time.

There was once an interesting debate about what constitutes a proper control group for psychotherapy, and although the issue was never resolved, I think the most clever solution was proposed by Paula Clayton. She suggested that, in order to control for time and attention, perhaps one should have the control group come in once a week for the same period of time as the psychotherapy patients, and play cards. (*Laughter.*)

Dr. Goldberg: I have a second question. This has to do with the possibility that psychotherapy and drugs affect different types of symptoms or measures. I wonder if that is a possible explanation for some studies showing that psychotherapy is better, and others showing that a drug is better. I think there is a pretty good literature on what particular kinds of symptoms or with what particular kinds of patients drugs are effective. And we know there is a large number of depressed patients who are not affected by drugs. Is it possible to analyze this?

Dr. Weissman: It is possible, since psychotherapy seems to have its effect in interpersonal areas, but cognitive therapy has its effect on cognition.

In fact, cognitive therapy outcome studies have been very sophisticated in looking at those aspects that are supposed to change—namely, change in thought. I don't think we can take what we know of what works in interpersonal psychotherapy or marital therapy as the only criterion of what should be used as outcome measures in studies of, perhaps, cognitive therapy or behavior therapy.

5

Opening Comments

ARTHUR K. SHAPIRO
Mount Sinai School of Medicine

I have been asked to begin the general discussion by preparing a lucid, profound, and written 5-minute discussion of the four thoughtful and stimulating papers which comprise 150 pages and 288 references. I therefore limit my discussion to brief, telescoped comments about several selected areas which are inadequately considered in much of the current research on psychotherapy.

In contrast to past conferences (and I have attended most of the major conferences, *naturally* because of my consuming interest in the placebo effect of treatment), which were concerned with only a few of the major psychotherapies, this conference is notable for its attempt to emphasize data-oriented studies of many new psychotherapies. They have exploded into 250 different types, variously referred to as CT, BT, IT, MT, RT, IPT, BFT, CBT, CCT, SCT, SST, TST, BM-T, even PP-T, and so on.

From the 288 references in three of the papers it would appear that psychotherapy research is only 10 years old, since 90% of the cited papers were published since 1973, and only one paper before 1966.

Although most comprehensive, especially data-oriented, conferences in the past included papers on the placebo effect of treatment, this basic factor underlying the applied practice of psychotherapy was not included in this or the previous APA conference on psychotherapy. It is an especially conspicuous omission because historic evidence leads to the conclusion that psychotherapy is probably the major placebo of our time, and, as you know, those who ignore the past are bound to repeat it. But it doesn't matter, because it is a law too that even if you know it you repeat it.

A major problem in reviews of studies assessing the efficacy of the psychotherapies is having to rely on the clinical judgment of the authors about the merit of the described studies, which are reminiscent of clinical discussions of individual patients, except that current discussion is couched in research parlance. A review should provide information about the methodology and include a rating about how well the studies fulfill the criteria for an adequate study, as described previously by Luborsky. Otherwise, the review deteriorates into mere clinical-research opinion.

As for the studies, they are often misleading in failing to specify whether the many results are predictive or retrospective.

Omitted from most studies and reviews is an assessment of the effect size of the treatment, or the amount of explained variance. Would the massive use of the 250 psychotherapies be warranted if only a very small amount of the improvement variance could be demonstrated, in comparison to the bulk of the variance being explained by placebo effects, spontaneous changes, and error?

The design of almost all studies does not fulfill the essential prerequisite for an adequate or double-blind study, which requires that there is no possibility that patients, clinicians, researchers, and statisticians can break the code before the statistical results are completely tabulated and analyzed.

Another shortcoming of the studies is the use of nonclinical samples—normal volunteers, patients with minor problems, studies for short periods and frequently in the laboratory rather than a clinic.

The placebo control in psychotherapy research is almost always inadequate since it tends to be a second-class procedure or pseudo therapy which guarantees positive results for the studied, invested-in therapy. For example, if the meta-analysis study by Glass & Smith were limited to studies with adequate placebo controls and clinical patients, I would predict that less than 10% of the studies would fulfill these criteria, and that there would be no difference between psychotherapy and placebo.

I would also suggest that retrospective examination of many variables, especially those with inadequate placebo and blind controls, could yield disparate results that would fit most preconceived hypotheses.

A major problem in studies of psychotherapy is the difficulty of devising a good placebo control. I have given it much thought during the past 27 years and believed that I had solved the problem many times, only to discover subsequently that someone was using that placebo as a specific treatment.

But I have finally solved the problem of an adequate placebo. It involves tilting one creditable therapy against another, such as psychoanalytic versus behavior therapy, or the use of therapies with a theory, practiced by enthusiastic, experienced, and committed therapists, which have captured the imagination of the public—that is, therapies such as pastoral, primal, orgone, Rolfing, Siegel and holistic types of therapy, and even dianetics or EST. The only problem is, are we willing to take the chance?

General Discussion

Dr. Donald F. Klein*: My recollection is that in none of the studies that Dr. Weissman reviewed in which drugs were superior to psychotherapy was there a placebo control that showed that the drug was indeed active in that subpopulation. We already know that it is not difficult to put together a study of depressed outpatients in which there is no drug–placebo difference whatsoever. All one has to do is to select patients who are either chronic hypochondriacs, nonmajor depressives, or, if they do have major depression, they have a Hamilton score of 14 or below. Under such circumstances you will not find, even with vigorous tricyclic treatment, any tricyclic-versus-placebo difference.

I would suggest that it is at least possible that what we have here is a problem in sampling. Further, in one of your studies, Myrna [Weissman], when you did subdivide the patients into whether they were endogenous or not, the psychotherapy effect disappeared. So I think there is rather good evidence from your own studies and from studies in the literature that the issue of the subdiagnosis of depression may be utterly crucial, and that the problem in psychopharmacology in general, in which we find differences between studies as to whether a drug is effective or not, is the marked variation among samples. I think that probably applies here as well.

The second point I'd like to make is that I am almost entirely in agreement with Dr. Shapiro in that I think that pitting credible therapies against each other is the real way to go. I do think his last suggestion, however, is unlikely to be effective. The reason for that is that I think there is some reasonable evidence that there has to be an ideological match between the preconceptions of the person going into therapy and what the therapy has to offer. For someone of the psychoanalytic persuasion to be in behavior therapy is unlikely, it seems to me, for behavior therapy would not hold much credibility for that particular patient. Even if it has a placebo effect, it wouldn't be a placebo for him. Similarly, if you did a study comparing dianetics with behavior therapy, the people who would come would likely be

*New York State Psychiatric Institute and College of Physicians and Surgeons, Columbia University.

pro-dianetic and would be quite disappointed with behavior therapy; therefore, any treatment differences you would get would actually be mismatch differences.

Dr. Arthur K. Shapiro*: There is little question about the importance of the experimental and placebo therapies being meaningful to patients in studies. There are very few things that stand up consensually in the placebo literature, and that is one of them. The placebo stimulus must make sense to the patient, or it won't work. This is a variable that should probably always be measured in all psychotherapy studies. Our studies indicate that it can be done.

Dr. Myrna M. Weissman†: I would like to address Don's [Klein] first point. The last part of my paper had to do with the various other types of information you could get from these studies in addition to the main effect issue of psychotherapy versus some other treatment. One of these has to do with just what you raised: differential outcome by patient subtype. In fact, although we may show some main effect for psychotherapy, that doesn't mean it works equally well for all patients.

What you reported, of course, is our study in which we found that patients with endogenous depression did slightly worse with psychotherapy than patients who had situational depression. Similarly, although not quite the same, in the Blackburn study, patients who were being seen in general practice (as opposed to psychiatric clinics) did very well with psychotherapy. They were probably the very mild primary care patients, whereas those in the hospital practice, which is probably equivalent to our outpatient clinic, required cognitive therapy plus drugs.

Kovacs has also looked at endogenous and nonendogenous patients, and did not find a correlation between endogenous depression and poor response to cognitive therapy, indicating a lack of specificity of cognitive therapy with regard to this distinction. In both the Blackburn and Kovacs studies, endogenous patients who were also situational were not separated out from those who were only endogenously depressed. So people are beginning to look at the data, and it looks as if the psychotherapy effect might not be present with endogenous patients, but might with those who are situational.

Dr. Samuel J. Keith§: I would like to raise a general question that has come up in the discussion this morning, and that frequently comes up—whether one has a "no therapy" condition. As Dr. Shapiro said, demonstrating that something is better than nothing may be a relatively easy thing to demonstrate. And I believe Dr. Klein once said that demonstrating the equivalence of two equally ineffective treatments is also easy. An example of

*Mount Sinai School of Medicine.
†Yale University School of Medicine and Connecticut Mental Health Center.
§National Institute of Mental Health.

this would be if you have two treatments, each of which produced the same result of no relapse, or relatively better improvement, how are you to judge whether they are equally effective or equally powerful?

Dr. Sol L. Garfield*: I don't think you can draw any definitive conclusions about the efficacy of treatment without some kind of standard control group. If you just compare two treatments and they don't show any differences, then you have to make a value judgment about whether they are equally effective or equally ineffective. If you have norms you can make some estimates; otherwise, you really can't. At least if you compare a long-term treatment with a short-term treatment, and one is either no more effective or no more ineffective, you can conclude that the short-term treatment may be more efficient.

Dr. Weissman: I think there may be times when you want to compare two treatments that seem to be similarly effective, but you're not sure, and they may be effective on different types of outcome, or with different populations. An example would be a pharmacotherapy study in which you compared weight gain on amitriptyline and imipramine. I think that would be a valid study. There are some interesting small questions that you can sometimes answer with a small study comparing two treatments, as long as you don't make generalizations about their differential efficacy with "no treatment."

Dr. Allen Raskin†*:* I think one of the big issues when you are looking at combined modality treatments today is what John Docherty alluded to, which is the sequencing, or timing, effect. I think this is particularly crucial, or at least has been pointed out more in studies of anxiety disorders, in which people are started off on an antidepressant to control the symptoms, and then are given behavior therapy at a later point to deal with avoidance behavior. If you use a repeated measurement model to look at any of these studies you do, in fact, find differential effects in terms of time. Myrna [Weissman] pointed that out as well in some of her work.

Dr. Harold I. Lief§*:* This question is addressed to Dr. Barlow. You cited the striking effect of introducing the spouse into the treatment, and I was wondering if you could comment on whether you thought this was just adding an additional support for the agoraphobic patient, or whether there was something in the marital interaction that maintained or augmented the phobia.

Dr. David H. Barlow‡*:* Yes, that has really been our major interest for the past 3 or 4 years, Dr. Lief. I can try to summarize it as briefly as I can by

*Washington University.
†National Institute of Mental Health.
§University of Pennsylvania School of Medicine.
‡State University of New York at Albany.

saying that the reason we included the spouse initially was because of the literature pointing out the possible etiological and maintaining factors associated with marital relationships and agoraphobia. A lot of the literature showed that if the agoraphobic woman got better, the marriage deteriorated, and the husband often got worse. What we found, in fact, was that when we included the spouses in treatment, the marriages, in addition to the patients, also got a bit better, but we are not yet at a point where we can say just what the mechanism of action is. Our original thought was, as you suggested, that the husband—all of our patients were women—would assist the patient in facing up to the feared situation and be supportive, and that we would be able to remove any sabotaging effect. However, when we looked more closely at the data, it was hard for us to confirm that, and it looked as if we might be effecting a general reduction of tension and stress in the marriage, and that might well be accounting for the gains. So the marriages do seem to get better, on the whole, along with the patients. But just why the patients are getting better, we are not yet sure.

Dr. Aaron T. Beck[*]*:* I agree with much of what has been said, and I just want to make a proposal. I would like to suggest that in looking at various outcome studies, and preferably in designing them, we think in terms of a mosaic that consists of numerous outcome studies over a whole variety of treatment modalities and treatment populations, including analogue studies as well as the severely clinically ill patients. The reason for this is that I don't think any one study can really conclusively answer any one question. But a variety of studies can answer a lot of questions.

To be more specific, in our own studies comparing cognitive therapy with drugs, we used a particular logic that was based on work that had previously been done. There had been at least 120 studies in which imipramine or other tricyclic antidepressants had been compared with control groups of various types, and also with placebo controls. We did not include a placebo control group because in the preliminary study in which we assigned patients randomly to a placebo control group or to cognitive therapy, the placebo patients deteriorated very badly. So in our particular setup we felt that for ethical and professional clinical-responsibility reasons, we could not include the placebo control. Our logic was that if we compared cognitive therapy with a drug treatment that had already been demonstrated to be superior to placebo, this would be a logical "plus" in favor of one or the other. Now this, of course, would have to be replicated elsewhere.

We did have the problem at the University of Pennsylvania that, after cognitive therapy got established as a glamour type of treatment in Philadelphia, patients would come with high levels of expectancy, and then we couldn't carry on that type of study there. But these studies were done in

*University of Pennsylvania.

St. Louis and Oklahoma, where the predilection of patients is toward drug treatment. No one of these studies can really answer any one question, but when all the studies are in, one can go through and use some kind of logical tool and see what they all add up to.

Dr. Solomon C. Goldberg*: I'd like to ask Dr. Weissman about differential dropout rates for drug treatment and psychotherapy treatment, and how they affect the interpretation of outcome.

Dr. Weissman: The dropout rates obviously affect the outcome and interpretation seriously, and in most of the studies they used end-point analysis, which is taking the clinical ratings of the patients at the points at which they drop out and entering those into all subsequent analyses, or used a life-table method so that you take into account when the patient actually did drop out. Some studies, like Bellack's, have actually used attrition as an outcome measure. I would have to look at each study in detail again to determine if taking attrition into account would change the results of the studies. There is often a differential dropout among treatments, but an impressive thing about these studies, for the most part, is the relative sophistication of design and analysis, and at least the discussion of this as an issue.

Dr. George E. Murphy†: I think the earlier comments about what has to be taken into account in evaluating outcome studies with depression are all very well taken, and I certainly agree. To take all those things into account, however, makes research in this field very difficult. Clearly, when different interventions are used we are going to be interested in a variety of process measures and differential outcomes on a variety of measures, but as far as I can see, the bottom line, if you are treating depression, is: Did the depression resolve, and to what extent? So it is important that investigators use the same measures that others have used. If they want to introduce new one, that's fine, but the Beck Depression Inventory, for example, and the Hamilton Depression Rating Scale, make it possible to compare outcomes from one study to another.

I would particularly like to emphasize, however, that mean values simply do not provide enough information; it is essential for investigators to report categorical outcomes. What I mean by this is how many patients improved to the point of a Beck depression score of 9 or less, or 6 or less, or whatever criterion they want to use? How many patients dropped their Hamilton scores from an initial value above 14 to, say, 7, or to Hamilton's current criterion of one-third or less of their initial level? Unless categorical outcomes are reported in terms of numbers of proportions of patients in the study, it is very difficult to know how much is being accounted for by a few

*Medical College of Virginia.
†Washington University School of Medicine.

patients with brilliant remissions, who are averaged in with people with indifferent kinds of remissions or hardly any remission at all.

Dr. Alan E. Kazdin*: At the risk of stirring controversy, I would like to say that the greatest disagreements in this area are precisely on methodological questions, and the fact that these questions have been tacit so far in the presentations is the basis for any illusion of clarity about any of the treatment effects. Let me mention some of these very briefly. First of all, I think the issues are far from resolved as to what measures should be used for any particular sort of problem. And then among the different measures, how to weight them is an issue. What has been raised before, of course, is if they are conducted in a blind or nonblind fashion. An issue that has not arisen at all, that perhaps deserves a prominent place on Dr. Weissman's chart, is the specification of the integrity of treatment. The integrity of treatment, which is rarely measured, refers to the extent to which the treatment was carried out as intended. A panel of the National Academy of Sciences recently evaluated all treatments of adult offenders, and concluded that no treatment is known to work in the rehabilitation of criminals. But a more important methodological conclusion that was elaborated in that report was that no treatment has been shown to have been fairly tested. I think that is the status of a number of interventions, still, in psychotherapy research. Many basic methodological issues still require resolution before any of the answers we have tried to come up with today can be formulated in even a tentative fashion.

*Western Psychiatric Institute and Clinic, University of Pittsburgh School of Medicine.

6

Paul Hoch Award Address

Cognitive Therapy, Behavior Therapy, Psychoanalysis, and Pharmacotherapy: The Cognitive Continuum[1]

AARON T. BECK
University of Pennsylvania

PHILOSOPHICAL SYSTEMS AND PSYCHOPATHOLOGY

To a large degree our scientific interpretations are based on a particular, often tacit, philosophical system. The philosophical system we use as investigators may differ widely from that we use as clinicians. Thus, the laboratory investigator who studies depression may work within the trappings of a materialistic (or monistic) model while he is in the laboratory. When he takes off his lab coat and replaces it with his sports jacket as he prepares to treat a patient in psychodynamic therapy, he switches to a new philosophical system— either dualism or mentalism.

Moreover, the philosophy that guides our scientific or clinical endeavors may be completely different from that which shapes the view of the practical realities of everyday life. Thus, when our investigator arrives home to confront a troubled wife, he may advise her to stop worrying or she will get an ulcer (interactionist system). In sum, we may jump from materialism in the laboratory, mentalism in psychotherapy, and interactionism outside our professional activities.

To find the common ground among the psychotherapies and pharmacotherapy we need to have some understanding of the philosophical background that shapes the quite diverse approaches to an individual case.

Psychopharmacology has drawn on a materialistic (or monistic) system; behavior therapy, also, predominantly utilizes a materialistic system; psychoanalysis depends primarily on a mentalist system; cognitive therapy has been primarily interactionist.

1. This chapter is an extended version of the Paul Hoch Award Address, American Psychopathological Association, March 3, 1983.

Despite the obvious philosophical, theoretical, and technical differences among cognitive therapy, psychoanalysis, behavior therapy, and pharmacotherapy, there are enough subtle but important similarities to justify attempts to construct a maxi-model to encompass those systems of therapy.

As a springboard for clarifying these similarities, let us take a typical case of a patient who showed a marked change during and after a particular intervention in cognitive therapy.

I will condense the description of the patient and interview to a few salient points in order to save space.

The patient was a 40-year-old married attorney who had been depressed for at least 6 months. He finally sought psychiatric evaluation after continuous prodding by his wife. Among the most salient features were insomnia, loss of gratification from any of the kinds of experiences that had brought gratification in the past (anhedonia), loss of appetite, loss of weight, early morning awakening, loss of libido, general slowing down, and difficulties in concentration. He was highly self-critical and pessimistic, and did not think that any kind of psychiatric treatment would be helpful because his depression was "realistic"—that it derived from his basic inadequacy and ineffectiveness on the job, his failure in all spheres of his life.

On interview, the patient appeared to be very depressed and slowed down in all of his observable behaviors. He scored near the top on the Depression Inventory (50). The patient's pervasive view of himself was that he was totally inadequate and incapable of dealing with even minimal demands or expectations. He believed firmly that he was incapable of performing any of his work at the office, that this would always be the case, and that if indeed he did attempt to do something he would be incapable of completing it or of doing an adequate job. His sense of hopelessness, inadequacy, and self-criticism also spread to his role as a husband and parent (he had two teenage sons).

Because of his sense of inadequacy and failure, he had been spending progressively less time at the office and had accumulated a pile of work that he had not attended to. He expected that he would be fired by the senior partners at any time, and he and his family would thus be destitute. He saw suicide as a way of relieving his family of the emotional burden he believed he had imposed on them and also a way to provide them some financial support from his life insurance policy.

The only indication of precipitating factors had been the death of a senior partner of the firm a few months prior to the onset of the depression. The patient had been very attached to him and probably dependent on him and "took his death very hard."

The patient was so suicidal that it was obvious that a quick intervention was indicated. This consisted essentially of starting cognitive–behavioral procedures immediately in the first interview. I discovered that the patient's belief that he would be fired in a day or two had a realistic basis. He was unprepared to try a case coming up for trial the next day and he had felt incapable of doing the necessary paperwork to request a continuation of the trial. He had tried many times to draft a letter or to make the appropriate phone call to the clerk of the court, but felt incapable of mobilizing the degree of concentration necessary for either action. He also had avoided telling his senior partners of the problem because of his sense of shame.

The therapeutic approach consists essentially of modified, graded, task assignments (Beck, Rush, Shaw, & Emery, 1979). Since he felt incapable of writing the letter, I asked him to give me some idea what he would say in the letter. As he "warmed up" to the project, he became unusually fluent and in a few minutes was able to produce orally an appropriate request. I took notes during this period of time and then handed him the written letter. He was surprised at this "success" and then we went on to dictate several other more complicated letters that he had been unable to attend to previously. After leaving the office he felt considerably better, more "alive," and more energetic. He started to walk through the campus and he noted a number of buildings that had been erected since he had graduated from the University of Pennsylvania. On an impulse he decided to go to the student cafeteria to see what the students were up to. As he went through the cafeteria line, he began to feel hungry and he had his first complete meal in several months. He later reported that he had enjoyed the meal and also enjoyed seeing various old familiar sights on the campus. These were the first experiences of pleasure that he recalled having had since his depression started.

Application of Philosophical Systems

How can we understand this particular case?

From the standpoint of the materialistic system (centralist type), we could say that the patient had some kind of biochemical disturbance that was responsible for his symptoms. The basic problem, according to current theories, might be variously ascribed to a disturbance in neurotransmitter functioning, a decreased sensitivity of specific receptors, a deficiency in steroid metabolism, some imbalance in the regulation of growth or thyrotropic hormones—or any combination of these or some other endocrine or normal neurochemical disturbance. According to the materialistic system, the treatment would consist of administration of a drug to correct the deficiency or imbalance.

The psychodynamic approach would work within a mentalistic system and assume that the symptoms evolved from certain unconscious forces such as "loss of a love object" or retroflected hostility. Behavior therapy would use a materialistic model (peripluralist type) and look for a deficit in reinforcements of positive behaviors. By environmental modification, the individual would be given positive reinforcements, particularly in constructive behaviors, and nonreinforcements for self-defeating behaviors.

The usual cognitive model is interactionist (Mahoney, 1982), but I personally favor the model I shall present in this chapter. Thus, the cognitivist assumes that the individual's primary problem has to do with his construction of reality. The remedy lies in modifying the cognitive set. This psychological modification then produces biochemical changes which in turn can influence cognitions further.

There are a number of reasons why none of the aforementioned philosophical systems can totally "explain" a phenomenon such as depression. For instance, the philosophical system dictates what type of instruments one uses for making observations, what kinds of observations are actually made, and how these observations are interpreted. If the investigator is interested in the phenomenon as a psychological entity, then all of the data and conceptualizations would be shaped to conform to the psychological mold. If he perceives of it as a biochemical entity, then the observations and inferences will deal with tangibles (neurons, synapses, neurotransmitters, etc.). This philosophical position may be illustrated by aligning the cognitive approach to the preceding case with the neurochemical.

The philosophical system that I endorse rests on the following postulates:

1. Nonmaterial, nonspatial phenomena or processes are just as "real" as material, spatial phenomena. "Nonspatial" means that the particular process cannot be located in space. "Nonmaterial" means that the phenomenon or process does not consist of stuff we can touch, see, or taste. Furthermore, these phenomena are private, and depend on the introspective report of the individual who is experiencing them and thus cannot be directly validated by another individual.

2. A phenomenon such as depression may be viewed alternately from a biochemical perspective, a psychological perspective, a behavioral perspective, or other perspectives. The biochemical and behavioral perspectives are similar insofar as they deal with public, spatial stimuli. The cognitive and psychoanalytic perspectives deal primarily with private, nonmaterial, nonspatial data. No one perspective is more correct or more "real" than the others.

3. The various perspectives have varying degrees of explanatory power. By relating them to each other we can attempt to construct an integrated model that will have greater explanatory power than the individual perspectives.

It is important to recognize that the thoughts and beliefs of the patient do not constitute the cognitive process any more than do the neurochemical changes that are taking place simultaneously. Thoughts do not cause the neurochemical changes and the neurochemical changes do not cause the thoughts. Neurochemical changes and cognitions are the same process examined from different perspectives. However, correspondences between one perspective and the other tend to validate the formulations of each perspective and provide a more complete explanation of the phenomenon.

We can now apply this unitary system to understanding how the "cognitive–behavioral intervention" improved the patient's anhedonia, sadness, and loss of appetite. We can conceptualize this as follows: The psychological intervention by the therapist was processed by the patient's information-processing apparatus. This processing involved changes in the brain, reflected in a biochemical modification and a simultaneous modification in the cognitive set. If we took a "psychological biopsy" after the cognitive–neurochemical modification, we would obtain cognitions such as "He really believes he can help me," and "I didn't believe I could write this letter—but I did." If we took a neurochemical biopsy at that point in time, we would find an intricate pattern of neurons firing and chemical changes at the synapses.

If we conceptualize depression as an abnormal or dysfunctional phenomenon, the cognitive processes *and* neurochemical processes are abnormal. This abnormality may be corrected in a variety of ways. The cognitive approach, expressed in terms of the verbal and nonverbal behavior of the therapist, produces cognitive–neurochemical changes. Similarly, the pharmacological approach—specifically, the administration of an antidepressant drug—leads to cognitive-neurochemical changes.

As we will see later, biochemical interventions have the same type of cognitive impact as does cognitive therapy. How do we explain the biological changes in this case after a psychological intervention? We can take anhedonia as an example. The lawyer–patient had a rigid idea: "Nothing matters . . . Life has gone stale . . . How can I enjoy anything when I'm a failure?" The cognitive–behavioral intervention reversed the cognitive set to "I can experience pleasure," and the patient did experience pleasure. A successful pharmacological intervention would produce the same cognitive changes (Simons, 1982). Couched in biological terms, the improvement in cognitive processing is expressed in a reversal of a biochemical chain reaction, leading further to a reversal of those biochemical processes involved in the experience of dysphoria.

THE UNIVERSAL DEFICIT

We can approach this case from the vantage point of the treatments listed in the title of this chapter. Each of these systems qualifies as a system of therapy, by which we mean a coherent theoretical framework, a body of clinical data to support it, and a therapeutic approach intrinsically related to the theory. As we shall see, each theory revolves around the concept of loss–deficit, and each approach includes a replacement therapy to fill in the gaps.

The psychoanalytic formulation of the case would rest largely on the loss of the "loved object" (death of the partner) and a consequent negative affect. This negative affect, presumably anger, is not overtly expressed but is turned against the self and is transformed into depressive affect. Similarly, behavior therapy would postulate that the loss of reinforcements from his senior partner and other members of the firm led to a reduction in the spontaneous behaviors (Lewinsohn, 1975); Rehm's (1977) self-control model would indicate that the patient's termination of self-reinforcement for achievement led to negative affect. Seligman's (1975) learned helplessness model would explain the patient's depressive behavior as the basis of loss of control over reinforcement (the partner) and attribution of responsibility to himself. According to these models, the positive reinforcement of constructive behavior by the therapist increased the patient's positive behavior (Lewinsohn) and the self-reinforcement (Rehm) and concept of control over reinforcement (Seligman).

The cognitive model postulates a similar deficit in this patient. As a by-product of the serious loss, the individual begins to overinterpret his experiences as losses; the usual positive constructions of reality have been deleted, and, thus, negative constructions become dominant. Since the negative constructions are presumably tied to negative affect, the individual not only makes negative appraisals of himself, his present, past, and future experiences, but also experiences unpleasant affect and loss of constructive motivation and suicidal impulses. According to the cognitive model, the positive deficits were counteracted by providing for more positive constructions of experience.

The psychopharmacological approach would also rest on an analogous hypothesized deficit. It would propose, for example, that the patient suffered from some disturbance in the availability or utilization of certain chemical transmitters at synaptic junctions in the brain. The derived remedy (not employed in this case) would be the administration of a monoamine oxidase inhibitor or tricyclic compound to counteract this defect. Other hypothesized deficiencies might involve defects in regulation of the entire neuroendocrine system or insufficient output of brain cells bearing noradrenergic receptors to meet increased demands resulting from stress (Stone, in press).

THE KEYS TO THE BLACK BOX

As was indicated above, clinicians of the major schools of thought have focused on the concept of loss or deficit in depression. In general, an external loss is postulated (loss of reinforcements or of control over them, or loss of loved object). If the loss leads to depression, there are certain processes that need to be stipulated to bridge the gap between the external deprivation and the depressive behaviors. Each of the theories either directly describes or alludes to some type of structure that mediates between the external situation (loss) and the ultimate depressive reaction. This intervening structure has been described in elaborate detail (psychoanalysis), in simplified terms (cognitive model), or simply alluded to as the "black box" (behavioral model).

The concept of the black box was applied originally to the unspecified "location" in the conditioning model in which stimuli connect up with the conditioned response. According to behavioral theories, it is here that the positive inputs (reinforcements) make their connections and produce the positive outputs (constructive behaviors). If the positive inputs (reinforcements) are inadequate for a sufficient period of time, then the outputs (behaviors) become extinguished and, according to the theory, the individual shows the typical slowing down of depression. The treatment prescribed by Lewinsohn attempts to increase the number of reinforcements through exposing the patient to potentially pleasant activities and thus increases the positive outputs. In the case described above, the patient's constructive activities were positively reinforced by the therapist and this led to more activity. Rehm's approach is to activate the patient to engage in activities for which he will reinforce himself, and this will tend to increase positive behavior.

The psychoanalytic and cognitive models presuppose several levels of organization, the lowest of which corresponds to the black box. Thus, the psychoanalytic version of the black box is represented by the complex formulation of the Unconscious, as the repository of the Id, or as the site of Primary Process thinking. Through the process of interpretation, the patient is able to lift the lid off the box and use his mature Ego to counteract these disruptive forces. The attempt is to "make the unconscious conscious," or to fulfill the dictum "where the Id was, there the Ego shall be." From a different standpoint, the Primary Process thinking (lower level) is subjected to contact with reality in the form of the Secondary Process (higher level) and is brought into a more logical and less disruptive framework. One psychoanalytic explanation of the lawyer's rapid symptomatic response is that he found a long lost father figure in the therapist, with whom he could identify. Another interpretation is that the therapist's nurturance neutralized the patient's overwhelming sense of emptiness and satisfied his dependence, his needs.

The theoretical framework of cognitive therapy is somewhat similar to that of psychoanalysis (Beck *et al.*, 1979). The constructs of "mature thinking" (higher level) and "immature or primitive thinking" (lower level) correspond to Secondary Process and Primary Process. The mechanism of successful treatment may or may not involve introspection. The thrust in this case was (1) to negate the hopelessness through behavioral experiments and thus undermine the negative bias, and (2) to promote, through the doctor–patient relationship and the assignment of success and pleasure experiences, a buildup of positive behavioral and affective experiences. According to the underlying rationale, as the patient's negative constructions diminish, the negative feelings diminish; as the positive constructions increase, the positive feelings increase.

In summary, in addition to having a common thematic content relevant to depression, the three systems of psychotherapy have a similar structural basis. The black box of the behavioral model corresponds to the Primary Process of psychoanalysis and the primitive thinking of the cognitive model. The neurochemical correlates of this construct constitute an area for future research.

The Common Pathway: Cognitive Processing

Another commonality among the systems of psychotherapy is the mechanism by which the specific therapy produces therapeutic results. There is considerable evidence accumulating that each of the effective therapies has an impact on cognitive processes. When measures of these cognitive processes show a shift from negative to positive, they are accompanied by a general improvement in depression and anxiety. Since only a few studies have been reported to date, I will have to cite disparate reports to illustrate my point.

Psychoanalytic therapy has not been studied to an extent using the kinds of measures that have been applied in other studies. However, a study by Carrington (1979) which used "insight" therapy based on psychodynamic principles, demonstrated that the depressed patients who improved on insight therapy showed changes in the cognitive items on the Depression Inventory.

A study by Hammen, Jacobs, Mayol, and Cochran (1981) using social-skills training for the treatment of socially anxious individuals showed significant positive changes on the Dysfunctional Attitude Scale, an instrument developed by Weissman and Beck (1978) to define the dysfunctional attitudes in depression.

If you randomly select two groups of depressed patients and one receives cognitive therapy and the other receives antidepressant medication, what changes take place? Cognitive therapy presumably affects cognition; antidepressant medication allegedly affects physiological processes. Is there a common denominator?

The most appropriate study to illustrate the cognitive impact of successful treatment was Simons's analysis (1982) of an outcome study conducted by Murphy and his associates at Washington University. Simons analyzed the data on the depressed outpatients who received cognitive therapy alone and those who received antidepressant medication alone. In looking at the change scores in the instruments specifically designed to measure automatic thoughts, dysfunctional attitudes, and negative expectancies, she found that the clinically improved patients showed a corresponding improvement in these measures of cognitive phenomena. More significantly, perhaps, the patients who did not improve did not show a change on the cognitive measures. What is most salient for our present discussion is that pharmacotherapy had essentially the same impact on the cognitive content as did cognitive therapy.

These findings are in line with those reported by Eaves and Rush (1982) in a study of depressed outpatients and inpatients. It should also be noted that Eaves and Rush found that the endogenous depressions showed as much cognitive distortion as did nonendogenous depression, a result supporting the thesis that cognitive processes are an intrinsic component of depressions, even those assumed by some writers to be biological in origin.

ANHEDONIA: FUSION OF THE PERSPECTIVES

A promising area for examining the overlap of the systems of psychotherapy with psychopharmacology is anhedonia, specifically as related to depression. Investigators have linked the presence of high concentrations of norepinephrine and dopamine to hypothetical pleasure centers in the brain. More recently, evidence that stimulation of specific brain areas containing high concentrations of the endorphins acts as a powerful positive reinforcer of behavior has suggested the importance of these substances as mediators of "pleasure." By inference, it could be hypothesized that depletion of the catecholamines or endorphins could lead to anhedonia. In fact, drugs designed to counteract the reduced availability or utilization of catecholamines in depression have been shown to be effective in this disorder.

In view of the progress in expanding the biochemical perspective, it would seem valuable to broaden the "psychological perspective." Moreover, comparison of these perspectives can serve as a guide to further research. Ultimately, the fusion of the perspectives on anhedonia should provide a more comprehensive model than is currently available.

A good deal of publicity has lately been attached to the biochemistry of anhedonia (Belson, 1983). Some writers appear to regard this condition as a primary biological phenomenon presumably due to some aberration of neuroendocrine. The reductionist models of this disorder seem to rest on the assumption that biochemical processes of the brain proceed in "splendid isolation" of environmental demands. It is more in keeping with contemporary concepts to analyze the phenomenon in terms of its functions and its relationships to normal processes. Furthermore, it would seem that anhedonia may well have—or has had—evolutionary value in order to have survived a multitude of selective pressures. Thus, a broad view of anhedonia should include not only concepts regarding internal regulatory mechanisms but also notions regarding adaptation to changing environmental stressors.

It should be noted that the reductionist explanation may also dictate notions regarding the appropriate therapy for this condition. Thus, part of the skepticism about the impact of cognitive therapy on primary affective disorders has been based on the notion that these are biochemical in origin. However, it has been found that even the endogenous depressives, characterized largely by loss of responsiveness to pleasurable stimuli, respond well to this type of psychological intervention (Rush, Beck, Kovacs, & Hollon, 1977). Furthermore, the item on the Beck Depression Inventory relevant to anhedonia shows an early responsiveness to cognitive therapy.

Anhedonia may be analyzed in terms of an elevation of the threshold for positive experiences. This relative imperviousness accounts, in part, for the selective focus on the negative. This type of response may be precipitated by an absolute subtraction from the domain (e.g., being abandoned by a "loved one") or by a hypothetical, relative loss (specifically, a disappointment, such as not performing as well as expected or not getting as much affection or approval as expected). Following a significant meaningful loss, the depression-prone individual is likely to make an overgeneralized *absolute* judgment (e.g., "I can never get what I want") even though the loss is only partial or relative, representing the discrepancy between anticipated and actual gain.

Such a conceptualization indicates the formation of a negative cognitive set, sometimes a prelude to depression. Positive experiences are blacked out, interpreted negatively, forgotten, or devalued on recall. Negative experiences are selectively abstracted or exaggerated. If the cognitive blockade becomes fixed, it sets in motion a sequence of other cognitive, motivational, and affective symptoms of depression.

It should be noted that in many situations we function with bias toward the positive: We tend to be optimistic and to have a somewhat elevated hedonic tone (the "illusory glow"). The dominance of positive processing appears to be a function, in part, of the reduction in negative processing. As the positive apparatus becomes less active (shows increased thresholds), the negative organization becomes relatively more prominent.

The Cognitive Blockade

Let us analyze the psychological mechanisms by which anhedonia and dysphoria may be produced in depression. Anhedonia, which is present in 92% of cases of severe depression, may be described along a dimension ranging from "I feel bored most of the time" to "I am dissatisfied with everything" (Beck, 1967); and dysphoria, present in 88% of cases of severe depression, from "I feel sad" to "I am sad, I can't stand it" (Beck, 1967).

The experimental and clinical studies cited below have suggested that there is a "cognitive blockade" that interferes with the reception and/or integration of positive data in depression. The term "cognitive" is used because the interference may occur at various points along the cognitive continuum: perception, recognition, interpretation, integration, learning, immediate recall, long-term memory. This refractoriness to the integration of positive aspects of experience increases with the severity of depression. The blockade against utilization of positive experiences may account for the loss of pleasure response associated with depression. If the positive experiences do not "get through," are diverted from active storage, or are minimized on recall, they are prevented from having any impact on the hedonic system. Sadness is a consequence of the relative predominance of negativity as a result of the blockage of the positive inputs. Thus, the elimination of positive factors from the conception of past, present, and future leaves the patient with an exclusively negative view, which leads to sadness.

The evidence suggesting a cognitive blockade in depression may be pieced together for a variety of experimental paradigms. Alloy and Abramson (1979) have reported that normal subjects have an "illusion of control" in contrast to realistic self-appraisals by nonclinical depressives. If generalized to normal experiences, their experiments suggest that we are generally inclined to be optimistic and thus maintain a somewhat pleasurable hedonic tone. If our bias toward the positive (e.g., the illusion of control) is negated, however, our hedonic tone is likely to drop to or below the baseline—as in the case of Alloy and Abramson's "depressives." Thus, in the mildly depressed state we have dropped our positive illusions and process negative information as readily as positive. Moreover, increasing depression is associated with increased refractoriness to positive inputs and a relative negative bias.

Analogue studies using induced-mood procedures to produce sadness or "minidepressions" indicate that normals or "elated" subjects have a positive bias that is eliminated in the sad subjects (Bower, 1981; Clark & Teasdale, 1982; Goodwin & Williams, 1982; Rholes, Riskind, & Lane, unpublished manuscript).

Stiles (1978) reported that depressed subjects recall experiences less positively with the passage of time. Although initial appraisals of enjoyment, performance, and success following an experience task were realistic, these assessments declined at subsequent testing up to 2 weeks following the task.

A different type of experiment (by Muller, 1982) supports the notion that normals have a positive bias that is vitiated in depressives. Using tachistoscopically presented scenes, he found that normals had a greater sensitivity to positive than to negative words. This positive bias (or, more precisely, "antinegative" bias) was eliminated in the depressed student volunteers who showed the same latency for positive exposures as for negative exposures.

An interesting study by Gilson (1983) presented evidence suggestive of the cognitive blockade. Using a binocularscope, he showed unpleasant and neutral or pleasant slides to "depressed" students and normals. The depressed subjects showed a significant main effect for the depressive slides (i.e., the "perception" of only depressed slides and "nonperception" of positive or neutral slides when presented simultaneously). The normals, in contrast, showed a main effect for the slides with the positive or neutral scenes. A subsequent, unpublished study by Gilson showed the same results with hospitalized depressed patients.

A variety of "state-dependent" studies indicate that *clinically* depressed patients have impaired recall of favorable feedback (e.g., DeMonbreun & Craighead, 1977), pleasant events (Clark & Teasdale, 1982; Lloyd & Lishman, 1975), self-referent positive adjectives (Bradley & Mathews, in press), and pleasant schemes in stories (Breslow, Kocsis, & Belkin, 1981).

Further support for the notion that depressives selectively block out positive aspects of experiences is found in a study by Butler and Mathews (in press). They reported that depressive and anxious patients attached much higher probabilities to mishaps occurring to them than did normals. Of interest to the present review, they found a trend for depressives to attach lower probabilities for positive events than did either anxious patients or normals. This finding is in line with Giles and Shaw's (1982) report that depressives underestimate probabilities of success on an experimental task.

The tendency of normals to block out negative self-references and of depressives to block out positive self-references is borne out in tests of social desirability response style. The normals tend to eschew items reflecting unfavorably on them, whereas depressives generally will not endorse favorable items. This tendency of depressives to give a fairly accurate statement of "socially undesirable" characteristics, such as symptoms, accounts for the validity of certain types of self-report instruments, such as the Depression Inventory.

Some of the aforementioned studies are reminiscent of an earlier trend in psychology subsumed under the rubric, "The New Look in Perception." The newer concepts of raising and lowering thresholds for recognition suggest earlier notions of "perceptual defense" and "perceptual vigilance." More recently, Erdelyi (1974) has reformulated these two phenomena as a special instance of selectivity in cognitive processing. His concepts are close to those presented here. Selectivity consists of multiple processes operating through varied mechanisms brought into play at multiple loci of the information processing sequence. Anticipating the studies reported here, he states: "Thus, selectivity is pervasive throughout the cognitive continuum, from input to output, and no single site is likely to provide exhaustive explanations of any substantial selective phenomenon" (p. 1). Thus, the slides cited above fit into the notion that a complex of sites and functions is involved in the selectivity observed in the cognitive processing of favorable and unfavorable information by the depressed individual. The influence of the negative cognitive set may be detected at multiple points along the pathway from perception to long-term memory. Thus, the depressives show a bias against positive at the level of recognition (Gilson, 1983; Muller, 1982), recent memory (Clark & Teasdale, 1982; DeMonbreun & Craighead, 1977), more remote memory (Lloyd & Lishman, 1975; Stiles, 1978), and expectancies (Butler & Mathews, in press; Giles & Shaw, 1982).

Mechanisms of Cognitive Blockade in Anhedonia

The addition of a "positive factor to the personal domain" represents a gain and ordinarily produces gladness; the subtraction of a positive (e.g., the departure of a valued person or the nonfulfillment of a positive expectancy) leads to sadness. If the subtraction is significant, the individual adjusts to the loss by reducing his or her expectations of pleasure or gain. Consequently, the individual's overall goal-oriented striving, which is derived from his or her expectations, is reduced. Another adjustment also occurs. The threshold for subjective satisfaction is raised ("loss of reinforcer effectiveness"— Costello, 1972). The previously cited experimental evidence suggests that this hedonic adjustment is derived from an increased threshold for the integration of positive inputs. In addition, there seems to be relative loss of the ability to assign positive *meaning* to events ordinarily regarded as positive. These cognitive changes may be regarded as expressions of the change from a positive to a negative cognitive set.

A serious question raised by this formulation is: Why does a loss lead to an *increased* threshold for positives? The increased threshold may, conceivably, be understood as a response to homeostatic or cybernetic regulation. The organism is "wired" to achieve a balance between action and passivity. The function of activity is related to goals relevant to long-term survival and reproduction. If the organism were not deterred by disappointment, it might continue in unending attempts to gain satisfaction and thus would be eventually exhausted (as in manic states).

The shift to negative expectations and the raising of minimal level of satisfaction following disappointment dampen spontaneous motivations and activity, and thus serve as a check against the runaway quest for gratification. The individual experience dysphoria not only following a deprivation but also in anticipation of a future deprivation. Individuals consequently anticipate further dysphoria if they attempt to undertake a project and, thus, they retreat more into an anhedonic passivity.

In a broader sense, we may view the intricate process of increasing and decreasing thresholds for positive experiences as playing a role in overall adaptation (and reproduction). The system of "rewards" regulated by enhanced sensitivity to positive stimuli enhances behavior directed toward these goals. The reduction of rewards reduces such behavior. Thus, in depression the increased thresholds for perceiving satisfying activities plus the negative expectancies lead to reduction in appetite for activities relevant to long-term survival (eating) and reproduction (sex).

In cognitive therapy of depression we attempt to exceed the thresholds along the cognitive continuum by providing a series of selected positive experiences (the "mastery and pleasure" principle). In "running the cognitive blockade," we seek to increase positive expectancies, which in turn increase motivation, leading to more success experiences, and consequent positive feedback. By swamping the thresholds with a series of immediate, concrete, unmistakable success experiences, we "force" the threshold and inject a positive view of the immediate and near future. We also instruct the patient to write down experiences relevant to pleasure and mastery, and to repeat them during the therapy sessions. These successful experiences stimulate increased positive expectancies, and the threshold for perceiving "positives" consequently drops; the writing down and forced recall increase the integration of positive experiences; and the patient experiences a gradual return of gratification.

Anhedonia is an interesting phenomenon to discuss from the perspectives of the various psychotherapies and psychopharmacology. The psychoanalytic perspective would focus on the antithesis of the "pleasure principle" versus the "reality principle." It could be suggested, for instance, that as a result of a series of disconfirmations of expectations, the pleasure principle is suspended temporarily: To bring cognitive processes more in line with the reality, the expectations are switched to a more realistic but negatively tinged "data-processing apparatus."

In essence, excesses resulting from regulation by the pleasure principle are counteracted by the imposition of the reality principle, which directs attention to scarcity rather than abundance, to failure and deprivation rather than success and fulfillment. The displacement of the pleasure principle by the reality principle inactivates the pleasure response mechanism. The "adjustment to reality," however, may overshoot the mark and lead to a negative cognitive set.

The cognitive model, as indicated above, spells out the consequences of the switch from positive to negative cognitive set. The behavioral model can account for anhedonia in terms of the removal of external reinforcements (Lewinsohn, 1975). As the self-reinforcing has become switched off, the individual no longer receives satisfaction for activities that were previously reinforcing.

It is of interest that the sequence of positive cognitive set to realistic set to negative set may culminate in depression. The road back to normal functioning appears to be based on a reversal of this sequence. Thus, cognitive therapy and psychoanalysis use techniques calculated to inject a more realistic perspective into the patient's thinking. It is of interest that the realistic perspective which is a link in the chain leading to depression is a crucial link in the chain back to normality.

The overlapping psychological theories of anhedonia may point the way for further brain research. It may be possible through some of the recent advanced techniques to pinpoint particular areas in the brain or neurochemical systems involved with the experience of pleasure. It would be interesting to demonstrate what the effects manipulating the cognitive set would have on the activity of such systems.

COGNITIVE COMPONENTS OF SPECIFIC TREATMENTS

Behavior Therapy

We are now ready to analyze the various therapies within the framework of the model I have just presented.

The traditional formulation of behavior therapy bypasses the role of cognitive processes in the therapeutic process. More recent writings by Wolpe (1982) suggest that in some cases of phobia, specifically those in which the patient has been exposed to erroneous information about the phobic situation, cognitive restructuring is valuable. However, Wolpe tends to equate cognitive with "conscious" ideas. The more comprehensive view presented in this paper treats the cognitive organization as composed of several levels. Only the higher levels (mature level) are characterized by free decision making, objectivity, rationality, and so forth.

According to the scheme I have presented (Beck *et al.*, 1979), the lower levels of cognitive organization (primitive level) are characterized by features attributed to "conditioned emotional responses"; that is, the cognitive reaction occurs as if by reflex, is automatic and maladaptive, and occurs despite the patient's considering it irrational and consciously opposing it. Hence, Wolpe's initial notion regarding cognitive processes is correct as far as it goes—in that the *higher-level* cognition is bypassed in the reflex arc; but he overlooks the concept of low-level cognition, a significant component of the "conditioned emotional response" (Beck, 1976). The agoraphobic demonstrates graphically how a patient can recognize at the higher, "rational" cognitive level that a situation is safe, but the lower, primitive level generates a sequence of automatic thoughts relevant to losing control or dying. The patient's experience and interpretation of physiological feedback such as rapid heartbeat or faintness further reinforce the primitive cognitive content such as fear of dying, losing control, and being abandoned, and swamp attempts at the mature level to view the situation realistically.

The therapeutic mechanism of behavior therapy may be readily analyzed within a cognitive framework. Let us turn to the treatment of the agoraphobic.

Exposure therapy—*in vivo* flooding, for example—switches on the primitive level: The individual experiences a sense of danger and intensification of symptoms of anxiety. The symptoms themselves trigger further cognitions about danger (Last & Blanchard, 1982). At that point the individual believes with close to 75–100% certainty that he or she is having or is about to have a heart attack, a stroke, loss of control, loss of sanity, or the like.

Within a therapeutic structure—that is, with a therapist present—the individual is enabled to assimilate the experience. Given a sufficient period of time during the exposure therapy, the patient receives cumulative feedback that indicates that he or she is *not* dying, losing control, having a heart attack, or going crazy—that the fear of disaster is unwarranted. Even without coaching, the patient can recognize increasingly that his or her fright is a false alarm. Incidentally, it is crucial that the patient experience anxiety in order to ensure that the primitive cognitive levels have been activated (since these levels are directly connected to the affects).

The repeated, direct, on-the-spot recognition that the danger signals do not lead to catastrophe eventually provides sufficient disconfirming evidence to enable the patient to switch off the alarm reaction. Subsequent practice sessions further reinforce the new learning experience. They enhance the responsivity of the primitive level to more realistic inputs from "above" (that is, from the mature cognitive level), which then turn off the alarm reaction. In the course of time, agoraphobics are able to switch off the alarm reaction at an early stage because they have learned that the physiological reactions are not signs of danger and that they can ignore their fearful cognitions. There is obviously much more to the cognitive component of behavior therapy than the foregoing, but this brief analysis demonstrates how its action can be brought within a cognitive framework.

Behavior therapy has shown that it is possible to "cure" a neurosis without the person's having insight into the origin of the disorder. Although behavior therapy explicitly short-cuts the high-level cognition insofar as it focuses exclusively on direct exposure to threatening situations, it actually provides the patient with a powerful framework to correct, cognitively, his unrealistic fears. The patients are aware of the unreasonableness of the primitive belief system as indicated by statements such as "I know that nothing will happen to me (in the crowded store), but I am still afraid of suffocating"; thus exposure therapy is able to produce cognitive restructuring.

It is important to emphasize the overlap between cognitive therapy and behavior therapy despite differences in terminology. The concept of primitive level (in the cognitive model) has much in common with the notion of conditioned reflex. The conditioning model postulates that the inappropriate response is due to the previous pairing of an innocuous stimulus with a realistically dangerous one. The cognitive model posits that the innocuous stimulus is construed as dangerous because of an idiosyncratic (low-level) cognitive set. Both the conditioning and cognitive models require low-level cognitive mediation because of the rapid, stereotyped, inappropriate response.

In both models, the response to the "innocuous" stimulus involves immediate motivational and affective components. In the cognitive model the automatic cognitive structuring determines the affect (anxiety) and the behavioral response (avoidance). In behavior therapy the affect (anxiety) and behavioral response (avoidance) are chained to the specific stimulus situation.

Psychoanalysis

The theory of cognitive therapy differs from psychoanalysis in several ways, but shares many similar concepts. Psychoanalysis, on the one hand, postulates that the content of the unconscious is diametrically opposite to that of the content of consciousness—in fact, that a variety of defenses such as reaction formation, displacement, rationalization, and sublimation are used to disguise any unconscious material that might leak through the wall of repression. The cognitive model, on the other hand, posits a continuity between the content of the more primitive levels and that of the more conscious levels. Thus, depressed patients may have dreams of being destitute, defective, or deserted; their conscious preoccupations deal with problems that are similar but of lesser magnitude, such as losing money, being inadequate, or losing affection. Even though their conscious appraisals of their domain may be totally at variance with reality, depressed patients may believe in them very strongly. They may have great difficulty in examining their distorted ideas objectively, which seem to them rational and reasonable. The therapy, thus, consists of using behavioral techniques, such as graded task assignments, to disconfirm the strongly held belief.

The division of the mental apparatus by psychoanalysis into *conscious = rational* and *unconscious = irrational* does not seem to fit depression. There is irrationality, of a particular type, at both levels. In anxiety, however, the psychoanalytic division into two antagonistic belief systems seems to hold. The "deeper" cognitive level is the source of the exaggerated or irrational cognitions, and the *highest* conscious level has the capacity to adapt a more realistic view. At the highest level, the anxious or phobic patient is able, without coaching, to examine the irrational constructions and align them with more rational constructions.

The theory of therapy in the two systems differs in emphasis. Psychoanalysis assumes that by continually working through the unconscious content by interpretation, a beneficial reorganization can occur. Working with only the rational component may serve only to bury the unconscious content more deeply.

In cognitive therapy, in contrast, the distorted content is exposed (e.g., by eliciting automatic thoughts), and the bulk of the work from there on is spent on fortifying this reality testing through behavioral experiments, checking observations, looking for evidence, and so on. Thus, the dominant emphasis is on the technical procedures sometimes referred to in the literature as "ego support" or "ego analysis."

In sum, psychoanalysis attempts to expose the unconscious processes (primary process) and assumes that the ego, relieved of the burden of trying to seal off the taboo material, will then spontaneously provide realistic corrections. Cognitive therapy explicitly attempts to induce the patient to draw continually on his or her rationality (logic, empiricism, etc.) to correct the irrationality.

Psychopharmacology

The system of psychopharmacology has been primarily empirically derived, and is not theoretical in any systematic sense. Many of the somatic treatments such as insulin coma therapy and electroconvulsive therapy were discovered serendipitously. When a drug was found to work, then it was refined to be more effective, with fewer side effects, and an attempt was made to map out mechanisms of action. Some of the current neurochemical theories of depression have been based in part on the known neurochemical effects of antidepressant drugs.

There has been a concerted attempt to apply findings regarding the nervous system as a basis for developing new and effective drugs. Progress has been limited by several factors: (1) The integrated knowledge of the central nervous system (CNS) is still limited although rapidly growing; (2) a broad schema which emphasizes a systems approach to CNS function is lacking; (3) there has been little attempt to utilize psychological findings or schemata as a guide for searching for or integrating biochemical findings. As a result of the tendency toward reductionist thinking prevalent in much scientific work, neurochemical abnormalities have often been labeled as *the* cause or *the* explanation for depression. An example of an attempt to link psychological and pharmacological data has been the development of the Dexamethasone Suppression Test and attempts to correlate neuroendocrine deviations with specific subtypes of depression.

Thus far, neuropsychopharmacotherapy has adopted a deficiency model for understanding depression. Certain deficiencies have been found (e.g., in pre- or postsynaptic neurotransmitter function) or in neuroendocrine response (as in the Dexamethasone Suppression Test). As the abnormal findings have not been woven into an adequate explanatory model, a comprehensive psychobiological model would integrate the psychological and neurochemical perspectives. It would enable the researcher to look at the psychological levels and correlate them with neurochemical findings and drug actions on the basis of these levels. It would also correlate neurochemical findings with the major spheres: cognitive, affective, motivational.

This maxi-model might, for example, prompt investigators looking for the equivalent of an ego deficit to search for an abnormality in the neocortex. Or, they might consider a dysfunction of the palecortex contributing to the cognitive distortions. We found that the initial change with drug therapy was in cognitions, not the affect of depression (Rush, Beck, Kovacs, Weissenburger, & Hollon, 1982). What are the cognitions being affected by drugs? Are they low-level (primary process) or high-level (secondary process) or both? A better model for understanding psychopharmacology may be found.

There is increasing evidence of a rapprochement between biological and psychological approaches. The theme of the 1983 meeting of the Society of Biological Psychiatry was "Biology of Information Processing." Gevins (1983) proposed a new model of neurocognitive functioning.

A promising line of research attempting to bridge the gap between psychosocial and psychopharmacological approaches has been the work by Kraemer and McKinney (1979), who found that the combination of a psychosocial stressor (maternal deprivation) and a drug (AMPT) that depletes brain catecholamines had a synergistic effect in producing "depression" in monkeys. This is an example of how loss or deprivation at an abstract symbolic level may be brought into apposition with "loss" or deficiency at the concrete biochemical level. Studies such as this by investigators well versed in the psychological perspectives as well as the biochemical perspectives may advance the day when the understanding and treatment of these psychiatric disorders can be encompassed within a sophisticated comprehensive model.

SUMMARY

Psychological observations are just as real as biological observations. The biological and psychological systems are different perspectives of the same phenomenon and use, respectively, a public, spatial, concrete focus, and a private, nonspatial, nonmaterial focus. Despite differences in the level of abstraction, there should be correspondences between the two, and a unified theory should provide clues as to where to look for these correspondences.

Commonalities across the systems of psychotherapy and pharmacotherapy and their underlying theories may be delineated. When we examine specific disorders such as depression, we find that each theory focuses on a relative deficit of the positive components of experience. This common concept is represented by terms such as loss of reinforcement (behavior therapy), loss of object (psychoanalysis), and deprivation or defeat (cognitive therapy). It is speculated that the psychological-deficit concept may have some relationship to deficits in neuroendocrine function.

Although different terms are used, there are other similarities in theory and therapy. Structurally, the locus of the problem in a disorder such as depression can be ascribed to the "primary process" or "unconscious"; to the "black box" of behaviorism; or to the "primitive cognitive organization." The key to therapy consists in correcting the negative balance through insight; through reestablishing positive reinforcements; through changing the negative cognitive set; or through increasing the availability of catecholamines and/or serotonin.

A common denominator of the various systems is the ascription of cognitive mechanisms to the process of therapeutic change. Research had indicated that improvement in the clinical condition is associated with changes in cognitive structuring of experience irrespective of the type of therapy. It is suggested that changes in the cognitive processes play an essential therapeutic role with each type of treatment.

REFERENCES

Alloy, L. B., & Abramson, L. Y. Judgment of contingency in depressed and nondepressed students. *Journal of Experimental Psychology: General*, 1979, *108*, 441–445.

Beck, A. T. *Depression: Clinical, experimental and theoretical aspects*. New York: Hoeber, 1967. (Republished as *Depression: Causes and treatment*. Philadelphia: University of Pennsylvania Press, 1972.)

Beck, A. T. *Cognitive therapy and the emotional disorders*. New York: International Universities, 1976.

Beck, A. T., Rush, A. J., Shaw, B. F., & Emery, G. *Cognitive therapy of depression*. New York: Guilford, 1979.

Belson, A. A. New focus on chemistry of joylessness. *New York Times*, March 15, 1983, Sect. C, p. 1.

Bower, G. H. Mood and memory. *American Psychologist*, 1981, *36*, 129–148.

Bradley, B., & Mathews, A. Negative self-schemata in clinical depression. *British Journal of Clinical Psychology*, in press.

Breslow, R., Kocsis, J., & Belkin, B. Memory deficits in depression: Evidence utilizing the Wechsler Memory Scale. *Perceptual and Motor Skills*, 1981, *51*, 541–542.

Butler, G., & Mathews, A. Cognitive processes in anxiety. *Advances in Behavior Research and Therapy*, in press.

Carrington, C. *A comparison of cognitive and analytically oriented brief treatment approaches to depression in black women*. Unpublished dissertation, University of Maryland, 1979.

Clark, D. M., & Teasdale, J. D. Diurnal variation in clinical depression and accessibility of memories of positive and negative experience. *Journal of Abnormal Psychology*, 1982, *91*, 87–95.

Costello, C. G. Depression: Loss of reinforcers or loss of reinforcer effectiveness? *Behavior Therapy*, 1972, *3*, 240–247.

DeMonbreun, B. G., & Craighead, W. E. Distortion of perception and recall of positive and neutral feedback in depression. *Cognitive Therapy and Research*, 1977, *1*, 311–329.

Eaves, G., & Rush, A. J. Cognitive patterns in symptomatic and remitted unipolar major depression. Submitted for publication, 1982.

Erdelyi, M. H. A new look at the new look: Perceptual defense and vigilance. *Psychological Review*, 1974, *81*, 1–25.

Gevins, A. *Shadows of thoughts: Towards a dynamic network model of neurocognitive functioning.* Paper presented at the meeting of the Society of Biological Psychiatry, New York, April 1983.

Giles, D. E., & Shaw, B. F. A test of the cognitive triad in Beck's cognitive theory of depression. Submitted for publication, 1982.

Gilson, M. Depression as measured by perceptual dominance in binocular rivalry. Submitted for publication, 1983.

Goodwin, A. M., & Williams, J. M. G. Mood-induction research—Its implications for clinical depression. *Behaviour Research and Therapy*, 1982, *20*, 373–382.

Hammen, C. L., Jacobs, M., Mayol, A., & Cochran, S. D. Dysfunctional cognitions and the effectiveness of skills and cognitive–behavioral assertion training. *Journal of Consulting and Clinical Psychology*, 1981, *48*, 685–695.

Kraemer, G. W., & McKinney, W. T. Interactions of pharmacological agents which alter biogenic amine metabolism and depression. *Journal of Affective Disorders*, 1979, *1*, 33–54.

Last, C. G., & Blanchard, E. B. Classification of phobics versus fearful nonphobics: Procedural and theoretical issues. *Behavioral Assessment*, 1982, *4*, 195–210.

Lewinsohn, P. M. The behavioral study and treatment of depression. In M. Hersen, R. M. Eisler, & P. M. Miller (Eds.), *Progress in behavior modification* (Vol. 1). New York: Academic, 1975.

Lloyd, G. G., & Lishman, W. A. Effect of depression on the speed of recall of pleasant and unpleasant experiences. *Psychological Medicine*, 1975, *5*, 173–180.

Mahoney, M. Personal communication, 1982.

Muller, R. L. *The recognition times to depressive and neutral stimuli by the depressed and nondepressed.* Unpublished master's thesis, Fairleigh Dickinson University, 1982.

Rehm, L. P. A self-control model of depression. *Behavior Therapy*, 1977, *8*, 787–804.

Rholes, W. S., Riskind, J. H., & Lane, J. W. *Depression and memory biases: The effects of cognitive priming and mood.* Unpublished manuscript.

Rush, A. J., Beck, A. T., Kovacs, M., & Hollon, S. D. Comparative efficacy of cognitive therapy and pharmacotherapy in the treatment of depressed outpatients. *Cognitive Therapy and Research*, 1977, *1*, 17–37.

Rush, A. J., Beck, A. T., Kovacs, M., Weissenburger, J., & Hollon, S. D. Differential effects of cognitive therapy and pharmacotherapy on hopelessness and self-concept. *American Journal of Psychiatry*, 1982, *139*, 862–866.

Seligman, M. E. P. *Helplessness.* San Francisco: Freeman, 1975.

Simons, A. *The process of change during the course of cognitive therapy or pharmacotherapy of depression: Changes in mood and cognitions.* Unpublished dissertation, Washington University, 1982.

Stiles, J. C. *Cognitive devaluation of past experiences in depression.* Unpublished dissertation, University of Texas, 1978.

Stone, E. A. Problems with current catecholamine hypotheses of antidepressant agents: Speculations toward a new hypothesis. *Behavioral and Brain Sciences*, in press.

Weissman, A., & Beck, A. T. *Development and validation of the Dysfunctional Attitude Scale.* Paper presented at the meeting of the Association for Advancement of Behavior Therapy, Chicago, 1978.

Wolpe, J. *The practice of behavior therapy* (3rd ed.). New York: Pergamon, 1982.

COMMENTARY

Dr. Joseph Zubin*: There are a couple of basic questions that need to be answered. First of all, why is it that not everybody benefits from cognitive therapy? Why is it that not everybody benefits from somatic or drug therapy? Why do some people experience spontaneous improvement? Why do some people benefit from placebos?

It seems to me that these questions can perhaps be integrated. There are two things: There has to be a cognitive component, and there has to be a physiologic or somatic component. It may very well be that it is the feedback from the somatic to the cognitive, or *vice versa*, that keeps the depression going. And therapy consists of breaking those two things apart. Perhaps by means of drug therapy you deaden the physiological churning within you, and you permit the cognitive to continue going by itself until it finally disappears because it has no feedback from the somatic, physiologic substrate. And *vice versa* to go the other way. And, of course, if you combine *both* the somatic treatment with the cognitive treatment, then you are on the best road of all. This would explain why cognitive therapy by itself can't always work, why drug therapy by itself can't always work, and why you need the combination.

Dr. Beck: I think that is very well taken. I think we can learn a lot, not only by recognizing the failures, but by seeing just what types of cases you get failures in. I think the outcome studies can help us with our theory, and that the theory can help us with the outcome studies. When a patient doesn't do well you don't necessarily need to discard this as a lost cause; you can try to find out why.

I think these process variables that we have been looking at, as in the study I just reported which is based on an outcome study, can tell us as much about theory as they do about the outcome. So I think there can really now be an interplay between theory and outcome along the lines you mentioned.

*University of Pittsburgh School of Medicine.

"NUTS AND BOLTS":
THE TECHNOLOGY MODEL
OF PSYCHOTHERAPY

7

Implications of the Technological Model of Psychotherapy

JOHN P. DOCHERTY
National Institute of Mental Health

The title of this chapter is "Implications of the Technological Model of Psychotherapy." What stands behind the choice of such a title? It is useful to consider the current social-political-economic climate which sets the context for this title and to note some general trends. To begin, 10 years ago it is likely this report would have had quite a different title. At that time interest abounded in altered states of consciousness, and the Psychosocial Treatment Research Section of the National Institute of Mental Health (NIMH) commissioned a series of papers on "alternative therapies—California style." What has happened? This is not an exhaustive analysis to be sure, but the following factors seem to have exerted a strong influence: (1) the clear effectiveness of the clinical trials model in psychopharmacology and the rapid development of that field in the context of enormous progress in the neurosciences, (2) the evocative and lucrative development of high technology in computer and other electronics industries, and (3) the "shrinking economy" with its growing emphasis on cost-containment, cost-effectiveness, and the concomitant application of the technology assessment procedures to the health and mental health field.

Let us consider then the term "technology." It derives from the Greek "$\tau\epsilon\chi\nu\eta$," meaning art, skill, device, craft, or cunning, and refers to "how" something is accomplished—that is, the principles, rules, or methods of procedure. This certainly sounds innocuous. There seems little in this definition to which the psychotherapeutic community or a sizable segment thereof would object—especially the "cunning" part. Why then has the conceptualization of psychotherapy as a technology been a cause for conflict?

In consideration of psychotherapy as technology there are several extremely important issues to consider. These may be usefully conceptualized as value issues. Furthermore, it is precisely because these value issues are involved that discussion of the proper role of technology in the conceptualization and conduct of psychotherapy has taken on a political form and

139

polemical tone. In hope of clarifying the politics and calming the polemics, I will consider three distinct value sets of relevance to psychotherapy which are strongly affected by and in turn influence the conceptualization of psychotherapy as a technology.

The first of these value sets is "materialism," the second "science," and the third "personalism." I will consider the first two relatively briefly. The third I will consider at greater length since it is the most problematic and also the most critical in determining the impact of a "technological model" on the future and practice of psychotherapy.

Let us begin with "materialism." The technological model of psychotherapy is highly consonant with this value set—the dominant value set in our society. This perspective values the acquisition and refinement of material resources and increased accessibility to and use of such resources. It values power and control of the physical world. Its direct aim is production. The functions of technology, as we understand that term, clearly serve this value system. What are the functions of technology? Generically, they entail the magnification of man's power in nature. Specifically they include (1) increased precision, (2) amplification, (3) acceleration–deceleration, (4) increased consistency, (5) extension, and (6) quantification. The technological model of psychotherapy seeks just such goals—that is, the establishment of psychosocial methods and procedures that can be consistently administered with precision of application to produce increasingly effective results with less effort in less time. In terms of this value set the technological model is sailing before the wind.

An even fuller sail is produced by the demand characteristics of the value set of "science." Science is the accumulation and systematic organization of empirically verified knowledge. It is a method for obtaining and organizing knowledge, a very effective method. It is a method which is based on and demands measurability and replicability—two functions strongly enhanced by technology. The great success of science in advancing knowledge of the physical world has reasonably led to its application to psychological and social phenomena. The application of the scientific method to such phenomena has, to this point, although clearly useful, been far less impressive than its application to the natural sciences. From a technological perspective, this is regarded as a methodological or technological problem. The assumption is made that as technical advance occurs to yield *measurability* and *replicability*, these phenomena too will become more suitable for study by—and profit from—the scientific method.

Let us consider, as a relevant case in point, the application of the clinical-trials model to psychotherapy. This model tests the efficacy or relative efficacy of two or more standardized, discriminably different treatments for the same condition. As I mentioned, this model has found wide acceptance and met with much success in the assessment and evaluation of pharmacological treatments. Consider further, then, the following criticisms of the use of the clinical trials model for a nonpharmacological treatment: (1) There is systematic bias in the expertise with which treatments are practiced and administered; (2) there is bias favoring technically simpler procedures; (3) the procedures are not uniform—"The title of procedures is deemed sufficient . . . to permit all [clinicians] to perform uniformly. It is common knowledge however that the same [therapy] may be performed in a variety of ways" (DeCosse, Donegan, Sedransk, & Claudon, 1980). Would it surprise you to know that these are all criticisms of the application of the clinical-trials model to the assessment of the efficacy of surgical procedures (DeCosse *et al.*, 1980; Fisher & Kennedy, 1982; Lacaine & Huguier, 1981; Van der Linden, 1980)? The issues identified should be familiar ones to psychotherapy researchers. They strike at the heart of the application of this experimental method of science to the psychotherapy procedure, namely (1) acceptable level of competence in skill in performing the procedure in all therapists, (2) equivalent skill in all therapists, (3) minimal change (i.e., consistency) in the skills of all therapists throughout the trial, and (4) a fully described procedure similarly applied by all therapists. Failure to meet these criteria undermines the very premise on which the scientific model is applied to psychotherapy research. Thus, these have been very vexing problems for psychotherapy and surgery, both of which hypothesize dependence on the skillful application of often complex procedures for clinical success.

Fortunately, faith in and the application of the technological model to the pursuit of a science of psychotherapy have led to some very important technical advances which go far to solving these problems. I will not "steal the thunder" of the subsequent chapters which will detail and illustrate these advances as they have occurred in the Collaborative Study of the Treatment of Depression other than to note that they represent the development of a multicomponent technology for standardizing the therapy and therapist.

However, lest I leave you with the pleasant but still fanciful image of psychotherapy and psychotherapy research sailing off peacefully into the sunset, I will raise the problematic issue of the implications of the technical model for the third value set critical to the conduct of psychotherapy and psychotherapy research: "personalism." It is not surprising that this issue should be problematical for psychotherapy. Kenneth Keniston (1971) has called the technologism–personalism dispute "the key ideological polarity of our time." It is also not entirely new. I could aptly subtitle this section of my presentation "*What does it profit a man if he gain the whole world but suffer the loss of his soul?*" "Personalism" refers to those values which recognize as important the depth, stability, and benignity of the relationships of human beings with one another. It involves such notions as caring, trust, attachment, loyalty, warmth, intimacy, nurturance, and understanding. It is a value system which emphasizes spontaneous interaction, subjective experience, knowledge based on intuition and acceptance. Psychotherapy as a technology has a major impact on these values and has been seen as posing a major threat to them.

For many years an ostensibly intellectual battle has raged in the field of psychotherapy. It has taken the form of the following question: What is of primary importance in producing positive changes in psychotherapy—specific techniques or relationship factors? There have been two major forms in which this issue has been represented: (1) The behaviorist–dynamicist contrast and (2) The "search for specificity."

The behaviorist–dynamicist opposition has most vividly and most radically represented this debate. As DeVoge and Beck (1978) have stated, "The behaviorist posture has been one of the centrality of technical procedure. Techniques have been seen as responsible for specific change, while relationship factors have been assigned a peripherally supportive but non-essential role."

At its height this perspective has led to the characterization of the therapist by Leonard Krasner (1962) as a "social reinforcement machine." Thus, the radical technological perspective devalues the patient–therapist relationship. It regards all curative influence as deriving from objective, impersonal procedures, at best enhanced by a relationship which renders the patient available for and cooperative with the potent procedure.

The "search for specificity" is, of course, not a behaviorist–dynamicist distinction. The field has avidly sought—usually as vindication of the superior grasp on "truth" by one school or another—to find a specific form of therapy which seemed to offer therapeutic advantage; the field had also been gravely disappointed when such results were not forthcoming, as indeed they have not been (Luborsky, Singer, & Luborsky, 1975; Smith, Glass, & Miller, 1980; Strupp & Hadley, 1979). Jerome Frank's (1973, 1974, 1979) decades of study has repeatedly demonstrated that variables indicative of the relationship between therapist and patient have greater association with the efficacy of the therapy than the specific therapy technique employed. This has earned him published comments from such a prominent psychodynamicist as Chessick (1981) as the following: "In spite of Frank's insinuations it is possible to distinguish between therapies that are successful due to the quasi-religious fervor of the founder and those which are scientific."

Note the values of the "search for specificity" disclosed in this statement. These are that the relationship is soft, fuzzy, and ubiquitous. It is not sufficiently special to be "elevated" to a professional activity. In the words of Fred Robbins, "Isn't psychotherapy the sort of thing that could be done by anyone's kindly grandmother?" or in the words of Morris Parloff, "Is psychotherapy just 'bubbamycin'?" This perspective is seen by a large segment of the psychotherapy community as frightening. It is perceived as antithetical to the most essential characteristic of psychotherapy: the therapeutic relationship. It is seen as a tendency to displace the interpersonal with the technological.

Plum (1981) has stated, "I argue that skill approaches to communication training mistakenly place skillfulness rather than meaning at the heart of personal communication." This proposition reflects a complex fear of the effect of a predominantly technological model on psychotherapy. This fear has two components: the fear of loss of the therapeutic relationship and its presumed power for profound psychological alteration, and the fear of the loss of meaning or personal significance. Together these combine to signify a loss of psychotherapy itself as a distinct phenomenon and activity. In this perspective psychotherapy may be thought to be dependent on a technology, *but* it is *not* a technology, and it is not a collection of technologies. It is an emergent phenomenon which produces its effects not because of its technology but because the technology supports its presence.

More specifically, it is felt to be a special "state of affairs" which emerges because of a "therapeutic relationship." It is further hypothesized that this state of affairs permits, facilitates, and, perhaps, creates those processes (such as accurate and deep empathy) which can bring about therapeutic change through relearning or profound transformation.

Additionally, it is felt that psychotherapy acts in the realm of meaning, and that a major function of psychotherapy is not simply to develop a device better able to decrease the presence of certain uncomfortable or otherwise unwanted behaviors, but that it is an activity to permit a person to review and revision the meaning of salient aspects of his or her life experience.

To make the extreme of this perspective clear, I must emphasize that the fears I have noted do not relate to a procedure's efficacy. Evaluation and assessment are irrelevant. The demonstration that a psychosocial procedure is capable of removing psychological distress is not the issue. How that removal is accomplished is held to matter more. This is reminiscent of the passage in Herrigel's *Zen and the Art of Archery* (1971) in which Herrigel describes the difficulty he is experiencing with the development of self-detachment and its reflection in an effortless loosing of the bow. He strikes on a "technical solution" which involves slowly loosening the pressure of fingers on thumb. He writes:

> I was able to convince myself very quickly that I must be on the right track. Almost every shot went off smoothly and unexpectedly, to my way of thinking. Naturally I did not overlook the reverse side of this triumph: the precision work of the right hand demanded my full attention. But I comforted myself with the hope that this technical solution would gradually become so habitual that it would require no further notice from me, and that the day would come when,

thanks to it, I would be in a position to loose the shot, self-obliviously and unconsciously, at the moment of highest tension, and that in this case the technical ability would spiritualize itself. Waxing more and more confident in this conviction I silenced the protest that rose up in me, ignored the contrary counsels of my wife, and went away with the satisfying feeling of having taken a decisive step forward.

The very first shot I let off after the recommencement of the lessons was, to my mind, a brilliant success. The loose was smooth, unexpected. The Master looked at me for a while and then said hesitantly, like one who can scarcely believe his eyes: "Once again, please!" My second shot seemed to me even better than the first. The Master stepped up to me without a word, took the bow from my hand, and sat down on a cushion, his back towards me. I knew what that meant, and withdrew.

The next day Mr. Komachiya informed me that the Master declined to instruct me any further because I had tried to cheat him. (pp. 73–74)

The rationale for such a position is that the achievement of a particular aim by an unsuitable method will lead ultimately to such untoward consequences as the increased development of a "false self," and the erosion of care of human beings for one another.

This latter worry touches on an even more basic and rarely articulated fear, namely that the essential social function of psychotherapy will be undermined, and that the enterprise itself will be jeopardized. This worry derives from an understanding that psychotherapy has an important role of advocating a minority value set in our society, the value set we have been discussing. Psychotherapy serves a societal function that is related to but separate from its efficacy. It stands for the importance of respecting human relationships and subjective human experience. This function is present whether psychotherapy works for focal goals or not. It is in consideration of this function that concern arises in the field regarding the "technologizing" of psychotherapy, which in its goal of heightening the power of psychotherapy may unwittingly place itself at odds with a major function and central values of the psychotherapy enterprise.

Since this presentation is being written from a research perspective and in the interests of forwarding psychotherapy research, I will consider some of the research implications of the value conflict I have been discussing. I should like at this point also to make clear that my affirmation of the validity of these value conflicts in no way disaffirms the validity of the scientific study of technically refined psychotherapy by technically improved and technologically dependent methods. It is, to repeat, in the interest of improving, fostering, and safeguarding the integrity of the research enterprise that this report is written.

What, then, are the research implications deriving from a consideration of the "personalism" value set?

First, though the defense of the relationship value set might appear antithetical to research, strong advocacy of it may preserve research integrity. It can protect us against the dangers inherent in a compelling draw along a research road to apparent but deceptive clarity and simplification of a "hard and clear" technology-based research. Daniel Yankelovich (Smith, 1972) described such a road:

> The first step is to measure whatever can be easily measured. This is okay as far as it goes. The second step is to disregard that which can't be measured or give it an arbitrary quantitative value. This is artificial and misleading. The third step is to presume that what can't be measured easily isn't very important. This is blindness. The fourth step is to say that what can't be measured really doesn't exist. This is suicide. (p. 286)

Specifically, the personalism value set foregrounds issues such as the following for our research attention, and I will note only a few:

1. Are we overlooking important variables in our current efforts to standardize psychotherapy for research purposes? For example:

a. Based on currently available empirically based information (Strupp & Hadley, 1979; Frank, 1973, 1974, 1979), is it not necessary to standardize the therapeutic relationship as well as the therapeutic technique? To accomplish this we must ask what type of therapeutic relationship? How do we measure it and how do we standardize it? All technological questions, but all too easily overlooked.

b. If psychotherapy is an emergent phenomenon how do we know when it is present? In some cases the technique is coextensive with the treatment—for example, simple surgical procedures. In others the technology produces a phenomenon that provides the treatment—for example, as analogy, the production of the laser beam by specific technology and the use of that laser beam for treatment of the detached retina. The problem for psychotherapy research is this: We can assess when the laser beam is present and when it is not; we cannot, however, assess directly when psychotherapy is present and when it is not.

c. In drug studies we have measures of bioavailability, but we lack the equivalent of those for psychotherapy research. We have begun to develop a technology form standardizing the treatment delivered. We have not yet developed a technology to assess the amount of therapy absorbed or the transformation it undergoes in the absorption process.

d. There are certain other seemingly arcane but potentially very important variables which should be considered. Jerome Frank (1974) has repeatedly pointed out, for example, that there do seem to be gifted therapists. He further notes that there are phenomena that may characterize such individuals which seem telepathic in nature and which should be investigated.

2. Psychotherapy research requires a tolerance for variability. The degree of variation or play, the unpredictability of therapy encounter, is vast. The technologized model would move us toward consistency and invariate performances. We must guard against the premature imposition of such invariability or the premature supposition we have achieved with it. The variability of the psychotherapy process remains a major technical problem.

3. Is there an inherent limit to the degree to which psychotherapy can be technologized? This question addresses the issue that the current structure of psychotherapy as it is practiced in this country generally intends and purports to address two aims: (a) the development of meaning or resolution of conflict, and (b) the enhancement or remediation of disordered functions. Mahoney (1980) has referred to these two aspects of therapy as "transformation" and "reformation." In the past there have been other terms used to indicate this same division—such as insight-oriented versus supportive, or expressive versus suppressive—or, in terms of technical emphasis, dynamic versus behavioral.

To the extent psychotherapy addresses the first of these aims, the role of technology may be more limited. Thus, although we might and should expect great advance in the techniques of and techniques for the study of psychotherapy, we might also expect that a sane and humane practice of psychotherapy must consider meaning. How to specify and study the process for the creation and transformation of meaning and the effects on physical and mental health of this process is a question that psychotherapy research must address. In this endeavor we might usefully look to the methods being developed in psychotherapy research that address the more traditional questions. Among other efforts, the Collaborative Study of the Treatment of Depression sponsored by the National Institute of Mental Health represents an important step in providing us with the tools to conduct carefully—with respect for the work we practice—a useful and credible scientific study of the specific effects and efficacy of two technically and theoretically different psychotherapeutic treatments of a particular disorder. This study and the model it exemplifies suggest the direction for a further refinement of research methodology allowing us to address just those concerns, reflected in the personalism value conflict, which have heretofore halted research progress in psychotherapy. Are we perhaps finally in a position to challenge the assumption of that question we earlier asked, and ask instead, "Must a man suffer the loss of his soul to gain the whole world?"

REFERENCES

Chessick, R. D. What is intensive psychotherapy? *American Journal of Psychotherapy*, 1981, *35*(4), 489–501.

DeCosse, J. J., Donegan, W. L., Sedransk, N., & Claudon, D. B. Operative procedures: Is standardization feasible or necessary? *Cancer Treatment Reports*, 1980, *64*(2–3), 419–423.

DeVoge, J. T., & Beck, S. The therapist–client relationship in behavior therapy. In M. Hersen, R. M. Eisler, & P. M. Miller (Eds.), *Progress in behavior modification* (Vol. 6). New York: Academic, 1978.

Fisher, L. D., & Kennedy, J. W. Randomized surgical clinical trials for treatment of coronary artery disease. *Controlled Clinical Trials*, 1982, *3*, 235–258.

Frank, J. D. *Persuasion and healing* (2nd ed.). Baltimore: Johns Hopkins University Press, 1973.

Frank, J. D. Therapeutic components of psychotherapy. *Journal of Nervous and Mental Diseases*, 1974, *159*, 325–342.

Frank, J. D. The present status of outcome studies. *Journal of Consulting and Clinical Psychology*, 1979, *47*(2), 310–316.

Herrigel, E. *Zen and the art of archery*. New York: Vintage, 1971.

Keniston, K. *Youth and dissent: The rise of a new opposition*. New York: Harcourt Brace Jovanovich, 1971.

Krasner, L. The therapist as a social reinforcement machine. In H. H. Strupp & L. L. Luborsky (Eds.), *Research in psychotherapy* (Vol. II). Washington, D.C.: American Psychological Association, 1962.

Lacaine, F., & Huguier, M. Randomized clinical trials: The right choice. *Surgery*, 1981, *89*(5), 641.

Luborsky, L., Singer, B., & Luborsky, L. Comparative studies of psychotherapies: Is it true that "everyone has won and all must have prizes"? *Archives of General Psychiatry*, 1975, *32*, 995–1007.

Mahoney, M. J. Psychotherapy and the structure of personal revolutions. In M. J. Mahoney (Ed.), *Psychotherapy process: Current issues and future directions*. New York: Plenum, 1980.

Plum, A. Communication as skill: A critique and alternative proposal. *Journal of Humanistic Psychology*, 1981, *21*(4), 3–19.

Smith, A. *Supermoney*. New York: Random House, 1972.

Smith, M. L., Glass, G. V., & Miller, T. I. *The benefits of psychotherapy*. Baltimore: Johns Hopkins University Press, 1980.

Strupp, H. H., Hadley, S. W. Specific vs. nonspecific factors in psychotherapy. *Archives of General Psychiatry*, 1979, *36*, 1125–1136.

Van der Linden, W. Pitfalls in randomized surgical trials. *Surgery*, 1980, *87*(3), 258–262.

COMMENTARY

Dr. Solomon C. Goldberg[*]*:* I have a question about what standardization can really mean. At one extreme, standardization can mean following a script, where the therapist says one and only one thing verbatim, which

[*]Medical College of Virginia.

seems a little silly. If we depart from that to some extent, I think we are talking about conceptual standardization. Has the technology to determine standardization of treatment been used in any experimental designs to determine to what extent a particular treatment has actually been delivered?

Dr. Docherty: It is possible to standardize not only the conceptual nature of a therapy, but also some of its therapeutic techniques, and then subsequently to develop devices to ensure that in fact different techniques and a different intensity, or frequency, of the technique's uses characterize two different therapy experiences. Your question touches on the variability of psychotherapy as it is currently given, and I think that with the development of these standardization procedures, we are able to capture some of that variability and permit a standardized yet flexible procedure.

The assessment of whether or not a therapy has actually been delivered can be done from recordings of the therapy, but we still need to develop techniques to measure what the patient has actually taken in. I think we could begin that now by simply asking people, in a systematic way, what it is they have experienced in the therapy, what they have gotten out of it, and so on. This should help us begin to develop useful measures of how much of the experience has been absorbed, and in what form.

Dr. Robert M. A. Hirschfeld*: I wonder if you haven't created something of a straw man. I get the image of an automaton or a computer somehow delivering the specific steps on the one hand, and a warm, empathic, insightful, helpful, caring human being on the other. I wonder if another way to look at it might be that you need a certain kind of context for these procedures to work, just as for a surgical procedure, to use your example, you need a sterile field, anesthesia, and so on. You couldn't perform a certain surgical procedure in the absence of those things. In terms of psychotherapy, I wonder if you don't need a certain amount of empathy and caring, and so on. But beyond that, for it to work, you need certain specific things that can be articulated, and then you could test to make sure you had this context of a good therapist. Two such therapists could be compared giving two different kinds of therapy. Wouldn't this fit into the conceptual model you have been describing?

Dr. Docherty: Yes, I think it would. And as I said before, we must keep in mind that the aspect of the therapy procedure should not be ignored.

Dr. Eugene I. Burdock†: The last speaker's comparison of psychotherapy with surgery, which he picked up from you, John [Docherty], suggests that perhaps psychotherapy is in a sort of pre-Semmelweis stage, in which we haven't yet laid out the necessary controls. In that connection, it seemed to me that your reference to the technological aspect of psychotherapy con-

---

*National Institute of Mental Health.
†New York University School of Medicine.

founded two different things: One is psychotherapy itself as a form of technology, and the other is the evaluation of psychotherapy. It seems to me that it is in regard to the latter that the technology is most important.

To my mind, one of the things that is lacking in most of the evaluative procedures is a reference point. We go about measuring the effectiveness of psychotherapy very much the way people used to measure temperature in primitive times: Something was hot if it felt hot to their hands, and cold if it felt cold to their hands. In time, however, we developed better scales, and now we have an absolute reference point for temperature in the Kelvin scale. It seems to me that what we need in our measuring instruments is something like that. We have a number of well-developed rating scales, self-report rating scales, rating scales by the therapist and by the evaluator. Most of them have been studied for their reliability, but they have not been standardized on a normal population, so we don't have a zero point at which we can say that the person has gone down to the stage where he or she is a normal person. It seems to me that some effort ought to be devoted to this.

Dr. Jerome Frank*: I wonder if part of our problem is that we are trying to define techniques without thinking of their place in the relationship. That is, it may be that what makes a technique work is that it is the best vehicle for the particular relationship with a patient. For example, if a patient has a specific symptom, then naturally a focused technique will make more sense to both the patient and the therapist. For another patient with vague, existential anxiety, the focused technique won't. So it is not in the technique. I guess it is really repeating what has been said before: It is the technique in a certain context that seems to be the crucial thing.

*School of Medicine, Johns Hopkins University.

8

Specification of the Technique Variable in the NIMH Treatment of Depression Collaborative Research Program

IRENE ELKIN WASKOW
National Institute of Mental Health

Psychotherapy research is an acknowledgedly difficult and complex area of endeavor. One of the sources of this difficulty lies in the need to carefully define often elusive although clinically important variables. This is especially true when we attempt to study the processes or mechanisms of change in psychotherapy. It is even, however, difficult to define clearly the most basic variables in outcome research as well. If we are to discover what forms of treatment are most effective in what ways, for which patients under the care of which therapists (the now famous litany in this field), we must be concerned about the careful definition of the patient population under study, the treatment intervention(s), characteristics of the therapists, and the criteria for successful outcome. Perhaps one of the knottiest problems has been that of the clear definition of the treatment intervention. Yet if we do not know what has actually transpired in the treatment, it is extremely difficult to draw any conclusions from our findings and to reproduce the treatment conditions in any attempts at replication. It is not very helpful to simply know that some type of "psychotherapy" has been successful, if our ultimate goal is to determine the best possible form of treatment for each patient. Thus, in our research, we must be able to specify the form of treatment we are studying.

I will, in this chapter, discuss the problem of defining the treatment intervention (or "technique variable") in psychotherapy research, and will present the ways in which we have attempted to address this issue in the NIMH Treatment of Depression Collaborative Research Program. I would like to stress that in focusing on the definition of the treatment intervention I do not in any way intend to downplay the importance of the other critical variables in psychotherapy research—variables related to the patient, the therapist, the nature of the therapeutic relationship, and the nature of therapeutic change. It is extremely important to carefully delineate, define, and measure all of these. For the purpose of this presentation, however, I will place major emphasis on the definition of the treatment intervention, partly because of the relative lack of attention to this variable in past research and partly because of the important part it has played in the Collaborative Research Program.

One of the major reasons it is difficult to draw conclusions and to generalize from past psychotherapy research is the vagueness and the lack of clear specification of the treatment variable. In reading the literature in this area, it is often very difficult indeed to know what transpired during the treatment, what the therapist actually did in his or her sessions with the patient. This is quite different from the situation in psychopharmacological research, where one at least knows that part—although by no means all—of the treatment consists in the specific medication given the patient. The description of the treatment was dealt with very casually in most of the older studies in psychotherapy: Sometimes there was only one line devoted to the description of a particular treatment approach; at other times there was no mention of the specific approaches used. Even some of the best studies that were carried out were scanty in their descriptions. The famous Phipps study defined the different treatment conditions largely in terms of amount of contact with the therapist and in terms of the individual versus group context of the psychoanalytically oriented treatment, although one paper (Frank, Gliedman, Imber, Stone, & Nash, 1959) further defined the individual and group therapy as focusing "on the resolution of the patients' current interpersonal difficulties, through discussion of relationships with other persons and feelings aroused by them," while the minimal contact therapy focused "on patients' symptoms and their alleviation."

Often the treatment was defined not in terms of specific therapeutic interventions but rather in terms of the therapists and their professed approach—"psychoanalytic" or "client-centered." The assumption must have been that the therapists carried out these approaches as they had been described in various books and articles. "Psychoanalytic" writings are, of course, so diverse that this label does not tell us much about what actually occurred in the therapy sessions. And although client-centered therapists— especially the group in Chicago in the 1950s—may have had a more clearly defined approach, even there therapists certainly differed in terms of their specific therapeutic interventions. As pointed out by Grummon (1954), the client-centered researchers decided to "side-step the difficult question of determining just who is and who is not a client-centered counselor by leaving this up to the individual. The counselor participated if he felt he was following essentially the client-centered orientation. A more careful study of the client-centeredness of the counseling was left to the later study of the recorded and transcribed therapeutic protocol" (pp. 48–49). And this group was, of course, one of the first to examine the actual interventions used by the therapists.

Other studies used a mixture of therapists with different approaches; one of the early VA reports mentioned that "most therapists in both studies had Freudian or Rogerian orientations" (McNair, Lorr, & Callahan, 1963). In all fairness, I should include in this list an early process study of my own (Waskow, 1963), in which I define treatment thus: "The orientations of the counselors were varied, including three or four who might be considered 'client-centered,' but more who were generally eclectic in their procedures."

More recent studies are mixed; some define the treatment interventions relatively carefully, and others continue with fairly broad definitions. The Penn Psychotherapy Project, for example, which is concerned with prediction of outcome, reports (Luborsky, Mintz, Auerbach, Christoph, Bachrach, Todd, Johnson, Cohen, & O'Brien, 1980) that therapists are "either eclectic . . . or Freudian and neoFreudian in orientation." Similarly, the investigators in the Vanderbilt study describe the professional therapist group as consisting of three analytically oriented psychiatrists and two experientially oriented psychologists (Strupp & Hadley, 1979), and state that "no constraints were placed on the therapeutic process proper, that is [therapists] were encouraged to use whatever verbal techniques they deemed most helpful." We should point out that these research groups later, of course, studied some of the actual therapeutic interventions made in the treatment sessions, but there were no further definitions or guidelines for the treatment before the studies began.

In a few areas of psychosocial treatment research, there have been significant advances in recent years, especially in the development of manuals that describe and define therapists' behavior in a particular treatment approach and which can be used to train therapists in that approach for research studies. Such manuals have been used most frequently in the behavioral approaches to treatment, with the early "mimeographed program which guided the treatment" reported by Lang and Lazovik (1963) being perhaps the first of these. In the area of individual treatment of outpatient depression alone, for example, there are now at least four different manuals describing various behavioral and cognitive behavioral approaches (Beck, Rush, Shaw, & Emery, 1979; Bellack, Hersen, & Himmelhoch, 1981; Fuchs & Rehm, n.d.; Lewinsohn, Antonuccio, Steinmetz, & Teri, 1982). The two psychotherapies being studied in the Treatment of Depression Collaborative Research Program, particular forms of cognitive behavior therapy and interpersonal psychotherapy, are defined in terms of very specific strategies and procedures in lengthy treatment manuals (Beck et al., 1979; Klerman, Rounsaville, Chevron, Neu, & Weissman, 1979). It is significant that there have recently been further attempts to develop manuals for psychodynamically oriented treatment of outpatients. In addition to the interpersonal-therapy manual developed by Klerman, Weissman, and their colleagues, there are now also two major manuals in this area which have been developed by Luborsky (in press) and by Strupp and Binder (1982). The need to clearly define the treatment intervention is accentuated in studies in which one is examining two or more different forms of therapy. If each treatment is not carefully described and differentiated from the other, what can we conclude, especially if there are no significant differences in outcome? Here, again, earlier studies were particularly scant in their descriptions—for example, the statement in one of the earliest studies of this kind that "the two types of treatment are adlerian and client-centered (or rogerian, if a personal title is desired)," supplemented by the fact that the patients were treated, respectively, at the Alfred Adler Institute of Chicago and the Counseling Center at the University of Chicago (Shlien, 1964). In recent years, there have been much more sophisticated attempts to deal with the need to define and to differentiate therapies being compared with one another. Sloane and colleagues (Sloane, Staples, Cristol, Yorkston, & Whipple, 1975), for example, using very experienced therapists in each of their approaches, the psychoanalytically oriented and the behavioral, presented some clear definitions, distinctions, and ground rules for the particular therapeutic approaches, and these were accepted by the therapists. Since, as the authors note, "these definitions merely set limits of allowable techniques and do not define what therapists actually did in treatment," they also studied actual differences between the treatments in the therapy session material. It is interesting to note, however, that although some of the measures they used were aimed at differentiating features of the two treatment forms, they explored very few of the variables included in their "stipulative definitions" for the treatments. Again, if we are to have confidence in our conclusions in regard to differences or lack of differences between two approaches, we want to know whether the therapists in each approach were doing what they were intended to do as well as whether the two approaches actually differed from one another.

Our concerns, then, when we talk about the need to have an adequate definition of the treatment intervention in psychotherapy research, focus on whether there are clear specifications of the techniques and strategies that the therapist is to use and whether the different therapists in a treatment approach are actually using these in a similar fashion. Only if this is the case can we be justified in drawing any conclusions from the study about this particular treatment approach. If more than one approach is being studied, we are also concerned about whether the therapists' behaviors in the different approaches actually differ from one another along those dimensions stipulated as distinguishing between them. Finally, there is a further question that must be asked if we are to compare or to combine data from studies carried out in different settings: Do we know, for example, that psychoanalytically oriented therapy in Washington, D.C., is the same as that in Boston or, for that matter, the same as that in nearby Baltimore? Do we know that behavioral therapy as practiced in Philadelphia is the same as that in Los Angeles or even the same as that in New Brunswick? This last question, that of the similarity of treatments in different locations, was particularly relevant to the issues we faced in designing the NIMH Treatment of Depression Collaborative Research Program.

To provide the context for the remainder of this discussion, I will briefly describe this NIMH Collaborative Study (Waskow, Parloff, Hadley, & Autry, 1983). As indicated by its title, it is a collaborative endeavor, in which three different research sites (University of Oklahoma—John Watkins, Principal Investigator; University of Pittsburgh—Stanley Imber, Principal Investigator; and George Washington University—Stuart Sotsky, Principal Investigator) are carrying out identical research protocols, studying the effects of two forms of brief psychotherapy for outpatient, nonbipolar, nonpsychotic depression, and comparing these to pharmacotherapy reference and control conditions. The two brief psychotherapies being studied are cognitive behavior therapy as developed by Aaron T. Beck and his colleagues in Philadelphia, and interpersonal psychotherapy as developed by Gerald Klerman, Myrna Weissman, and their colleagues in the Boston–New Haven Depression Research Project. The comparison reference and control conditions consist of imipramine and pill–placebo treatments, each combined with a clinical management component.

The fact that we are trying to study the same therapeutic approaches as they are carried out at three different research sites has led to our intensive focus on the issue of defining the treatment interventions. It is important that the therapists in a particular approach be doing pretty much the same thing, not only within but also across sites. We must have some confidence in the fact that interpersonal therapy as practiced in Washington, D.C., will be the same as that practiced in Pittsburgh and Oklahoma City—and similarly for cognitive therapy and the pharmacotherapy conditions. Only if this is the case will it be possible to consider the study at each of the sites a replication of those at the other sites and will we be justified in pooling data across sites for the purpose of predictor analyses.

The ultimate test of whether the therapists are actually practicing the same approaches will rest on the analysis of tape recordings of the therapy sessions. An independent researcher (Steven Hollon of the University of Minnesota) is currently developing scales to tap the major dimensions of each of the treatment approaches. When these scales are applied to the taped treatment sessions, it will be possible to see whether the therapists are actually carrying out the therapy as prescribed in each of the approaches and whether the treatment conditions can be clearly differentiated from one another.

We could not afford, however, to wait for the analysis of the tapes to discover whether the treatments had actually been carried out in an adequate and a fairly uniform fashion across sites. What if we were to discover at the completion of the study that they had not? What conclusions could we draw? Some measures had to be taken at the beginning of the study to provide assurance, or at least to make it more likely, that therapists within a treatment condition would be carrying out the same approach both within and across research sites and that each of the treatments would be carried out in a competent fashion. How were we to accomplish this? That was one of the major problems that we faced in the early stages of designing the Collaborative Study.

The first method we considered was one frequently used in the past—to recruit therapists who profess to practice the particular types of therapy we proposed to study. How would we know, however, if the different therapists would indeed be similar in what they actually did in the therapy sessions, if their treatment interventions would be in accord with those defined by the major proponents and developers of each of the approaches, and if they could carry out their respective approaches consistently and competently throughout the study? In interpreting our results, how representative could we say these therapists were of a particular treatment approach? Additional problems arise, in regard to recruiting therapists who already practice an approach, when one is interested in very *specific* therapeutic approaches, such as those being studied in this research program. It would, in fact, be extremely difficult to find a sufficient number of therapists at each of several geographical locations who already profess to be carrying out cognitive behavior therapy as defined by Beck and colleagues or—even more unlikely —interpersonal therapy as defined by Klerman, Weissman, and colleagues. For all of these reasons, we abandoned the idea of defining our treatment conditions in terms of therapists who profess to practice a particular approach.

Our focus shifted to the definition of the treatment itself, rather than to the therapists who would be carrying it out. First of all, it seemed important for therapists to use the same general instructions and guidelines for carrying out their respective treatments as those had been defined in treatment manuals for each of the approaches. For the two psychotherapy conditions, manuals were already available—one in a fairly advanced form, the other at that time in a more preliminary form, but in the process of extensive expansion and revision. The existence of manuals was not, of course, an accident; it had indeed been one of the criteria for choosing the psychotherapies in the study. For the third approach, our reference pharmacotherapy condition, we enlisted a well-known and expert pharmacotherapy researcher (Jan Fawcett) to develop a manual defining this treatment condition, including the "clinical management" component.

Although these manuals stipulate guidelines for treatment, including goals and general strategies and procedures, as well as specific techniques, their use in a treatment study does not necessarily ensure that therapists will, in fact, carry out the therapy as stipulated, and that they will be able to use the framework provided by the manual in a flexible and competent fashion. And, once more, there is no guarantee that different therapists (within or across sites) will interpret the stipulations in a similar way. So we went one step further and decided to make sure not only that therapists would use these manuals to provide the framework for their treatment but also that they would receive standard training in their respective treatment approaches.[1] By asking therapists in each approach to undergo a standard training program we hoped that we could increase the probability of their carrying out the treatment in a similar fashion, that there would be some consistency, both within and across sites, in the particular approach as it was used by study therapists, and that we might thus have more faith in our definition of each of the treatment conditions.

The therapists to be trained were already experienced clinicians; the requirements for prospective therapists included at least 2 years of clinical experience past the PhD in clinical psychology or the psychiatric residency, with specific experience in treatment of depressed patients. (In fact, most therapists selected for the study had far more experience than this, ranging up to 25 years.) In addition, prospective therapists had to have training, experience, and interests relevant to their respective treatment approaches and had to submit, in addition to vitae and references, a videotape of a treatment session with a depressed patient. Principal investigators at each research site made the final selection of therapists, but they relied heavily on recommendations from the training sites (at Yale University for IPT—Myrna Weissman, Principal Investigator; University of Western Ontario for CB—Brian Shaw, Principal Investigator; and Rush Presbyterian St. Luke's Medical Center for pharmacotherapy—Jan Fawcett, Principal Investigator), based in part on viewing these videotapes.

A general format was established for training the therapists in all three of the approaches; training began with an initial didactic (and in some cases partly experiential) institute in which therapists from all sites received basic instruction in the treatment method, utilizing discussions of the manual, other reading materials, videotapes, role playing, and so on. Following the initial institutes, therapists were assigned several practice cases in their own

1. The decision to develop standard training programs for the Collaborative Study evolved from a series of discussions among NIMH staff and with colleagues in the field. I would like to acknowledge, especially, the contributions made by A. John Rush and by my NIMH colleagues, Morris Parloff, Suzanne Hadley, and Joseph Autry.

research sites, which were supervised by their respective trainers. One of the unusual aspects of this program involved the use of long-distance supervision based on the trainers' viewing of videotapes followed by telephone supervisory sessions. This system allowed for all therapists to be supervised by the same teams of trainers.

Finally, each therapist had to meet competence criteria in his or her respective approach in order to participate in the outcome study. The evaluation of competence included ratings of therapy tapes by experts in each of the treatment approaches who were independent of the training program. By requiring that study therapists pass competency criteria, we hoped to ensure that therapists would not only be doing something similar and fairly clearly defined but be doing it reasonably well. Only if this condition were met could we be confident that the study would provide a fair test of the effectiveness of each of the approaches.

The implementation of these plans for the training programs, the actual programs that evolved, and their results will be described in the next two chapters, by Bruce Rounsaville *et al.* for IPT and Brian Shaw for CB therapy.

The final test of whether the therapists do indeed carry out the therapy in a similar fashion within and across sites and whether they do this with competence and flexibility, will, of course, have to await the examination of the therapy sessions themselves by independent researchers and evaluators. We will know what happened in the sessions only by looking at what happened in the sessions. We feel, however, that we have greatly improved our chances of obtaining competent and consistent treatments across as well as within sites by having carefully selected therapists receive standard training and meet specific competence criteria.

If our efforts prove successful, the therapists who have met the competence criteria and are taking part in the outcome study will continue to carry out their respective treatment approaches, as defined, in a competent and consistent fashion.[2] If this occurs, we may have greater confidence than has been possible in the past in the definition of our "technique variable" and in any conclusions that may be drawn about the effectiveness of these specific treatment approaches as they have been defined in this study. Finally, for those of us who have a special interest not only in studying the effectiveness of psychotherapy but also in understanding the processes and mechanisms through which therapeutic change comes about, this research will provide us with a wealth of material for studying processes that may be specific to different well-defined therapy approaches as well as those which may be common to the different approaches.

---

2. Monitoring of selected sessions and limited consultation will continue for the duration of the outcome study, to ensure the maintenance of the required competence levels.

ACKNOWLEDGMENTS

The NIMH Treatment of Depression Collaborative Research Program is a multisite program initiated and sponsored by the Psychosocial Treatments Research Branch, Division of Extramural Research Programs, NIMH, and is funded by cooperative agreements to six participating sites. The principal NIMH collaborators are Irene Elkin Waskow, PhD, Coordinator; John P. Docherty, MD, Acting Branch Chief; and Morris B. Parloff, PhD, Former Branch Chief. Tracie Shea, PhD, George Washington University, functions as Associate Coordinator. The principal investigators and project coordinators at the three paticipating research sites are: George Washington University—Stuart M. Sotsky, MD, and David Glass, PhD; University of Pittsburgh—Stanley D. Imber, PhD, and Paul A. Pilkonis, PhD; and University of Oklahoma —John T. Watkins, PhD, and William Leber, PhD. The principal investigators and project coordinators at the three sites responsible for training therapists are: Yale University—Myrna Weissman, PhD, Eve Chevron, MS, and Bruce J. Rounsaville, MD; Clarke Institute of Psychiatry—Brian F. Shaw, PhD, and T. Michael Vallis, PhD; and Rush Presbyterian St. Luke's Medical Center—Jan A. Fawcett, MD, and Phillip Epstein, MD. Collaborators in the data management and data analysis aspects of the program are C. James Klett, PhD, Joseph F. Collins, ScD, and Roderic Gillis of the Perry Point, Maryland, VA Cooperative Studies Program.

REFERENCES

Beck, A. T., Rush, A. J., Shaw, B. F., & Emery, G. *Cognitive therapy of depression*. New York: Guilford, 1979.

Bellack, A. S., Hersen, M., & Himmelhoch, J. Social skills training for depression, a treatment manual. *Journal of Selected Abstract Service Catalogue of Selected Documents*, 1981, *11*, 36.

Frank, J. D., Gliedman, L. H., Imber, S. D., Stone, A. R., & Nash, C. H. Patients' expectancies and relearning as factors determining improvement in psychotherapy. *American Journal of Psychiatry*, 1959, *115*(11), 961–968.

Fuchs, C. Z., & Rehm, L. P. *Self-control therapy manual*. (Document No. 02937, ASIS/NAPS, c/o Microfiche Publications, New York, N.Y. 10016.)

Grummon, D. L. Design procedures, and subjects for the first block. In C. R. Rogers & R. F. Dymond (Eds.), *Psychotherapy and personality change*. Chicago: University of Chicago Press, 1954.

Klerman, G. L., Rounsaville, B., Chevron, E., Neu, C., & Weissman, M. *Manual for short-term interpersonal therapy (IPT) of depression* (fourth draft preliminary). New Haven–Boston Collaborative Depression Project, June 1979.

Lang, P. J., & Lazovik, A. D. Experimental desensitization of a phobia. *Journal of Abnormal and Social Psychology*, 1963, *66*(6), 519–525.

Lewinsohn, P. M., Antonuccio, D., Steinmetz, J., & Teri, L. *The coping with depression course: A psychoeducational intervention for unipolar depression*. Eugene: University of Oregon, 1982.

Luborsky, L. *Principles of psychoanalytic psychotherapy: A manual for supportive-expressive treatment*. New York: Basic Books, in press.

Loborsky, L., Mintz, J., Auerbach, A., Christoph, P., Bachrach, H., Todd, T., Johnson, M., Cohen, M., & O'Brien, C. P. Predicting the outcome of psychotherapy: Findings of the Penn Psychotherapy Project. *Archives of General Psychiatry*, 1980, *37*, 471–481.

McNair, D. M., Lorr, M., & Callahan, D. M. Patient and therapist influences on quitting psychotherapy. *Journal of Consulting Psychology*, 1963, *27*(1), 10–17.

Shlien, J. M. Comparison of results with different forms of psychotherapy. *American Journal of Psychotherapy*, 1964, *18* (Suppl. 1), 15–22.

Sloane, R. B., Staples, F. R., Cristol, A. H., Yorkston, N. J., & Whipple, K. *Psychotherapy versus behavior therapy*. Cambridge, Mass.: Harvard University Press, 1975.

Strupp, H. H., & Binder, J. L. *Time-limited dynamic psychotherapy (TLDP): A treatment manual*. Nashville, Tenn.: Center for Psychotherapy Research, Vanderbilt University, 1982.

Strupp, H. H., & Hadley, S. W. Specific vs nonspecific factors in psychotherapy: A controlled study of outcome. *Archives of General Psychiatry*, 1979, *36*, 1125–1136.

Waskow, I. E. Counselor attitudes and client behavior. *Journal of Consulting Psychology*, 1963, *27*(5), 405–412.

Waskow, I. E., Parloff, M. B., Hadley, S. W., & Autry, J. H. The NIMH Treatment of Depression Collaborative Research Program: Background and research plan. In preparation, 1983.

9

Specification of Techniques
in Interpersonal Psychotherapy

BRUCE J. ROUNSAVILLE, EVE S. CHEVRON, AND MYRNA M. WEISSMAN
Yale University School of Medicine
and Connecticut Mental Health Center

INTRODUCTION

If all of the many research issues of the NIMH Treatment of Depression Collaborative Research Program were to be boiled down to a single question it would be, "Do differences in psychotherapeutic technique matter?" That there are over 200 "brand names" of psychotherapy practiced in America today (Parloff, 1980) suggests that clinicians believe that technical differences are important. However, this is a controversial issue as some have emphasized the common elements shared by different psychotherapies and consider theoretical and technical differences to be comparatively unimportant (Frank, 1974). Despite decades of debate, there are few data that really address the question. Those who emphasize common elements point to the fact that different types of psychotherapy, when tested separately, tend to show comparable improvement rates. However, it is not possible to determine from these findings if the same types of patients or the same types of problems are treatable by the different psychotherapies.

For a rigorous test of the properties of different psychotherapeutic techniques, there are basically two kinds of experimental designs. Within a given case or across different cases, techniques can be systematically varied. Hence, for example, interpretations could be removed from a session or from a course of psychotherapy. This finely tuned approach can determine the "active ingredients" of psychotherapy. This design is highly difficult to put into practice in that the large number of potentially important techniques would require an impractically large number of studies to be performed. A variant of this plan which has been used relatively frequently has been to evaluate psychotherapeutic process across cases for the degree to which different techniques are used. This variation is then correlated with outcome. The problem with interpreting this kind of information is that the use of techniques across cases is not randomly determined but may be influenced by important patient characteristics. For example, a very insightful patient may elicit a greater number of interpretations from a psychotherapist and may, in turn, derive more benefit than a less insightful patient. However, the differential improvement may be less a factor of differences in technique than in preexisting differences in the patients.

A second research design to evaluate the type of effects produced by different psychotherapeutic techniques is that utilized by the NIMH Collaborative Study, which is to compare two types of psychotherapies with demonstrably different theoretical orientations and techniques. For this study cognitive therapy (Beck, Rush, Shaw, & Emery, 1979) and short-term interpersonal psychotherapy (Klerman, Rounsaville, Chevron, Neu, & Weissman, 1979) are being evaluated. To understand if and how they are effective these two psychotherapies are also compared to each other and to a pharmacotherapy and a placebo standard reference condition. In that the two types of psychotherapy differ in many techniques, this is a less finely tuned design than varying one technique at a time. There have been comparisons of this type in the past, but the difference in the present study is the extent to which attention is paid to ensure that the therapists carrying out the different treatments will be using the techniques that are definitive of those treatments and to reduce the likelihood that the therapists in different treatment conditions will be making heavy or exclusive use of techniques which are essentially the same. In this presentation we will describe the procedures devised for defining interpersonal psychotherapy (IPT), and for selecting, training, and monitoring psychotherapists to participate in this study. These procedures have been devised to ensure that IPT is being carried out as defined consistently across different cases, consistently within each case, and consistently across psychotherapists and across sites in the collaborative study.

DESCRIPTION OF INTERPERSONAL PSYCHOTHERAPY

Before describing the methods we have utilized to define IPT, we will review some of its characteristics. IPT is a brief individual psychotherapy devised for treatment of ambulatory patients who are in a current major depressive episode (Weissman, Klerman, Rounsaville, Chevron, & Neu, 1982; Klerman *et al.*, 1979; Rounsaville & Chevron, 1982). It attempts to achieve two kinds of goals: (1) alleviation of depressive symptoms, and (2) improvement in interpersonal functioning. IPT is explicitly eclectic and utilizes techniques and strategies common to many types of psychotherapy. To give a sense of the work, it is useful to describe the four major influences that have been brought together to make up IPT.

The first is the recognition of depression as a psychiatric disorder which, in common with other medical disorders, is characterized by distress and disability. It is not simply a transient mood or an epiphenomenon of problems in living but is characterized by abnormal behavior or functioning. The so-called "medical model" of depression is not simply utilized to determine diagnosis or eligibility for treatment with IPT but is incorporated into the treatment itself. This involves educating the patient about characteristics of the depressive syndrome such as its prognosis, prevalence, course, symptom constellation, and effects on interpersonal functioning. While patients are encouraged to take steps that will reduce depressive symptoms, they are not blamed for bringing on their own depression as a manipulative act. Moreover, they are temporarily allowed the "sick role," which involves being relieved of some social obligations. This is justified by the debilitating characteristics of the syndrome.

The second major influence on IPT is the belief that depression is closely associated with impaired interpersonal functioning. Problems in the patient's current interpersonal relationships are seen as contributing to the cause or perpetuation of the depression. Most of the work of IPT is aimed at identifying a limited number of key problems in the patient's current interpersonal relationships and helping the patient to develop less dysfunctional ways to understand and manage them. Four paradigmatic problem areas are identified: pathological grief, role disputes, role transitions, and interpersonal deficits. Strategies are spelled out for managing each type of problem. At a practical level, IPT also includes the use of reassurance, attempts at social manipulation, and the teaching of problem-solving skills.

The third major influence on IPT is the fact that all of its practitioners have had prior training and experience in an insight-oriented approach to psychotherapy. The most important way in which this has influenced IPT is through the use of techniques and a therapeutic stance that are common to many types of exploratory therapies. For example, although the therapist is comparatively active, he or she takes the patient's lead in choosing the topics in any given hour. The therapist adopts a comparatively neutral role and attempts to encourage the patient to talk freely and in an exploratory manner about a given interpersonal topic in order to discover unexpected thoughts or affects that are associated with it. Although advice may be offered, this is sparing, and homework is not assigned. To distinguish IPT from other insight-oriented psychotherapies it includes more active, practical interventions and is less ambitious in the nature of change sought. The IPT therapist does not attempt to bring about major personality change through the achievement of insight into underlying conflicts. Rather change is sought through education, combating demoralization, social manipulation, or problem solving, and the IPT therapist addresses underlying psychological conflict if work at these levels is stalled or if the patient is showing strong resistance to the treatment which must be managed.

The fourth major factor influencing the nature of IPT is its attempt to bring about a change in a limited number of sessions and brief amount of time. Many of the characteristics of IPT are determined by its short-term nature and are shared with other forms of brief treatment. For example, these include setting limited treatment goals, developing a structured and comparatively concrete treatment plan, not seeking a full understanding of determinants, focusing on the here and now, fostering an early positive relationship, and having the therapist take a relatively active stance (Butcher & Kolotkin, 1979). Although the brevity of IPT is certainly not a unique feature, it is seen as an important mobilizing force that encourages both the patient and the therapist to be more energetic in bringing about change.

DEFINING IPT IN A TRAINING MANUAL

The major instrument used to define, specify, and transmit the strategies and techniques of IPT is the training manual (Klerman *et al.*, 1979). In common with others books that describe different types of psychotherapy, the IPT manual includes a discussion of the theoretical background and general characteristics of the treatment. However, it differs from most other types of books about psychotherapy by providing detailed instructions and guidelines about the actual conduct of the treatment. One way of describing the intent of the manual is that it demarcates both the external and the internal boundaries of IPT. Within the IPT approach there are an operationalized list of techniques which may be drawn upon, a detailed outline of four general strategies for approaching the patient's interpersonal problems depending on the type of issues presented, a set of guidelines for handling specific problems (e.g., silence, lateness) which commonly arise in the conduct of psychotherapy, instructions regarding the sequence of events to be followed in the different phases of therapy, and a description of the defining features of the relationship the IPT therapist attempts to form with the patient. Moreover, the external boundaries of IPT are delimited and techniques that are not part of IPT are described such as assignment of homework, thought stopping, or interpretation of dreams, to name a few. Also outside the boundaries of IPT is the failure to adopt a therapeutic stance consistent with IPT, such as being overly active or directive, or failing to be supportive and active enough. The manual includes a detailed table of contents to facilitate its use as a working guide to the therapist, who can refer to it when issues of definition arise. An important point about the manual is that there is much that is not defined, such as tactical decisions of how to handle an hour in detail or how to form a therapeutic alliance with patients with a wide range of personality types. These are considered general therapeutic skills and outside the domain of the manual which was designed to outline the characteristic features of a particular treatment.

SELECTING IPT PSYCHOTHERAPISTS

The IPT training manual and the IPT training program were not designed to train inexperienced therapists in the fundamentals of psychotherapy. Rather, they are intended to shape and focus the existing repertory of skills of experienced psychotherapists while also selectively adding to this repertory. In comparison to basic psychotherapy training of novices, the IPT training program in the NIMH Collaborative Program is comparatively brief and nonintensive in the sense of requiring only three to four completed supervised cases before passing competence criteria. Because of this, *selection* of appropriate therapists was of the utmost importance. As defined by NIMH protocol, prospective IPT therapists had to meet the following criteria at minimum: (1) to be fully qualified psychiatrists or PhD clinical psychologists; (2) to have had a minimum of 2 years of clinical experience following completion of their professional training; (3) to have received training in a psychodynamically oriented framework; (4) to have had experience treating at least ten cases of ambulatory depression with a psychotherapeutic approach; (5) to have good general clinical competence; and (6) to show interest in and commitment to this therapeutic approach. In addition to the NIMH requirements, we required that therapists show a lack of attachment to techniques or theories incompatible with the IPT approach (e.g., use of gestalt or behavioral techniques).

To screen therapists for inclusion in the training program the research sites provided us with three sources of information: (1) the applicant's resume, with primary attention paid to clinical training and experience; (2) the therapist's responses to an attitudes and expectations questionnaire, which evaluates techniques and strategies which the therapist feels are useful for depressed patients; and (3) a single videotaped sample of the therapist's conduct with a depressed patient in a psychotherapy session or in an evaluation interview. On the basis of the videotapes we made two kinds of ratings: therapist empathy—that is, the therapist's ability to relate to the patient, and therapist IPT potential, including use of a therapeutic stance and of techniques that are compatible with IPT and, conversely, the failure to use techniques that are definitive of some other type of treatment.

We relied heavily on videotape ratings in making recommendations for selecting therapists. In the collaborative study 27 applicants were evaluated and six were found to be outstanding, 15 acceptable, and six unacceptable.

Table 1. Differences among Therapist Subgroups on Age and Experience

	Mean of group 1 outstanding ($n = 6$)	Mean of group 2 acceptable ($n = 15$)	Mean of group 3 unacceptable ($n = 6$)
Age	44.3	47.3	37.2
Experience	14.2	15.5	7.3

Note. From Chevron, Rounsaville, Rothblum, & Weissman (1983).

The unacceptable therapists were excluded either because of their use of techniques incompatible with the IPT approach or because they were perceived as lacking general therapeutic skills. It is worthy of note that the ratings of IPT potential were independent of the therapist's attitudes and expectations (e.g., therapists who believed that biochemical factors might play an important role in the cause of depression were not rated differently from those who did not). Moreover, most other therapist characteristics examined were also related to ratings of how the therapist actually performed with the videotaped patient, including sex of therapist, type of degree, or work primarily in an academic or clinical setting. The key factors that distinguished among our ratings of the therapists were age and experience. We found that highly rated therapists had an average of 14 years of experience and that low-rated therapists averaged 7 years (see Table 1) (Chevron, Rounsaville, Rothblum, & Weissman, 1983). In subsequent training efforts we have continued to be impressed with the importance of psychotherapist's experience for this psychotherapy. Experience may lead to improvement as therapists refine their skills over the course of their careers. Alternatively, there may be a self-selection process by which those who find the work gratifying will continue with clinical work while less able therapists do not.

In that this was the first time we have actually attempted to systematically select psychotherapist for IPT training, we are currently attempting to evaluate the predictive validity of our screening procedures by assessing their ability to predict therapists' performance in training and therapist effectiveness with patients both in the training phase and in the main study. This exploratory analysis is in progress at this time.

TRAINING IPT PSYCHOTHERAPISTS

The major task of IPT training is shaping and boundary marking in that the therapists are already highly experienced and highly selected. There are two primary components to the training program: (1) a 5-day didactic seminar, and (2) supervision on the basis of review of videotaped psychotherapy sessions.

In the 5-day seminar, we attempt to help the therapists identify what it is they are already doing that is like IPT, what they are doing which is not IPT, and what new skills they need to incorporate to conform to the IPT approach. This takes the form of an exegesis of the manual with extensive clinical illustration using videotaped case material. We have found that IPT turns out to seem quite reasonable and acceptable to experienced, psychodynamically trained psychotherapists.

There have been three main areas in which the therapists have had difficulty:

1. Adjusting to the short-term focus, which includes being quick to offer feedback and to focus the patient's efforts. This, ultimately, is best learned when the therapists come to believe that meaningful work can be accomplished in 16 weeks.

2. Giving up certain ways of handling an hour which are more characteristic of an open-ended, psychoanalytically oriented treatment For example, some therapists initially found it difficult to resist the temptation to spend sessions primarily interpreting the transference relationship, interpreting dreams, or placing exclusive emphasis on past relationships with the family of origin.

3. Avoiding a rigid, cookbook compliance with the manual. In regard to this point, the important thing about IPT is that although the manual defines the boundaries, the therapist is free to make use of individual variations in stance and timing. Some therapists missed the opportunity to find ways of forming a therapeutic alliance by spending too much energy going "by the book" (Weissman, Rounsaville, & Chevron, 1982).

Following the didactic portion, each therapist is assigned training cases on which he or she receives weekly supervision. This is done over the telephone and follows the supervisor's having reviewed the videotape of the therapy session being discussed. Both parties have videotape equipment and tapes available so that they can watch specific segments together. The primary purpose of the supervision is boundary marking. One technique that helps with this is going over the supervisor's research ratings of the session with the trainee, to help the trainee understand in more detail what is expected of him or her.

In a pilot training program we demonstrated the importance of basing supervision on review of videotapes. In this project supervision had been carried out in the traditional manner, on the basis of review of process notes.

After each supervisory session the supervisor made ratings of the therapist's use of IPT techniques and strategies. Videotapes were also made of the sessions, and several months following the training the two supervisors reviewed them, making ratings using the same format. What we found was that, whereas the interrater reliability of the supervisors' ratings of the videotapes were highly significant (Pearson's $r = .88$), there was no significant relationship between the videotape ratings of the psychotherapists and those made on the basis of traditional supervision. Therapists were also asked to rate their own performance in sessions based on recall immediately after the sessions and these ratings agreed with neither the supervisor's ratings nor the ratings based on review of the videotape. Two kinds of discrepancies between traditional supervision and viewing videotapes were noted. Several therapists who, on review of videotape, were felt to be excellent had underrated their own work, whereas others, who could talk about IPT theories and techniques well and made a good presentation of their therapies, were rated less highly when actual sessions were viewed. We feel that this independence of the impressions gained from supervision and from viewing videotapes is a key issue that needs to be taken into account in other types of clinical training (Chevron & Rounsaville, 1983). It is noteworthy that we dropped a written multiple-choice examination from the training and evaluation procedures because improvement on this instrument was found to be negatively correlated with ratings of therapist's skill in actually performing IPT.

ASSESSING THERAPISTS' COMPETENCE IN IPT

After viewing the videotaped psychotherapy session, and on the basis of the entire psychotherapy hour, the supervisor rates the trainee's performance. The reason for viewing the entire hour is that the areas being rated encompass more than the nature of the therapeutic relationship, which could be assessed in a shorter period. Evaluating the appropriateness of the use of specific techniques and strategies requires a knowledge of the context. Moreover, given an emphasis in IPT on the sequencing of strategies across sessions and focusing on targeted problems, it is really desirable that ratings be made with knowledge of what has occurred before in the treatment and what the therapist had in mind. Although this is possible for the supervisor, it is not done with independent evaluators.

The rating forms cover three levels of compliance with the IPT manual: (1) broadly defined use of appropriate IPT strategies; (2) appropriate use of the specific IPT techniques; and (3) use of techniques that are not part of the IPT approach. In each of these areas, the strategy or technique is rated as having been utilized or not, and the quality of the use is also rated. In addition, ratings of general psychotherapeutic skills and of patient receptivity are made.

INDEPENDENT EVALUATIONS OF COMPETENCE

In addition to ratings of the therapist by his or her supervisor, ratings are completed by other supervisors to monitor reliability. Additional ratings are made by independent evaluators who have not participated in the training in order to verify that therapists are performing the treatment in accordance with the IPT manual. The use of raters who are not invested in the training process is felt to be necessary in order both to evaluate the rating system and to ensure that aspects of the supervisory relationship have not biased the rater in favor of his or her supervisees. Our experience with this process is that the ratings have been made in a highly reliable fashion with agreement across raters quite good (Pearson's r ranged from .71 to .87).

The independent evaluators have also been used as ultimate judges of whether any given therapist is competent to use IPT in a clinical trial. In three separate training programs, therapists have been excluded for two types of reasons: (1) failure to use IPT strategies and techniques consistently or skillfully, and (2) persistence in using techniques that are incompatible with IPT. A minimum cutoff level of competence has been devised. In the collaborative program using this system, only one of the ten therapists who participated in the didactic training supervised practicum failed to achieve acceptable ratings for performing IPT.

MONITORING TO PREVENT DRIFT

To ensure further that trained IPT therapists continue to practice what they have learned throughout the clinical trial, a monitoring procedure has been adopted. Supervisors continue to monitor a reduced number of videotaped psychotherapy hours and to make all ratings made during the training phase. They have individual contact with the psychotherapists on a monthly basis and by participating in monthly case conferences of all IPT therapists at a site. However, the interaction is limited to pointing out when the therapist has missed opportunities to make use of IPT strategies and techniques and when he or she has made use of non-IPT techniques. A "red line" concept has also been devised so that, when quality ratings of two consecutive sessions are shown to fall below a minimum standard, the therapist is more intensively supervised until his or her ratings are once again above the "red line." In addition, therapists are contacted any time they demonstrate a significant deviation from protocol. So far, there have been only two cases in which therapists have drifted to a degree that required non-scheduled contact, and in both cases a single telephone contact was sufficient to correct the problem.

EVALUATING THE TRAINING AND EVALUATING THE EVALUATIONS

Although there was a 1-year pilot training program, some of the training procedures and rating instruments were previously untried. Because of this, we are paying close attention to evaluation of our selection, training, and assessment procedures.

Evaluating the Training

The primary ways that we will attempt to evaluate the training is to assess if change in the trainees took place over time. For example, did ratings of therapists' later sessions indicate better use of IPT than ratings of earlier sessions? Were ratings of the third case higher than ratings of the first case? Finally, although not necessarily related to a training effect, were there any changes in the rank order of trainees from the initial screening to the completion of training? If the rank orders do not change this may simply mean that all trainees improved equally, or it may mean that their performance was virtually unchanged over the training and was more related to skills they brought to the training.

Evaluating the Evaluations

Aside from evaluating reliability of the ratings of IPT therapist's competence, we are also assessing validity of two kinds: (1) discriminant validity, and (2) predictive validity. Regarding discriminant validity, we have attempted to determine if ratings cover features that are specific to IPT rather than related to several psychotherapy processes. For this purpose we have assessed general characteristics of session quality, of therapist performance, and of patient receptiveness, using the Vanderbilt Psychotherapy Process Scale (VPPS; Strupp, Hartley, & Blackwood, 1974). To evaluate the extent to which IPT ratings are directed at issues that are specific to IPT we will compare ratings made using our scales with those made using general process measures. It is possible, for example, that the ratings of use of IPT techniques are contaminated by a general "good therapist" factor. Another interpretation of this finding, if this were discovered, would be that "good therapists" also usually make good use of IPT. A second type of analysis will be to evaluate the extent to which ratings of therapists' IPT competence in the training phase are predictive of ratings made during the actual conduct of the study.

CONCLUSIONS

The steps we have described above have all been devised for one purpose: to reduce the variance in IPT therapist's performance in a clinical trial. Unless we can be sure that IPT and only IPT is actually being performed, we cannot really know if this type of treatment is successful; nor can we hope to find any unique advantages or disadvantages that this form of psychotherapy offers in comparison to another form. Of course, simply knowing that IPT is being consistently performed does not ensure efficacy. In addition, it may turn out that IPT is being performed consistently and that it is effective, but that the psychotherapists did not show a training effect by improving over the course of the training.

This kind of work—training therapists to participate in a treatment outcome study—has never been done before at this level of effort and detail, and it has been a kind of bootstrap operation in some respects as we have found it necessary to revise and to validate as we go along. For example, we are completing the training program before we have determined if our ratings of IPT skill are specific to IPT or whether they represent general "good therapist" and "good session" characteristics. However, regardless of how this particular analysis turns out, we feel that the greatly increased attention paid to specifying psychotherapy techniques in this study will have allowed the Collaborative Study to provide a serious test of the original question, "Do differences in psychotherapeutic technique matter?"

ACKNOWLEDGMENTS

The NIMH Treatment of Depression Collaborative Research Program is a multisite program initiated and sponsored by the Psychosocial Treatments Research Branch, Division of Extramural Research Programs, NIMH, and is funded by cooperative agreements to six participating sites. The principal NIMH collaborators are Irene Elkin Waskow, PhD, Coordinator; John P. Docherty, MD, Acting Branch Chief; and Morris B. Parloff, PhD, Former Branch Chief. Tracie Shea, PhD, George Washington University, functions as Associate Coordinator. The principal investigators and project coordinators at the three participating research sites are: George Washington University—Stuart M. Sotsky, MD, and David Glass, PhD; University of Pittsburgh—Stanley D. Imber, PhD, and Paul A. Pilkonis, PhD; and University of Oklahoma —John T. Watkins, PhD, and William Leber, PhD. The principal investigators and project coordinators at the three sites responsible for training therapists are: Yale University—Myrna Weissman, PhD, Eve Chevron, MS, and Bruce J. Rounsaville, MD; Clarke Institute of

Psychiatry—Brian F. Shaw, PhD, and T. Michael Vallis, PhD; and Rush Presbyterian St. Luke's Medical Center—Jan A. Fawcett, MD, and Phillip Epstein, MD. Collaborators in the data management and data analysis aspects of the program are C. James Klett, PhD, Joseph F. Collins, ScD, and Roderic Gillis of the Perry Point, Maryland, VA Cooperative Studies Program.

REFERENCES

Beck, A. T., Rush, A. J., Shaw, B. F., & Emery, G. *Cognitive therapy of depression.* New York: Guilford, 1979.

Butcher, J. N. & Kolotkin, R. L. Evaluation of outcome in brief psychotherapy. *Psychiatric Clinics of North America,* 1979, *2*(1), 157–169.

Chevron, E., & Rounsaville, B. J. Evaluating the clinical skills of psychotherapists: A comparison of techniques. *Archives of General Psychiatry,* 1983, *40,* 1129–1132.

Chevron, E., Rounsaville, B. J., Rothblum, E., & Weissman, M. M. Selecting psychotherapists to participate in psychotherapy outcome studies: Relationship between psychotherapist characteristics and assessment of clinical skills. *Journal of Nervous and Mental Disease,* 1983, *171,* 348–353.

Frank, J. D. *Persuasion and healing.* New York: Schocken, 1974.

Klerman, G. L., Rounsaville, B., Chevron, E. S., Neu, C., & Weissman, M. M. *Manual for short-term interpersonal psychotherapy (IPT) of depression.* Mimeographed distribution, 1979.

Parloff, M. B. Psychotherapy research: An anaclitic depression. *Psychiatry,* 1980, *43,* 279–293.

Rounsaville, B. J., & Chevron, E. Interpersonal psychotherapy: Clinical applications. In A. J. Rush (Ed.), *Short-term psychotherapies for depression.* New York: Guilford, 1982.

Strupp, H., Hartley, D., & Blackwood, G. *Vanderbilt Psychotherapy Process Scale (VPPS).* Unpublished manuscript, Vanderbilt University, 1974.

Weissman, M. M., Klerman, G., Rounsaville, B. J., Chevron, E. S., & Neu, C. Short-term interpersonal psychotherapy (IPT) for depression: Description and efficacy. In J. C. Anchin & D. J. Keisler (Eds.), *Handbook of interpersonal psychotherapy.* New York: Pergamon, 1982.

Weissman, M. M., Rounsaville, B. J., & Chevron, E. Training psychotherapists to participate in psychotherapy outcome studies. *American Journal of Psychiatry,* 1982, *139*(11), 1442–1446.

COMMENTARY

Dr. John P. Docherty*: Bruce [Rounsaville], you discussed the validation of training toward the end of your presentation, and you indicated two methods for accomplishing that: One is by the change in performance itself, and the other is by the change in outcome. I want to expand on that a little bit, because it has the potential for being somewhat confusing.

*National Institute of Mental Health.

One of the important advantages that this degree of standardization of the treatments has is that it permits us to assess whether or not a treatment is being performed competently, independent of the treatment's effect. This is a critical issue, and an important advance in the field, and one that we have discussed previously as having important implications for training because it allows you to develop a treatment in which you demonstrate what has been called the integrity or purity of the treatment—that the treatment is being performed the way it is supposed to be performed by its description, without prejudging the issue of whether or not it works. This is critical for a comparative achievement outcome study, because you want to be able to demonstrate without regard for outcome whether or not these several different treatments are each being performed competently, and you want to have ways of validating that the training has taken place to permit competent performance, independent of outcome.

10

Specification of the Training and Evaluation of Cognitive Therapists for Outcome Studies

BRIAN F. SHAW
University of Toronto

Cognitive therapy (Beck, Rush, Shaw, & Emery, 1979) is a system of psychotherapy (Ford & Urban, 1963) and thus is based on a theoretical foundation (Beck, 1967; Beck & Shaw, 1977), a body of scientific and clinical knowledge (see Kovacs & Beck, 1978; Shaw, 1979), and a set of well-defined therapy interventions (Beck, Rush, Shaw, & Emery, 1979). This chapter outlines our efforts toward the specification of cognitive therapy appropriate for outcome studies on patients with major unipolar depressive disorders.

The cognitive theory places a major emphasis on the individuals' phenomenology (e.g., view of the self, experiences, and the future) in the maintenance of the depressive episode. An oversimplified cognitive position is that as a function of certain schemata (attitudes and/or self-constructs), the individual, when faced with a loss from his or her personal domain, adopts a rigid, dysfunctional cognitive set. This cognitive set includes both a distinct content (particularly concerning personal abilities) and process of thinking. Rather than promoting a reduction in stress, the response accentuates the person's coping inadequacy and sense of personal failure. It is assumed that as the disorder worsens, major changes in the individual's affect, biochemistry, and behavior are related to this negative cognitive set. The negative set has a learning history developed as a function of significant past experiences with loss and/or failure. If the individual persists in maintaining his or her dysfunctional attitudes, the negative experience may progress into a full-blown depressive episode. The types of attitudes observed in depression are well described elsewhere (see Beck, 1967). For example some individuals believe that one's self-worth is contingent on achievements. The depressed individual may be observed to make negative predictions and yet to persist with *increasing* personal demands to achieve in the hope of reversing past errors. The stress engendered by such a strategy is even more likely to debilitate the individual. The more functional approach is to

173

decrease demands, approach the problems in a graded way, and disengage the self-worth/achievement contingency.

While this theoretical stance is unidimensional, and as such is unlikely to account for all depressions (Craighead, 1980), there is literature strongly supporting the cognitive theory of depression (Beck, 1967). At this time an intensive assessment of the cognitive changes associated with depression is both theoretically and therapeutically valuable (Shaw & Dobson, 1981).

Table 1 provides a brief overview of the major studies supporting the cognitive theory. Only studies employing clinically depressed subjects are

Table 1. Major Empirical Studies Supporting Beck's Cognitive Theory of Depression

Study	Conclusion
Negative view of self	
Loeb, Beck, & Diggory (1971)	Outpatients with depression have lower expectancies for success
Lobitz & Post (1979)	Depressed patients had lower expectations and self-evaluations
Giles & Shaw (1983)	RDC depressed female inpatients have lower expectations for success that are distinct from other patients
Derry & Kuiper (1981)	Depressed patients make negative self-referent judgments
Lewinsohn, Mischel, Chaplin, & Barton (1980)	Depressed outpatients' self-evaluations of lower social competence *confirmed* by others
Negative view of experiences	
DeMonbreun & Craighead (1977)	Depressed inpatients receiving high positive feedback made negative distortions
Lunghi (1977)	Depressed inpatients evaluate their relationships negatively compared to nonpsychiatric controls
Breslow, Kocsis, & Belkin (1981)	Depressed inpatients have lower recall of positive themes in story
Krantz & Hammen (1979)	Depressed inpatients manifested more cognitive distortions than psychiatric controls
View of future	
Dilling & Rabin (1967)	Depressed patients less oriented to the future
Vatz, Winig, & Beck (1969)	Depression significantly correlated with pessimism
Minkoff, Bergman, Beck, & Beck (1973)	Hopelessness is a strong indicator of suicidal intent
Wetzel (1976)	Hopelessness correlated more highly with suicide intent than depression
Hauri (1976)	Even in remission depressed patients are past-oriented

included following my longstanding argument against prematurely equating analogue and clinical studies. In general, depressed patients have a rather unique, negative view of their abilities (Giles & Shaw, 1983) and themselves (Derry & Kuiper, 1981), a negative bias in their recall of events (DeMonbreun & Craighead, 1977), and a strong sense of hopelessness (Beck, Kovacs, & Weissman, 1979; Wetzel, 1976). While it may be that nondepressed people have a normal, positive (yet equally unrealistic) bias (Lewinsohn, Mischel, Chaplin, & Barton, 1980), the depressed person's negative set is remarkable. The fact that depressed patients differ from others is of course not unique to cognitive variables. They also exhibit major interpersonal deficits (Lewinsohn *et al.*, 1980), dramatic neuroendocrine changes (Carroll, Curtis, & Mendels, 1976a, 1976b), and sleep pattern abnormalities (Kupfer, Foster, Coble, McPartland, & Ulrich, 1978), which are other state markers. To date there have been no convincing demonstrations of the etiologic importance of any factor in depression, and the search for trait markers continues with particular increasing interest in genetics (Weitkamp, Stancer, Persad, Flood, & Guttormsen, 1981).

In time our efforts will focus on identifying individuals who have both a pattern of cognitive symptoms of depression and cognitive vulnerability to depression. These efforts may help to identify depressed patients who will preferentially benefit from cognitive therapy for symptom reduction, prophylaxis, or both. The influence of cognitive change on the course of the disorder is also of interest. At present, the interventions to alter the depressed individual's cognitive set have been well defined and have been shown to be efficacious for many unipolar depressed outpatients (e.g., Blackburn, Bishop, Glen, Whalley, & Christie, 1981; Kovacs, Rush, Beck, & Hollon, 1981). Nevertheless, the therapy is by no means uniformly successful. Factors such as the chronicity of the disorder and associated psychopathology have been seen as important negative predictors of response (Blackburn *et al.*, 1981; Fennell & Teasdale, 1982) although Simons, Lustman, Wetzel, and Murphy (1983) did not find strong relationships between chronicity and outcome. A discussion of efficacy of cognitive therapy compared to other approaches and of the patient types most likely to benefit is beyond the scope of this chapter, however (see Kovacs, 1980). It is certainly not unusual for clinical interventions to develop more quickly than the theoretical or empirical substrates. In fact, the theory may be clearly wrong and yet the clinical intervention may be of value (e.g., systematic desensitization). Demonstrating the efficacy of a therapy does not provide support for the theory (Mahoney, 1974), but the therapist is guided by theory in considering the mechanism and extent of change he or she would like to facilitate.

One purpose of specifying therapeutic interventions for psychotherapy research is to increase the fidelity of the independent variable. In group design research it is assumed that each subject receives the same procedures. In psychotherapy outcome research, however, there is considerable variability in the procedures for each subject. This variability is reduced by defining procedures, by training therapists in these procedures, and by ensuring a minimal level of performance (quality assurance).

In the first instance, it is important to determine whether cognitive therapy is indeed a recognizable system of psychotherapy. The most difficult discriminations for the novice observer would be between rational–emotive therapy (Ellis, 1962), self-control therapy (Rehm, 1977), and Lewinsohn's (Lewinsohn, Biglan, & Zeiss, 1976) behavior therapy. With skilled observers and a reasonable observation period, however, these discriminations are not difficult. Other systems of psychotherapy such as nondirective therapy and gestalt therapy are more easily discerned.

DeRubeis, Hollon, Evans, and Bemis (1982) differentiated cognitive therapy from interpersonal psychotherapy (IPT; Klerman, Rounsaville, Chevron, Neu, & Weissman, 1979) using 12 naive observers. Each rater listened to four tapes (two from each psychotherapy) from a pool of 12 tapes. They used the Minnesota Therapy Rating Scale (MTRS), a 48-item, Likert-type format scale designed to reflect "good, typical" cognitive or inter-personal therapy. Four factors were identified: cognitive behavior therapy technique, general therapeutic skills, therapist directiveness, and IPT technique. DeRubeis *et al.* (1982) concluded that clear procedural differences exist between the two types of therapy. These differences were in line with those predicted by experts associated with each school.

It is important to distinguish between efforts to detect differences among therapies and efforts designed to judge the quality of cognitive therapy. In the NIMH Treatment of Depression Collaborative Research Program (TDCRP), my group has the responsibility of training cognitive therapists and assuring that the quality of the therapy remains acceptable during the clinical trial phase of the program. As will be seen later, efforts to assure quality demand different and, in our view, more specialized judgments about therapist behavior. The work completed for the TDCRP will be outlined in the following sections. It is hoped that the knowledge gained from this research will be applied to other clinical trials employing cognitive therapy.

It is critical in the TDCRP that the therapists employ cognitive therapy in an orthodox manner. In a clinical practice wider variation would be expected, but research therapists must behave consistently with the research protocol (Weissman, Rounsaville, & Chevron, 1982). Trained therapists are expected to use the treatment manual (Beck, Rush, Shaw, & Emery, 1979) as a guide rather than a rigid doctrine. Too little attention in past psychotherapy studies has been given to the issue of quality assurance. Do psychotherapists do what they say they do? Do the interventions consistently reflect the protocol? Are there breaks in the protocol? Can we measure competency in delivery of cognitive therapy? Is there a prototype cognitive therapist? What is the effect of different patient types on therapist behavior? These questions are of considerable interest to our research group.

In the past, published studies using cognitive therapy utilized therapists who were closely monitored and supervised (e.g., Rush, Beck, Kovacs, & Hollon, 1977) or who were also the principal investigators of the study (e.g., Blackburn *et al.*, 1981; Shaw, 1977). This strategy led to understandable concerns about the influence of factors such as intense supervision and commitment to the therapy under study. The plan for more recent studies is to evaluate the efficacy of cognitive therapy using therapists who have a more "independent" practice (i.e., independent in the sense that their practice more closely approximates a field trial). We recognize of course that there are limits to the generalizability of any clinical trial. The nature of a research protocol conducted at the university-based clinical setting is different from typical outpatient office practice. Nevertheless, the mandate from the field was clear: Evaluate cognitive therapy with well-trained, competent therapists functioning within a peer consultation system. Unfortunately, at that time there were few well-trained cognitive therapists, competence hadn't been defined, and it was known that therapist behavior is not a constant. There was a need to select and train therapists in this complex system of therapy relatively quickly (hopefully within 1 year), to develop measures of competence, and to design a system to specify when the therapist deviated from the treatment protocol. The rest of this chapter will outline some of our early efforts in the TDCRP to define criteria for therapist selection of cognitive therapists, competence, and acceptable deviance from the treatment protocol for outcome studies.

THERAPIST SELECTION

Judgments about therapist behavior must be based on observations of the therapist's behavior. This statement appears obvious but many arguments have been used to keep videotape equipment out of the psychotherapist's office (Strupp, 1978). There are many advantages of videotaped over audio-taped observations, the most obvious being that videotape provides non-verbal data. While it is important to study videotapes of the therapy it is also important for the researchers to recognize that their observations may have an effect on the therapeutic procedures they want to study (a psychotherapy variant of the Heisenberg [1927/1971] uncertainty principle). If researchers are to inform the field about efforts to help people with psychotherapy, the data must include observations of the therapist–patient interaction. It is desirable in our experience to observe the complete 50-minute CB therapy session. Specific attention is paid to three major segments of a session: (1) a review of recent events and agenda setting; (2) problem-oriented, cognitive, and/or behavioral intervention; and (3) summary and homework assignment.

TDCRP therapists were recommended for specialized training in cognitive therapy following reviews of their curriculum vitae, a form of evaluating their attitudes and expectations about psychotherapy, and a videotape of recent work. Two experts in CB therapy assessed the therapist's behavior using three ratings: (1) a judgment of overall psychotherapeutic skills; (2) a judgment of conceptualization ability (i.e., the ability to translate patient symptoms and problems into an understandable form); and (3) the mean probability estimate that the applicant would become a CB therapist. Interrater reliability across raters on the probability that a therapist would be successfully trained in CB therapy is .88 based on an *n* of 21. Therapists who are comfortable working within a short-term therapy framework and who can establish a problem-oriented working alliance tend to be evaluated positively for CB therapy training. These judgments are understandably not infallible. Two TDCRP therapists initially not recommended for CB training were later trained to a criterion of competence, and one of the recommended therapists did not meet the criterion as a CB therapist after training. One clinical observation about selection is that therapists who report a cognitive or schematic fit after reading the treatment manual (Beck, Rush, Shaw, & Emery, 1979) or observing a training videotape are good bets for training. The way in which the therapist conceptualizes psychological problems with the patient provides important information about the likelihood of a successful training in CB therapy. A general impression is that therapists who are either overly directive or nondirective or who are resistant to phenomenological approaches to therapy tend to have a poor prognosis for training in CB therapy.

THERAPIST TRAINING

Once selected, trainees attended a intensive didactic/experiential training institute lasting 1–2 weeks where they were exposed to lectures, videotapes, demonstrations, and role-play situations concerning CB therapy. Interestingly, in the first cohort of ten, the trainees' knowledge of cognitive therapy interventions (measured by a written examination) and their application of the methods in control situations (e.g., role playing) were of little value in predicting a successful outcome of training. On the other hand, the evaluation of expert cognitive therapists after observing the trainees in the initial institute was a useful predictor. The finding that an examination score has little relevance to observed therapeutic behavior is not new. Hogan (1979) reviewed the use of written and oral examinations to license U.S. psychologists and reported that "substantial evidence is mounting that these more traditional methods do not provide useful measures of competence" (p. 160).

The CB therapy training procedure is a complex interaction between the trainees' conceptualization of the patient problems, their selection of target symptoms for immediate treatment, and their judgment of which cognitive or behavioral intervention to employ. The interaction of these variables is at a level of abstraction beyond simple behavioral observation (i.e., you can't teach CB therapy by simply showing videotapes and modeling interventions). As a result the major method of training involves clinical supervision with an emphasis on the trainee's conceptualization of the case and treatment planning. Some training videotapes are available, but for the most part learning occurs as a function of trial and error and discussion.

The technical acquisition of new CB interventions is rapid whereas judgment about when to apply these interventions develops slowly. Novice therapists tend to use 1–2 favorite methods and have difficulty with novel situations (e.g., what happens when the patient does not respond to methods designed to alter his or her negative overgeneralizations). As with many skilled activities, timing is essential and the combination of interventions into a logical flow is important.

The initial cohort of CB trainees in the TDCRP were supervised individually for 12–18 months. External evaluations occurred every 6–8 months using a group of independent experts in CB therapy. During the supervised practice stage trainees treat 4–6 depressed patients in which every session is observed and rated, with subsequent supervision in a weekly 1-hour meeting. Notably, the supervision occurs at long distance. Except for the first institute and one on-site supervision session per year, the trainees and trainers interacted via telephone using simultaneous videotape review. (For more details see Shaw & Dobson, in preparation.) Before each supervision session the trainers reviewed the most recent videotapes (mailing results in 1–2 weeks' delay) to provide detailed feedback to the trainees.

MEASURING COMPETENCE: THE COGNITIVE THERAPY SCALE

The Cognitive Therapy Scale (CTS; Young, Beck, & Budenz, 1983) was designed to assess the therapist's level of competence in cognitive therapy. This 11-item scale taps both general psychotherapy skills (e.g., understanding, empathy) and specific cognitive therapy skills (e.g., agenda setting, cognitive and/or behavior techniques). To achieve a high score trainees must identify the key cognitions or behaviors relevant to the patient's problems or symptoms. He or she then must design a custom-made intervention strategy including an appropriate homework assignment.

As with any scale the main concern was to establish item-total and interrater reliability and construct validity. We have conducted a number of such studies demonstrating a high internal consistency ($\alpha = .95$, $n = 42$), and acceptable interrater reliability on the total CTS score .71 ($n = 59$, $p < .01$). Furthermore, the CTS's construct validity as measured by the relationship between CTS total score and global judgment of competency is good. The global judgment–total CTS correlation for expert raters was .91 ($n = 143$, $p < .001$); for trainers it was .82 ($n = 644$, $p < .001$).

Each use and assessment of the Cognitive Therapy Scale as a measure of competence in cognitive therapy has been encouraging. As a result we have continued to use this scale to document the progress of training and the quality of cognitive therapy provided by therapists. To date, our group has only employed a group of recognized experts in cognitive therapy to make judgments of competency on the assumption that the ratings required considerable judgment based on experience.

Our expert raters have various backgrounds with respect to basic training (psychology and psychiatry), past supervisors, and years of experience. Nevertheless, the interrater agreement on independent, global, yes–no judgment such as cognitive therapy competence (if you were conducting an *outcome* study in cognitive therapy, would you select this therapist to participate at this time, assuming this session is typical?) and acceptability as a cognitive therapist (how would you rate the clinician *overall* in this session as a cognitive therapist?) has been 100%. It is also notable that our experts make similar constructive suggestions for improvement and future training. In other words there appears to be a cognitive therapist prototype, an individual with a set of skills selected and combined in a way that maximizes an understanding of the depressed patient's phenomenology while challenging the negative, dysfunctional aspects of his or her construction.

Two efforts have been directed toward a better understanding of the relative importance of aspects of this prototype. First, we determined the items that related most to the raters' global judgments of cognitive therapy competence. Second, we obtained the rationally derived ratings of the importance via rank ordering of the items from five experienced cognitive therapists. The two sources of data (stepwise regressions and expert rankings) are compared in Table 2.

Note that there are interesting differences in the two rankings. Clearly the focus on key cognitions is important as it is rated highly by ranking and contributes most to the overall judgment of the competency of the cognitive therapist. General therapeutic skills are not highly ranked in considering the competence of the therapist in the rationally derived rankings, yet empirically they are major contributors to the overall score. This finding reinforces the notion introduced by Beck, Rush, Shaw, and Emery (1979) that in order to be a good cognitive therapist it is important to have good general skills. Notably collaboration, an aspect of CB therapy that is seen as important rationally does not play a major role in the empirical derivation. Future studies are needed to confirm this ranking.

Table 2. Rationally and Empirically Derived Hierarchies of the Items from the Cognitive Therapy Scale

Rank	Rationally derived hierarchy	Empirically derived hierarchy[a]
1	Focus on key cognitions	Focus on key cognitions
2	Strategy for change	Understanding
3	Implementation of strategy	Interpersonal effectiveness
4	Empiricism	Empiricism
5	Understanding	Strategy for change
6	Collaboration	Implementation of strategy
7	Interpersonal effectiveness	Feedback
8	Homework	Pacing
9	Feedback	Agenda
10	Agenda	Homework
11	Pacing	Collaboration

[a]Determined by a stepwise regression procedure. CTS items were used to predict overall therapist competency.

QUALITY ASSURANCE AND THE RED LINE CONCEPT

Quality assurance ratings are essential to ensure that the therapists behave in a consistent manner within a research protocol. In an outcome study investigators want the therapists to perform in a way that will allow generalization to the field. This requirement means that therapists should have limited contact with the trainers, whose task becomes one of monitoring the therapist's behavior. At this stage the trainers' job is to identify problems or inadequacies in the delivery of the therapy. We needed a plan to monitor the CB therapists and to handle two situations. The first was a serious protocol deviation involving the use of methods that were not part of CB therapy. The serious protocol deviation is an obvious compromise of the independent variable. As a result in the TDCRP the trainer contacts the therapist immediately, informs him or her of the problem, and files a report.

The second situation involves a sub-par performance. The latter situation arises when the therapist performs poorly (i.e., does not follow the protocol, makes errors in judgment) or the patient's problems, symptoms, or personality (i.e., patient difficulty factors) extend the therapist beyond his or her capabilities. If the therapist simply performs poorly independent of patient factors the therapy is not getting a fair test in the outcome study (i.e., the independent variable is compromised). It may be that the training was not adequate, or the criteria for competence was not valid, or the therapist's performance for whatever reason is not up to standards. If on the other hand, the therapist has difficulty because of factors related to the patient then the therapy is getting a fair test. We would simply find that some patients do not respond to the procedures. This example illustrates the importance of making competency judgments that are taken across various levels of patient difficulty during the training phase. Relatively stable and competent therapist behavior across a variety of patients is required in the outcome study. Thus, competency judgments must be made independently of patient variables and outcome (i.e., you want judges to rate the quality of therapy and not just therapists who get good outcome). Otherwise the quality assurance judgments are confounded.

To monitor the quality with which the therapists provide CB therapy the concept of a red line was borrowed from auto racing to indicate a dangerous situation—namely, that CB therapy is not being provided at a level above our standard. The red line is defined as a point one standard deviation below the mean CTS score of certified CB therapists. If the trainers observe two consecutive sessions in which the CTS score falls below the red line then they contact the therapist and the research site to express concern and to arrange for an added consultation time until the performance improves. Details on the calculation of the red line will be provided later.

The red line procedure serves several functions: (1) It is a quantitative method of describing the level of performance or competence along a number of specific CB therapy dimensions. (2) It controls for individual differences in the level of skill across CB therapists. (3) It provides a methodology for determining if the therapist *drifts* from the protocol—that is, if forms of less adequate cognitive therapy or other modes of therapy are occurring. (4) It gives the trainers a replicable, concise method for determining when, and if, the therapist in question should be contacted for further consultation and/or questioning of the therapy he or she is providing. (5) It provides a minimum quality assurance of any given therapist's performance level so that the researchers will have confidence in the quality of CB therapy being delivered in the study.

To develop a red line for each therapist, every CB therapy session conducted by each CB therapist during the training phase of the project (i.e., more than 720 1-hour tapes) was rated. Thus we were able to plot the CTS scores for each patient over all therapy sessions, as well as compute the average (mean) CTS scores. Originally, we were going to base the red line on an average level of competency across *all* training cases (4–6 in number). Since training was ongoing and assumed to be cumulative, however, the level of performance expected should increase with successive training cases. As an example, Figure 1 shows the plot of CTS total scores as a function of session. In the first case, Dr. A showed an increase in his level of cognitive therapy skills, as there was a generally positive increase in his CTS score. In

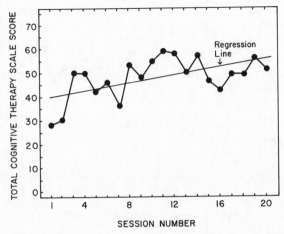

Figure 1. General improvement in competence across first case during cognitive therapy training.

fact, the best-fit regression line illustrates an increase in skill across the sessions. By the time of his fourth (last) training case, however, it can be seen (Figure 2) that there is no further increase in his CTS scores (note the regression line). Dr. A's mean level of CB competence, as measured by the CTS, is, therefore, more likely to be accurately reflected in his performance with the fourth case than the first. This general pattern of training, followed by the attainment of a particular level of performance, occurred across therapists. Consequently, it was decided to use the *final* training case for each therapist as the basis for defining red lines. The last training case illustrated in Figure 2 will serve as an example for the red line calculation. In this case the therapist's average CTS score is 52.1 with a standard deviation of 5.4. Therefore, this therapist's individual red line was calculated to be 47 (52.1 − 5.4; rounded off to the nearest whole number to provide the most conservative minimum CTS score). Assuming consistent behavior of the therapist across cases 16% of his or her sessions will fall below 47. The next step is to calculate the CTS grand mean of the study therapists (i.e., therapists certified as competent CB therapists). At present for the TDCRP we are using a CTS value of 39 as the group red line. Thus, if we observe two consecutive sessions below this value, we voice our concern.

As yet we have not determined how many sessions below red line would result in rejecting the therapist's behavior as not representative of cognitive therapy. Figure 3 illustrates using the red line concept to advise the cognitive therapists (and the research sites) of weak performance. In this example a red line of 44 was in use and two consecutive below red line sessions were observed. Feedback appears to have had a positive effect in reestablishing

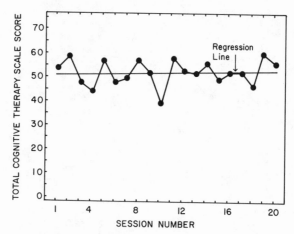

Figure 2. Stabilization of competence across fourth case during cognitive therapy training.

the therapist's behavior. Note that for sessions 6 and 7 two raters evaluated the session independently and both observations were graphed.

In addition to the total CTS score, we are interested in the relationship between general psychotherapy skills and cognitive therapy technical skills. Clearly a therapist can manifest strong relationship skills and yet be technically weak in providing cognitive therapy. Many of our trainees were experienced psychotherapists who had good relationship skills. Notably, early on in training, the technical demands of cognitive therapy were frequently seen to diminish the trainees' other skills. This finding may not be surprising. Competent cognitive therapy involves *both* relationship and technical skills (and probably others as well), yet the trainee's attention initially is directed toward technique. A strong technical performance early in training, however, is frequently stilted and naturally does not receive a high overall rating. In general, the relationship between general therapeutic skills and CB technical skills is strong ($r = .71$, $n = 606$, $p < .001$). This finding is consistent with expectation that in order to be a competent cognitive therapist, an individual first must have strong general psychotherapeutic skills.

To summarize, we have focused our efforts on the specification of cognitive therapy (Beck, Rush, Shaw, & Emery, 1979) for a research protocol, an intensive successful training program for therapists, and a procedure for quality assurance. A scale to evaluate the competence of cognitive therapists continues to be developed. Through the careful determination of competence in cognitive therapy, researchers interested in the efficacy and process of this psychotherapy will know with a degree of certainty that the therapy was delivered as planned.

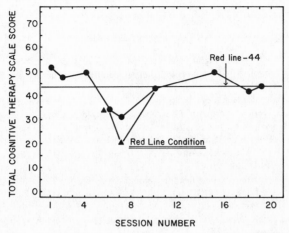

Figure 3. Examples of therapist meeting red line condition.

FUTURE WORK

As this book concerns future directions in psychotherapy research, a brief comment will be made about the necessary work to advance the study of therapeutic competence with specific reference to cognitive therapy. As previously noted, it is important to separate therapy outcome from judgments of therapeutic competence. While some psychotherapists are particularly gifted we are also interested in a good psychotherapist's use of an effective method of therapy. The hope is that cognitive therapy is a powerful method to treat many depressions and that it is a therapy that with training can be used effectively not just by a few but by many therapists. As such, the methods must be transportable and we have to determine the specific criteria for competence. The alternative would be to identify those individuals who are "naturals" (i.e., effective cognitive therapists with minimal training). It may be of course that as in many other skilled behaviors both natural ability and training are necessary.

Future research questions related to the therapeutic competence are (1) Does training make a difference? (2) What is the impact of frequent monitoring and consultation? (3) How do patient variables affect our judgments of therapist competency?

This work may have an influence on such varied areas of investigation as the use of telecommunications in training, methods of supervision, and criteria for certification. Our major goal, however, continues to be the assessment, through rigorous evaluation, of the best methods to help depressed patients.

ACKNOWLEDGMENTS

The NIMH Treatment of Depression Collaborative Research Program is a multisite program initiated and sponsored by the Psychosocial Treatments Research Branch, Division of Extramural Research Programs, NIMH, and is funded by cooperative agreements to six participating sites. The principal NIMH collaborators are Irene Elkin Waskow, PhD, Coordinator; John P. Docherty, MD, Acting Branch Chief; and Morris B. Parloff, PhD, Former Branch Chief. Tracie Shea, PhD, George Washington University, functions as Associate Coordinator. The principal investigators and project coordinators at the three participating research sites are: George Washington University—Stuart M. Sotsky, MD, and David Glass, PhD; University of Pittsburgh—Stanley D. Imber, PhD, and Paul A. Pilkonis, PhD; and University of Oklahoma —John T. Watkins, PhD, and William Leber, PhD. The principal investigators and project coordinators at the three sites responsible for training therapists are: Yale University—Myrna Weissman, PhD, Eve Chevron, MS, and Bruce J. Rounsaville, MD; Clarke Institute of Psychiatry—Brian F. Shaw, PhD, and T. Michael Vallis, PhD; and Rush Presbyterian St. Luke's Medical Center—Jan A. Fawcett, MD, and Phillip Epstein, MD. Collaborators in the data management and data analysis aspects of the program are C. James Klett, PhD, Joseph F. Collins, ScD, and Roderic Gillis of the Perry Point, Maryland, VA Cooperative Studies Program.

REFERENCES

Beck, A. T. *Depression: Clinical, experimental, and therapeutic aspects.* New York: Harper and Row, 1967.

Beck, A. T., Kovacs, M., & Weissman, A. Assessment of suicidal intent: The scale of suicide ideation. *Journal of Consulting and Clinical Psychology*, 1979, *47*(2), 343–352.

Beck, A. T., Rush, A. J., Shaw, B. F., & Emery, G. *Cognitive therapy of depression.* New York: Guilford, 1979.

Beck, A. T., & Shaw, B. F. Cognitive approaches to depression. In A. Ellis & R. Grieger (Eds.), *Handbook of rational-emotive therapy.* New York: Springer, 1977.

Blackburn, I. M., Bishop, S., Glen, A. I. M., Whalley, L. J., & Christie, J. E. The efficacy of cognitive therapy in depression: A treatment trial using cognitive therapy and pharmacotherapy, each alone and in combination. *British Journal of Psychiatry*, 1981, *139*, 181–189.

Breslow, R., Kocsis, J., & Belkin, B. Contribution of the depressive perspective to memory function in depression. *American Journal of Psychiatry*, 1981, *5*, 227–230.

Carroll, B. J., Curtis, G. C., & Mendels, J. Neuroendocrine regulation in depression: I. Limbic system—Adrendocortical dysfunction. *Archives of General Psychiatry*, 1976, *33*, 1039–1044. (a)

Carroll, B. J., Curtis, G. C., & Mendels, J. Neuroendocrine regulation in depression: II. Discrimination of depressed from nondepressed patients. *Archives of General Psychiatry*, 1976, *33*, 1051–1058. (b)

Craighead, W. E. Away from a unitary model of depression. *Behavior Therapy*, 1980, *11*(1), 122–128.

DeMonbreun, B. G., & Craighead, W. E. Distortion of perception and recall of positive and neutral feedback in depression. *Cognitive Therapy and Research*, 1977, *1*(4), 311–329.

Derry, P. A., & Kuiper, N. A. Schematic processing and self-reference in clinical depression. *Journal of Abnormal Psychology*, 1981, *90*, 286–297.

DeRubeis, R. J., Hollon, S., Evans, M. D., & Bemis, K. M. Can psychotherapies for depression be discriminated? A systematic investigation of cognitive therapy and interpersonal therapy. *Journal of Clinical and Consulting Psychology*, 1982, *50*, 744–756.

Dilling, C. A., & Rabin, A. I. Temporal experience in depressive states and schizophrenia. *Journal of Consulting Psychology*, 1967, *31*(6), 604–608.

Ellis, A. *Reason and emotion in psychotherapy*. New York: Lyle Stuart, 1962.

Fennell, M. J. V., & Teasdale, J. D. Cognitive therapy with chronic, drug, refractory depressed outpatients: A note of caution. *Cognitive Therapy and Research*, 1982, *6*, 455–460.

Ford, D. H., & Urban, H. B. *Systems of psychotherapy*. New York: Wiley, 1963.

Giles, D. E., & Shaw, B. F. *A test of the cognitive triad in Beck's theory of depression*. Unpublished manuscript, 1983.

Hauri, P. Dreams in patients remitted from reactive depression. *Journal of Abnormal Psychology*, 1976, *85*, 1–10.

Heisenberg, W. *Physics and beyond*. New York: Harper and Row, 1971. (Originally published, 1927.)

Hogan, D. B. *The regulation of psychotherapists* (Vol. 1). Cambridge, Mass.: Ballinger, 1979.

Klerman, G. L., Rounsaville, B., Chevron, E., Neu, G., & Weissman, M. M. *Manual for short-term interpersonal psychotherapy (IPT) of depression*. Unpublished manuscript, Yale University, 1979.

Kovacs, M. The efficacy of cognitive and behavior therapies for depression. *American Journal of Psychiatry*, 1980, *137*, 1495–1501.

Kovacs, M., & Beck, A. T. Maladaptive cognitive structures in depression. *American Journal of Psychiatry*, 1978, *135*, 525–533.

Kovacs, M., Rush, A. J., Beck, A. T., & Hollon, S. D. Depressed outpatients treated with therapy or pharmacotherapy: A one-year follow-up. *Archives of General Psychiatry*, 1981, *38*, 33–39.

Krantz, S., & Hammen, C. L. Assessment of cognitive bias in depression. *Journal of Abnormal Psychology*, 1979, *88*(6), 611–619.

Kupfer, D. J., Foster, F. G., Coble, P., McPartland, R. J., & Ulrich, R. F. The application of EEF sleep for the differential diagnosis of affective disorders. *American Journal of Psychiatry*, 1978, *135*, 69–74.

Lewinsohn, P. M., Biglan, A., & Zeiss, A. M. Behavioral treatment of depression. In P. O. Davidson (Ed.), *The behavioral management of anxiety, depression, and pain*. New York: Brunner/Mazel, 1976.

Lewinsohn, P. M., Mischel, W., Chaplin, W., & Barton, R. Social competence and depression: The role of illusory self-perception. Journal of Abnormal Psychology, 1980. *89*, 203–212.

Lobitz, W. C., & Post, R. D. Parameters of self-reinforcement and depression. *Journal of Abnormal Psychology*, 1979, *88*(1), 33–41.

Loeb, A., Beck, A. T., & Diggory, J. Differential effects of success and failure on depressive and nondepressed patients. *Journal of Nervous and Mental Disease*, 1971, *152*(2), 106–114.

Lunghi, E. The stability of mood and social perception measures in a sample of depressive inpatients. *British Journal of Psychiatry*, 1977, *130*, 598–604.

Mahoney, M. J. *Cognition and behavior modification*. Cambridge, Mass.: Ballinger, 1974.

Minkoff, K., Bergman, E., Beck, A. T., & Beck, R. Hopelessness, depression, and attempted suicide. *American Journal of Psychiatry*, 1973, *130*, 455–459.

Rehm, L. P. A self-control model of depression. *Behavior Therapy*, 1977, *8*, 787–804.

Rush, A. J., Beck, A. T., Kovacs, M., & Hollon, S. D. Comparative efficacy of cognitive therapy and imipramine in the treatment of depressed outpatients. *Cognitive Therapy and Research*, 1977, *1*, 17–37.

Shaw, B. F. A comparison of cognitive therapy and behavior therapy in the treatment of depression. *Journal of Consulting and Clinical Psychology*, 1977, *45*, 543–551.

Shaw, B. F. The theoretical and experimental foundations of a cognitive model for depression. In P. Pliner, I. Spigel, & K. Blankstein (Eds.), *Perception of emotion in self and others*. New York: Plenum, 1979.

Shaw, B. F., & Dobson, K. S. Cognitive assessment of depression. In T. V. Merluzzi, C. R. Glass, & M. Genest (Eds.), *Cognitive assessment.* New York: Guilford, 1981.

Shaw, B. F., & Dobson, K. S. Selection and training of cognitive therapists for an outcome trial. In preparation.

Simons, A. D., Lustman, P. J., Wetzel, R. D., & Murphy, G. E. *Predicting response to cognitive therapy of depression: The role of learned resourcefulness.* Unpublished manuscript, Washington University School of Medicine, 1983.

Strupp, H. H. Psychotherapy research and practice: An overview. In S. L. Garfield & A. E. Bergin (Eds.), *Handbook of psychotherapy and behavior change: An empirical analysis.* New York: Wiley, 1978.

Vatz, K. A., Winig, H. R., & Beck, A. T. *Pessimism and a sense of future time constriction as cognitive distortions in depression.* Unpublished mimeograph, University of Pennsylvania, 1969.

Weissman, M. M., Rounsaville, B. J., & Chevron, E. Training psychotherapists to participate in psychotherapy outcome studies. *American Journal of Psychiatry,* 1982, *11,* 139.

Weitkamp, L. R., Stancer, H. C., Persad, E., Flood, C., & Guttormsen, S. Depressive disorders and HLA: A gene of chromosome 6 that can affect behavior. *New England Journal of Medicine,* 1981, *305,* 1301–1306.

Wetzel, R. D. Hopelessness, depression and suicide intent. *Archives of General Psychiatry,* 1976, *33,* 1069–1073.

Young, J., Beck, A. T., & Budenz, D. *Assessment of competence in cognitive therapy.* Unpublished manuscript, University of Pennsylvania, 1983.

COMMENTARY

Dr. Robert L. Spitzer*: You mentioned that you had a way of evaluating your therapists on a continuum. How satisfied are you with these therapists? How many would you say are excellent or mediocre? I would ask the same question of Bruce [Rounsaville] about the IPT therapists.

Dr. Shaw: I am satisfied with the therapists. What I have noticed is that we do have an interaction between our judged competency and patient difficulty factor. Patient difficulty in this sense is not related to the severity of depression, but a judgment of a patient's difficulty. What we are finding is that for the most part—and we have randomly selected tapes—these are good therapists who are doing a good job. I wouldn't want to say that they are uniformly excellent, just as I wouldn't want to say that I am uniformly excellent. We are still finding that there are some cases with which the therapist simply has a great deal of difficulty, and we are still finding a greater variability in the therapist's performance than I am willing to tolerate at times.

Dr. Kenneth Altshuler†: I have a question about what happens to the patients in this study after the 20th session. Are they continued in the same modality of treatment, or are they switched over to another treatment? And in either event, are they followed and counted in some fashion thereafter?

---

*College of Physicians and Surgeons, Columbia University, and New York State Psychiatric Institute.

†Southwestern Medical School.

Dr. Irene Elkin Waskow*: Why don't we answer that in general for the whole collaborative study? The period of treatment is 16 weeks across all of the treatment conditions. At that time the research staff makes a judgment based on input from the therapist, from the clinical evaluator, and so on, as to whether the patient is in real need of further treatment at that time, in which case an appropriate referral is made. If the patient doesn't seem to be in real need, but has some interest in going on in treatment, he or she is asked to wait a little while, if possible, explaining that sometimes people do feel better in a little while, and so on. But all patients are followed in terms of possible later referrals.

We have, during the training phase, done a 6-month follow-up. In our renewal applications, which are now in and about to be reviewed, we have asked to do an 18-month follow-up of all patients in the study.

Dr. Sol L. Garfield†: I am interested in how you, in a sense, apportion the amount of variance in outcome between the training of these therapists and their previous training and experience and personal skill. In other words, it is going to come out that they were trained in cognitive therapy or IPT, and the results are supposedly due to training to some degree. But how much could be said to be due to the fact that there were certain kinds of therapists who came in with certain kinds of experience, background, and training. Who knows? Some of them may even have gone through Washington University! That would make a difference.

So how do you interpret the findings? In a similar way, you have training of a certain kind, and you have supervision that goes on for a long time. To what extent can you generalize about either kind of therapy, and how will it be translatable in the field, because you have very unique conditions in this situation. I am not saying it is good or bad; I'm just asking a question.

Dr. Shaw: What we have here is clearly a group of therapists who have had a lot of attention paid to them. And they are well trained and well monitored. I think that an emphasis on continued quality assurance is important for our field.

In terms of the exportability of cognitive therapy, one of the things that has impressed me is that these therapists were not all our selections, and despite the fact that we didn't have high probabilities of success for some of them, the training had an impact. So I would say that, while in this case there has been very specialized training, it would be my guess that we could export that training to other therapists. I don't know how this would compare to somebody who had just picked up the manual and read it and practiced, although I have seen a number of "naturals" in terms of cognitive therapy.

*National Institute of Mental Health.
†Washington University.

11

Opening Comments

SOLOMON C. GOLDBERG
Medical College of Virginia

It is interesting that the developmental course of research in psychotherapy has paralleled the development of standardized rating scales for psychopathology and diagnosis, toward greater specification and standardization. There was much resistance to the standardization of rating scales because it seemed to call into question the need for the acumen brought to the interview of the trained clinician. Up until World War II, observer rating scales might have consisted of an enumeration of global concepts, such as anxiety, depression, motor retardation, hostility, and so on which the clinical observer used as a very general guide to the interview. The particular questions used to elicit information about any one of these concept areas differed among clinicians, as did the order in which he or she inquired about the information. There was no specification as to whether observations were to be based only on the interview or on everything that could be learned about the patient whether from relatives or the police. There were few distinctions between inferred and manifest behavior. Recording scales were sometimes of frequency, sometimes of severity, sometimes present versus absent, and sometimes whether or not the behavior was disruptive to life processes. It would come as no surprise to anyone today that such scales were highly unreliable simply because the various observers were not operating under the same ground rules. Furthermore, if the clinician had to form a diagnosis from some patterned combination of observations of history and psychopathology, the algorithm that was used differed among clinicians and accordingly reduced diagnostic reliability.

There has been considerable progress in the development of observation scales and diagnostic instruments in the past 35 years, accomplished by standardizing and making more specific the questions that are asked and placing severe restrictions on inferential judgment. There has been an analogous movement in research on psychotherapy, although it is far more difficult to standardize and to specify the operations of the therapist. We are currently at a stage where the specification of what the therapist does and says is at a conceptual level: The therapist does not operate from a script. Detailed manuals for therapeutic operations still require a therapist with clinical acumen to carry through the procedure, making it likely there will be therapist differences of some degree in the way the therapy is administered. A test of therapist differences still needs to be built into any study. We have heard much discussion on separating out the specific from nonspecific aspects of a therapy, but before doing so we must ask whether the package as a totality is effective regardless of which therapist is used and regardless of which of its components may be the active ingredient.[1]

Going counter to the specificity hypothesis are the results of Jerome Frank and then Hans Strupp to the effect that it doesn't make much difference what is said in the therapeutic process as long as a therapeutic relationship is established. There seems to be agreement about the value of the relationship between therapist and patient, yet this has been one aspect of the therapeutic process that has been less specified. Some would maintain that it cannot be specified at all. It is an interpersonal quality that therapists have to one degree or another. General guidelines certainly exist for clinicians in training on the establishment of rapport, but nothing so specific as a training manual. Like anything else, this, too, can probably be taught. In so doing, it will be made more explicit and standard.

I personally doubt that there are no specifics in the therapeutic process that make a difference. I think it does make a difference what is said to whom, beyond the establishment of the therapeutic relationship. I can best illustrate the reasons that I think so by pointing out that cognitive and interpersonal therapy so far seem to be effective with depressed patients; however, judging from the Phillip May study on schizophrenia, a form of individual psychodynamically oriented psychotherapy had no demonstrable effect in schizophrenia. In the more recent literature, there are now two controlled studies contending that family therapy with the families of schizophrenic patients is effective in forestalling relapse in the schizophrenic patient. I personally would doubt that this kind of family therapy would have a comparable beneficial effect on depressed patients. This would be a clear demonstration that the therapeutic operations appropriate for depression are very different from the therapeutic operations appropriate for schizophrenia, and it does make a difference what is said and to whom.

I would like to finish with a methodological point that stems from the question discussed in some of the presentations today of what is the appropriate control group to control for nonspecific effects. Donald Klein made the point aptly that in order to know the nonspecific effects to define such a control group, one also had to know what the active ingredient was in order to make certain that it did not enter the control group. If we knew what the specific active ingredient was, we would not need the study. I should like to offer an alternate design to the ones that have been used so far which seem to be a comparison of a total treatment package with a control group which has only the nonspecific process. My proposal is to compare two different therapies on the kinds of patients for whom each is considered appropriate. This would be analogous to the drug study by Donald Klein in which depressed and schizophrenic patients were randomly assigned either to imipramine or to chlorpromazine. To no one's surprise, the responders on chlorpromazine tended to be schizophrenic and the responders on imipramine tended to be depressed. Analogously for psychotherapy, one could have a study of, say, interpersonal therapy versus the kind of family therapy that was effective with schizophrenic families by Ian Falloon and by Julian Leff. Depressed and schizophrenic patients would be randomly assigned to both kinds of therapy. My expectation is that the depressed patients would do best on the interpersonal therapy and that the reverse would be true for the schizophrenia patients. The differences observed in the form of a therapy-type by diagnosis interaction would certainly indicate that the active ingredients in the two therapies were quite different.

Such a design would also have merit in overcoming the fact that in psychotherapy research it is virtually impossible to have the patient be blind to the kind of therapy he or she is getting. We can easily blind the outside observer. Even under these conditions, however, patients themselves do know what they are getting; although patients may have some bias regarding the active treatment received, the worst bias is in knowing that one is in the nonactive control group. To overcome this bias the patient must be convinced he or she is receiving an active treatment. It would be a distinct advantage to be able to tell the patient in the informed consent that in all cases he or she will receive an active treatment. Short of this, as in studies like the NIMH Collaborative Study, the inability to have the patient blind to his or her assignment can possibly bias the nonspecific control group in the negative direction.

I recall a chapter in the *Annual Review of Psychology* a number of years ago on psychotherapy research in which the author began with the words: "All is chaos!" Reading his review, one would have to agree. Hearing many of the reports today, the field can justifiably take pride in accomplishments.

General Discussion

Dr. Irene Elkin Waskow*: I'd like to respond to some of the other questions Sol [Garfield] raised. We plan to relate things like experience level and previous training to our outcome results as well, so that we will be looking at a number of variables. In terms of the role of the specific skills, as I mentioned, we are going to have an independent researcher who is looking to see how much each of the therapists is carrying out the approaches as they have been specified, also look at some "nonspecific" factors. So we will be able to look at how much therapists' carrying out of the techniques is related to outcome, how much some general therapeutic skills are related to the outcome, and so on.

Dr. Bruce J. Rounsaville†: Right. The question, as I see it, is: Do techniques really matter? And the only way that you can really test that is to make sure that the therapists are as qualified as possible, and doing the therapy as well as possible. I think that it is important that the therapists have as much experience and as much training as possible, although this is not necessarily generalizable to clinical programs or to what people are doing out in the field, to test whether this kind of therapy, which has these kinds of techniques, when practiced under these relatively specific conditions, affects patients in different ways than this other kind of therapy.

Dr. Myrna M. Weissman†: Also in answer to Dr. Garfield's question, I do believe that Don Klein had suggested adding to the original design, a cell to test out the need for training, and, in fact, that wouldn't be hard to do. You would have to have two cells: one in which you gave the therapist the cognitive therapy book by Beck to read, and the other in which you gave them the IPT manual to read. Then you would have each therapist do the respective therapy they read about without the elaborate training program. Although that would have been expensive to do (adding those two more cells) it would have been feasible. We are not sure that training makes a

*National Institute of Mental Health.
†Yale University School of Medicine and Connecticut Mental Health Center.

difference; just having experienced therapists who read the various manuals may be all we need. In fact, they may not even have to read the manuals. However, the decision was made to bias in favor of all the hypotheses, and that is to have the most experienced therapists, well trained by the people who developed the therapies. Then, if the therapies don't work under those conditions, or don't differ relative to each other as well as relative to the placebo management group, there can be less complaint about those biases. And I think that was a wise decision.

Dr. Waskow: We haven't yet said anything about our pharmacotherapy training. I would like to mention that Jan Fawcett, who is carrying that out, just mentioned to me the other day that although the therapists in general are getting much closer to the protocol, they continue to vary a good bit from time to time in what they do when they are giving the patient the pill, depending upon the particular patient they get.

Dr. Arthur K. Shapiro*: My understanding is that you are going to have cognitive therapy with imipramine and placebo.

Dr. Waskow: They are separate conditions. There are four separate conditions: cognitive therapy, interpersonal therapy, imipramine plus clinical management, and pill–placebo plus clinical management. At this time we are not studying the interactions of the drugs and the therapies.

Dr. Shapiro: So you don't really have an adequate control for the effectiveness of both cognitive therapy and interpersonal therapy. The control for it is what some might consider an inadequate placebo condition because you don't have manuals for clinical management.

Dr. Waskow: Yes, we do.

Dr. Shapiro: Are you going through the same procedures, and are the therapists committed to it and believe in it?

Dr. Waskow: Yes.

Dr. Shapiro: And does it involve the same amount of management and the same amount of time? In other words, are all the conditions the same? Is it a good placebo control?

Dr. Waskow: We have the imipramine in there as a "standard reference conditon," feeling that there is a certain amount of efficacy data available for outpatient depression using imipramine. And we had Jan Fawcett, who is a well-known person in this area, develop a manual. As things developed, it became apparent that we couldn't treat that training any more casually than we could the training for the psychotherapies, because pharmacotherapists do just as many varied things as do psychotherapists. So the pharmaco- therapy training became more intensified and is really much more on a par with the psychotherapy training. Also there was a didactic institute, there is a very clear manual, and there were supervised cases. The pharmacotherapists

*Mount Sinai School of Medicine.

were chosen as also having experience in that area, as being committed to that approach, and so on.

Dr. Shapiro: Are they being seen as frequently and for as long?

Dr. Waskow: They are being seen once a week for the 16 weeks. The only real deviation has to do with the fact that the sessions, after the first one, are not as long, because what we decided in this study was to try to keep the integrity of the particular treatment approaches. So we kept the interpersonal therapy as it had been reported and researched; the same with cognitive; and the same with the pharmacotherapy.

Certain parameters, like the 16-week treatment, we felt were very important to hold constant. There are slight variations in numbers of sessions, and some variation in the amount of time for the pharmacotherapies. We do have sessions once a week, which is not necessarily done in pharmacotherapy, but we thought that frequency of contact was very important to keep constant. What we have tried to do is keep as many parameters as constant as we can without violating the integrity of any of the treatment conditions. That is our basic principle of design.

Dr. Shapiro: Except you do now have for the clinical management condition some substantial variables that differ from the other condition. The amount of time is a significant variable.

Dr. Waskow: The amount of time for each session is different, and is close to what is being done in the field. We are using the standard reference condition the way pharmacotherapy treatment has been done in the field, just as we are using the IPT the way it has been done, yes.

Dr. Shapiro: I think you are defending the adequacy of that placebo condition. I don't know that I would accept that.

Dr. Waskow: Every clinical research study is a matter of compromise. One always has to walk a line between clinical meaningfulness on the one hand and scientific rigor on the other. And one has to make a decision based on a particular study. One school of thought, for instance, says that you should use the same therapist across treatment conditions, because then you control the therapist variable. Our own option, in this case, was to go with the idea that it is the commitment and the experience of the therapist relative to that approach that is the important variable. They are both defendable positions. In a particular study you simply have to make your choices and then interpret your results on the basis of the choices made.

Dr. John P. Docherty*: I want to underline the comment that Irene [Waskow] just made, because I think it is a very important one in understanding the state of the art of clinical research.

There are a number of issues that demand compromise in research design. What is important is that the various possibilities and options be

---

*National Institute of Mental Health.

spelled out, and that the rationale for the ones that are selected be spelled out if we are going to advance the field.

It is in that task that the sophistication of clinical research has advanced. The various choices, then, can be evaluated in terms of the rationale for the option selected. And it would put the burden on the researcher or on the critics of the research to demonstrate that the alternative options were really superior in that context, for that particular study.

Dr. Ronald Lipman*: I would like to go back to the theme of having need for a mosaic of studies. At Hopkins, for example, Dr. Covi and I looked at a comparison between group cognitive behavior therapy, either alone or with imipramine, and traditional group psychotherapy as a control. I think this gets to Dr. Shapiro's comments. That traditional group psychotherapy had a manual, and had an experienced therapist who was an adherent of traditional dynamic psychotherapy. However, we found a very clear superiority, at least in the pilot study, in favor of group cognitive behavior therapy.

In reference to Dr. Garfield's point about generalizability, look at the training of the therapists. You will find, if my memory serves me correctly, that for the most part they were relatively inexperienced clinicians, not very well trained in cognitive behavior therapy. Yet the results of that, in terms of outcome—and I know there have been some concerns about the control aspects of the study—nevertheless are quite impressive. So to some extent I think we have a clue as to what we are likely to find in the field.

Dr. Waskow: Those therapists were also very intensively supervised during the course of the study, and I think that is something you also would not find out in the field very frequently.

Myrna [Weissman] earlier today mentioned Ivy Blackburn's study in which they found real differences when they compared cognitive therapy and drug therapy in the outpatient psychiatric department and in the private practitioners. I just looked back at the data recently, and the reason things look so different is because drug treatment does so abysmally when it is being done by private practitioners.

Dr. Robert A. Neimeyer†: You had mentioned earlier, Dr. Waskow, your interest in studying the mechanisms of change over the course of these therapies in the collaborative study. I would like to invite the panelists to say something about their differential predictions concerning IPT, CT, and pharmacotherapy in terms not only of symptomatic remission, but also cognitive and interpersonal change, and about how those are being assessed, if that is part of the thrust of the study.

*Johns Hopkins University.
†Memphis State University.

Dr. Waskow: For the study as a whole, let me speak first in terms of outcome measures, which are taken at interim periods as well as at the end. Some of the things we are particularly interested in, for instance, are things like the Dysfunctional Attitudes Scale, which is something that the cognitive therapists have been using, although of course we will be looking at changes on it across all the treatment conditions. We are particularly interested in things like the Social Adjustment Scale, which has various effects posited for interpersonal therapy, although, again, we will be looking at it across treatments. Those are being done at 4 weeks, 8 weeks, 12 weeks, and so on, as well as at the end of therapy.

In terms of more detailed process studies, those are really more in the thinking stage, and will include trying to develop and to use measures that are already available that may tag those changes in cognitions and those changes in interpersonal relationships as they are related by the patients in therapy during the actual therapy sessions. Those are, however, much more in the conceptualization stage, and the measures have not been chosen. We have all the videotapes, however, and it would be possible to do a lot of direct process studies based on the tapes.

Dr. Thomas Williams*: As one of the architects of an earlier collaborative study on the psychobiology of the depressive illnesses, I can understand a lot of what you are doing. But at this point in history I find myself a registered voter and an unregistered lobbyist with a very sympathetic congressman who represents our district in Tampa.

I don't know how to sell this project to him, because if everything comes out the way you want it to, and you reject all the null hypotheses, what one thing are we going to know? How do I sell this project instead of tanks? What are we going to know when you are done with all this?

Dr. Waskow: That's a good question. I think there are several things we are trying to do in this project. Our ultimate goal is to find the best treatments for each patient. And we are also trying to find the best ways of doing research to come up with those answers.

So far we have not gotten too many answers in the area of psychotherapy research, and one of the things we are trying to explore is other models of trying to get those answers, one of them being the idea of having replicated studies in different places so that we can at least try to see if there is some consistency in the answers that come up.

I don't know if you can sell this part of it to the congressman, but I think one of the most important things coming out of the collaborative study is that by doing the same study at different research sites, and trying to train

*Veterans Administration Medical Center, Tampa, Florida.

therapists across research sites, we are coming up against an awful lot of procedural, methodological, and conceptual problems in psychotherapy research that can often be treated very lightly at a particular site because you don't know you are doing this differently from the guy down the street or in another city. So we are hoping that in many ways we are going to be able to help address (if not resolve) and try to find some temporary resolutions to some problems that will help in psychotherapy research more generally so that we can get some of the answers about treatment effectiveness, and especially, I hope, eventually some of the answers that I think are more important in the long run, about the mechanisms of change. Only if we start to learn something about the mechanisms of change can we start to develop better and more efficient and more effective kinds of treatment.

Dr. Docherty: I would like to make a quick comment about this. There are a couple of things. One is that I would wonder why it was a question. Is it a question about research, and health research? There is a standard question in response to that, which is if you think the costs of health research are high, consider the cost of disease.

The research being undertaken here is research to try to determine the efficacy of some reasonably well-developed treatments for very serious disorders. We fully expect, because we have a long history of the usefulness of this kind of work, that we will get some answers regarding the efficacy, and in the process of that get, in this particular study, some answers regarding differential efficacy.

We can already demonstrate that in this study we have significantly advanced the methods that permit us to carry out treatment efficacy studies, and has positioned us well, were the funding available to carry out a whole series of those studies and to advance significantly the state of knowledge in the field.

I would point out to the congressman that the total amount of federal expenditure for psychotherapy research since 1948 has been $70 million. The amount budgeted for military bands for this single 1983 year was $89 million! (*Applause.*)

Dr. Gerald L. Klerman[*]*:* As someone who has been in the position of talking with congressmen, let me add that this is a very pertinent question. First of all, the very fact that this study is being done has enhanced the credibility of the field. When I was in Washington, the psychotherapy field had relatively low credibility before Congress because of the apparent unwillingness of the field to subject itself to systematic studies. And very often, when hearings were held before Congress, members of the field said why it couldn't be done, why psychotherapy was so different from other health procedures that doing trials was a mistake, or that randomization was

---

[*]Harvard Medical School, Harvard School of Public Health, and Massachusetts General Hospital.

inhumane, etc. The very fact that this study has been done, I think, has raised the credibility of the field.

Secondly, if the study confirms the current trend in the field it will show that there are some forms of patients for whom psychological techniques are relatively as effective as medication, which I think has gone against the conventional wisdom. But there are now at least five trials, some of which were reviewed by Dr. Weissman this morning, that show that in selected patients both cognitive and interpersonal therapy are about as effective as a tricyclic.

Let me also point out that depression is about as prevalent as hypertension, and the Public Health Service, after many years, has launched a very intensive program on the early detection and reduction of morbidity and mortality of hypertension. And it wouldn't surprise me if we would be in the position, in 5 or 10 years, to advocate something similar for at least ambulatory depressives.

"IF ONLY WE KNEW THEN WHAT WE KNOW NOW": STRATEGIES OF PSYCHOTHERAPY RESEARCH—LESSONS FROM THE PAST FOR THE FUTURE

12

Psychotherapy versus Behavior Therapy: Implications for Future Psychotherapy Research

R. BRUCE SLOANE AND FRED R. STAPLES
University of Southern California School of Medicine

DESCRIPTION OF STUDY

This study (Sloane, Staples, Cristol, Yorkston, & Whipple, 1975) was planned and carried out in the late 1960s. At that time behavior therapy was looked upon largely as a mechanistic technique, unhumanistic, and somehow distinct from "talking psychotherapy." It was also seen as a procedure that might have relevance only for phobias or other rather narrowly defined aspects of behavior. Few saw it as a useful treatment for the mixed bag of problems of living which constitute the bulk of therapeutic practice. The issue of symptom substitution was raised if such patients were not treated with more intensive "in-depth" procedures. On the other hand, behavior therapists saw dynamic psychotherapy as an esoteric, unscientific enterprise with little or no empirical justification for its procedures or its treatment effects.

The study was designed to evaluate the effectiveness of these two therapies, given by experienced practitioners, with real patients who presented a broad range of typical outpatient problems.

Ninety-four outpatients suffering from moderately severe neuroses and personality disorders were assigned randomly with equalization of sex and a rough measure of severity of pathology to a waiting list, behavior therapist, or an analytically oriented psychotherapist. All the therapists were experienced. The minimum qualification was 6 years of behavior therapy practice and 250 patients, and 8 years of psychoanalytically oriented psychotherapy and 300 patients. The maximum was 6,000 patients in 35 years of practice for the senior analyst and 2,000 patients and 20 years practice for the behavior therapist.

The patients were rated on severity of illness on many different scales and also completed the Eysenck Personality Inventory (EPI), Minnesota Multiphasic Personality Inventory (MMPI), and California Psychological Inventory (CPI) together with the Mill Hill Vocabulary Scale. There were two principal measures of psychological change, the Structured and Scaled Interview to Assess Maladjustment (SSIAM) and assessment of target symptoms. All the patients were assessed by independent assessors and a research assistant interviewed a close friend or relative of the patient, the informant, who also made ratings of patient's work and social adjustment.

The patients were treated for 4 months, an average of 14 sessions. At 4 months all three groups had improved significantly on the severity of the target symptoms, but the two treated groups had improved significantly more than the waiting list group. There was no significant difference in the amount of improvement between the psychotherapy and the behavioral therapy groups. On the work scale of the SSIAM, behavior therapy patients improved significantly, whereas psychotherapy and waiting-list patients showed only marginal improvement. On the SSIAM social scale only the behavior therapy and waiting-list patients improved significantly; *however, there was no significant difference in the amount of improvement among the three groups, either for work or for social adjustment.* There was no significant effect on improvement due to sex of the patient, severity of the neuroticism, or the amount of the therapist's experience.

At the 1-year follow-up, improvement was maintained or continued in most patients. It was difficult to evaluate these 1-year results since many members of each group had different therapeutic experiences after the initial 4 months. If only the patients who had no therapy after 4 months were compared, the results were substantially similar. All groups maintained significant symptomatic improvement. Behavior therapy and psychotherapy patients were significantly improved in work adjustment; waiting-list patients only marginally so. Psychotherapy patients were significantly improved in social adjustment but behavior therapy and waiting-list patients showed only marginal change. However, the groups did not differ significantly in the amount of improvement with any measure.

There was no evidence of any symptom substitution in any group. On the contrary, patients whose target symptoms improved often reported improvement in other less important symptoms as well.

At the 2-year follow-up only 61% could be interviewed. The great majority in all groups had increased or maintained significant improvement both on symptomatic and adjustment measures. Unfortunately the psychotherapy patients who could be reassessed at 2 years proved to be those who had already shown the most improvement at 1 year. This bias prevented a comparison between them and behavior therapy and waiting-list patients who were representative of their original samples. However, the results did indicate that the initial improvement was not a transitory phenomenon and was maintained by most patients without further supportive therapy between the 1- and 2-year assessments.

PROCESS VARIABLES AND OUTCOME

On the Truax dimensions behavior therapists were rated as providing significantly higher levels of accurate empathy and self-congruence and a significantly greater degree of interpersonal contact than the psychotherapists. Levels of warmth or unconditional positive regard were not significantly different between the two groups. None of these variables were correlated with degree of patient improvement.

The Lennard and Bernstein ratings showed that the topic discussed was more often initiated by the patient in psychotherapy and by the therapist in behavior therapy. None of the categories were significantly related to improvement on target symptoms, indicating that this difference in style might be simply that, with no important effect on the outcome of therapy.

Behavior therapists and their patients spent roughly equal amounts of time talking, in contrast to psychotherapy patients who talked about three times as much as their therapists. This too characterized behavioral therapists' greater control over and direct participation in therapy. In both treatments patients who spoke in longer utterances improved significantly more on their target symptoms than patients who spoke in short utterances.

CONTENT

Behavior therapists made more statements giving information not directed at the patient's problem than did psychotherapists. This indicated a greater readiness to answer the patient's questions directly, whereas psychotherapists tended to reflect such questions. Behavior therapists used more statements in the imperative mode directing the patient to do something. This is in keeping with the general impression that behavioral therapists are more directive than psychotherapists.

In the psychotherapy group, patients receiving fewer "clarifications" or "interpretive statements" improved significantly more than those receiving many, but this paradoxical result did not hold true for the behavior therapy patients.

PATIENT AND RELATIONSHIP CHARACTERISTICS
AND OUTCOME

There were interesting differences in the types of patients who responded to psychotherapy and to behavior therapy. Using a composite rating of target symptom changes as the criterion of improvement, we found that in psychotherapy patients with more severe pathology as measured on the MMPI improved less on their target symptoms than did initially relatively healthier patients. This was especially so for the hysteria and psychopathic deviate scales which often indicate antisocial acting-out behavior. For behavior therapy patients, on the other hand, the amount of improvement was much less affected by the general level of pathology as measured by the MMPI. Also behavior therapy patients with more initial pathology on acting-out scales improved more than those with lower scores on these scales. There was a consistent tendency for patients with relatively greater pathology on those MMPI scales to improve more with behavior therapy. These results were also true of a composite severity score of target symptoms plus MMPI pathology.

There was some tendency for psychotherapy patients with higher self-acceptance, greater self-control and sociability, and less neuroticism to show more symptomatic improvement than more disturbed patients. There was no such tendency for behavior therapy patients.

Relatively greater success in psychotherapy was associated with greater youth, higher intelligence, higher income, being female, being married, coming from a smaller family, and being not the firstborn. Although these results were not all statistically significant, they were much more marked and consistent for psychotherapy than behavior therapy. Psychotherapy patients improved more who were more liked by their therapists, who were rated as resembling the therapist's usual patients, and who were considered suitable for this treatment. This had no effect on the outcome of behavior therapy patients, but there was a tendency for the latter to improve more if their therapists felt comfortable with them and found them interesting.

CONCLUSIONS

There was rather clear evidence that therapy in general "works" and that the improvement of patients in therapy was not entirely due either to "spontaneous recovery" or to the placebo effect of the nonspecific aspects of therapy such as arousal of hope, expectation of help and an initial cathartic interview, which were also present for the control or minimal-treatment patients.

Behavior therapy was at least as effective and possibly more so than psychotherapy with the sort of moderately severe neuroses and personality disorders that are typical of clinical populations. This should help to dispel the impression that behavior therapy is useful only with phobias and "restricted" unitary problems. It is a *"generally useful treatment,"* and symptom substitution did not occur.

There was some suggestion that behavior therapy could effectively deal with a broader range of patients than could psychotherapy. Both treatments were apparently effective for the classical stereotype of the good patient: a young, well-educated woman who was verbal, intelligent, successful, and less severely disturbed to begin with. Her disorder tended toward neurosis and introversion rather than personality disorder or any kind of acting-out behavior. However, psychotherapists had more success with patients like this than those with opposite characteristics, whereas these differences did not seem to matter to behavior therapists, who tended to achieve more symptomatic improvement with disturbed acting-out patients than did the psychotherapists.

It is clear that behavior therapists and psychotherapists provided distinctive treatments. We were impressed with the similarity among therapists in each group. Differences between behavior therapists and psychotherapists were evident not only in their formulations of their patient's problem and their clinical strategies but also in their pattern of interaction with patients.

The patient–therapist relationship appeared to be a critical factor in the success of psychotherapy and important in behavior therapy too. Although Truax variables rated in therapy sessions were unrelated to outcome, patients in both groups who themselves reported higher levels of warmth, empathy, and genuineness in their therapists tended to show greater improvement. *Successful patients in both therapies rated the personal interaction with the therapist as the single most important part of their treatment.* Thus the personal interaction, the "relationship," may well have been the essential ingredient overshadowing differences of style and theoretical and technical approaches.

IMPLICATIONS FOR FUTURE RESEARCH

Of the two questions asked by Dr. Spitzer, namely what are the implications of this study for future research and practice, it is perhaps easier to answer the second. It is unlikely to have much effect on the practice of psychotherapy. Thus in the 15 years since Strupp and Bergin (1969) published their critical review of psychotherapy research in 1969, there is little evidence that any findings of any outcome study have had much influence on the *practice* of psychotherapy in the last decade, and certainly not our one. Some therapists might have been encouraged to do behavior therapy with patients without phobias, but in all probability they would have done this anyway. We stand in the same position today as we did when Colby (1969) commented on Strupp and Bergin's 1969 review that very few clinicians read or believed research studies and that it certainly had no effect on their practice of psychotherapy anyway. Change in therapeutic procedures seems more the produce of the imaginative conceptualization of clinicians than the results of psychotherapy studies, good or bad.

The study received both praise and blame. It might be instructive to review some of the critiques in considering implications for future research.

1. The major criticism was that the study focused on analytically oriented psychotherapy and behavior therapy as usually practiced, rather than limiting therapists to a few specific techniques. Similarly patients were not restricted to those with specific symptoms, but included the whole range of neurotic problem areas usually encountered in clinical practice. Use of such omnibus treatment packages with mixed patient groups makes it difficult to identify the critical variables producing change in specific patient behaviors.

This criticism is valid but of little practical significance for this study. In the first place one of the major aims was to see how well the two approaches, in the hands of experienced therapists, coped with everyday clinical problems —a hot issue in the late 1960s, when the study was conducted. Instead of restricting patients or therapies, attempts were made to define admissible techniques for each approach and to analyze tapes to determine empirically what therapists actually did in treatment. Extensive analyses were also conducted post hoc to evaluate the effect of specific techniques on specific problem areas.

More importantly from a practical point of view, the study could not have been done any other way. When asked to limit their treatment to a few specific techniques with patients with restricted problems, our therapists simply refused. This issue became whether it was worthwhile to do the study as it was done or to not do it at all. Thus, "if we had known then what we know now," we probably would have designed the study in much the same way. This points out the main difficulty of doing clinical research, namely that every study must depart from the ideal because of the practical realities of getting the study done. This does not justify poorly designed studies, but does affect the kinds of research questions that can be asked. These problems have led many to analogue research where technique and subject characteristics are more readily controlled. However, such studies risk throwing the baby out with the bath water, and their results may have little relevance for a clinical population. Advances in measurement techniques make it increasingly possible to gain useful information from studies of real therapists with real patients. We believe that this is the only way to go. On the other hand, how far to go with increasingly rigorous methodology aided by "a cookbook or two" (May, 1974) or a manual or two becomes problematical. The "conflict between research demands of reproducibility and standardization" and the clinician's need for "flexibility, creativity, and sensitivity" (APA Commission on Psychotherapies, 1982, p. 224) may in fact never be reconciled.

2. The correlations between the ratings made by the different types of assessors (self, therapist, significant other, and independent assessor) are close to zero, suggesting either the different goals of these assessors or the possible unreliability of the measures (Bergin & Lambert, 1978).

Partially false, partially true. Only the therapists' correlations were very low—.13, .21, and .04—with ratings made by assessors, patients, and informants respectively. The ratings of assessors were significantly correlated with the patient ($r = .65$; $p < .001$) and with the informant ($r = .40$, $p < .01$) The patient and the informant also showed lower agreement ($r = .25$). We believe that these relatively low correlations did support the hypothesis that different raters might have different goals in treatment or use different criteria for improvement.

However, the informant who correlated poorly with the patient often did not have a close enough relationship *through time* with the patient. A "meaningful other" at one time in a young population might have had much less contact later on. Parents certainly were not able to report much of sexual and interpersonal behavior, and were often unaware of what the patient's target symptoms were. Ideally, one might have a stable marital situation with a faithful spouse reporting every detail. Such marriages are rare in a psychiatric population and even rarer in California. Possibly, as Kazdin and Wilson (1978) suggest, the ratings are unreliable. However, we think these other vagaries are more important.

To us these findings underlined the necessity of having multiple vantage points to view the outcome of therapy. The therapist's concept of outcome will be influenced by his or her goals, and much research has certainly shown that these are quite often discordant from those of the patient and may be colored by countertransference feelings.

3. Our follow-up data were of little value because patients and treatments were confounded by the time of the follow-up assessment (Bergin & Lambert, 1978).

True and false. It is true that groups were confounded, but not that follow-up data were of little value. Ethics demanded treatment after 4 months. It is difficult to stop treatment arbitrarily for someone who still needs treatment. At the 4-month assessment the groups were relatively pure but between 4 months and 1 year many patients became involved in other treatment, vitiating the comparison among original treatment groups. However, the main purpose of the 1- and 2-year follow-ups was to determine if the 4-month gains remained stable. The pattern of change between 4 months and 1 year did appear to be consolidation of improvement shown during the first 4 months. At 2 years, attrition led to only 61 persons being followed up. At this time the great majority of patients in all groups had increased or maintained significant improvement on both symptomatic and adjustment measures. Only seven of these patients had any substantial amounts of therapy since their 1-year assessment, yet there were few relapses and many had continued to improve, which was clear evidence that the earlier significant improvement was neither transitory nor maintained only by continued supportive therapy.

Such follow-ups are essential in psychotherapy research even if clear comparisons of original treatment groups cannot be made. Many patients will continue to obtain help—either formal therapy or informal sources of support in the community. The latter may at times be more influential than the 1 hour per week spent with the therapist, and should be carefully documented.

4. Process observations were limited to a single interview and in the case of the Truax variables to four 4-minute samples of this interview (Bergin & Lambert, 1978).

True. We had intended to sample three interviews, one each in early, middle, and late therapy, but were outwitted by gremlins. Studies which show changes in process measures during the course of therapy illustrate the importance of frequent sampling.

CONSIDERATIONS FOR FUTURE RESEARCH

The Efficacy of Minimal-Contact Therapy

The minimal contact afforded the control group in our study proved to be surprisingly helpful to them. Seventy-seven percent were considered by the independent assessor on a global judgment to be improved or recovered. On many measures of outcome, these patients showed significant improvement equal to that of treated groups. These patients received an initial assessment interview, a test battery, and periodic phone calls during the 4 months to maintain contact.

These results suggest that future studies might be designed to determine the minimum amount of intervention necessary to produce results equivalent to those produced by full-scale therapy. Minimal treatment could be defined in terms of therapist training or experience, amount of patient contact, length of treatment, depth of interaction, and so on. Such studies could provide information with both practical applications (particularly in conjunction with a cost–benefit analysis) and theoretical import (what is necessary for change to occur).

The whole issue of control groups in psychotherapy research is a difficult one. The basic problem is to determine what specific things we want to control for: amount of patient contact, certain therapeutic techniques, expectation of improvement, or what have you. A recent review (Prioleau, Murdoch, & Brody, 1983) has suggested that the only appropriate control for psychotherapy effectiveness is a placebo group, and judged by this standard there is no evidence that psychotherapy works with real patients. Use of a placebo control seems appealing at first glance, but is not as practical or straightforward as it appears. First, since the active ingredients of psychotherapy remain largely unknown, it is difficult to design an appropriate placebo control. There is no clear parallel of a chemically inert pill in a double-blind study for use in psychotherapy research. One man's placebo may be another's active ingredient.

Use of treatments that are not specific for the particular disorder, those that may be helpful but not the treatment of choice, or group discussions that avoid the targeted problem area may have more relevance for determining the role of potential active ingredients than for evaluating the efficacy of therapy per se. If, for example, use of interpretations making the parent–transference link is critical for success in short-term analytic therapy, as Malan (1973) suggests, then an appropriate control group would be one in which the therapist treats the patient similarly but withholds the "active ingredient," the making of the parent–transference link. This type of control might be considered placebo therapy by some and not by others, but would provide valuable information on the role of parent–transference interpretations. Whether skilled experienced therapists would or could do this is questionable. Such controls might prove an insuperable shackle to their skills.

Second, in these days of patients' rights and extensive informed-consent documents, it is difficult to manipulate patients' expectations of control treatments. A study we are currently conducting compares patients treated by psychotherapy or by a psychoactive drug, or by a drug placebo. In both the active and placebo drug groups, patients must be told that they may or may not be receiving a drug that will likely be helpful: neither group can be told that what they are receiving will provide effective treatment. Therefore, this placebo group is not, strictly speaking, receiving placebo therapy.

The Relationship

Whatever the modality of therapy, the patients considered that the relationship with the therapist who provided encouragement, advice, and reassurance was the most crucial in both the therapies. Frank, a staunch advocate of these "nonspecific" ingredients of all therapies, believes that they raise the patients' morale to try new ways of coping with their difficulties (Frank, 1969).

All psychotherapy patients who improved more were more liked by their therapists, but this did not obtain for behavior therapy. However, there was a tendency for behavior therapy patients to improve more where the therapist felt comfortable with them and found them interesting. Moreover, patient and therapist ratings need to be made fairly early in therapy; when they are made at the end of the therapy the therapist might be likely to like a patient because the patient improved just as the patient might improve as an indirect result of the therapist's liking him or her.

This suggests that future studies must pay particular attention to the relationship—how the patient thinks about the therapist, and vice versa. Whether these are expressed in transference–countertransference terms or some other nomenclature seems to be immaterial.

Variations of Severity of Symptoms

The suggestion that behavior therapists in our study dealt successfully with greater psychopathology and acting-out syndromes suggests that future research might well be directed to exploring these variables.

Style Differences

The considerable difference in style between the behavior therapists and the psychotherapists suggests that the temple of truth can be approached, and perhaps also reached, by apparently widely differing pathways. How much such process variables might be overshadowed by something as important as the "relationship" is another matter. Nevertheless, we were impressed by the great similarity in style among the behavior therapists, although they expressed some divergent views with each other, and its sharp contrast with that of the psychotherapists.

Skill and Experience

Although we examined to some extent the effect of the experience of the therapist on therapeutic outcome, we had poorer measures of skill. Certainly there seems little evidence to date that the experience of the therapist after a certain period of time is very important. However, it seems implausible to us that the skill is not important. In most fields of human endeavor the skilled person does better than the unskilled or those of modest accomplishments. Whether rigorous methodology with unskilled if experienced therapists will ever reveal the truth is questionable. We would like to see studies with experienced and skilled therapists compared to experienced and nonskilled. In the absence of better criteria for skill, a peer review might suffice. In every community there are many qualified experienced therapists to whom colleagues are reluctant to refer patients and, conversely, others in whom they have great confidence. This may be misplaced or well placed, but perhaps the best we can go on at present.

Particular Techniques

Our finding that the more frequent interpretations in brief analytically oriented therapy were associated with less improvement was anticipated by Malan by more than a decade (Malan, 1963). He found that the frequency of undirected interpretations was negatively correlated with improvement. The reasons for this are not clear. It may be that too-frequent interpretations evoke resistance in patients. Alternatively, therapists may attempt to stimulate patients who have little insight or inclination to look into psychological causes of their own behavior by increasing the frequency of interpretive statements. Such patients are less likely to improve.

Although the crucial role of transference interpretation and resolution is a widely held belief in psychoanalysis, there is a dearth of data both in this and in analytically oriented therapy. Malan did in fact find a significant relationship between better outcome of treatment and frequency of the transference–parent link interpretation in brief analytically oriented therapy. By this he referred to a transference interpretation linking the therapist with the patient's relationship with is parents or significant figures. He later replicated this study with another sample of patients using independent judges (Malan, 1976). These studies have been criticized, since the frequency with which such transference statements are noted by therapists may depend on a number of factors and the relationship has yet to be replicated using direct measures of actual therapy sessions. Nevertheless, this remains a promising avenue for further work. Such studies would need to define precisely what the transference interpretation and resolution were and to use broadly based measures of outcome as have been advocated by many writers.

Finally, throughout the psychotherapy literature there remains a search for the symbolic "ring," that elusive technique that carries with it the power to change patients' lives. In the mists of Wagnerian mysticism, we believe that it will remain elusive. If indeed it is found, might it fit only a Procrustean finger?

In conclusion, I recall the no doubt apocryphal story of the famous American Professor, Dr. Smart, who visited the famous British Professor of Psychiatry, Sir Acerbic, in London. Sir Acerbic said, "I understand, Professor Smart, that you spent a mere 6 months in clinical psychiatry. Do you feel that that is a sufficient background for research in the area?" Professor Smart replied, "Sir Acerbic, anybody with half a mind who spent half a month in clinical psychiatry has enough unsolved research problems to last him the rest of his life." Sir Acerbic could not but smile.

REFERENCES

APA Commission on Psychotherapies. *Psychotherapy research: Methodological and efficacy issues.* Washington, D.C.: American Psychiatric Association, 1982.

Bergin, A. E., & Lambert, M. J. The evaluation of therapeutic outcomes. In S. L. Garfield & A. E. Bergin (Eds.), *Handbook of psychotherapy and behavior change: An empirical analysis* (2nd ed.). New York: Wiley, 1978.

Colby, K. M. Researchers are weeded out. *International Journal of Psychiatry,* 1969, 7(3), 116–117.

Frank, J. D. Common features account for effectiveness. *International Journal of Psychiatry,* 1969, 7(3), 122–127.

Kazdin, A. E., & Wilson, G. T. *Evaluation of behavior therapy: Issues, evidence, and research strategies.* Cambridge, Mass.: Ballinger, 1978.

Malan, D. H. *A study of brief psychotherapy.* London: Tavistock, 1963.

Malan, D. H. The outcome problem in psychotherapy research. *Archives of General Psychiatry,* 1973, 29, 719–729.

Malan, D. H. *Toward the validation of dynamic psychotherapy: A replication.* New York: Plenum, 1976.

May, P. R. A. Psychotherapy research in schizophrenia—Another view of present reality. *Schizophrenia Bulletin,* summer 1974, 126–132.

Prioleau, L., Murdoch, M., & Brody, N. An analysis of psychotherapy vs. placebo studies. *Behavioral and Brain Sciences,* 1983, 6(2), 275–310.

Sloane, R. B., Staples, F. R., Cristol, A. H., Yorkston, N., & Whipple, K. *Psychotherapy versus behavior therapy. A Commonwealth Fund publication.* Cambridge, Mass.: Harvard University Press, 1975.

Strupp, H. H., & Bergin, A. E. Some empirical and conceptual bases for coordinated research in psychotherapy: A critical review of issues, trends, and evidence. *International Journal of Psychiatry,* 1969, 7(2), 18–90.

COMMENTARY

Dr. George Gardos[*]*:* Was I correct in understanding that you had 77% improvement on the waiting list?

Dr. Sloane: I think it was 77% on a global improvement scale, yes.

Dr. Gardos: It seems to me there is a major problem with baseline, which I suppose is probably true in a lot of studies. But when you have that kind of an improvement rate on baseline, maybe the best thing to do is a discriminant function analysis between the people who improve versus the people who don't improve, and assign only the people who didn't improve to therapy, to try and find out why your waiting list is such a powerful therapeutic tool! (*Laughter.*)

[*]McLean Hospital, Belmont, Massachusetts.

Probably a lot of studies, not just in psychotherapy research, have a problem with baseline, because once you have people enter a study at their most symptomatic, it is very difficult to disentangle specific from nonspecific factors. Maybe some other kind of design might be more conducive to demonstrating the power of your therapy technique: one that first allows nonspecific improvement to take place and then measures baseline, which in episodic or chronic conditions is not the peak of a particular condition, but more an average.

Dr. Sloane: Yes. I do want to stress that although you might call this a baseline, it really was minimal therapy. But I agree that this is the sort of study that should follow after it; you start them all again after 4 months.

13

A Phase II Study of Cognitive Therapy of Depression

A. JOHN RUSH
University of Texas Health Science Center

This chapter has two major objectives. The first is to review the background, context, major results, and problems of execution and interpretation in our previous study comparing cognitive therapy with imipramine (Rush, Beck, Kovacs, & Hollon, 1977). The second is to discuss the implications of this study for future research and to put it in context in terms of the developmental steps of psychotherapy research as a whole.

Our initial study was conducted in 1973–1976 at the University of Pennsylvania in collaboration with Drs. Beck, Kovacs, and Hollon. It came at a time when two prior studies had already shown that supportive group therapy (Covi, Lipman, Derogatis, Smith, & Pattison, 1974) and marital therapy (Friedman, 1975) did little to reduce symptomatology in depressed outpatients. Interpersonal therapy (Klerman, DiMascio, Weissman, Prusoff, & Paykel, 1974) improved social adjustment of depressed patients. At that time, several years had been invested in developing and refining particular techniques that became known as cognitive therapy for depression. These techniques had been standardized, placed in a treatment manual (Beck, Rush, Shaw, & Emery, 1979), and subsequently refined by many hours of interaction between the therapists under Dr. Beck's supervision. This approach was derived from Beck's many years of clinical work with depressed patients. This codification of treatment methods allowed, for the first time, clear definitions of therapist behavior that fell under the rubric of a cognitive approach to depression. The question at hand was whether this particular treatment package either (1) reduced depressive symptomatology or (2) provided prophylaxis—two objectives predicted by cognitive theory (Beck, 1976; Beck & Rush, 1978).

Table 1 provides a brief overview of the four potential major objectives of psychotherapy (Rush, 1983c). While cognitive techniques can also be used to reduce the consequences of a prior medical or psychiatric disorder,

Table 1. Objectives of Psychotherapy

A. Symptom reduction
   1. Direct symptom change: behavior therapy
      (Example: Modify contingencies for bedwetting)
   2. Indirect symptom change: interpersonal therapy
      (Example: Clarify patients' response to ongoing role conflict to reduce depression)
B. Prophylaxis: Modify factors that contribute to relapse
   1. Behavior therapy: Improve social skills
   2. Cognitive therapy: Modify silent assumptions or schemata
   3. Supportive therapy: Reduce environmental stresses and increase access to resources
C. Reduction of secondary consequences of the disorder
   1. Marital therapy: Marital tensions that have resulted from the illness (e.g., manic–depressive illness)
   2. Occupational or skill training to increase employability of previously psychotic patients
D. Increase compliance with pharmacotherapy
   1. Provide information about treatment and illness
   2. Provide direct "rewards" for compliance
   3. Change attitudes about medication and/or the disorder
   4. Use a cuing or reminder system for medication taking

Note. The examples provided for each major objective are exemplars. Other techniques or treatments not listed may also accomplish one or more of the above objectives.

as well as to increase compliance, the objectives to be evaluated in this study were symptom reduction and subsequent prophylaxis.

To answer these two questions, a contrast or comparison group was needed. Only a few analogue studies of cognitive therapy in nonpsychiatric patient populations had been conducted or were ongoing at that time (see below). This lack of efficacy data for cognitive therapy in a psychiatric population led us to compare cognitive therapy against a standard active treatment as the most appropriate and ethical design. Furthermore, this two-cell comparison required the lowest number of patients to reveal the *ineffectiveness* of cognitive therapy. Since the standard in the field for the treatment of moderately to moderately–severely depressed outpatients was tricyclic antidepressant medications, we chose to contrast the cognitive treatment package with a standard antidepressant drug, namely imipramine (Morris & Beck, 1974). Should the symptom-reducing powers of cognitive therapy not equal or exceed that of imipramine in depressed psychiatric outpatients, then only one question would remain—whether prophylaxis ensued following termination of treatment. That is, this initial study was designed to reveal the *ineffectiveness of* cognitive therapy.

To put the study in further context, the technology to measure circulating blood levels of imipramine and desipramine was not available at the time of the start of this study. Furthermore, the question of whether there is a therapeutic window or lower threshold level for circulating levels of imipramine and/or its metabolites was unanswered at that time and remains controversial even today. Thus, blood level determinations for the tricyclic-treated group were not conducted.

Let us review briefly the study itself and its results. The initial report involved 41 subjects, 19 of whom were assigned to cognitive therapy and 22 of whom were assigned to pharmacotherapy. At the time of the initial report (Rush *et al.*, 1977), 18 had completed cognitive therapy and 14 had completed pharmacotherapy. This sample was subsequently expanded so that 18 completers in cognitive therapy and 17 in pharmacotherapy were finally obtained—in order to obtain a sizable sample for the ensuing 1-year follow-up (Kovacs, Rush, Beck, & Hollon, 1981). However, the results relevant to symptom reduction are equivalent whether one uses the expanded or the initial sample.

What sorts of subjects were involved in this study? These were all psychiatric outpatients, two-thirds of whom were female, who were seen at the University of Pennsylvania Outpatient Clinic. Most patients had multiple prior episodes of depression and a high incidence of suicidal ideation. A little less than half the sample had been in their current depressive episode for over a year. *All patients were required to have both a 17-item Hamilton Rating Scale for Depression (HRSD) score of at least 14 and a 21-item Beck Depression Inventory (BDI) of at least 20.* A history of a poor response to an adequate trial of tricyclic antidepressants, as well as medical contraindications to antidepressant treatment, constituted bases for exclusion. Evidence of hallucinations or delusions, bipolar illness, or severe depression that required hospitalization excluded some patients as well. Finally, patients had to agree to accept either of two treatments, which were randomly assigned.

The population on the average was in their mid-30s, and about one-fifth reported psychiatric hospitalization in the past. All cases would have met the DSM-II description for neurotic depression, although a number of patients showed some evidence of endogenous symptoms, such as reduced weight, appetite, sleep, and libido. However, Research Diagnostic Criteria for endogenous symptomatology were not employed that time (Spitzer, Endicott, & Robins, 1978).

The treatment consisted of cognitive therapy dispensed over roughly 12 weeks to a maximum of 20 individual 50-minute sessions. Pharmacotherapy was dispensed over 12 individual once-a-week 20-minute sessions. Pharmacotherapy included imipramine in a flexible dose usually given once a day that ranged between 75 and 250 mg. Maximum dose was maintained up to week 10; weeks 11 and 12 were used to taper and discontinue the medication.

Hamilton Rating Scales for Anxiety and Depression (Hamilton, 1959, 1960, 1967), the Raskin Depression Scale (Raskin, Schulterbrandt, Reatig, & McKeon, 1970), and the 21-item BDI (Beck, Ward, Mendelson, Mock, &

Erbaugh, 1961), as well as other scales, were used to determine outcome. Considering the full sample of 35 completers (Kovacs *et al.*, 1981), a differential attrition rate was found with cognitive therapy losing only 5% and pharmacotherapy losing 32% of patients assigned to treatment. The majority of those who left treatment did so between the first and fourth weeks of treatment. The 32% loss from pharmacotherapy compares very well with other studies of tricyclics in depressed outpatients. McLean and Hakstian (1979) also found a lower attrition rate with a behavioral–cognitive approach than with amitriptyline. However, a more recent study (Blackburn, Bishop, Glen, Whalley, & Christie, 1981) did not find that attrition was lower with cognitive compared to antidepressant treatment.

Patients completing cognitive therapy had on the average five more treatment sessions than patients who completed chemotherapy as a result of the initial design. However, the duration of treatment did not distinguish the two groups (about 75 days). The average maximum daily dose of imipramine was 215.6 mg prior to tapering.

A series of one-way analyses of covariance revealed a significant advantage to cognitive therapy based on the BDI ($F_{1,31} = 6.67, p < .02$) and on the 17-item HRSD ($F_{1,25} = 5.83$, $p < .02$). Trends favoring cognitive therapy were obtained with the Raskin Scale ($F_{1,27} = 3.89, p < .06$) and the Hamilton Anxiety Scale ($F_{1,23} = 3.75$, $p < .07$). Also the above findings were based on actual scores without end-point analysis.

End-point analysis further accentuated the effects in favor of cognitive therapy. Using end-point analysis, the BDI, the HRSD, and the Raskin Scale all very significantly favored cognitive therapy over imipramine (Kovacs *et al.*, 1981).

Finally, we attempted in retrospective analysis to determine whether the presence of endogenous symptoms or endogenomorphic depression as defined by Klein (1974) might distinguish responders and nonresponders in each of the two groups. However, this was a reconstruction of the endogenomorphic status based on several items chosen by Dr. Klein (items 5–9, 16, 18, 23) from the HRSD at initial evaluation. Thus, each subject was given an endogenomorphic score. These scores ranged from 4 to 13, with a median of 8. Those who completed cognitive therapy had a mean score of 8.33 ± 1.24, whereas dropouts from cognitive therapy had only 4.0 ± 0.00. Completers in pharmacotherapy had a mean score of 8.82 ± 2.24 and dropouts averaged 8.50 ± 1.51. A median split based on the full sample was developed with a cutoff score of 8 or less or 9 and above. A two-way analysis of variance showed no main effect for treatment assignment, for termination status, and no interaction effect between the two. Thus, an endogenomorphic score was not predictive of whether the patient would complete the protocol.

The three-way analyses of variance using the BDI and Raskin Scale at termination showed a main effect for treatment and termination status, but no main effect for endogenomorphicity. In addition, a three-way analysis of variance on the BDI data revealed an interaction between treatment and termination status and between termination status and endogenomorphic classification. However, these interactions were not significant on the Raskin Scale data. High endogenomorphic patients who completed treatment had the lowest self-rated depressive symptomatology at the end of the trial and did better in both cells than those with low endogenomorphic scores at initiation of treatment. Thus, overall endogenomorphic score was not *differentially* predictive of good or poor outcome, but a higher score was suggestive of a better outcome in both treatment cells.

Follow-up study over the ensuing year was reported by Kovacs et al. (1981). In summary, there was suggestive but not convincing evidence that cognitive therapy induced prophylaxis for at least some patients who initially responded to this treatment. Tables 2, 3, and 4 summarize these published data. Perhaps the most convincing of these data are those showing that the risk of relapse ratio was a little over 2:1 no matter how risk of relapse was defined. One year following treatment termination, the BDI, but not the HRSD, distinguished these two groups at that point in time.

Let us turn now to the question of putting this study into hypothetical historical context. To accomplish this task, we need a model for how psychotherapies aimed at symptom reduction might be developed (Table 5). This model is based on the assumption that no single psychotherapy study is sufficient either to develop the treatment package or to document efficacy and is restricted to symptom-reducing psychotherapies. In addition, while analogy to drug development is suggested, there are specific differences between developing and testing a drug and a psychotherapy. Phase I drug studies are conducted in normal controls to identify side effects and to ensure safety. The agent that enters a phase I drug study has already been shown to have central

Table 2. Cumulative Relapse in 1-Year Follow-Up for Patients Who Completed Treatment[a]

Definition of relapse met at any point during 1-year follow-up	Treatment assignment	Follow-up classification		χ^2	Ri ratio
		Relapse	No relapse		
Depressed[b]	Cognitive therapy	7	11	2.33	2.11
	Chemotherapy	11	6		
Received psychiatric–psychological treatment	Cognitive therapy	9	9	2.62	2.09
	Chemotherapy	13	4		
Met either definition	Cognitive therapy	10	8	2.91	2.14
	Chemotherapy	14	3		
Met both definitions	Cognitive therapy	6	12	2.29	2.19
	Chemotherapy	10	7		

[a]Taken from Kovacs, Rush, Beck, & Hollon (1981).
[b]Patient had a BDI score of 16 or greater. The values are based on constant or proportionate risk in each group.

Table 3. Clinical Status at End of Treatment and 1-Year Follow-Up of Patients Who Completed Protocol[a]

State of depression[b] and time of assessment	Cognitive therapy (n = 18)	Chemotherapy (n = 17)
No clinical symptomatology		
End of treatment	15	5
12-month follow-up	12	6
Mild symptomatology		
End of treatment	2	7
12-month follow-up	4	5
Moderate–severe symptomatology		
End of treatment	1	5
12-month follow-up	2	5
Unknown		
End of treatment	0	0
12-month follow-up	0	1

[a]Taken from Kovacs, Rush, Beck, & Hollon (1981).
[b]No clinical symptomatology indicates a BDI score of 9 or less; mild symptomatology, a BDI score between 10 and 15; and moderate–severe symptomatology, a BDI score of 16 or greater.

nervous system (CNS) activity. Furthermore, a fair idea as to the ultimate target population has been formed from various animal laboratory screening tests. Thus, at the start of a phase I drug trial, activity is better documented than is safety. I would argue that the psychotherapy analogue to phase I drug trials consists of the earliest attempts to find one or more psychotherapy techniques derived from a psychological model that have any effect in single-case studies of students or patients. In essence, in psychotherapy the analogue of animal laboratory work done to identify drug activity must be done in humans with mild or significant problems. Just as in pharmacologic screening, a theo-

Table 4. One-Year Longitudinal Clinical Course of Patients Who Completed Treatment[a]

Clinical course of depression[b]	Cognitive therapy (n = 18)	Chemotherapy (n = 17)
Remission	10	6
Intermittently symptomatic	5	5
Chronically symptomatic	3	6

[a]Taken from Kovacs, Rush, Beck, & Hollon (1981).
[b]Remission indicates no BDI score greater than or equal to 16; intermittently symptomatic, less than 50% of the BDI scores were greater than or equal to 16; and chronically symptomatic, 50% or more of the BDI scores were greater than or equal to 16.

Table 5. Hypothetical Development of Psychosocial Treatments Aimed at Symptom Reduction

Phase I		
Clinical work	Identify techniques	Experimental investigation
Open trials in patient groups (single cases) →	Several treatment strategies are identified and packaged and patient groups specified	← Open trials in analogue studies (single cases)
	↓	
Early phase II		
Selection of techniques →	Package revised; technique ordered	← Selection of techniques; new techniques identified
	↓	
Single-case psychiatric patients →	Test package in patient groups (i.e., open trial)	Compare to waiting list in ← analogue groups
	↓	
Replicate initial findings with active → control groups	Specify objectives and target group for package	
Late phase II	↓	
	Test against active standard if available	
	↓	
	Further comparisons with active treatments	
Phase III	↓	
	Psychotherapy contrast and placebo control conditions	Develop and test ← training methods and assess transmissibility of techniques
Phase IV	↓	
	Assess generalizability of findings	

retical experimental model guides the conduct of this level of investigation. That is, one begins with a theory and works with both patients one at a time and analogue populations, such as depressed students, in order to develop and define particular techniques, to discard those techniques that are ineffective, and to gradually shape a treatment package. In addition, one searches for negative effects of treatment. For example, in cognitive therapy we found that certain strategies made delusional patients worse (Hole, Rush, & Beck, 1979).

After phase I, safety continues to be an issue as does dose in drug development. Thus, open-label dose-finding studies are conducted in early phase II drug trials. This phase is analogous to testing, revising, and retesting a preliminary psychotherapeutic treatment package in open-label analogue (student) and in single-case psychiatry patient studies. One is trying to define the nature, structure, and content of the treatment package. I would call this early phase II. Since the treatment package is undergoing revision, and efficacy is not yet well established, single-case studies are still called in for psychiatric patients. However, waiting-list or nonspecific treatment controls can be used in analogue studies. In mid-phase II development, the treatment is being tested in patient populations for final refining before comparative efficacy studies are conducted. This open-label testing was done with cognitive therapy in a prior report (Rush, Beck, Kovacs, Khatami, & Wolman, 1975). It was in this report that we found that treatment twice a week for the first 4 weeks showed more favorable results than treatment once a week (see Figure 1), although treatment assignment was not randomized in this developmental protocol.

Once the treatment package has been finalized, one contrasts this package (now in the form of a rather detailed treatment manual) against another active treatment and/or a credible placebo. For drugs once activity, safety, and dose are known, one also proceeds to a contrast test condition.

Figure 1. Once versus twice weekly cognitive therapy.

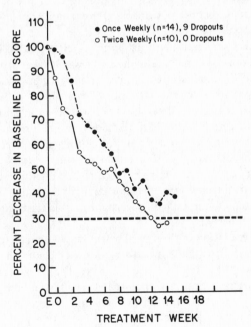

With drugs, the control is a placebo initially (late phase II). This placebo group is used to control for expectations, the act of intervening, milieu, natural remission, and so on. Subsequently, another standard active drug and a placebo cell are used in phase III trials. This second (active drug) contrast group is used to gauge relative efficacy and safety (i.e., does the new agent measure up to what is available?).

In psychotherapy, depending on the objectives of the treatment, one is confronted with the need for at least two comparison groups. The first comparison would logically be a placebo to control for the effects of expectation, natural remission, and the like. However, finding such a "placebo" for psychotherapy, or psuedo psychotherapy, is not an easy task. Furthermore, this placebo would only be indicated if one had preliminary data that the psychotherapy package was "active." The second comparison group needed is a standard treatment to answer the question of whether the package had activity that was at least close to available treatments. Thus, ideally a four-cell design is needed (psychotherapy package, standard treatment, placebo for standard treatment, placebo for psychotherapy). Obviously, the expense is too great at this phase of development. Since cognitive therapy was alleged to reduce symptoms, the least expensive way to test this hypothesis in a preliminary manner was to compare the therapy with an established active treatment (imipramine). Given the well-known fact that doing anything is more effective than doing nothing (that is, a waiting list contrast condition typically fares more poorly than active treatment no matter what form of treatment), we decided to exclude a waiting list condition in this phase II trial.

Previous case studies (Rush, Khatami, & Beck, 1975; Rush & Beck, 1978) were indicative of some treatment effect with this approach. If we had chosen a two-cell comparison (cognitive therapy versus waiting list) and found efficacy greater than waiting list, the question still would have remained as to the degree of efficacy in comparison to available alternative treatments. Furthermore, it would have made it more difficult to get Human Experimentation Committee permission for a three-cell study (drugs, waiting list, and cognitive therapy), as that would still be viewed by most as two placebos against one active treatment—that is, as unethical and too risky. On the other hand, if cognitive therapy fared well against an active drug contrast group, then fewer ethical concerns would be raised about the above three- or four-cell designs.

The logical extension of this initial work was, of course, to proceed with further studies of this treatment in settings unrelated to the place of origin, to determine whether the initial finding could be replicated, and to add contrast or control comparison groups. Since that time, several studies have been conducted, many of which appear to show that cognitive therapy or behavioral cognitive techniques at least equal the efficacy of antidepressant medication and, depending upon the particular patient population (Blackburn *et al.*, 1981), may even exceed the effects of antidepressant medication. Table 6 enumerates these studies and their overall results in psychiatric patients treated with individual cognitive therapy. The efficacy of cognitive therapy in a group format has also been evaluated (Taylor & Marshall, 1977; Shaw, 1977; Rush & Watkins, 1981) with findings indicative of effect in this format, although perhaps individual therapy is more effective than group treatment (Rush & Watkins, 1981).

Three additional studies in Baltimore (Drs. Covi and Lipman), Minneapolis (Dr. Hollon), and St. Louis (Dr. Murphy), have been conducted, but the results are not yet published. In addition, Dr. Beck's group has compared cognitive therapy alone with cognitive therapy plus amitriptyline for acute symptom reduction and prophylaxis. Preliminary results of this study appear to suggest that the addition of amitriptyline does not further augment the effect of cognitive therapy alone (Beck *et al.*, 1979). These findings are in agreement with a small study we conducted at the University of Oklahoma (Rush & Watkins, 1981) and with the findings of Blackburn and colleagues (Blackburn *et al.*, 1981; Blackburn & Bishop, 1981) in depressed general-practice outpatients.

Table 6. Individual Therapy—Clinic Patients

Study	Measures	Treatment	Sessions		Results
			n	Weeks	
Schmickley (1976)	BDI, MMPI ($n = 11$)	1. Cognitive modification	4	2	Within-subject improvement
Rush, Beck, Kovacs, & Hollon (1977)	BDI, HRSD ($n = 41$)	1. CT 2. Imipramine	20	11	CT > imipramine
Beck, Rush, Shaw, & Emery (1979)	BDI, HRSD ($n = 26$)	1. CT 2. CT + A	20	12	CT = CT + A
McLean & Hakstian (1979)[a]	BDI, DACL ($n = 154$)	1. A 2. RT 3. BC 4. I	10	10	BC > A = RT I
Blackburn, Bishop, Glen, Whalley, & Christie (1981)	BDI, HRSD ($n = 64$)	1. CT 2. Med 3. Comb	16–17	12–15	Hospital clinic: comb > CT = med General Practice: CT = comb > med

Note. Explanation of abbreviations: MMPI, Minnesota Multiphasic Personality Inventory; DACL, Depression Adjective Check List; CT, cognitive therapy; BC, behavioral–cognitive therapy; A, amitriptyline; comb, combination; med, medication; I, insight therapy; RT, relaxation training.

[a]Included community volunteers and clinic patients.

Whether cognitive therapy offers advantages over other forms of psychotherapy is unknown. Only one study (McLean & Hakstian, 1979) has compared a behavioral–cognitive approach (not a treatment following the Beck manual exactly, but a similar approach to depression involving cognitions, behaviors, and homework) to other psychotherapies (relaxation training and insight therapy). In this study, both relaxation training and the behavioral–cognitive therapy exceeded the effects of amitriptyline, and all exceeded the effects of insight therapy. While design and execution problems (e.g., using newspaper respondents, the lowish and less flexible drug dosing pattern, etc.) preclude making strong generalizations from this study one can infer that either the form (e.g., degree of structure) or the content of a psychotherapy will lead to differences in outcome.

RETROSPECTIVE REGRETS AND FUTURE HOPES

Looking back on this study from the perspective of several years, I still do not think that a third comparison condition, such as relaxation training, to control for therapist exposure, therapy structure, homework, and number of treatment sessions would have been ethically justifiable in this first study. Obviously without this comparison, the interpretation of our results is complex. As it turned out, cognitive therapy exceeded the effects of imipramine, which reduced the number of interpretations available. Had cognitive therapy only equaled the imipramine, or come close to but not quite equaled that of imipramine, the interpretation of our initial study would have been even more complex. A third treatment cell would have been justifiable in terms of cost and patient risk only if previous comparative studies had shown some efficacy of cognitive therapy in reducing symptoms. At the time of the study, no such data were available. It is obviously premature to try to control for nonspecific factors that might produce symptom reduction, when the psychotherapy package itself had not been shown to be effective at all. Thus, ethical considerations argued against adding this third cell *at the time*.

A second criticism is that we tapered patients off imipramine over the last 2 weeks of the study. Only one patient in the pharmacotherapy group worsened during this tapering. Thus, the tapering is not likely to have caused the result. Follow-up studies after termination of medication treatment by Weissman and associates (Weissman & Kasl, 1976; Weissman, Kasl, & Klerman, 1976; Weissman, Prusoff, & Klerman, 1978; Paykel, DiMascio, Klerman, Prusoff, & Weissman, 1976; Paykel, DiMascio, Haskell, & Prusoff, 1975) also suggests that relapse following discontinuation of antidepressant medications is not acute. In fact, the relapse rate in the first months off drug is virtually identical to that seen in the eighth or even the twelfth month off drug in their extensive outpatient follow-up study. We did wish to stop both active treatments at the same time to allow equivalent times between treatment termination and the 1-year follow-up, and to equate the two groups at termination with regard to the knowledge that treatment was ending (i.e., to avoid bias with regard to differential expectations about treatment status).

The study has also been criticized because of our failure to use antidepressants of clinician's choice. While Blackburn *et al.* (1981) have taken this factor into account in their study by allowing the physician to choose the antidepressant, one can still argue that that physician's choice would not equal that of a skilled psychopharmacologist doing clinical practice. This, however, is limitation of all clinical research studies in which one must control or restrict each treatment condition and, thereby, to reflect actual clinical practice only incompletely. In addition, by allowing clinicians to use first one antidepressant and then another should the first fail (a situation that is typical in clinical practice), one is attempting to maximize antidepressant drug effect. This argument should then allow for additional strategies to maximize the effect of cognitive therapy—for example, seeing patients three times a week, involving more of the couple or family social system immediately in treatment, the extensive use of milieu therapy during treatment, and so on. Thus, we were at the time comparing a reasonable standard of practice, although not an exact replica of all practitioners with regard to imipramine, and a reasonable standard of cognitive therapy. Neither treatment cell would or could reflect the wide variations in practice that different clinicians employ, given particular patients.

Another concern is that we studied drug-resistant patients, therapy artificially making cognitive therapy look too good. The diagnosis of primary depression by St. Louis critieria (Feighner, Robins, Guze, Woodruff, Winokur, & Muñoz, 1972) was thought by most at the time to identify drug-responsive depressions. In addition, we established severity criteria to increase the likelihood that drugs would be both appropriate and effective (recall that we needed to ensure an active, effective, contrast condition). The mean HRSD score on admission was 21, and the mean BDI was 31 (numbers that compare favorably with many drug studies). Furthermore, we excluded patients who had previously failed on an adequate trial of any tricyclic agent. Adequate drug dosages were given.

This concern is not raised so much on the basis of our design, however, as on our results. While the number of patients attaining *complete* symptomatic remission was only five of 17 (final BDI of 9 or less), those with a good response (final BDI of 15 or less) totalled 12 of 17, or 70.5%. Recall that a good drug response was, at the time, regarded as at least a 50% reduction in initial symptom severity by most at the time. Thus, the response rate for imipramine was really rather good.

Finally, perhaps the major retrospective regret is that we did not have a large enough study at the outset to discern statistical significance in some of the between group differences noted in the 1-year follow-up study (Kovacs *et al.*, 1981). This, however, would be a natural course of events in early research, and subsequent larger studies obviously have been launched to answer this question.

There is one retrospective joy—namely, we used standard diagnostic and assessment instruments. It is now possible to pool our study data with those gathered from a variety of other centers in order to do a combined data analysis. This combined data analysis might allow us to search more effectively for predictors of response and/or prophylaxis that are not detectable in smaller samples.

Future directions in the area, I think, include further attempts to determine whether there are differential effects obtained with cognitive as compared to medication or other forms of psychotherapy (Rush, Beck, Kovacs, Weissenburger, & Hollon, 1982; Rush, Kovacs, Beck, Weissenburger, & Hollon, 1981), to identify indications for or predictors of response as well as contraindications for this form of treatment (Rush, Hollon, Beck, & Kovacs, 1978; Rush & Shaw, 1983), and, finally, to define the potential negative consequences of being in cognitive therapy (Rush, 1983b).

Having failed to find symptom or psychological indicators of response in our previous work, our research group has spent the last several years investigating biologic derangements in depressed inpatients and outpatients. While the implication of these derangements is far from clear in identifying candidates for cognitive or other forms of psychotherapy, a brief word on our current studies and hopes for the future is in order.

In a recent study of 66 outpatients and four inpatients (Rush, Giles, Roffwarg, & Parker, 1982) we found a higher incidence of dexamethasone nonsuppression (Carroll, Feinberg, Greden, Tarika, Alballa, Haskett, James, Kronfol, Lohr, Steiner, deVigne, & Young, 1981) in the endogenous (41%) than in the nonendogenous (4%) group. This finding was confirmed in a larger outpatient study of nonpsychotic nonbipolar patients with major depression (Giles & Rush, 1982). The dexamethasone nonsuppression in 95 nonendogenous outpatients was 4%; 44% of the endogenous group showed dexamethasone nonsuppression (Figure 2). Furthermore, we found that the endogenous group were more likely to evidence a reduction in REM latency, as well as other sleep EEG disturbances. Figure 3 shows our overall results in this regard.

We took a number of these subjects and gave them cognitive therapy. This was an uncontrolled, nonblinded study. To date, we have assigned nine patients to cognitive therapy, who showed *neither* a reduction in REM latency (i.e., a REM latency greater than 70 minutes) nor dexamethasone nonsuppression. Eight of these nine patients, all of whom were nonendogenous by Research Diagnostic Criteria, responded completely to cognitive therapy in terms of symptom reduction (end of treatment BDI Score of 9 or less).

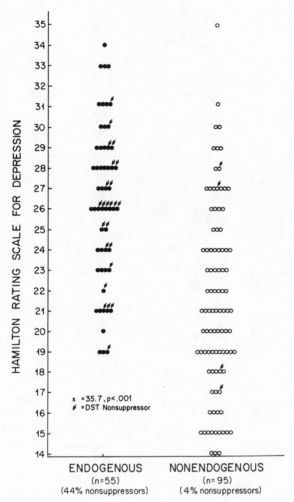

Figure 2. Relationship of Hamilton scale scores to endogenous/nonendogenous depression.

On the other hand, again in a nonrandomized and nonblind fashion, over the years we have treated five patients, all of whom were endogenous by RDC, and all of whom evidenced *both* biologic derangements (dexamethasone nonsuppression and a REM latency of less than 60 minutes) with cognitive therapy alone. All of these patients had previously failed on at least one tricyclic agent. The alternative considered was electroconvulsive therapy. None of these patients responded to cognitive therapy; in fact, four of the five patients could not complete treatment.

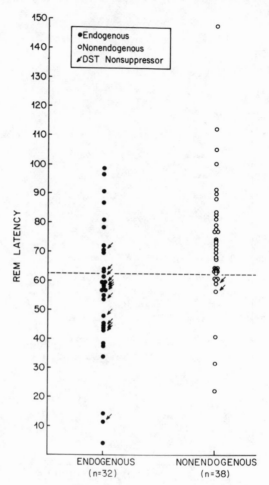

Figure 3. Relationship of REM latency to endogenous/nonendogenous depression.

Whether biologic laboratory tests will provide better clues to cognitive therapy response than severity, the endogenous–nonendogenous dichotomy, or other clinical subdivisions is far from clear. However, the patients most likely to show these derangements by at least some studies are those who have a positive family history for depression. One might speculate that those genetically disposed to depression, while perhaps being helped by cognitive therapy temporarily, will not attain either a thorough symptomatic remission or ongoing, long-lasting prophylaxis. With subsequent research, we hope to address these questions more directly in the future.

In conclusion, the development, testing, subsequent revision and retesting, and the identification of candidates for a particular psychotherapy is an expensive and time-consuming process. However, the results in the end hold the promise, at least, of our being able to select specific patients with particular disorders for well-defined forms of psychotherapy. The ultimate cost–benefit justification is that obviously patients who are not in need of extensive or expensive psychotherapy might avoid it, and those who do require such treatment can be identified early and not be subjected to multiple, unnecessary medication trials.

While many answers are still out with regard to cognitive therapy, the bulk of evidence now from a number of psychiatric outpatient studies certainly suggests that there is substantial promise in this approach. Perhaps the task at hand is how to identify those candidates for whom this treatment is in fact especially and/or uniquely effective.

ACKNOWLEDGMENTS

The author would like to express his appreciation to Ms. Marie Marks and Anita Roman for their secretarial support, and to Kenneth Z. Altshuler, MD, Professor and Chairman, for his administrative support. Some of the studies reported herein received partial support from National Institute of Mental Health (MH-19989, MH-27759, and MH-35370).

REFERENCES

Beck, A. T. *Cognitive therapy of the emotional disorders.* New York: International Universities Press, 1976.

Beck, A. T., & Rush, A. J. Cognitive approaches to depression and suicide. In G. Serban (Ed.), *Cognitive defects in development of mental illness.* New York: Brunner/Mazel, 1978.

Beck, A. T., Rush, A. J., Shaw, B. F., & Emery, G. *Cognitive therapy of depression.* New York: Guilford, 1979.

Beck, A. T., Ward, C. H., Mendelson, M., Mock, J. E., & Erbaugh, J. K. An inventory for measuring depression. *Archives of General Psychiatry,* 1961, *4,* 516–571.

Blackburn, I., & Bishop, S. Is there an alternative to drugs in the treatment of depressed ambulatory patients? *Behavioral Psychotherapy,* 1981, *9,* 96–104.

Blackburn, I., Bishop, S., Glen, A. I. M., Whalley, L. J., & Christie, J. E. The efficacy of cognitive therapy in depression? A treatment trial using cognitive therapy and pharmacotherapy, each alone and in combination. *British Journal of Psychiatry,* 1981, *139,* 181–189.

Covi, L., Lipman, R., Derogatis, L., Smith, J., & Pattison, I. Drugs and group psychotherapy in neurotic depression. *American Journal of Psychiatry,* 1974, *131,* 191–198.

Carroll, B. J., Feinberg, M., Greden, J. F., Tarika, J., Alballa, A. A., Haskett, R. F., James, N. M., Kronfol, Z., Lohr, N., Steiner, M., deVigne, J. P., & Young, E. A specific laboratory test for the diagnosis of melancholia. *Archives of General Psychiatry,* 1979, *38,* 15–22, 1981.

Feighner, J. P., Robins, E., Guze, S. B., Woodruff, R. A., Winokur, G., & Muñoz, R. Diagnostic criteria for use in psychiatric research. *Archives of General Psychiatry,* 1972, *26,* 57–63.

Friedman, A. S. Interaction of drug therapy with marital therapy in depressive patients. *Archives of General Psychiatry*, 1975, *32*, 619-637.

Giles, D. E., & Rush, A. J. Relationship of dysfunctional attitudes and dexamethasone response in endogenous and nonendogenous depression. *Biological Psychiatry*, 1982, *17*, 1303-1314.

Hamilton, M. A rating scale for depression. *Journal of Neurology, Neurosurgery and Psychiatry*, 1960, *12*, 56-62.

Hamilton, M. Development of a rating scale for primary depressive illness. *British Journal of Social and Clinical Psychology*, 1967, *6*, 278-296.

Hamilton, M. The assessment of anxiety states by rating. *British Journal of Medical Psychology* 1959, *32*, 50-55.

Hole, R., Rush, A. J., & Beck, A. T. Cognitive change methods with delusional patients. *Psychiatry*, 1979, *42*, 312-319.

Klein, D. Endogenomorphic depression. *Archives of General Psychiatry*, 1974, *32*, 447-454.

Klerman, G. L., DiMascio, A., Weissman, M., Prusoff, B., & Paykel, E. Treatment of depression by drugs and psychotherapy. *American Journal of Psychiatry*, 1974, *131*, 186-191.

Kovacs, M., Rush, A. J., Beck, A. T., & Hollon, S. D. Depressed outpatients treated with cognitive therapy or pharmacotherapy, a one-year follow-up. *Archives of General Psychiatry*, 1981, *38*, 33-39.

McLean, P. D., & Hakstian, A. R. Clinical depression: Comparative efficacy of outpatient treatments. *Journal of Consulting and Clinical Psychology*, 1979, *47*, 818-836.

Morris, J. B., & Beck, A. T. The efficacy of antidepressant drugs: A review of research (1958-1972). *Archives of General Psychiatri*, 1974, *30*, 667-674.

Paykel, E. S., DiMascio, A., Klerman, G. L., Prusoff, B. A., & Weissman, M. M. Maintenance therapy of therapy of depression. *Pharmacopsychiatry*, 1976, *9*, 127-136.

Paykel, E. S., DiMascio, A., Haskell, D., & Prusoff, B. A. Effects of maintenance metriptyline and psychotherapy on symptoms of depression. *Psychological Medicine*, 1975, *5*, 67-77.

Raskin, A., Schulterbrandt, J. G., Reatig, N., & McKeon, J. J. Differential response to chlorpromazine, imipramine, and placebo: A study of subgroups of hospitalized depressed patients. *Archives of General Psychiatry*, 1970, *23*, 164-173.

Rush, A. J. Biological markers and treatment response in affective disorders. *McLean Hospital Bulletin*, 1983, *8*, 38-61. (a)

Rush, A. J. Cognitive therapy for depression. In M. R. Zales (Ed.), *Affective and schizophrenic disorders*. New York: Brunner/Mazel, 1983. (b)

Rush, A. J. Pharmacotherapy and psychotherapy. In L. Derogatis (Ed.), *Psychopharmacology in clinical practice*. New York: Addison and Wesley, 1983. (c)

Rush, A. J., & Beck, A. T. Cognitive therapy of depression and suicide. *American Journal of Psychotherapy*, 1978, *32*, 201-219.

Rush, A. J., Beck, A. T., Kovacs, M., & Hollon, S. Comparative efficacy of cognitive therapy and imipramine in the treatment of depressed outpatients. *Cognitive Therapy and Research*, 1977, *1*, 17-37.

Rush, A. J., Beck, A. T., Kovacs, M., Khatami, M., & Wolman, T. *A comparison of cognitive and pharmacotherapy in depressed outpatients: A preliminary report*. Presented at Society for Psychotherapy Research, Boston, Mass., June 1975.

Rush, A. J., Beck, A. T., Kovacs, M., Weissenburger, J., & Hollon, S. Differential effects of cognitive therapy and pharmacotherapy on hopelessness and self-concept. *American Journal of Psychiatry*, 1982, *139*, 862-866.

Rush, A. J., Giles, D. E., Roffwarg, H. P., & Parker, C. R. Sleep EEG and dexamethasone suppression test findings in outpatients with unipolar major depressive disorders. *Biological Psychiatry*, 1982, *17*, 327-341.

Rush, A. J., Hollon, S. D., Beck, A. T., & Kovacs, M. Depression: Must pharmacotherapy fail for cognitive therapy to succeed? *Cognitive Therapy and Research*, 1978, *2*, 199-206.

Rush, A. J., Khatami, M., & Beck, A. T. Cognitive and behavior therapy in chronic depression. *Behavior Therapy*, 1975, *6*, 398–404.

Rush, A. J., Kovacs, M., Beck, A. T., Weissenburger, J., & Hollon, S. D. Differential effects of cognitive therapy and pharmacotherapy on depressive symptoms. *Journal of Affective Disorders*, 1981, *3*, 221–229.

Rush, A. J., & Shaw, B. F. Failures in treating depression by cognitive behavioral therapy. In P. M. Emmelkamp & E. B. Foa (Eds.), *Failures in behavior therapy*. New York: Wiley, 1983.

Rush, A. J., & Watkins, J. T. Group versus individual cognitive therapy: A pilot study. *Cognitive Therapy and Research*, 1981, *5*, 95–103.

Schmickley, V. G. *The effects of cognitive behavior modification upon depressed outpatients*. Unpublished doctoral dissertation, Michigan State University, 1976.

Shaw, B. F. Comparison of cognitive therapy and behavior therapy in the treatment of depression. *Journal of Consulting and Clinical Psychology*, 1977, *45*, 543–551.

Spitzer, R. L., Endicott, J., & Robins, E. Research diagnostic criteria: Rationale and reliability. *Archives of General Psychiatry*, 1978, *35*, 773–782.

Taylor, F. G., & Marshall, W. L. Experimental analysis of a cognitive–behavioral therapy for depression. *Cognitive Therapy and Research*, 1977, *1*, 59–72.

Weissman, M. M., & Kasl, S. V. Help-seeking in depressed outpatients following maintenance therapy. *British Journal of Psychiatry*, 1976, *129*, 252–260.

Weissman, M. M., Kasl, S. V., & Klerman, G. L. Follow-up of depressed women after maintenance treatment. *American Journal of Psychiatry*, 1976, *133*, 757–760.

Weissman, M. M., Prusoff, B. A., & Klerman, G. L. Personality and the prediction of long-term outcome in depression. *American Journal of Psychiatry*, 1978, *135*, 797–800.

COMMENTARY

Dr. Donald F. Klein*: John Rush reminds us how important it is that the supposedly active treatment control is in a group of patients in whom the treatment would be effective, and he went to some lengths to choose patients who apparently should be imipramine-responsive. However, the findings were that five of the 17 patients on imipramine were responders, which is a very low imipramine response rate. Therefore, my question is: Do you really think that your methods were successful in culling out a group of potentially imipramine-responsive patients?

Dr. Rush: I do. I have some doubts about it, obviously, because we don't have the third cell comparison. But I don't think the study should be cited as having only five of 17 responding. I tried to get at that by discussing the Beck Inventory, a self-report measure.

In most drug studies that show effects, for example, with the Hamilton Rating Scale, or drug–placebo differences, if you try to define response as an

*New York State Psychiatric Institute and College of Physicians and Surgeons, Columbia University.

end-of-treatment Beck of 9 or less, I think you will find relatively small numbers of patients. In fact, in many studies, the self-report of the patients after 3 or 4 weeks will often fail to discriminate placebo from drug.

The other reason, I think, that it is a drug-responsive group is the statistical analysis itself. That is, statistical analysis showed a significant drug effect, by weeks, on the Hamilton, Raskin, Hamilton Anxiety, Beck Inventory, and a number of other measures. The mean post-treatment Hamilton for that group was something on the order of, I think, 13. So we are having an effect.

Now the question is one of evenness of effect; that is, how much of the sample had a pretty good drug effect. And that is why I would argue that if you look at Beck scores of 15 or lower, you are getting a 70% response rate, which is pretty good.

Dr. Klein: I don't understand why you refer to that as a drug effect, because you have no placebo group, and the improvement during drug treatment may not have anything to do with drug effect.

Dr. Rush: I refer to that as a drug effect because the assumption was that the therapy was the placebo group. But I agree with you that a third cell is necessary to determine which one is, if you will, active, or whether both are active.

My only contention is that at this phase of development of a therapy, that third cell is fraught with some problems until one shows semiefficacy, at least. And then one adds cells to assure that the treatment is active, and to control for nonspecific factors.

Dr. Robert A. Neimeyer*: I was curious if your move toward the search for a biologic predictor of treatment response indicated that you had given up looking for cognitive predictors. And I was wondering, if that was the case, what sort of cognitive predictors you had searched for and not found.

Dr. Rush: We had searched for, in this former study, some items off of the Hamilton. We didn't have a Dysfunctional Attitudes Scale, or a lot of other measures. No, we haven't given up on it, and Dr. Murphy's group has some data with regard to a self-control scale that look rather healthy on first pass at potentially predicting. No, we haven't given up on it—I think we just took another track at this point.

*Memphis State University.

14

The Vanderbilt Psychotherapy Research Project: Past, Present, and Future

HANS H. STRUPP
Vanderbilt University

The early years of my career in psychotherapy research (beginning around 1953) were marked by a special interest in the therapist's contribution to the treatment process. On the basis of my clinical experience (as both analysand and young therapist) as well as the existing literature I sensed intuitively that the person of the therapist had to play an important part in the therapeutic process, determining its quality and outcome. I never went so far as Carl Rogers (1957), who declared that the "therapist-offered conditions" of warmth, empathy, genuineness, and unconditional positive regard were the "necessary and sufficient conditions," but as my experience grew and as I began to carry out a series of analogue studies (summarized in Strupp, 1960) I came to believe even more firmly that any meaningful definition of psychotherapy would have to accommodate personal qualities of the therapist that are brought to bear on the therapeutic interaction with a given patient. Thus to describe psychotherapy in terms of its theoretical orientation or techniques, as was common then and still is now, provides a truncated view of what is always a complex human relationship. By this reasoning, what the therapist communicates by attitudes, gestures, and innuendo must be studied and understood as carefully as the techniques he or she uses. In brief, psychotherapy is never adequately defined as a "treatment modality" or as a set of "technical procedures." This position has important implications for currently fashionable attempts to describe psychotherapy as a "health care technology" and the "clinical trials" approach to research. Progress has been made in studying the nature of the therapeutic influence—the primary task of research—but we have a long way to go in capturing the elusive qualities of what is therapeutic, antitherapeutic, or simply inert.

My early research, limited as it was in terms of resources, access to process and outcome data, and available technology, made a beginning

235

contribution to the documentation of important differences among therapists and led to methodological advances in assessing the therapist's contribution (Strupp, 1957). In short, I began to differentiate between "technical" (specific) and "nontechnical" (nonspecific) factors, the latter referring to the therapist's human qualities that subtly but decisively suffused and were integrally related to his or her techniques. Others, notably Jerome Frank (Frank, Hoehn-Saric, Imber, Liberman, & Stone, 1978), were pursuing similar conceptualizations and inquiries. Basically, however, as I learned later, this way of looking at the therapist's contributions has serious limitations. For conceptual and research purposes it may be useful to differentiate between specific and nonspecific factors, but in practice the two cannot be pried apart; they must always be studied in conjunction. Moreover, lest we get caught up in an unfortunate reification, I now feel that we should abandon or reformulate the problem.

The origins of what came to be known as the Vanderbilt Psychotherapy Project or, more specifically as the Vanderbilt I study (Strupp & Hadley, 1979), are found in my collaboration with Allen Bergin which extended over a period of several years, beginning in the late 1960s, and culminated in our book, *Changing Frontiers in the Science of Psychotherapy* (Bergin & Strupp, 1972). We were commissioned by the National Institute of Mental Health (NIMH) to explore whether large-scale collaborative studies were feasible—we concluded that the time was not ripe—and where the field might be going, that is, where significant advances might be made. This quest led to several years of pilot work, preliminary to the Vanderbilt I study which was initiated in the early 1970s and lasted almost 10 years. A certain amount of research involving these data is still going on.

Using a control-group design, the Vanderbilt group sought to explore the hypothesis that, with a reasonably specific patient population (in this case, male college students suffering from moderately severe anxiety, depression, and social withdrawal), the technical expertise of professional therapists, when compared to the activities of untrained (in psychotherapy) college professors would yield superior therapeutic results. We reasoned that professional therapists as well as carefully selected college professors would provide a comparable therapeutic "climate" (analogous to Rogers's "facilitative conditions"); therefore, systematic differences in outcome favoring professional therapists would constitute evidence for the unique importance of technical factors. The therapy was time-limited (up to 25 hours) and techniques were allowed to vary freely. The professional therapists who had no special expertise in time-limited therapy were either psychoanalytic or client-centered/humanistic in their theoretical orientation.

The major results of the study, together with its unintended extrapolations to professional training and contemporary political trends, are well known: We replicated the common finding that some form of psychotherapy is better than no treatment, but it seemed to make little difference who administered it. In retrospect and in the light of more recent advances in research, neither the conceptualization nor the experimental design was felicitous. Had we stopped with the traditional group comparisons which, on the basis of subsequent reanalyses of the data, were judged particularly inadequate (Suh & Strupp, 1982), we would have learned very little. However, in contrast to most studies previously undertaken, we had made careful assessments of patients at intake, termination, and follow-up; we had collected assessments from multiple perspectives—patient, therapist, and evaluating clinician; and, most importantly, we had complete sound recordings of every therapy hour and videotapes of selected ones. I was also blessed with several generations of unusually gifted, creative graduate students and postdoctoral fellows. Finally, NIMH's continuing confidence and support proved indispensable. With this auspicious constellation of factors, we carried out a sizable number of studies which explored in detail and depth the vagaries and vicissitudes of the patient–therapist interaction in individual cases; particularly fruitful were comparisons between high and low changers treated by the same therapist. To aid these explorations we developed several new methodological tools, notably the Vanderbilt Psychotherapy Process Scale (VPPS) and the Vanderbilt Negative Indicators Scale (VNIS), which were used in assessing salient aspects of the therapist's and the patient's behavior as well as their interaction. And, by deliberately weaving between the quantitative measures and the clinical data we sought to advance our understanding of both. Time allows me to mention only the highlights of our findings; however, I wish to emphasize that the lessons we learned have been built into our new Vanderbilt II study, pilot work for which has been under way for about 2 years. If NIMH concurs with our judgment that we are ready for this ambitious project, Vanderbilt II will be inaugurated in a matter of months. Now, to the highlights:

1. Neither professional therapists nor college professors were notably effective in treating patients with more pervasive personality problems (whose suitability for time-limited therapy emerged as questionable in our retrospective assessments). On the other hand, professional therapists were most effective with patients showing the following characteristics: high motivation for psychotherapy; ability to form a good therapeutic relationship (working alliance) early in treatment; and relative absence of long-standing maladaptive patterns of relating. The latter were defined by such qualities as pronounced hostility, pervasive mistrust, negativism, inflexibility, and antisocial or asocial tendencies.

The foregoing is not meant to imply that professional therapists were most effective with the *least* disturbed patients. Rather, these therapists were particularly effective with patients whose personality resources and capacity for collaboration allowed them to take maximal advantage of the kind of relationship and traditional techniques proffered by the therapists. These findings are in general agreement with the literature (Luborsky, Chandler, Auerbach, Cohen, & Bachrach, 1971; Kernberg, Burstein, Coyne, Appelbaum, Horwitz, & Voth, 1972).

2. The quality of the therapeutic relationship, established early in the interaction, proved to be an important predictor of outcome in this time-limited context. In particular, therapy tended to be successful if by the third session the patient felt accepted, understood, and liked by his or her therapist (Waterhouse, 1979). Conversely, premature termination or failure tended to result if these conditions were not met early in treatment. In addition, we obtained preliminary evidence that reasonably accurate predictions of process and outcome can be made from initial interviews, specifically in terms of judgments relating to the patient's motivation for therapy (Keithly, Samples, & Strupp, 1980) and quality of interpersonal relationships (Moras & Strupp, 1982). Stated differently, we found no evidence that an initially negative or highly ambivalent patient–therapist relationship was significantly modified in the course of therapy under study. Furthermore, the patients' perceptions of the therapeutic relationship were found to remain fairly stable throughout therapy and to the follow-up period.

3. The quality of the therapeutic relationship appeared to depend heavily on the patient's ability to relate comfortably and productively to the therapist in the context of a traditional therapeutic framework. This capacity, in turn, seemed to be a function of the patient's personality resources and suitability for time-limited therapy (see 1 above). In short, there was compelling evidence that the quality of the patient–therapist relationship was significantly, although not entirely, determined by *patient* variables.

4. Professional therapists gave little evidence of adapting their thera-peutic approach or techniques to the specific characteristics and needs of individual patients. Instead, the kind of relationship they offered and the techniques they employed were relatively invariant. Similarly, therapists did not tailor their techniques in specific ways to the resolution of "target symptoms," and they did not seem to formulate specific therapeutic goals of their own that were then systematically pursued in therapy.

5. Professional psychotherapists, in general, had little success in con-fronting or resolving the marked negative reactions characteristic of the more difficult patients. Instead, they tended to react negatively and counter-therapeutically to a patient's hostility, mistrust, inflexibility, and pervasive resistances, thereby perhaps reinforcing the patient's poor self-image and related difficulties. The result of such interactions tended to be (a) negative attitudes on the part of the patient toward the therapist and therapy; (b) premature termination; and/or (c) a poor therapeutic outcome (i.e., no change or negative change). For detailed analyses, see Strupp (1980a, 1980b, 1980c).

These results have significant implications for research and clinical practice.

PATIENT SELECTION

Patients with substantial personality resources, high levels of motivation for therapy, relatively circumscribed problems, and the capacity to work productively within a traditional therapeutic framework are likely to show the greatest and the most rapid improvement. From the therapist's standpoint, these persons generally constitute the most desirable and rewarding patients. And when viewed from the broader perspective of the needs of society and the future development of psychotherapy, these are the least problematic cases.

By contrast, patients falling short of optimal suitability for short-term approaches (according to the criteria mentioned above) represent by far the largest segment of the patient population. Paradoxically, while these individuals are in the greatest need of professional services, they are also the ones who have been most neglected by mental health professionals (Rabkin, 1977). This judgment applies with particular force to short-term dynamic psychotherapy which has traditionally focused on the selection and treatment of the most promising candidates (Butcher & Koss, 1978). (It is noteworthy in this regard that the extensive contemporary literature dealing with borderline conditions and narcissistic personality disorders is almost entirely devoted to long-term intensive therapy; see, e.g., Giovacchini, 1979; Kernberg, 1975; Kohut, 1971.)

CONCLUSION 1

In order for psychotherapy to meet more adequately the needs of patients as well as society, it is essential to focus attention on patients who have typically been rejected as suitable candidates for short-term psychotherapy and to explore systematically the extent to which such patients can be treated more effectively by a well-defined, time-limited approach.

PATIENT ASSESSMENT

Considering the complexity of the human personality, it is perhaps not surprising that even when assessment procedures are designed to select a homogeneous group of patients, the resulting samples are likely to include individuals who differ widely on a number of dimensions considered critical to their suitability for time-limited psychotherapy. For example, the initial patient selection was based on significant elevation ($T \geq 60$) of scales 2 (Depression), 7 (Psychastenia), and 0 (Social Introversion) of the Minnesota Multiphasic Personality Inventory (MMPI). Although we did not insist that all patients be "pure" 2-7-0's, marked variability was observed in the subsample that met this criterion. It emerged that patients showed wide variations in terms of character structure, ranging from mild neurotic disturbances in a relatively well-functioning personality organization to severe obsessionals, character disorders, and even a few borderline conditions.

In light of our findings and those of others (Davanloo, 1978, 1980; Malan, 1976, 1979; Sifneos, 1972, 1979), additional criteria of crucial significance for treatment planning should include (1) severity of character disturbances (negativism, pervasive mistrust, rigidity), (2) degree of impairment in coping ability, (3) quality of past interpersonal relationships, (4) motivation for change, and (5) presence of "core conflictual themes" (Luborsky, 1977) or central issues that allow for the establishment of a dynamic focus. Despite the importance of these qualities to the determination of a patient's suitability for a particular treatment approach, such careful assessments are typically not made in clinical practice. McLemore and Benjamin (1979) present a strong argument that traditional nosology, instead of focusing on *interpersonal behavior*—the proper focus for planning and executing psychotherapy—employs categories which, in the view of numerous authors (e.g., Adams, Doster, & Calhoun, 1977; Carson, 1969, p. 224), are "largely meaningless."

CONCLUSION 2

Psychiatric assessments must be sharpened to include (1) evaluations of the patient's interpersonal functioning; (2) determinations of the patient's suitability for time-limited psychotherapy in terms of the criteria that have been identified as important prognostic indicators; and (3) reformulation of patients' presenting complaints in terms of central issues or themes which lend themselves to focused therapeutic interventions. To effect more specific treatment planning, these determinations must become an integral part of the assessment process. Through this step, a closer link will be forged between diagnosis, formulation of therapeutic goals, techniques, and outcomes.

THERAPEUTIC OPERATIONS

As shown by our analyses of patient–therapist interactions, therapists tended to use a broad-gauged approach aimed at helping patients achieve insight into certain aspects of their current difficulties. Except for the fact that the treatment was time-limited, psychodynamically trained therapists typically followed the analytic model of long-term intensive psychotherapy. Accordingly, they adopted a passive–expectant stance, left the initiative for introducing topics to the patient, and largely confined their activity to clarifications and interpretations of conflictual patterns. Therapists tended to provide relatively little warmth and support, did not focus on the specific problems identified at the beginning of treatment, rarely acquainted patients with the nature of the therapeutic process, and infrequently confronted patients' negative personal reactions. In sum, the therapists' approach tended to be relatively invariant and patients were expected, without significant effort on the therapist's part, to feel comfortable with and respond favorably to the requirements of this therapeutic framework. It should be noted that, with relatively few exceptions, this approach reflects the model followed in most training centers for psychologists and psychiatrists, despite the fact that the majority of patients are unable to take optimal advantage of this regimen. Furthermore, as shown by our research results, the absence of a good "fit" between pertinent patient characteristics and the therapist's framework frequently leads to an impasse early in treatment, such as poor therapeutic alliance, premature termination, and/or poor outcome.

Of particular significance to the course and outcome of treatment were therapists' negative personal reactions to patients whose resistance took the form of anger, hostility, negativism, and pervasive mistrust. In view of these findings, we believe that systematic efforts must be made to help therapists deal with this problem.

CONCLUSION 3

To realize the full potential of short-term dynamic psychotherapy, therapists should receive specialized training, with particular emphasis on the following elements:

1. Techniques should be geared optimally to the achievement of reasonably specific therapeutic objectives identified early in the course of treatment. Crucial here is the isolation of a central issue, dynamic focus, or "theme."

2. The therapeutic process should be designed to meet the unique needs of the individual patient, as opposed to the tacit assumption that the patient conform to the therapists's notions of an "ideal" therapeutic framework. Techniques should be applied flexibly, sensitively, and in ways maximally meaningful to the patient.

3. Steps should be taken to foster a good therapeutic relationship (working alliance) from the beginning of therapy, thus enhancing the

patient's active participation and creating a sense of collaboration and partnership.

4. Negative transference reactions should be actively confronted and defused at the earliest possible time.

5. Concerted efforts should be made to help therapists deal with negative personal reactions which are characteristically engendered by patients manifesting hostility, anger, negativism, rigidity, and similar resistances.

6. While time-limited psychotherapy poses particular challenges to all therapists (especially demands for greater activity and directiveness), they should resist the temptations to persuade the patient to accept a particular "solution," to impose their values, and to diminish the patient's strivings for freedom and autonomy in other respects.

7. Rather than viewing psychotherapy predominantly as a set of "technical operations" applied in a vaccum, therapists must be sensitive to the importance of the human elements in all therapeutic encounters. In other words, unless the therapist takes an interest in the patient as a person and succeeds in communicating this interest and commitment, psychotherapy becomes a caricature of a good human relationship.

8. Closely related to the foregoing, therapists should keep in mind that all good therapeutic experiences lead to increments in the patient's self-acceptance and self-respect; consequently, continual care must be taken to promote such experiences and to guard against interventions that might have opposite effects.

The foregoing terse summary does scant justice to the empirical bases which form the foundation for our inferences, conclusions, and recommendations. The best I can do is to refer the interested reader to the body of articles, chapters, dissertations, and manuals that undergird my assertions.

In conclusion, I wish to present a cursory outline of our new project which embodies our best judgment of one promising direction for future research. In essence, our proposed investigation is anchored in the conviction that, above all, researchers must pursue the goal of achieving a better understanding of the therapeutic process and the ingredients that account for good or poor outcomes. To this end, we must obtain a clearer picture of those patient characteristics that facilitate (or impede) a patient's entry into a human relationship aimed at providing a "corrective emotional experience." Next, we must seek sharper specifications of therapeutic interventions and the interpersonal context in which they come to fruition (or fail to do so). In short, we must keep our gaze riveted on the all-important problem of therapeutic change—how it can be brought about, why in some cases therapy succeeds and in others it fails, and what factors in patient and therapist account for success or failure. To this end, we must find new and better ways of capturing the intricacies of the dynamic interaction between patient and therapist, a task to which existing research techniques and methodologies are not yet equal. Another way of stating this is to counsel the abandonment of simplistic conceptions of psychotherapy as a set of techniques that can be administered mechanically to modify impersonal syndromes, symptoms, or "conditions." Our thinking and our research strategies must accommodate the conceptualization of psychotherapy as an exquisitely interpersonal endeavor.

How do we plan to pursue these objectives in the Vanderbilt II project? First, in keeping with the teachings of the "interpersonal school" (Anchin & Kiesler, 1982), we view the patient's presenting difficulties as integrally related to the perpetuation of maladaptive patterns of interpersonal behavior. Because of disturbed relationships with significant others in the past, the patient tends to reenact maladaptive and self-defeating scenarios with significant others in the present. By assuming an appropriate stance and because of the patient's desire for help, the therapist presently becomes a significant other for the patient. Because of the universal tendency toward reenactment (transference), the therapist is able to turn a seeming liability to therapeutic advantage. Through skillful "analysis of the transference in the here and now," the patient is enabled to modify his or her cognitions, feelings, attitudes, and patterns of behavior. Such changes are forged in the crucible of the patient–therapist interaction.

Second, we have developed a treatment manual (Strupp & Binder, 1983) which sets forth basic principles and procedures of what we call time-limited dynamic psychotherapy. TLDP is based on our view of the most advanced thinking in psychoanalytic theory, short-term analytic therapy, object relations theory, system theory, and interpersonal theory. Although for practical and strategic reasons we work with time limits, we believe that the model is equally compatible with long-term efforts. The delineation of a "dynamic focus" which helps define treatment goals and activities aimed at the achievement of reasonably specific goals is central, as is the emphasis on the understanding and management of interpersonal transactions in the here and now. The lessons mentioned earlier are embedded in the contents of this manual. We propose to train a sample of therapists in the use of TLDP and study their performance before and after training.

Third, we are vitally interested in exploring the range of patients who might be suitable for this form of therapy. Recall that in the Vanderbilt I study, professional therapists were particularly effective with patients who had good "ego resources" but they appeared to be relatively ineffective in dealing with patients who approached therapy with attitudes of negativism, hostility, and significant anger. It should also be kept in mind that, with few but notable exceptions (Davanloo, 1978; Malan, 1976), short-term dynamic psychotherapy has generally been reserved for patients who fall into the first group. Thus, from a scientific as well as a public-health standpoint it is important to explore systematically whether the "rich get richer" phenomenon, which is still widely believed, is indeed an immutable fact of life. Can we empirically demonstrate the value of training therapists in the management of transference and countertransference problems? Even moderate success in this arena might yield a rich harvest.

Finally, I wish to emphasize that the proposed research is aimed at building a stronger bridge between psychotherapy research and practice. Perhaps the time is not too far off when practicing clinicians will be able to make use of the insights gained by researchers, thus consummating a partnership that has been slow in developing.

REFERENCES

Adams, H. E., Doster, J. A., & Calhoun, K. S. A psychologically based system of response classification. In A. R. Ciminero, K. S. Calhoun, & H. E. Adams (Eds.), *Handbook of behavioral assessment*. New York: Wiley, 1977.

Anchin, J. C., & Kiesler, D. J. (Eds.). *Handbook of interpersonal psychotherapy*. New York: Pergamon, 1982.

Bergin, A. E., & Strupp, H. H. *Changing frontiers in the science of psychotherapy*. Chicago: Aldine, 1972.

Butcher, J. N., & Koss, M. P. Research on brief and crisis-oriented psychotherapies. In S. L. Garfield & A. E. Bergin (Eds.), *Handbook of psychotherapy and behavior change: An empirical analysis*. New York: Wiley, 1978.

Carson, R. E. *Interaction concepts of personality*. Chicago: Aldine, 1969.

Davanloo, H. (Ed.). *Basic principles and techniques in short-term dynamic psychotherapy*. New York: Spectrum, 1978.

Davanloo, H. (Ed.). *Short-term dynamic psychotherapy*. New York: Jason Aronson, 1980.

Frank, J. D., Hoehn-Saric, R., Imber, S. D., Liberman, B. L., & Stone, A. R. *Effective ingredients of successful psychotherapy*. New York: Brunner/Mazel, 1978.

Giovacchini, P. *Treatment of primitive mental states*. New York: Jason Aronson, 1979.

Keithly, L. J., Samples, S. J., & Strupp, H. H. Patient motivation as a predictor of process and outcome in psychotherapy. *Psychotherapy and Psychosomatics*, 1980, *33*, 87–97.

Kernberg, O. F. *Borderline conditions and pathological narcissism*. New York: Jason Aronson, 1975.

Kernberg, O. F., Burstein, E. D., Coyne, L., Appelbaum, A., Horwitz, L., & Voth, H. *Psychotherapy and psychoanalysis: Final report of the Menninger Foundation's psychotherapy research project*. Topeka, Ks.: Menninger Foundation, 1972.

Kohut, H. *The analysis of the self*. New York: International Universities Press, 1971.

Luborsky, L. Measuring a pervasive psychic structure in psychotherapy: The core conflictual relationship theme. In N. Freedman & S. Grand (Eds.), *Communicative structures and psychic structures*. New York: Plenum, 1977.

Luborsky, L., Chandler, M., Auerbach, A. H., Cohen, J., & Bachrach, H. M. Factors influencing the outcome of psychotherapy: A review of the quantitative research. *Psychological Bulletin*, 1971, *75*, 145–185.

Malan, D. H. *The frontier of brief psychotherapy: An example of the convergence of research and clinical practice*. New York: Plenum, 1976.

Malan, D. H. *Individual psychotherapy and the science of psychodynamics*. London: Butterworths, 1979.

McLemore, C. W., & Benjamin, L. S. Whatever happened to interpersonal diagnosis? A psychosocial alternative to DSM-III. *American Psychologist*, 1979, *34*, 17–34.

Moras, K., & Strupp, H. H. Pre-therapy interpersonal relations, a patient's alliance, and outcome in brief therapy. *Archives of General Psychiatry*, 1982, *39*, 405–409.

Rabkin, J. G. Therapists' attitudes toward mental illness and health. In A. S. Gurman & A. R. Razin (Eds.), *Effective psychotherapy: A handbook of research*. New York: Pergamon, 1977.

Rogers, C. R. The necessary and sufficient conditions of therapeutic personality change. *Journal of Consulting Psychology*, 1957, *21*, 95–103.

Sifneos, P. *Short-term psychotherapy and emotional crisis*. Cambridge, Mass.: Harvard University Press, 1972.

Sifneos, P. *Short-term dynamic psychotherapy: Evaluation and technique*. New York: Plenum, 1979.

Strupp, H. H. A multidimensional system for analyzing psychotherapeutic techniques. *Psychiatry*, 1957, *20*, 293–306.

Strupp, H. H. *Psychotherapists in action: Explorations of the therapist's contribution to the treatment process*. New York: Grune & Stratton, 1960.

Strupp, H. H. Success and failure in time-limited psychotherapy: A systematic comparison of two cases (comparison 1). *Archives of General Psychiatry*, 1980, *37*, 595–603. (a)

Strupp, H. H. Success and failure in time-limited psychotherapy: A systematic comparison of two cases (comparison 2). *Archives of General Psychiatry*, 1980, *37*, 708–716. (b)

Strupp, H. H. Success and failure in time-limited psychotherapy: Further evidence (comparison 4). *Archives of General Psychiatry*, 1980, *37*, 974–954. (c)

Strupp, H. H., & Binder, J. L. *Time-limited dynamic psychotherapy: A treatment manual*. Unpublished manuscript, 1983. (Available from H. H. Strupp, PhD, Department of Psychology, Vanderbilt University, 134 Wesley Hall, Nashville, Tenn. 37240.)

Strupp, H. H., & Hadley, S. W. Specific versus nonspecific factors in psychotherapy: A controlled study of outcome. *Archives of General Psychiatry*. 1979, *36*, 1125–1136.

Suh, C., & Strupp, H. H. *Appropriateness of residual gain scores in psychotherapy research: An analysis with special reference to the Vanderbilt Psychotherapy Project*. Paper presented at the Conference of the Society for Psychotherapy Research, Burlington, Vermont, 1982.

Waterhouse, G. J. *Perceptions of facilitative therapeutic conditions as predictors of outcome in brief therapy*. Paper presented at the European Conference of the Society for Psychotherapy Research, Oxford, England, 1979.

COMMENTARY

Dr. Sol L. Garfield*: Hans, I am interested in why you didn't follow up and do comparable analyses with the college professors. They are such a gifted group that it is hard to understand why you didn't do that.

Dr. Strupp: To let you in on a secret, Sol [Garfield], I never really had a great interest in college professors as therapists. They were really being used

*Washington University.

for a purpose. That doesn't necessarily explain why such an analysis of the kind you are suggesting should not be done, but their purpose was, at the time, to represent the nonspecific factors in relatively pure culture. So I didn't find them all that interesting.

We did learn quite a few things about what differentiates college professors from professional therapists in their performance, which provides an answer to the public criticism which, unfortunately, no one in *The New York Times* or *Time* magazine ever pointed out. For example, these college professors ran out of material to talk about after 5 or 6 hours. They had difficulty keeping these patients in therapy. Their conceptual thinking was very limited. "This fellow seems to have girl trouble" was one of the more sophisticated formulations. (*Laughter.*) I think we could make a very nice case why these people should not be let loose on the public as therapists.

Dr. Garfield: It is interesting that you say that when they got just as good results as the trained therapists.

Dr. Brian F. Shaw*: I admire your attempt to look at patient difficulty. We know, though, that idiosyncratically therapists determine their own patient difficulty in clinical practice. Are you going to be measuring the therapists' perceptions of the patient difficulty in addition to diagnosis and other external measures?

Dr. Strupp: We believe that we have some measures for assessing patient difficulty in an objective way. Of course, therapists' assessments could and should be taken into account also. I guess that if we are interested in research that has a broad applicability, we would like to have objective procedures that are not idiosyncratic which can be applied by clinical raters, and which would assess the patient's difficulty in a reasonably objective way.

*University of Toronto.

15

From the Menninger Project to a Research Strategy for Long-Term Psychotherapy of Borderline Personality Disorders

OTTO F. KERNBERG
New York Hospital-Cornell Medical Center, Westchester Division,
Cornell University Medical College,
and Columbia University Center for Psychoanalytic Training and Research

METHODOLOGY AND FINDINGS OF THE MENNINGER FOUNDATION'S PSYCHOTHERAPY RESEARCH PROJECT

The sample of the psychotherapy research project consisted of 42 adult hospital patients and outpatients treated at the Menninger Foundation (Kernberg, Burstein, Coyne, Appelbaum, Horwitz, & Voth, 1972). Diagnosed as suffering from neurotic conditions, latent psychoses, or characterological disturbances, all patients underwent treatment designed within the framework of psychoanalytic theory ranging from supportive psychotherapy to psychoanalysis.

In addition to the quantitative studies based largely on the method of paired comparisons that permitted us to carry out traditional statistical analysis of our findings, we also applied facet theory and the technique of multidimensional scalogram analysis (MSA) to a comprehensive study of the quantitative and the nonquantifiable data of the project.

The statistical analyses revealed that a high level of initial *ego strength* of the patient indicated a good prognosis regardless of which treatment method had been carried out; that is, psychoanalysis, expressive psychotherapy, expressive–supportive psychotherapy, and supportive psychotherapy were all helpful to patients with good ego strength. As a result of the factor analysis of our patient variables, "ego strength" was defined as a combination of three intimately linked characteristics: (1) the degree of integration, stability, and flexibility of the intrapsychic structures (including variables

247

such as *patterning of defenses and anxiety tolerance*): impulse control, thought organization, and sublimatory channeling capacity are subsumed under these categories; (2) the degree to which relationships with others are adaptive, deep, gratifying of normal instinctual needs, which corresponds to the variable *quality of interpersonal relationships*; and (3) the degree to which the malfunctioning of the intrapsychic structures is manifested directly by symptoms, which corresponds to the variable *severity of symptoms.*

The MSA similarly led us to conclude that there exists an overriding relationship between overall outcome (change) and ego strength especially regarding those aspects of ego strength related to the quality of interpersonal relationships: Patients with low initial ego strength (particularly low initial quality of interpersonal relationships) showed the least improvement. The MSA differentiated one modality of treatment from another, and suggested that while supportive treatment of patients with high initial ego strength was related to a good outcome, the greatest improvement was evidenced by patients with high initial ego strength who had undergone psychoanalysis. The MSA also concluded that patients with high ego strength improved less with supportive psychotherapy, supportive–expressive psychotherapy, or expressive psychotherapy than with psychoanalysis.

A general conclusion was that while high initial ego strength implied a good prognosis for all modalities of treatment within the psychoanalytic frame of reference, psychoanalysis may bring about the highest degree of improvement in such patients. This overall finding, supported by both methods of study (i.e., the statistical and the MSA) might raise the question of whether psychoanalysis may be considered the ideal treatment for patients who need it least—that is, those with high initial ego strength. High ego strength is not to be confused, however, with freedom from severe symptoms. High initial ego strength in these studies refers to one extreme of a continuum within our patient population and not to an ideal, or optimum, of normal psychological functioning.

The combined statistical analysis of the relationship between outcome, on the one hand, and focus on the transference, therapist's skill, and initial ego strength, on the other, revealed that patients with low initial ego strength treated by therapists with high skill improved to a significantly greater extent when the focus on the transference (as assessed by the variable *transference resolution*, considered as a process variable rather than an outcome variable) was high. Therefore, we concluded that the lower the initial ego strength of the patient, the more important is the work with the transference by a skilled therapist in determining the outcome of the treatment. The MSA revealed that patients with low ego strength who had been given supportive treatment, as well as patients with low ego strength who had been treated by psychoanalysis, belonged to the group of patients with the least degree of improvement. In contrast, patients with low ego strength tended to improve when treated with an expressive–supportive approach, and a group of patients with low initial ego strength who underwent supportive–expressive psychotherapy belonged to the region of high or highest degree of improvement.

The MSA showed that patients with low ego strength who received supportive–expressive psychotherapy with concomitant hospitalization belonged to the group showing a high increase in ego strength as measured at the follow-up point. In contrast, ego strength was not highly increased at follow-up among patients with low initial ego strength who were treated with supportive psychotherapy outside the hospital, with the therapist actively structuring the patient's daily life. These findings support the conclusion that the best treatment for such patients may be the combination of an expressive approach (with little structure during the treatment hours) and concomitant hospitalization as the patient needs it. This approach is in contrast to a purely supportive treatment, in which a good deal of structure is provided during the treatment hours and there is no hospital support.

Both methods of study concluded that patients with ego weakness require a special modality of treatment which could be described as a modified expressive or supportive–expressive approach. This approach focuses especially on work with the transference phenomena in the treatment hours. During the later phases of the project, the patients originally identified as those who had "ego weakness" were found on review of diagnostic data either to have been schizophrenic or to possess the cluster of attributes which has since been recognized as a special organization of the personality—the borderline personality organization (Kernberg, 1967). Actually, most of the patients in the project who were identified as having low initial ego strength conformed to the diagnosis of borderline personality organization, since schizophrenic patients were excluded from the study by design, and only one such patient found his way into a research sample.

One rather unexpected finding of the Menninger Foundation's Psychotherapy Project was that a relatively simple, quantitative measure of outcome —namely, the health–sickness rating scale—correlated so highly with paired comparisons of variables drawn from the major qualitative write-ups of change (involving multiple, individualized criteria) that the costly and tedious paired comparison method was largely superfluous. We had thought, on theoretical grounds, that psychotherapy outcome implied change along various dimensions which could not be integrated into one global measure of improvement; our findings convinced us that an integrated and quantified measure of improvement was a reasonable reflection of change.

SOME IMPLICATIONS FOR FUTURE RESEARCH

The naturalistic study of psychotherapy, of which the Menninger Project is probably a most sophisticated example, served the important purpose of defining significant variables and generating hypotheses for further experimental investigations. While some practitioners in our field are already convinced that psychoanalysis and psychotherapy are effective when conducted by skilled therapists with properly selected patients, others, and critics from outside the field, remain highly skeptical of the effectiveness of psychotherapy in general, and of whether its technical aspects are any more significant in helping patients than the ministrations of any well-meaning listener to the complaints of a troubled client. It is questionable whether further naturalistic studies will generate new knowledge or convince our critics of the value of what psychotherapists do. Studies of what good clinicians customarily do well at best demonstrate the obvious regarding transference, therapeutic alliance, and so on, which would hardly convince those critics who require scientific rigor before taking seriously any pronouncements about the effects of psychotherapy or any other intervention. At the same time, experienced practitioners and innovative theoreticians within our field will be bored by naturalistic studies that contribute nothing new. Experimental designs rather than naturalistic ones are therefore to be strongly preferred at the present stage of our development as a discipline.

Pure process analysis of psychotherapy or psychoanalysis that is not connected with outcome evaluation may lead to time-consuming investments on the part of research groups while the crucial question of the relationship among technique, process and outcome is left aside. Should a clear-cut relationship emerge from an experimental design involving both process and outcome variables, the rigorous critics of long-term psychotherapy are likely to be interested in such findings.

Treatment Variables—The Therapist's Skill

Research on long-term psychotherapy should focus on psychotherapy carried out by experienced therapists; otherwise the potential waste of time, the patient dropout rates, difficulties in evaluating specific treatment techniques, and so on, would not only be excessively costly, but would undermine the validity of whatever findings might have emerged. By the same token, however, psychotherapy research involving senior clinicians over a long time at the same institution may maximize the natural uneasiness that even highly experienced therapists develop when their work is inspected by others. The need to believe in the value of a psychotherapeutic approach to which a clinician has dedicated many years of training, and the reluctance to participate in a research effort that may prove clincians' convictions to be unfounded, are powerful motives for many senior clinicians to avoid involvement in research efforts evaluating the effectiveness of their particular approach.

On the basis of my experience, however, it is not true that this is the major reason for the reluctance on the part of senior clinicians to participate in psychotherapy research. For every rigid and dogmatic believer who has been successfully indoctrinated by an authoritarian training institution, I have found a self-questioning psychotherapist interested in ongoing critical evaluation and reevaluation of theories and techniques. Experienced, yet open-minded clinicians at advanced levels of training are present in most training centers, and can form the core of research groups to study psychotherapy. The best of the clinician/researchers in the field of long-term psychotherapy and psychoanalysis would wish to evaluate their work not only in terms of confirmation or disconfirmation of the general value of what they are doing, but in terms of generating new knowledge. This would be most interesting for the clinician, yet at the same time most controversial. My point is that for the purpose of studying the effect of psychotherapy we need to select and encourage senior, experienced clinicians who are raising challenging questions regarding their field and the nature of their own work, rather than selecting the "most representative" experienced therapists within a certain modality of treatment.

Experienced and skillful clinician/researchers will not carry out long-term psychotherapy according to preset technical standards unless they believe that what they are doing is the best for their patients; they cannot be cajoled into practicing treatment techniques they experience as hampering the exercise of the skills they have earned over years of study and practice. Thus, the problem is to provide alternative modalities of treatment that are equally prestigious in the institution where the research takes place. If this can be done, then clinicians can be recruited who are fully confident about the usefulness of what they are providing for their patients and who at the same time are committed to a design geared to develop new knowledge in the field rather than to a "horse race" between two competing and well-known treatment modalities.

Treatment Variables—Treatment Techniques

One major theoretical assumption within psychoanalytic theory regarding the specific effects of psychoanalysis is that of the development of structural intrapsychic change. Although the exact definition of what is meant by "structural intrapsychic change" may vary from author to author, the common features of these concepts include the assumption that, though change in psychotherapy may come about by various means, symptomatic change based on a significant restructuring of the patient's personality achieved in psychoanalytic treatment provides such change with depth and stability, so that it transcends change reflecting direct behavioral influences on the patient, "transference cures," and placebo effects. Structural intrapsychic change refers to a significant modification in the assumed, underlying, unconscious intrapsychic conflicts that determine the development of symptom formation.

One could argue, of course, that what matters to the patient is symptomatic and character change, and that the concept and related complications of structural intrapsychic change could be avoided if research on psychoanalytic treatment demonstrated the relevance of psychoanalytic technique for such symptomatic and character change. It might be added, perhaps cynically, that only psychoanalysts are concerned about the concept of structural intrapsychic change, and that the evaluation of the effectiveness of psychoanalytic technique in producing patient improvement could be researched regardless of such psychoanalytic assumptions.

New learning about himself or herself on the part of the patient in psychoanalysis emerges in the context of the systematic examination of transference paradigms. At some point, that new understanding should lead to a change in the obligatory nature of the reptition of a certain sequence of behavior patterns, to an actual disruption of the rigidity of the sequence, and the emergence of new, unexpected behavior, to be followed by further exploration regarding the unconscious meaning of this new behavior and a shift away from the previously obligatory behavioral sequence. Insight and shifts in the transference are thus intimately linked, and the transfer of the knowledge acquired in this context to the patient's behavior outside the sessions would be an important indicator that structural intrapsychic change is occurring.

In the light of the analysis of structural intrapsychic change formulated above, the specific aspect of the relation between interpretation and structural intrapsychic change is the emergence of new information, spontaneously provided by the patient in the context of the exploration of the transference, information that indicates new understanding of the patient's present behavior as well as its linkages to other experiences of the patient in the present and in the past. The unpredictability, the spontaneous emergence and expansion of this understanding as a precondition for changes in the transference, and the transfer of such change and understanding into other areas of the patient's behavior are what differentiate insight into unconscious conflicts derived from interpretation from other, cognitively induced change in the patient's present understanding, and from direct instructions for behavioral change by the therapist with which the patient complies. In other words, structural intrapsychic change may bring about behavioral change that generalizes more than that specifically and directly induced in the therapy.

To reiterate an issue that provided one of the starting points for conceptualizing an experimental study of psychotherapy for patients with borderline personality organization, one of the major initial predictions of the Menninger Project was that patients with low ego strength would benefit most from a supportive modality of treatment. This prediction was in accordance with the prevalent thinking at the time the Menninger Project started. Since the group of clinicians/researchers of the project were widely respected for their understanding of the complexities of psychoanalytic treatment, their findings have influenced the field; and what they found was that patients with low ego strength benefited most from a particular kind of expressive therapy. Since then the treatment of borderline patients in this country has gradually shifted away from the predominantly supportive modality of 20 years ago toward a more purely expressive psychotherapeutic approach, although in practice, a mixture of interpretive and supportive techniques is often carried out under the label "supportive–expressive psychotherapy." Indeed, most clinicians working with patients with borderline personality organization probably describe their work by this label (Kernberg, 1978).

One interesting function of long-term psychotherapy research may be to contribute to the differentiation of supportive and expressive techniques, and the study of their specific effects. Thus, for example, a consistent relationship between structural intrapsychic change and interpretive techniques on the one hand, and direct symptomatic and behavioral change on the basis of supportive techniques on the other, may strengthen the general theory of psychoanalytic treatment as well as sharpen the analysis of the psychotherapeutic process of various types of dynamic psychotherapy.

An experimental design to study expressive and supportive psychotherapy, then, requires definition of the interventions in each modality. This involves the construction of manuals that set forth the theory underlying the techniques, specify the key techniques that differentiate supportive from expressive work, and provide operational definitions of these key interventions. Since such manuals will be addressed to researchers in the field of psychotherapy rather than serve as textbooks for beginners, a generally high level of expertise and experience on the part of those who will use the manuals may be assumed.

There is no need, for research purposes, to prepare manuals describing psychotherapy in general, laying out such basic techniques as listening, accepting patients' communications, responding empathically, and so on. Manuals on crucial supportive and expressive interventions, however, may prove relevant and highly informative, particularly if various treatment modalities are compared that have the same underlying theory of technique but different specified technical approaches. One enormous advantage to such a restricted and specialized approach to manuals would be that controversial, clinically interesting aspects of technique may be evaluated in the process, thus conforming to the general principle proposed that research on long-term psychotherapy should deal with problems on the cutting edge of the field and not with demonstrating what will seem obvious or trivial to experienced clinicians.

Selection of Patients

The patient population to be studied should be selected on the basis of convergence of clinical criteria with DSM-III criteria, and a restrictive spectrum of severity of illness, thus circumscribing by the combination of overlapping clinical, research, and classificatory–bureaucratic considerations a patient population easily recognizable by the professional field at large. Such overlapping selection criteria by which all patients have to fit simultaneously into several diagnostic criteria, stemming from different viewpoints, should include characterological, symptomatic, and demographic features.

A PROPOSAL FOR RESEARCH ON LONG-TERM PSYCHOTHERAPY OF BORDERLINE PERSONALITY DISORDERS

This proposal has been developed by the author, in collaboration with Ann Appelbaum, MD; Arthur Carr, PhD; John Clarkin, PhD; Paulina Kernberg, MD; Harold Koenigsberg, MD; Andrew Lotterman, MD; John Oldham, MD; Lawrence Rockland, MD; Jesse Schomer, MD; and Michael Selzer, MD (Kernberg, Goldstein, Carr, Hunt, Bauer, & Blumenthal, 1981).

Goals and Objectives

The overall goal of this research is to study the effects of two distinct psychotherapeutic techniques on the process of long-term psychotherapy with patients suffering from borderline personality disorder. A related goal is to contribute to the study of process and outcome of long-term psychotherapy.

Specific objectives subsumed under these overall goals include (1) to describe in manual form two parallel types of therapeutic techniques derived from psychoanalytic theory of psychotherapy—expressive psychotherapy and supportive psychotherapy—both of them specifically modified for borderline patients; (2) to develop instruments with confirmed validity and reliability to measure these psychotherapeutic techniques, and to measure intrapsychic structure and its change over time; (3) to predict, in the light of a theory of psychotherapy that is common to both, the specific effects of each technique on the patient–therapist interaction; (4) to compare the predicted effects of these interventions with actual effects observed in the course of psychotherapeutic sessions; and (5) to study the overall effects on outcome of psychotherapy of these two psychotherapeutic techniques and, in this context, evaluate specific relations between psychotherapeutic process and outcome.

Rationale

The present effort is a continuation of research carried out originally at the New York State Psychiatric Institute and later at the Westchester Division of New York Hospital on the diagnosis of borderline personality disorder. Working with a psychostructural hypothesis of personality organization, our research group developed a special interview ("structural interview") with the purpose of differentiating "borderline personality organization" from neurotic and psychotic personality organizations (Kernberg, 1977, 1981a).

The diagnosis of borderline personality organization arrived at on the basis of this interview was significantly correlated with the diagnosis of borderline personality disorder on the basis of Gunderson's diagnostic interview for borderlines (DIB) and clinical diagnoses carried out independently with a hospitalized patient population at Westchester Division. In the process, we were able to define the variables of reality testing, identity diffusion, and predominance of primitive defensive operations as three personality characteristics which we feel differentiate borderline personality organization. In our view, this may be a heuristically valuable contribution to the present study of the still controversial diagnostic entity of borderline personality disorder. It is our intention to select for further study a group of patients diagnosed as "borderline" on the basis of DSM-III criteria, the DIB, and our structural interview. These patients will thus correspond to a "core" group of borderline conditions common to various classifications and criteria currently undergoing intense investigation throughout this country.

We are planning to carry out long-term psychotherapy with patients presenting borderline personality disorder thus selected, and to evaluate psychotherapy outcome in relation to the actual process of psychotherapy. Long-term psychotherapy with borderline patients is a prevalent modality of treatment for these patients, and empirical research on the effectiveness of this treatment is a major need.

We plan to develop two mutually contrasting yet equally interesting and desirable modalities of treatment. Both modalities will be based on a common theoretical frame. Insofar as that common frame, a psychoanalytic theory of psychotherapy, represents researcher bias, there exists a risk of unconscious attempts to "demonstrate" the value of this theoretical frame influencing this psychotherapy research. However, insofar as this frame is translated into differentiated techniques that, by design, are constrasting, and insofar as we hypothesize favorable but different effects of each technique, the problem of comparing psychotherapy outcome (i.e., is one modality better than the other?) is changed into the question whether or not different techniques produce different courses and outcomes. This approach should reduce the risk of research bias toward one modality of treatment. Absence of differentiable outcome of such contrasting techniques may indicate the ineffectiveness of both techniques, the equal effectiveness of both, or the overriding importance of "nonspecific" or non-accounted-for effects of psychotherapy in contrast to specific, predicted effects of such techniques.

EXPRESSIVE AND SUPPORTIVE PSYCHOTHERAPY: MUTUAL DIFFERENTIATION AND HYPOTHESIZED DIFFERENTIAL EFFECTS

Expressive and supportive psychotherapies in our conception are modalities of treatment derived from psychoanalysis (Kernberg, 1981b, 1982).

On this basis, expressive psychotherapy, particularly as applied to the treatment of the borderline personality disorder, is defined as a treatment modality characterized by the use of clarification, confrontation, and interpretation as major tools—similar to psychoanalysis, but with clarification and confrontation predominating over interpretation in the early stages of the treatment, and a predominance of the interpretation of unconscious meanings in the "here and now" over the genetic tracing of these unconscious meanings back into the patient's past throughout the major part of the treatment. The transference is interpreted in expressive psychotherapy (as in psychoanalysis), but transference interpretations are partial, codetermined by (1) the predominant transference paradigm, (2) the patient's immediate external reality, and (3) the particular long-range treatment goals.

In expressive psychotherapy with borderline patients one tries to maintain technical neutrality but is continually challenged by the severity of acting out and the need to structure the patient's life outside the treatment setting. It becomes necessary to reinstate this technical neutrality repeatedly by means of interpretation, including the reasons for necessary departures from technical neutrality.

In contrast, supportive psychotherapy for borderline patients is defined as a treatment modality that does not use interpretation; instead, clarification and confrontation are used to highlight the inappropriate or unrealistic aspects of the transference in order to dispel, disperse, reduce, or deflect outside the treatment situation such inappropriate transference.

In addition, cognitive and emotional supports are used in helping patients to apply their developing knowledge about the inappropriate nature of their interactions with the therapist (the transference). The goal is to improve the patients's relations in reality with the therapist, as well as with significant others in his or her external life situation. Cognitive support should strengthen cognitive functions that are often swept aside in borderline patients. Emotional support implies the communication of sympathy and encouragement in dealing with their conflicts.

Supportive psychotherapy for borderline patients also uses the techniques of advice giving in areas where the patient is unable to understand or react appropriately in dealing with life problems, and of direct environmental intervention in dealing with external circumstances that exacerbate the patients' pathological behavior or undermine his or her efforts to control it.

In supportive psychotherapy then, while the therapist must remain acutely aware of the transference, monitor its vicissitudes, and carefully consider transference resistances in relation to his or her technique in dealing with the patients' character problems and their connection to life difficulties, the transference is not interpreted. The use of suggestion, advice, and environmental intervention eliminates technical neutrality by design. In supportive psychotherapy, mutual influences of the learning regarding the patient's interactions in external reality and in the transference reinforce each other and may lead to behavioral change as a direct consequence of the guidelines set forth by the therapist in his or her exploration of these patterns and his or her attempts to modify them.

In expressive psychotherapy, in contrast, we expect the development of "structural intrapsychic change," namely, a change in the sequence of pathological behavior patterns derived from the interpretation of their unconscious meaning, and particularly, from the interpretation of intrapsychic conflicts expressed in the alternation of contradictory behavior patterns in the relation to the therapist. Here, in contrast to supportive psychotherapy, the psychotherapist does not directly suggest changes in the patient's behavior and does not support, reward, discourage, or suppress aspects of it; rather, one expects spontaneous changes to occur in response to the increase of knowledge of unconscious meanings.

In simple terms, in expressive psychotherapy, the therapist does not tell the patient how to behave. The patient is expected to alter his or her functioning in new, unexpected ways, and solutions may spread from one area to another according to change in associated meanings rather than related behavioral directions. The amount of suggestive influence of the therapist on the patient is expected to be much greater in supportive psychotherapy; the behavioral change outside the hours will be much more a direct consequence of behavior the therapist attempts to strengthen in the patient; and unexpected, new knowledge "spontaneously" evolving in the patient as a consequence of the exploration of unconscious meanings is not expected to develop.

One major weakness of our design is the potential similarity between the two techniques. This relates to their derivation from a common theory. It may be argued that even if these two techniques can theoretically and operationally be clearly differentiated from each other, the therapists may not carry out clearly differentiated treatment procedures. Avoidance of this pitfall will require a very detailed monitoring of the relation between specific interventions and their short-term and long-term effects. It may well be that the overall outcome may be the same with both techniques. If so, this research should contribute to clarifying the question to what extent final common effects may be reached by seemingly different roads.

If there are clearly differentiated short-term responses related to techniques, the study will have contributed to clarifying the question of "specific" versus "nonspecific" effects of psychotherapy. The "nonspecific" effects of psychotherapy (such as the activation of hope, the therapist's strength of conviction, commonly shared goals of patient and therapist, and a friendly atmosphere) can be assumed to operate equally in both treatment modalities proposed; if these effects were of overriding influence over the specific effects of the contrasting techniques to be investigated, these nonspecific effects should become clearer as we evaluate processes signaling change unrelated to the predicted effects of specifically designed, contrasting techniques.

A detailed approach to process, session by session, over a long period of time, seems to us indispensable as part of our methodology. By the same token, this research, at least in the first phase, implies a design involving a small number of patients to be studied intensively over a long period of time, rather than a study of large experimental groups (where the specific effects of differential techniques on overall outcome may be submerged in simple statistical comparisons between the two groups).

REFERENCES

Kernberg, O. Borderline personality organization. *Journal of the American Psychoanalytic Association*, 1967, *15*, 641–685.

Kernberg, O. The structural diagnosis of borderline personality organization. In P. Hartocollis (Ed.), *Borderline personality disorders*. New York: International Universities Press, 1977.

Kernberg, O. Contrasting approaches to the treatment of borderline conditions. In J. Masterson (Ed.), *New perspectives in psychotherapy of the borderline adult*. New York: Brunner/Mazel, 1978.

Kernberg, O. Structural interviewing. In M. Stone (Ed.), *Psychiatric clinics of North America* (Vol. 4). Philadelphia: Saunders, 1981. (a)

Kernberg, O. The theory of psychoanalytic psychotherapy. In S. Slipp (Ed.), *Curative factors in dynamic psychotherapy*. New York: McGraw-Hill, 1981. (b)

Kernberg, O. Supportive psychotherapy with borderline conditions. In J. O. Cavenar & H. K. Brodie (Eds.), *Critical problems in psychiatry*. Philadelphia: Lippincott, 1982.

Kernberg, O., Burstein, E. D., Coyne, L., Appelbaum, A., Horwitz, L., & Voth, H. *Psychotherapy and psychoanalysis: Final report of the Menninger Foundation's psychotherapy research project*. Topeka, Ks.: Menninger Foundation, 1972.

Kernberg, O., Goldstein, E., Carr, A., Hunt, H., Bauer, S., & Blumenthal, R. Diagnosing borderline personality. *Journal of Nervous and Mental Disease*, 1981, *169*, 225-231.

COMMENTARY

Dr. Sol L. Garfield*: Dr. Kernberg, in the monograph reporting the Menninger study, I wasn't able to see what was the relative improvement rate for the two different forms of therapy that were studied and evaluated.

Dr. Kernberg: We didn't organize the data in terms of relative improvement rate, but compared the degree of improvement or worsening of each patient in relation to the total sample and in relation to the particular techniques selected. The basis for the factor analyses were paired comparisons of change, and these comparisons didn't give us absolute rates of improvement, but a comparison of all the patients in terms of who did better than who. So at the lower end there was worsening of the cases, and at the upper one the most improvement.

So we don't have data that would come from direct rates of improvement: high, low, or zero. In fact, there was a strong bias against establishing such overall rating systems in order to avoid excessive simplification of psychotherapy outcome. I am not defending that design necessarily, but I am explaining why you didn't find that.

Dr. Garfield: Don't you have to have some baseline, though, to relate your inferences to some level of improvement? Otherwise, do you really know if the therapy is effective, or effective enough with a certain percentage of cases? I mean, if you continue to do internal analyses, you never really have some general statement about the overall effectiveness of the therapy, which, in some sense, one needs if one is going to look at process variables.

Dr. Kernberg: Sure. The design didn't call for a study of overall effectiveness of the therapy, but the design called for the overall effect on patient change of X number of variables derived from the entire spectrum of psychoanalytic treatments.

Of course, I could give you an answer clinically, but that has no specific statistical value, which is very similar to the findings in most psychotherapy projects: Somewhere between two-thirds and three-fourths of the patients

*Washington University.

improved to some extent, probably half of the patients improved very significantly, and approximately one-fourth worsened, including several patients who committed suicide or died from the effects of their symptoms, directly or indirectly.

One striking finding, against our predictions, was that the weaker the patient's ego, the better he or she responded to a combined analytic therapy with supportive elements in the treatment. In other words, expressive therapy was very important for the sickest patients. The institutional bias was that the sicker the patient the more supportive you have to be, which is what used to be thought 20 or 30 years ago in the field at large. In fact, I think that was a reassuring finding in the sense that it ran against all our biases at that time. It certainly influenced my views and my whole approach to the treatment of borderline patients.

16

Opening Comments

GEORGE E. MURPHY
Washington University School of Medicine

It is increasingly clear that the question "Is psychotherapy effective?" is an insufficiently specific question. Whether we are dealing with studies of process or studies of outcome, a part of what is always being asked is "Is this psychotherapy effective for this patient or this problem?" A meaningful addressing of this question had to await a reliable diagnostic system, whether it be the Feighner criteria, Research Diagnostic Criteria, or DSM-III. It is now possible to test psychotherapies of carefully defined conditions, such as major depression. We are beginning to accumulate evidence to suggest that certain psychotherapies just may be effective in alleviating depression, although we are still a long way from satisfying our critics.

As Dr. Sloane pointed out, Colby remarked some time ago that therapists neither read nor believe research studies, so that these studies have no effect on their practice. I submit that up to the present, no reasonably critical therapist has found much to believe or much that would move him or her to change his or her practice, let alone to give up one form of therapy for another.

However, there are some hints of progress. Both Bruce Sloane's and Hans Strupp's studies showed that where psychoanalytic therapists are concerned, there are certain nonillness patient variables that are very important to treatment outcome: the YAVIS variables, or, as I prefer to think of them, YAVIE, for Young, Attractive, Verbal, Intelligent, and Educated. The patient who fits the therapist's expectations may benefit the most; the patient who is not so blessed or obliging, fares poorly. But I don't think this means that psychoanalytic therapy is only for the YAVIE, or modal patient.

Strupp has shown that psychoanalytically trained therapists seem not to accommodate themselves to the angularities of the nonmodal patient, and he would probably trace that behavior to their training rather than the method itself. It may be that the better results that behavior therapists got in Sloane's study were merely the result of the therapists' paying greater attention to the patients' concerns. Strupp is now proposing that psychoanalytic therapists adopt a more flexible approach to the patient, a modification of therapy that might sell to practicing therapists. It may be that part of whatever efficacy cognitive behavior therapy has is a function of the very focused attention that is given to the patient in developing a problem list and pursuing it item by item to the resolution, to the patient's satisfaction, of what it was he or she came for. There must be a way of controlling for that variable in testing what is efficacious in this therapy.

Finally, there is still not enough reason for therapists to change their entire approach to practice, even if CBT, IPT, or another therapy should convincingly prove as effective for the treatment of depression as its most euphoric adherents would have us believe. Depression, after all, is not the main or only problem therapists confront. If, however, we were to learn that there are specific factors of therapy that benefit depression, then it might behoove therapists to incorporate those specific interventions into their repertoires for this specific problem when they encounter it.

It is not the aim of psychotherapy outcome research studies to prove one therapy better than another. Rather, our aim is ultimately to discover what each has uniquely to offer and to find those possibly specific features of each that may be incorporated into other therapies and result in smoothly effective and flexible psychotherapies.

General Discussion

Dr. Hans H. Strupp*: I would like to address a comment to you, Dr. Murphy. You made a comment early in your discussion referring to the importance of nonillness variables in patients that are predictive of therapeutic outcome. There is, of course, a long literature relating to what the analysts have called analyzability, which is composed of variables that have to do with a patient's previous adaptation, ways of relating to significant others, relating to himself or herself, motivation, and ability to become involved in a particular kind of interpersonal relationship that makes up psychoanalytic or psychodynamic or interpersonal psychotherapy that is based on verbal interaction.

I would say that these are not nonillness variables. They are, in a sense, perhaps, but they are also critically intertwined with at least what we view as the difficulties that the patient brings to psychotherapy. It is disturbances in interpersonal relationships, the difficulties that people have with significant others, that are the ones that are treated by psychoanalytic psychotherapy. Now, true, these are interpersonal difficulties, and they are also intrapsychic factors. I think this is just one of the things I would like to take issue with. When we talk about depression, or the discouragement, or whatever symptoms the patient may have, these are interpersonally anchored.

So the distinction you are making between nonillness variables and illness variables, I think, is an artificial one and a potentially misleading one. And I would like to correct it, or at least take issue with it.

Dr. George E. Murphy†: Thank you, Dr. Strupp. I was referring particularly to the YAVIS or YAVIE characteristics, and the modal characteristics of patients that therapists like particularly. Now, have I confused that with the things you are saying?

Dr. Strupp: I think when we talk about YAVIS variables, "young" is very tricky. I think Freud unfortunately introduced a myth, but I don't think there is much evidence of it, that older people aren't particularly treatable. I don't think there is much evidence that young people are the only ones who are responsive to verbal interactional psychotherapy. And you can go down

*Vanderbilt University.
†Washington University School of Medicine.

the list—I mean, some of these are sort of seemingly discrete variables, but what I was really wanting to call attention to was the artificiality of these so-called nonillness variables.

Dr. Murphy: The distinction is clear in my mind. I would like to take this opportunity to ask Dr. Kernberg: How do you measure structural intrapsychic change?

Dr. Otto F. Kernberg:* That is, of course, the most difficult question, as your smiles indicate. What is it that psychoanalytic theory assumes specifically on which it must stand or fall? That each patient has a few basic conflicts that are hardened in his or her personality or character structure that will show up in the treatment again, and again, and again, and again, and either these change and everything will be all right, or they don't change. If they don't, the patient may smile and act happier, but basically nothing will have changed. Now, that may be right or wrong. I am just saying what psychoanalysis says.

I happen to believe, on the basis of clinical experience treating very sick patients over a long period of time, that there is some truth to it. To put it more specifically, each patient has a limited repertoire of significant patterns that repeat themselves again and again that require some time to be diagnosed. I mean, if you see the patient for a total of 15 sessions, you may never know what these are. But after you see him or her for 50 sessions, you know. Sometimes you know even after ten sessions, but not always.

So first of all, in long-term treatment, you start redefining what your symptoms are, and you discover, as was said before, that the patient who is depressed may be depressed for many reasons, that depression is just an entrance to get into psychotherapy, but nothing more than that (except if you have a major affective illness—then it is certainly much more than that).

Structural intrapsychic change would refer to the following process: First, the diagnosis of dominant and repetitive patterns clearly specified and documented in the treatment situation, and awareness that these patterns are relevant to what happens outside the sessions as well. If a male patient depreciates everything he receives from the therapist, and the patient at the same time has sexual promiscuity, at one point we may discover that the sexual promiscuity has to do with an unconscious devaluation of women, which is similar to the unconscious devaluation of the therapist that shows up every three or four sessions. That is step 1.

Step 2: The therapist attempts to analyze, explain, and formulate reasons for these patterns in the course of which the patient acquires new knowledge and understanding about himself. The therapist doesn't tell the

*New York Hospital–Cornell Medical Center, Westchester Division; Cornell University Medical College; and Columbia University Center for Psychoanalytic Training and Research.

patient "be nice to women." He analyzes what is going on with depreciation as a character trait. That is step 2.

Step 3: The patient understands past reasons for his devaluation of the therapist, and by the same token realizes that he has similar attitudes toward women. And, lo and behold, there is a change in his behavior toward women. That, I would see, is an illustration of structural intrapsychic change.

One final comment. We are talking about patients who are really sick, whose relations with others are chronically aggressive, disturbed, self-defeating. YAVIE patients are patients who probably can improve with anything, with common sense, with Hertz Rent-a-Friend, and I think these patients are inappropriate for psychotherapy research. If psychotherapy has anything to offer, it should start where common sense and an ordinary slap on the shoulder end. Unless we deal with those patients, we are dealing with something trivial, and I don't think anybody should give us money for it. That is my bias.

Dr. Murphy: Thank you for that comprehensive answer. As I understand it, then, it might be possible for a therapist in long-term therapy within the first 3 or 4 months, perhaps, to specify what some of these structural difficulties are, and then at the end of treatment to be able to specify to what degree those had changed. Is that it?

Dr. Kernberg: Yes. In fact, this already is being done, and Luborsky has been working on this, and Mardi Horowitz has been working on this. And it may well be that it may take much less than we are really focusing our attention on—that we might diagnose it after a few sessions. I don't know. In any case, I think Luborsky has contributed a very important, hopeful opening in this field.

Dr. Strupp: Dr. Kernberg, I agree very much with you on the identification of recurrent patterns of behavior of interacting, which I really think is where it's at. And that's what needs to be studied. A question that comes up is the extent to which it might be possible to expedite the identification and modification of such patterns, or whether this has to take its natural course over a long period of time. And I don't think we have really good evidence for that at this point.

Dr. Kernberg: I think we don't, but I think there are ways of diagnosing this quickly. What I have called "structural interviewing" as part of the diagnostic technique might be one way to quickly bring about the sickest pattern in the patient. In other words, to start out the treatment pressing the patient for the limits of his or her self-understanding and awareness of pathological behaviors and interactions. A stressful technique, but not an artificial induction of stress—rather an open focusing on where the problems are greatest.

Very often psychotherapists start out with the assumption that first you have to establish a friendly relationship with the patient by being nice to him or her. I think that is questionable.

Dr. A. John Rush*: A comment about recurrent patterns. I think that most patients who seek out treatment, at least those we see in the area of psychiatry at a medical center, have recurrent patterns. That is, in fact, the reason that they show up for treatment. If it is a one-time problem that lasts 2 or 3 months, it comes and goes, and they don't go for treatment. So I would concur that that is the critical focus of not just psychoanalytic therapy, but really all major therapies. And I think, in fact, that is probably, ultimately the cost justification for the therapy. In other words, if we cannot show prophylaxis, but only symptom reduction that is somewhat greater than, equal to, or less than chemotherapy for certain syndromes for which drugs are available, I think we would be hard pressed to sell our skills in the cost–benefit equation.

Dr. Strupp: John's question and other comments remind me of a conference I attended a few months ago sponsored by NIMH, in which there were people of various orientations present. The one thing people of different orientations agreed on quite well was precisely this idea of maladaptive, chronic patterns that people bring to therapy and that manifest themselves in their daily lives and lead to difficulties with significant people. And what we have here, I think, is a modern-day reformulation of one of Freud's greatest insights, the transference idea—namely, that people have the uncanny tendency to reenact with people who become significant to them emotionally, difficulties that they have built up over the years. And that these people make the therapist as a significant person, a co-actor in their difficulties. The tendency of people unwittingly or unconsciously to enact with significant others, the very difficulties that are the illness for which they are typically being treated, also allows their resolution.

Now, as to how to modify these patterns, I think we know as yet very little. But I think this is the direction that is perhaps a common ground, where behavior therapists and psychodynamicists as well as a lot of other people can begin to operate.

It is also an area that is beautifully operational—there is nothing esoteric or mysterious about it. What the patient enacts with the therapist as the significant other is empirical. It is there for people to see; we can study it, we can understand it, and we can begin to operate on it.

Dr. Rush: You and I agree that the patterns are critical. I think where there may be some divergence of opinion that could be investigated is whether the method to modify these patterns is exclusively transference and its interpretation, or, possibly, development of another kind of a model, say, with schemata, and then modifying behavior in the experiential world and in

---

*University of Texas Health Science Center.

the relationship to see whether one can intrude on those patterns. So I might differ a little with the conceptualization, but not the target.

Dr. Joseph Zubin*: It seems to me that as a result of the last 2 days' discussion, what is happening is we have now developed systematic structured interviews to the point where they are reliable. We are now beginning to develop systematic structured therapies to the point where they might be equally conventionalized, standardized, so that we can look upon them as a systematic approach to therapy. It seems to me we have three reasons for doing this. First, there is a *specific* reason for trying to establish a scientific basis for what we are doing, both in the interviewing and in the therapeutic situation. We have a *pragmatic* reason for trying to develop these techniques to the point where they can be spread over to many more people than the innovators themselves. And we have also *third-party-payment* reasons for engaging in this kind of systematic approach.

From the point of view of the scientific approach to the problem, we have two aspects that Rachenbach pointed to a long time ago: the realm of discovery and the realm of verification. The realm of discovery can perhaps be exemplified by the storming of a beachhead with a new idea. The realm of verification is where the foot soldiers come on shore and bring peace and quiet, and organize the land.

It seems to me that what we are doing now is in the realm not so much of discovery, but verification. We are moving along in that direction. But let's not forget where the sources of what we know now came from. Let's continue to bring new ideas into the field. Let's try and replenish, as I believe Dr. Strupp tried to point out, the current conventionalized, standardized approach with new ideas. Let's go back to phenomenology, both in the area of the interviewing and diagnosis, and the area of therapy, because that is where the ideas come from.

We are now living on top of three to four centuries of accumulated knowledge, both on the diagnostic side and on the therapeutic side. Let's not conventionalize and standardize things as of 1980. Let's move ahead and come back to the phenomenology for new insights.

Dr. Kernberg: I would like to comment on what was said regarding different methodologies and theories of change. I think it is really very important that we identify the same patterns from a cognitive, from a behavioral, from a psychoanalytic viewpoint, and then work on them with different techniques and see whether they change.

Dr. Donald F. Klein†: I would like to follow up on Dr. Garfield's question of Dr. Kernberg.

One of the great promises of psychoanalysis was just what you were talking about: its ability to understand that there is a structural problem with

*University of Pittsburgh School of Medicine.

†New York State Psychiatric Institute and College of Physicians and Surgeons, Columbia University.

the patient, and that structural intrapsychic change can be brought about. Such structural intrapsychic change, one would hope, would be accompanied by a symptomatic remission and by functional competence, interpersonal competence, the restoration of what Freud talked about—the ability to work and love.

Now, indeed, those are wonderful goals. I think that although it was referred to before as simplistic to be concerned about outcome, nonetheless that is what we have to be concerned about. There is no reason to put a tremendous amount of time, effort, money, and professional skill into studying something that is not very promising. It seems to me that the Menninger study of some 42 people could give us some guidelines as to just how promising these methods are.

I was interested in hearing Dr. Kernberg say that 25% of the patients seem to get worse. I don't think that is the general conviction as to what these forms of therapies will do with apparently suitable patients. I would like to have an estimate of what proportion of the patients had structural intrapsychic change accompanied by symptomatic remission and functional competence.

Dr. Kernberg: I very much agree with every point you made, and that is one of the problems with psychoanalysis. Psychoanalysts have been terribly reluctant to do research, to give us the data. And there is only a small proportion of psychoanalysts willing to do any research on this at all.

The Menninger project was the first psychoanalytic effort to work on this. It started in 1954, in the infancy of technology of psychotherapy research.

Dr. Klein: The Menninger project has my entire admiration. I think it was a wonderful start. Nonetheless, you do have outcome data on 42 people, and you should be able to answer the question.

Dr. Kernberg: I think the task we have is definitely to evaluate outcome. I didn't say that evaluation of outcome alone was simplistic. I just said it would be worthless if long-term psychotherapy, at this point, is studied only in terms of outcome, in the same way as I think it is worthless to do pure process studies that are not linked to outcome. I would even imagine that that is not controversial to say this. Methodologically, of course, it is extremely difficult, how to combine the two. And the proof of the pudding is that we don't yet have good studies in this regard.

Dr. Klein: Dr. Kernberg, is there any chance we can get this worthless data? (*Laughter.*) I think it would be very interesting to many people as to just what proportion of the patients had structural intrapsychic change accompanied by remission.

Dr. Kernberg: No, I don't have the data beyond clinical impressions and clinical communications. No study has been carried out answering that, and that is precisely what we have to do. I mean, are you complaining because that which we have to do has not yet been done? I am not following you.

Dr. Klein: I am sorry; I can't accept the idea that you don't have the data. Those patients were analyzed, they were followed, they had complete psychotherapy work-ups. You have tremendous rating scales on them before and after. You have got the data.

Dr. Kernberg: Yes, I understand you now. You are saying this study was carried out with the patients of the Menninger Psychotherapy Research Project?

Dr. Klein: Right.

Dr. Kernberg: The method, the quantitative analysis that I reported, was not dealing with the issue of structural intrapsychic change. It was not a question raised at that time. It is a formulation that has evolved after the completion of that project. However, Dr. Robert Wallerstein is, at this time, reviewing all of these cases in terms of these very questions, and I hope that his book will be published within the next 9–12 months.

Dr. Strupp: Not ever having been connected with the Menninger study, but having some knowledge about it, I would like to make a comment. I have read Dr. Wallerstein's reanalysis of this study, and a lot of these patients, as Wallerstein himself points out, were very sick people; also, the changes they underwent were rather modest. So I think that by their own account there wasn't great success.

As a more general comment, I don't know what intrapsychic or structural change means. The only way we can ever demonstrate it, it seems to me, is through the patient's feelings, cognitions, and behavior. I think we have yet to go some considerable distance in specifying, first of all, what those changes are, and secondly, what in particular cases we want to achieve. I think that we have to arrive at some understanding of the kinds of changes we are looking for, what we want to achieve, what we are satisfied with. And that is a very, very complex question.

Dr. Kenneth Altshuler*: It was interesting to hear all the panelists focus on the identification of maladaptive behavior patterns in different groups to elicit change. It seems to me that the theoretical difference between analytic therapies and the learning therapies has to do with the idea that the maladaptive patterns are purposeful, in a sense, and resultant of an effort to repress unconscious aspects of motivation.

I wonder, in that connection, if one approaches such problems by interpretation of the transference and reiteration and exhortation, if that is not just another way of attacking, in a cognitive fashion, the same thing that the cognitive therapists attack when they recognize a cognitive schema that is distorted and suggest an alternative way of behavior.

So I wonder if either Dr. Strupp or Dr. Kernberg, who were focusing on the dynamic, insightful methods of therapy, are focusing on the resistance to changing these patterns or bringing them into awareness.

Dr. Kernberg: I think we have the task to define structural intrapsychic

*Southwestern Medical School.

change operationally. Otherwise it is just a fantasy. And that should permit a comparison of psychoanalytic and behavioral treatments around the same objective variables.

Let me illustrate this with what we are doing in our present study. We are planning to measure the intrapsychic changes as reflected in three structural characteristics of borderline patients that we have identified before—identity integration, predominance of primitive defensive operations, and reality testing. We have operationalized these three structural intrapsychic variables in terms of a self-report measure, about 39 items on a questionnaire that we are giving the patients initially, and that we are planning to give them every 3 months. In addition, we are planning to use a modified version of the Beck Depression Inventory and a semistructural interview, to evaluate the same structural characteristics. And it will be possible to compare changes on these three variables in the expressive and supportive treatment. Our assumption is that they should change more significantly in the expressive treatment.

This is, it seems to me, a task that psychoanalytic research cannot avoid, to operationalize what is meant by structural intrapsychic change, and test it.

Dr. Robert A. Neimeyer*: In listening to Drs. Kernberg, Strupp, and Sloane speak, it seems clear that you have distilled from your own work and from your clinical impressions some notions about what effective psychotherapy ought to be doing, and I was wondering if any of you would care to share any impressions regarding potential deficiencies in a cognitive, behavioral approach; ways in which it does not match up to your best predictions now as to what an effective therapy is. Are there certain things that seem to be sorely lacking in a cognitive approach? Then perhaps Dr. Rush could provide a rejoinder.

Dr. Murphy: Before these panelists respond to that, I would like to say that I would certainly not be competent to discuss in what ways psychoanalysis does not measure up, and I think perhaps those psychoanalytically trained may not be prepared to answer that question.

Dr. Neimeyer: Well, don't take it so easy, Dr. Kernberg.

Dr. Kernberg: I think there are some ways in which psychoanalysis is not measuring up. I can talk about that. I think the cognitive and behavior therapists should talk about how their treatments don't measure up.

Psychoanalysis, I think, doesn't measure up because of the potential for arbitrary interpretations and fancy theories that are given to patients and practically indoctrinate them. In other words, we educate the patient toward our theories. The problem psychoanalysis has is how can we differentiate what comes from the patient from our own indoctrination of him? And we haven't solved that problem. I see that as the major problem with the relation between psychoanalytic theory and technique. Now I would like to hear from the other side where your problems lie.

*Memphis State University.

Dr. R. Bruce Sloane*: Before he says that, I would say that there is nothing wrong with cognitive therapy, but why do we have to make it antipodal? I am not an analyst. In therapy you may have to make an interpretation—you might have to make it quite a lot. You may also make cognitive or behavioral interventions. Why do we have to—why can't we embrace each other, in a sense? If you have been trained in a number of ways, this is what you do in practice.

Dr. Neimeyer: Maybe I could just say something to sharpen the question. I am not meaning to invite conflict that is to no purpose, but I think there are certain things that can come from constructive criticism that may not come from just a pseudo mutuality, that we are all working toward common goals, when in fact real differences may exist.

So, for example, some of Luborsky's work has demonstrated that whether the treatment is cognitive–behavioral or more analytically oriented, support seems to be an important predictor of outcome in therapy. And support, I think, had not been really taken into account as sufficiently as it might have been in cognitive–behavioral formulations. So I think there may be deficiencies in theorizing that can be pointed up and perhaps corrected by a critical dialogue.

Dr. Murphy: John, will you respond specifically to that?

Dr. Rush: Yes. The development of a therapeutic package is not a one-time, stamp-it and test-it and roll-it-out-on-the-assembly-line kind of exercise. One starts with some ideas, interacts with patients, refines techniques, and gets a sense of for which sorts of patients with what kinds of problems these sorts of strategies might be helpful.

That leads us to a second problem, which maybe is a rephrasing of your question, and that is perhaps a "package" or delimited series of strategies and conceptualizations that are good for a subset of patients, but not for all patients. We have run, in fact, some borderline patients with cognitive therapy, and our recommendation, in writing, for several years has been try not to use it with these patients. We feel that it is too confrontive and demanding, and one doesn't have a chance to develop some sort of trust and mutuality to hold the patient in therapy. Many of these patients, for example, start to balk at all sorts of demands that we are placing on them.

One can deal with that as resistance through a cognitive maneuver which we have tried with these patients, but that doesn't seem to work. So I think it is a question of not just what's deficient in a package, as if there is supposed to be an ideal therapy package where we just put everything in the can and eventually come out with a delicatessen of cures for everybody. I think, rather, it is a matter much more like psychopharmacology, where certain sorts of conditions respond to certain sorts of agents. Other conditions may respond partly to them. And I think the issue is, in addition to

*University of Southern California School of Medicine.

sharing techniques and getting some sense of deficiencies back and forth, also to try to specify for whom, once you've got an approximation of a treatment, is it likely to be more or less effective.

Dr. Arthur K. Shapiro*: One of the major advances in medicine, as documented by some historians in the 1950s, is the development of the methodology for the evaluation of treatments, thus avoiding the age-old problem of substituting one placebo for another. Of course, this has developed considerably, and we know a lot about how to do it: randomization, predictive hypotheses, et cetera.

One thing that has also become apparent is that one is able to evaluate the reliability and validity of your concepts. In regard to the study of that in psychoanalysis, I am reminded of the work of Hartvig Dahl, who had excellent credentials as a card-carrying New York psychoanalyst, and also as a well-trained methodologist who tried to study the problem. And the study, as some of you remember because he presented his material many times, involved five very senior analysts having transcripts of the record—maybe audio recordings—to see if they could come to a consensus about what was going on in the patient; that is, what were the unconscious mechanisms, what was the transference, what could one expect? And as of a few years ago, when I last heard of them, the results were practically zero; that is, hardly anybody ever agreed with anyone. And the one time the five raters agreed, the therapist disagreed, and had a completely different interpretation. It led to one conclusion: that perhaps every analysis should be conducted by a therapist who never says anything until he consults with the raters, and if they all agree, he should say something.

It is very easy to develop ideas, and most ideas in the world, and certainly ideas in regard to the history of medicine, have been absolutely wrong. There's maybe one out of 10,000 that is correct. One indication that you are dealing with placebo effects is when researchers and therapists and people in medicine develop one hope and substitute it for another; that is, one idea to keep them going. And one indication that you are dealing with a placebo effect is to deal with process to the exclusion of efficacy. So the two have to go hand in hand, and the question is, what provisions are you making for carefully studying the reliability and validity of all these interpretations in order to relate it to what you are trying to study?

Dr. Kernberg: I am absolutely in agreement, and the research that Dr. Dahl is doing is the kind that will not lead anywhere because it is only process research, and because we are asking analysts to agree rather than forcing the analysts to make clear definitions, and having independent raters to rate whether this is observable or not.

---

*Mount Sinai School of Medicine.

17

Presidential Address

Psychiatric Diagnosis:
Are Clinicians Still Necessary?

ROBERT L. SPITZER
*College of Physicians and Surgeons, Columbia University,
and New York State Psychiatric Institute*

INTRODUCTION

The American Psychopathological Association is steeped in tradition. One tradition is that the president plays a major role in selecting the theme for the annual meeting. When I joined Joe Zubin's Biometrics Research Department at the New York State Psychiatric Institute, after completing my psychiatric residency, my long-term goal was psychotherapy research, the topic I proposed for this meeting. Another tradition is that the president of the association delivers a presidential address at the annual meeting on a topic of his or her choice. By yet another tradition, the printed program notes only "Presidential Address," thereby allowing the president the option of deciding the actual topic of the talk only moments before it is given.

I did not take advantage of this option, and first began brooding (having automatic thoughts, to use the terminology of cognitive therapy) about the topic of this talk when I accepted the nominating committee's choice of me as a candidate for vice president and realized that an inevitable chain of events would finally lead to this moment. Although presidential addresses usually involve an aspect of the theme of the annual meeting, my initial career goal of doing psychotherapy research was not to be, and my work since that time has focused on problems of assessment of psychopathology and, more recently, diagnosis. I therefore decided to talk about what I know best with the happy realization, as this meeting makes clear, that psychotherapy researchers no longer regard issues of diagnostic assessment as irrelevant to the central problems of psychotherapy research.

It occurred to me that a historical review of the development of structured interviews for assessing psychopathology and diagnosis, culminating in several important recent developments, would be useful. I asked my mentor, Joe Zubin, if he knew of the very first use of structured interviews. According to him, he believed that their first use was in the Inquisition and ensured that potential witches and heretics were systematically assessed. If true, it is a chilling thought and a reminder that genealogic research frequently uncovers unsavory ancestry.

Undaunted, the topic of the history of structured interviews still seemed promising, and with a certain narcissistic glee, I looked forward to reviewing my own contribution to this area, the development in 1961 (with Eugene Burdock and Anne Hardesty) of the first structured interview for the comprehensive assessment of mental status, the Mental Status Schedule (Spitzer, Fleiss, Burdock, & Hardesty, 1964). By coincidence, a few months ago, as I was musing about this early work, my mother presented me with a faded copy of a July 28, 1963, article that appeared in the *New York Post*. The title was "The Mental Health Quiz: Question and Answer Approach Holds Promise for Standardized Diagnostic Aid." That my mother should save a copy of the article is no surprise since, according to the reporter, "a young doctor at Columbia University's New York State Psychiatric Institute has developed a tool which may become the psychiatrist's thermometer and microscope and X-ray machine rolled into one. It is simply an 11 page questionnaire and rating scale." In fact, like the proverbial bear who can dance—one should marvel that a bear can dance at all and not judge its lack of grace too harshly—the Mental Status Schedule itself was little used in research and is primarily of historical interest in tracing the genealogy of some instruments that have been more widely used, such as the Psychiatric Status Schedule (PSS) (Spitzer, Endicott, Fleiss, & Cohen, 1970), the Current and Past Psychopathology Scales (CAPPS) (Endicott & Spitzer, 1972), and the Schedule for Affective Disorders and Schizophrenia (SADS) (Endicott & Spitzer, 1978).

Further study of the history of structured interviews for evaluating psychopathology revealed the (to me) unpleasant fact that the first edition of John Wing's structured interview schedule, the now well-known Present State Examination (PSE) (Wing & Giddens, 1959), antedated by several years my own Mental Status Schedule. All was not lost. I could still claim to have developed the first structured interview for eliciting psychopathology *in this country*. However, I then found out that Eli Robins and other Washington University investigators in St. Louis in the mid-1950s had developed structured interviews for use in several studies they were conducting. These early structured interviews were not published. With this new piece of information I would have to further qualify that I developed the first *published* interview schedule for use in this country, etcetera, etcetera.

The lack of narcissistic gratification that I experienced in my brief research into the history of structured interviews made me decide that I would rather discuss with you only the most recent developments in the use of structured interviews for psychiatric diagnosis. These new developments raise an issue that was unthinkable only a few years ago, namely: Are clinicians still necessary for making psychiatric diagnoses? This topic will also enable me to share with you some preliminary work I have begun with my colleague Dr. Janet Williams. We are developing yet another structured interview for psychiatric diagnosis, but one predicated on the self-serving hypothesis that clinicians are indeed still necessary (or at least highly desirable) to make the most valid psychiatric diagnoses. This topic allows us to describe the approach we are taking in developing this new instrument, and to use this audience, many of whom use structured interviews in their research and are therefore potential users, as consultants (unpaid, of course).

STRUCTURED INTERVIEWS FOR MAKING PSYCHIATRIC DIAGNOSES

Structured interviews for making psychiatric diagnoses are hardly a new development and go back to the computer program DIAGNO (Spitzer & Endicott, 1968), which simulated a DSM-I diagnosis using data from the Psychiatric Status Schedule (again—remember the dancing bear), and the widely used computer program CATEGO (Wing, Cooper, & Sartorius, 1974) based on data collected by John Wing's Present State Exam, which yields a syndromal diagnosis. In both these efforts the clinician was used only to collect the necessary data using the structured interview. It was the computer program that summarized the data into a diagnosis.

The next attempt to use structured interviews to make diagnoses involved the clinician more directly: A clinical interviewer using the Schedule for Affective Disorders (SADS) made a psychiatric diagnosis based on the data collected after consulting the Research Diagnostic Criteria (RDC) (Spitzer, Endicott, & Robins, 1978). In all of these efforts the research strategy was basically the same. Information variance was minimized by the use of a structured interview which ensured that the clinician systematically covered all of the relevant areas of psychopathology; observation and interpretation variance were minimized by ensuring that the interviewers had training in recognizing psychopathology; and criterion variance, which results when different rules are used to summarize the clinical information into a psychiatric diagnosis, was minimized by the use of specified diagnostic criteria.

These and other similar instruments using structured interviews for making psychiatric diagnoses were developed by psychiatrists and clinical psychologists. They were convinced that their clinical colleagues would make more reliable and valid diagnoses if they used interview schedules to collect the clinical data and if specified diagnostic criteria were used to summarize the information into diagnoses. But it is hardly surprising that it never occurred to any of them that a clinically trained person was not necessary to administer the interview schedule and make the ratings of psychopathology; that perhaps the structure of a specially designed interview schedule and the use of a computer program to summarize the data might make it possible to dispense with the requirement that the interview schedule be administered by a clinically trained professional.

The Washington University Department of Psychiatry in St. Louis, not content with one major assault on the grandiosity of clinicians by starting the revolution of specified diagnostic criteria (Feighner, Robins, Guze, Woodruff, Winokur, & Muñoz, 1972), did the unthinkable. Under the leadership of Lee Robins (a distinguished medical sociologist with extensive experience in designing survey instruments, but not herself a clinician), and with two psychiatrist collaborators, John Helzer and Jack Croughan, an interview schedule has been developed that can be administered by individuals without any clinical experience—only a week or two of intensive training is necessary. The data are analyzed by a computer program which applies the criteria of Feighner, the RDC, and DSM-III, and makes a large number of diagnoses according to these systems. This instrument is called the NIMH Diagnostic Interview Schedule, or more colloquially, the DIS (Robins, Helzer, Croughan, & Ratcliff, 1981). It was developed at the request of the Division of Biometry and Epidemiology for use in several large-scale epidemiologic studies that are now under way, the Epidemiologic Catchment Area Program (Regier, Myers, Kramer, Robins, Blazer, Hough, Eaton, & Locke, 1982). (Dr. Williams and I were fortunate to have been able to play a small role in the development of the DIS; we served as consultants to review drafts and made suggestions for changes in the questions and the computer algorithms.)

Although originally developed for use in epidemiologic studies in which the cost of employing clinically trained interviewers is prohibitive, the DIS is now being used by many investigators in nonepidemiologic studies as well. (If the DIS is another bear trying to dance, it does not want for dancing partners!)

To answer the question raised by the title of this report—are clinicians still necessary to make psychiatric diagnoses?—we will first examine the innovations in the DIS that allow it to be administered by nonclinicians, and will contrast this approach with the one we are taking in developing our new structured interview for clinicians; then we will examine the validity evidence that has been presented for the DIS and discuss the harsh demands that are placed on the use of a diagnostic instrument in epidemiologic studies. Finally, we will discuss the kind of validity evidence that will tell us what advantages, if any, there are in using clinicians to make psychiatric diagnoses.

CONTRASTING APPROACHES IN STRUCTURED
INTERVIEWS FOR PSYCHIATRIC DIAGNOSIS

It is now time to tell you the name of our new instrument. In order to emphasize that it is modeled on the clinical interview (even more than its ancestors, such as the SADS), and to give it a classy Germanic flavor, we first considered the Structured Klinical (with a "K") Interview for Diagnosis. Several esteemed colleagues remarked that acronym, SKID, suggested to them that the "downward drift hypothesis" might well apply to the authors and that we had better consider other possibilities. We did. They included (1) Diagnostic Interview Guide (DIG) (a bit too canine); (2) Structured Interview for Diagnosis (SID) (how would Sidney Malitz, the acting chairman of our department, feel?); and (3) Comprehensive Hierarchical Assessment for Diagnosis (CHAD) (the name of a Third World country). A colleague thought we should capitalize on our acknowledged authority in nosological matters and suggested Guided Observations for Diagnosis (GOD). Another suggested a name with a more technical referent and an uplifting acronym, Structured Interview for Nosological Groups (SING). Finally, yet another colleague suggested abandoning any defense against narcissism, and proposed Structured Psychiatric interview To Zealously Enhance Research (SPITZER). Unable to decide this issue ourselves, we polled a large group of consultants who are helping us develop this instrument. The consensus seemed to be in favor of the original name—with two modifications: Clinical, not Klinical, and more specifically, "for DSM-III" rather than "for Diagnosis." So, Structured Clinical Interview for DSM-III (SCID) it is.

Now for the comparison between the DIS and the SCID. The reader will note that the DIS attempts to overcome the limitations of using lay interviewers by thoroughly structuring the interview and by using the computers to summarize the information into diagnoses. The SCID, in contrast, allows for greater flexibility in the interview by taking advantage of the strengths of the traditional clinical diagnostic interview.

Data Base

The DIS interviewer obtains all of the clinical information about the subject from the subject. This is clearly necessary since a lay interviewer would not be in a position to evaluate other sources of information, such as a note from a referring physician, the observations of ward personnel (if the subject has been hospitalized), or previous hospital or clinic records. In contrast, the SCID interviewer (unless contrary to the needs of a particular study) is encouraged to use all sources of information available about the subject in making the ratings. If there is a discrepancy between the subject's account and some other source of information (e.g., a family member) the interviewer is told to (gently) confront the patient with the discrepancy. In such a situation it is the interviewer who makes the final decision as to the most likely state of affairs.

Ideally, as suggested by Brockington (Brockington & Meltzer, 1982), when the SCID is used to document an episode of psychiatric illness, the final ratings should also take into account information collected from all of the clinical staff that have had contact with the patient.

Type of Questions and Interviewer Judgments

All DIS questions to determine whether a symptom has been present are close-ended (i.e., the lay interviewer describes the symptom in the question and the subject responds with a simple "yes" or "no" answer). Further close-ended questions are used to see if the symptom meets certain criteria for clinical or diagnostic significance, such as severity, frequency, and clustering in time with other symptoms. The DIS interviewer reads the questions as they are written. If the subject seems not to understand what is meant by a question it is repeated or broken down into segments. Only rarely does a question need to be rephrased by the interviewer. Thus, the fully structured interview requires only that the DIS interviewer make the relatively simple judgment that first, the subject understood the question being asked, and second, the answer to the question was "yes" or "no." (One clinician trained to administer the DIS admitted that it held promise for use in epidemiologic studies, but complained that it reduced the subject to a "yes and no machine.")

In contrast, in the SCID, as in most clinical interviews, there are many open-ended questions to encourage subjects to describe symptoms in their own words rather than merely agree or disagree that a symptom described by the interviewer is present. For example, the first question in the affective-disorders section of the SCID is "What's your mood been like?" The SCID interviewer is encouraged to rephrase an interview schedule question whenever the subject seems not to understand the intent of the question.

Figure 1 shows the beginning of the affective-disorders portion of the SCID. The left side of each page contains the interview questions with directions to the interviewer. In the middle of the page are the corresponding DSM-III criteria. The purpose of the questions is to elicit from the subject all of the necessary information to enable the interviewer to make a judgment about the DSM-III criteria. The right-hand column of each page contains codes for rating the criteria as either YES (present), NO (absent), or ? (uncertain). Thus in the SCID the judgments made by the interviewer are as complex as the individual DSM-III diagnostic criteria. The diagnostic criteria are used, as noted in DSM-III, as "guides" and not as rigid rules. If

AFFECTIVE DISORDERS
CRITERIA

**CURRENT MAJOR
DEPRESSIVE EPISODE**

Now I am going to ask you some specific questions about how you have been feeling recently (*or specify other definition of "current," e.g., "past month"*) . . .

		No	?	Yes

What's your mood been like?

A. Either (1) or (2):

Have you been feeling depressed or down?
If yes: Since this began, has there been a 2-week period when you felt this way every day?

(1) Depressed mood (e.g., sad, blue, hopeless, low, down in the dumps) every day for at least 2 weeks   No 1   ? 2   Yes **3**   xx

Have you been not interested in things or unable to enjoy the things you used to?
If yes: Since this began, has there been a 2-week period when you felt this way every day?
Since (date of onset of present illness), when was this the worst?

(2) Loss of interest or pleasure in all or almost all activities every day for at least 2 weeks   1   2   [Go to past MDE, p. 10]   3   xx

For the worst period of current episode, ask about associated SXs. If a SX may have been only intermittent, ask: Was this nearly every day for 2 weeks or more?

B. During the depressive period, at least four of the following symptoms have been present nearly every day:

How has your appetite been? (What about compared to your usual appetite? Do you have to force yourself to eat? Eating more than usual?)

(1) Poor appetite or significant weight loss or increased appetite or significant weight gain   1   2   3   xx

Figure 1. Portion of affective-disorders section of the SCID.

an interviewer uses the DSM-III criteria other than as exactly written (e.g., considering two items coded as uncertain as being equivalent to one coded as definitely present), this is recorded so that it can be reviewed at a later time when a decision can be made as to whether or not the interviewer's diagnosis should be revised.

Chief Complaint and History of Present Illness

Even when the DIS is administered to a patient in an initial evaluation, the patient is never asked what the problem is that is causing him or her to seek clinical care. In contrast, at the beginning of a SCID interview, the interviewer first obtains an overview of the history of the present illness and past episodes of psychopathology before systematically inquiring about specific symptoms. This overview of the present illness is pursued, often with questions improvised by the interviewer, until the following are fairly clear: the environmental context in which the present episode developed; when the height of the current episode occurred; whether the current episode is a recurrence of a previous episode; the symptoms that accounted for the referral or admission; and the likely differential diagnosis. (If the SCID is used in community studies, the overview section can be replaced with a portion that inquires about personal problems without an assumption of patienthood.)

Period under Study

In the DIS, for all symptoms, the interviewer first asks if a given symptom has ever been present, and if so, how recently. The computer program uses this information to calculate both lifetime prevalence and current prevalence according to several definitions of "current." The SCID focuses on the clinical concept of the "current episode of illness," which is assumed to have occurred in the past year, and diagnostic judgments are based on the symptom pattern when the episode of illness was at its worst. The SCID also covers past episodes of affective disorder and psychotic disorders. (Eventually the SCID will also include a module for evaluating personality disorders.)

Screening Questions and Cutoffs

The DIS avoids screening questions and cutoffs so that the subject is asked about a large number of symptoms that may be diagnostically irrelevant. The SCID has a large number of screening questions and cutoffs so that if a subject does not meet the entry requirements for a disorder (e.g., the sustained dysphoric mood or loss of interest or pleasure or a major depressive episode), associated symptoms are not inquired about (e.g., the B symptoms of a full depressive syndrome). The sequence of questions in the SCID is designed to approximate the differential diagnostic process according to the DSM-III decision trees. Therefore, the presence of a disorder that hierarchically preempts another disorder allows the interviewer to skip over that preempted disorder (e.g., the presence of agoraphobia preempts a diagnosis of generalized anxiety disorder; the presence of bipolar disorder preempts a diagnosis of cyclothymic disorder).

Figure 2 shows how the SCID decision tree for affective disorders enables the interviewer, like an experienced clinician, to consider sequentially the various affective disorders according to these principles. After the overview, the subject is asked about a current major depressive episode. If any of the criteria are lacking the subject is then asked about a past major depressive episode. If a current major depressive episode is judged present, the subject is asked if there have been similar episodes in the past, but individual symptoms are not to be inquired about. The same approach is taken toward asking about current and past manic episodes. If there is a current or past manic episode then the interviewer goes to the anxiety disorders portion of the SCID, skipping over consideration of both dysthymic or cyclothymic disorder. In doing this the interviewer is also jumping over the psychotic disorders portion of the SCID, as psychotic features would already have been considered in assessing the exclusion criteria C and D for both a manic and a major depressive episode (this is not shown on the figure). If a manic episode has never been present, then cyclothymic disorder is considered, whether or not there has ever been a major depressive episode. If the hypomanic symptoms of cyclothymic disorder have been presented then dysthymic disorder is skipped over. After cyclothymic or dysthymic disorders are considered the interviewer goes to the psychotic disorders portion of the SCID (if the interviewer has not already been there while considering the exclusion criteria C and D for a manic or major depressive episode) or to anxiety disorders.

Who or What Makes the Diagnosis

The DIS computer program makes the diagnosis on the basis of algorithms that translate the DSM-III diagnostic criteria into inflexible rules which are then applied to the coded data after the interview has been completed. The lay interviewer therefore does not need to know anything about psychiatric diagnosis. In contrast, the SCID interviewer is expected to be familiar with DSM-III, to assess the DSM-III criteria as the interview progresses, and to make a provisional DSM-III diagnosis during the course of the interview, pending other diagnostic information that may become available.

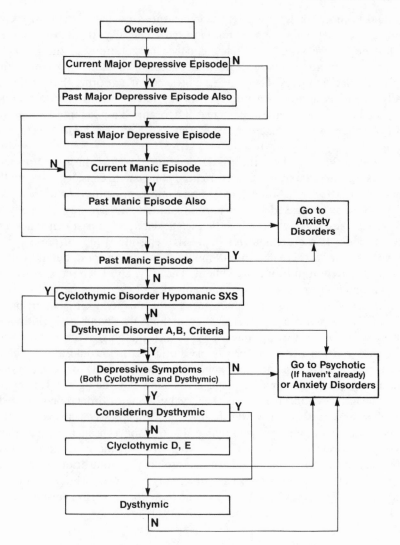

Figure 2. SCID decision tree for affective disorders.

VALIDITY EVIDENCE FOR THE DIS

Validity evidence always requires one or more external criteria that can be applied to the issue under study. Our St. Louis colleagues have already clarified the criteria to be used in assessing the validity of diagnostic concepts, such as course of illness and differential response to treatment. However, the issue of the validity of a diagnostic assessment instrument such as the DIS or the SCID is a very different matter, since the validity issue here is of the assessment procedure itself, not of the diagnostic categories. (Elsewhere, Williams and I have suggested the term "procedural validity" for issues of this kind; cf. Spitzer & Williams, 1980.)

In assessing the validity of a diagnostic interview, such as the DIS or SCID, it is not at all clear what the external criterion should be. What we would like to have is some already established diagnostic procedure that we could use as the criterion and compare the results of this established procedure on a sample of patients with the results obtained with our new instrument. Since the major impetus for developing structured interviews for assessing psychopathology and diagnosis is premised on lack of faith in the validity of the usual unstructured clinical interview, it can hardly be the ultimate standard against which our new diagnostic assessment instrument is to be measured. All we can say in this regard is that a modest degree of concordance between the results obtained with our new assessment procedure and the results of unstructured clinical interviews would be expected if our new assessment procedure is valid.

Let us now turn to the validity evidence that has been presented by the developers of the DIS. As noted by Robins in the first report describing the validity evidence for the DIS (Robins *et al.*, 1981), no existing diagnostic instrument was available to compare with the DIS that made the full range of DSM-III diagnoses made by the DIS. Instead, they first asked the modest but crucial question of whether the lay interviewer could administer the DIS, using as a yardstick the DIS administered by psychiatrists who had the option of asking additional questions after the DIS interview whenever they felt that the DIS questions were inadequate for them to resolve diagnostic uncertainties. In a large sample of diagnostically heterogeneous patients, using a test–retest design, the results differed little whether the DIS was administered by a psychiatrist or a lay interviewer. In addition, the DIS results with the psychiatrist differed little from the clinical impression of the psychiatrist recorded after his or her DIS interview. (A skeptic remarked that these results did not show that the DIS enabled lay interviewers to make clinical diagnoses, but rather than with the DIS clinicians could abandon and forget all of the clinical skills they had acquired over their years of training.)

In another paper on the validity of the DIS (Robins, Helzer, Ratcliff, & Seyfried, 1982), the DIS diagnoses were compared with the chart diagnoses given to the same patients to determine the extent to which the DIS results were in accord with common clinical practice. The results were encouraging: For those diagnoses appearing with adequate frequency, the DIS (whether administered by lay interviewers or by a psychiatrist) had a modest agreement with the chart diagnoses. However, examination of the discrepancies between the DIS and the chart diagnoses suggested that frequently the clinician failed to note a secondary diagnosis after making a principal diagnosis, and that clinical diagnoses were often based on fewer symptoms than required by the DSM-III criteria. Robins and her colleagues concluded that "clinical practice is not an adequate standard against which to measure the validity of a research instrument." I would heartily agree, if by the phrase "clinical practice" is meant "usual" clinical practice.

THE GRIM REALITY OF DIAGNOSTIC ASSESSMENT IN EPIDEMIOLOGIC STUDIES

The harsh demands placed on a diagnostic instrument used in community surveys of specific mental disorders is apparent after some fairly simple calculations (Fleiss, 1981). Let us take the case of schizophrenia, a relatively rare condition in the community, and assume a base rate of approximately 1%. Let us make the fairly generous assumption that our diagnostic instrument has a sensitivity of 80% for this disorder. That would mean that in a sample of 1,000 cases, assuming the base rate of 1%, there would be ten actual cases and our instrument would correctly diagnose eight of them as having the disorder. Now let us consider the specificity of our instrument—the proportion of noncases that are correctly identified as noncases. If the specificity is 99%—an extremely high value—it would mean that only one of 100 noncases would incorrectly be diagnosed as a case—for example, an eccentric or religious fanatic who is incorrectly diagnosed as having schizophrenia. But in our sample of 1,000 cases it would mean that we incorrectly diagnosed approximately ten noncases (actually, 9.9) as having schizophrenia. In this example our instrument would have diagnosed approximately 18 cases in the community as having schizophrenia, when actually only eight of the 18, less than half, would have been true cases.

The proportion of cases that our instrument diagnosed as having the disorder that actually had the disorder is called the predictive value of the test, and it is sobering to see how it plummets as the specificity drops. With the assumption of a sensitivity of 80% and a base rate of 1%, with a specificity of 99% the predictive value was only .44 (the eight true cases of the 18 diagnosed in our example). With a specificity of 98% the predictive value drops to .29, with a specificity of 95% it is .15, and with a specificity of 90% it is only .07!

This mathematical reality indicates the difficulty that is imposed on the use of any diagnostic assessment procedure for detecting relatively rare disorders in the community (Shrout & Fleiss, 1981). It also indicates the disastrous consequences of even a relatively small departure from the ideal of having 100% specificity. Obviously, these problems are further compounded if there are also serious problems in the sensitivity of the instrument.

Because of the absence of any direct comparison between the DIS and an established research procedure for making DSM-III diagnoses, we do not know to what extent the problems noted above may hinder the use of the DIS in epidemiologic studies. However, my clinical bias leads me to suspect that, despite the remarkable innovations in the DIS that allow it to be used by lay interviewers, there may be serious problems in both its sensitivity and its specificity that are inherent in its nonclinical, thoroughly structured approach. I suspect that the sensitivity of the DIS is fairly high with obvious cases of nonpsychotic disorders, but may be rather poor with individuals with psychotic disorders or with ambiguous or confusing clinical presentations. This is only a hypothesis but is consistent with the findings of a study done by Pulver and Carpenter (1983). They found that with the DIS only about half of a sample of patients who 11 years previously had been admitted to the hospital with a psychotic diagnosis acknowledged ever having had a psychotic symptom. The authors note that the design of their study did not enable them to determine if the low recall of psychotic symptoms was due to the DIS structured-format approach. Clinicians are certainly not always entirely successful in overcoming the reluctance of patients to discuss prior psychotic experiences. However, I would expect that the SCID approach, which would have enabled a clinician to ask, in detail, about past psychiatric hospitalizations and the reasons for them, would have been far more successful.

My clinical bias also leads me to suspect that the main advantage of the clinical SCID approach as compared to the highly structured DIS approach is the ability of the SCID interviewer to minimize false positives by focusing on the intent of the diagnostic criteria and not merely accepting a yes or no answer to a question. I would expect that the DIS might make many more false-positive diagnoses of mental disorder in the community than would a SCID interviewer; that is, the SCID would have greater specificity than the DIS. Again, this is only a hypothesis. In the NIMH Epidemiologic Catchment Area Program, the DIS diagnoses are being compared with an independently administered structured psychiatric evaluation that includes a modified PSE. The results will provide important information on the specificity and sensitivity of the DIS.

STRATEGIES FOR ASSESSING THE VALIDITY OF DIAGNOSTIC INTERVIEWS

Another Structured Interview as the Validity Criterion

Unfortunately, the SCID was not available when the DIS was being developed, and therefore it was not used as a criterion to determine the sensitivity and specificity of the DIS. Dr. Williams has started a study in which the DIS is being compared with the SCID in a group of psychiatric inpatients, and discrepancies are being examined in great detail in order to understand the nature of the disagreements. We hope that this study will provide suggestions for improving both instruments.

Because of my clinical bias, I believe that a strong case can be made for using the SCID, or some other structured clinical interview, as a criterion for evaluating the DIS. But what criterion can be used to evaluate the SCID—having already concluded that usual clinical practice is a flawed standard?

The LEAD Standard as a Criterion: A Proposal

There are only a few organic mental disorders for which a laboratory test can be the ultimate criterion, or "gold standard" for evaluating the validity of a diagnostic assessment instrument. In the absence of such a gold standard for most of the mental disorders, I propose the following more modest LEAD standard. (The acronym LEAD involves three essential concepts: Longitudinal, Expert, and All Data.)

Longitudinal. This means that the diagnostic evaluation is not limited to a single examination done at one point in the evolution of the illness, such as an initial evaluation performed on admission to the hospital. Symptoms that only emerge or are identified after an initial evaluation are also taken into account in diagnosing the entire episode of illness.

Expert. The criterion diagnoses are made by expert clinicians who have demonstrated their ability to make reliable diagnoses. These expert clinicians will make independent diagnoses based on thorough clinical interviews, discuss the reason for diagnostic disagreement, and then make consensus diagnoses that will constitute the criterion measure.

All Data. The expert clinicians will not only systematically evaluate the subject, but will interview other informants, such as family members, and will have access to data provided by other professionals, such as ward personnel and previous therapists. The evaluation will systematically assess the same diagnoses that are assessed by the SCID.

We have discussed with our consultants how the concept of the LEAD standard might be applied to evaluating the validity of the SCID as an initial assessment procedure. Consider a clinical service devoted to the study of, for example, patients with anxiety disorders or with psychotic disorders. The SCID is administered on admission with the SCID interviewer having access to whatever clinical information is available at that time, such as referral notes and previous case records. The patient is studied intensively for several months by the senior clinical staff (each of whom has previously participated in a systematic diagnostic reliability study in which adequate reliability was attained). This includes conducting independent diagnostic interviews with the patient and family members or friends, observing changes in the patient's condition over time. Finally, all of this material is reviewed and a consensus diagnosis for the episode of illness is made by the senior clinical staff after careful review of the DSM-III diagnostic criteria. This comprehensive longitudinal clinical assessment is then used as the diagnostic standard for evaluating the procedural validity of the SCID in a series of patients with a range of diagnoses.

Advances in psychiatric nosology, such as specified diagnostic criteria and the many recent changes in nomenclature and classification, always represent a challenge to cherished beliefs. So it is with the innovations of the DIS. The DIS has put the proverbial ball in the clinician's court and the score is 40–love in favor of the DIS. The burden of proof is now on the clinician to show that advances in technology have not made the clinician superfluous in the task of diagnostic assessment. Whatever the outcome of this game, a rematch is inevitable.

ACKNOWLEDGMENTS

I thank Drs. Jeffrey Boyd, John Helzer, Donald Klein, Lee Robins, and Janet B. W. Williams for their many helpful suggestions.

REFERENCES

Brockington, I. F., & Meltzer, H. Y. Documenting an episode of psychiatric illness: Need for multiple information sources, multiple raters, and narrative. *Schizophrenia Bulletin*, 1982, *8*, 485–492.

Endicott, J., Spitzer, R. L. Current and Past Psychopathology Scales (CAPPS): Rationale, reliability, and validity. *Archives of General Psychiatry*, 1972, *27*, 678–687.

Endicott, J., & Spitzer, R. L. A diagnostic interview: The Schedule for Affective Disorders and Schizophrenia. *Archives of General Psychiatry*, 1978, *35*, 837–844.

Fleiss, J. L. *Statistical methods for rates and proportions* (2nd ed.). New York: Wiley, 1981.

Feighner, J. P., Robins, E., Guze, S. B., Woodruff, R. A. Jr., Winokur, G., & Muñoz, R. Diagnostic criteria for use in psychiatric research. *Archives of General Psychiatry*, 1972, *26*, 57–63.

Pulver, A. E., & Carpenter, W. T. A study of the recall and report of lifetime psychotic symptoms as assessed with the Diagnostic Interview Schedule. *Schizophrenia Bulletin*, 1983, *9*(3), 377–382.

Regier, D. A., Myers, J. K., Kramer, M., Robins, L. N., Blazer, D. G., Hough, R. L., Eaton, W. W., & Locke, B. Z. *The NIMH Epidemiologic Catchment Area (ECA) program: Historical context, major objectives, and study population.* Paper presented at the annual meeting of the American Public Health Association (APHA), Montreal, Canada, November 1982.

Robins, L. N., Helzer, J. E., Croughan, J., & Ratcliff, K. S. National Institute of Mental Health Diagnostic Interview Schedule. *Archives of General Psychiatry*, 1981, *38*, 381–389.

Robins, L. N., Helzer, J. E., Ratcliff, K. S., & Seyfried, W. Validity of the Diagnostic Interview Schedule, version II: DSM-III diagnoses. *Psychological Medicine*, 1982, *12*, 855–870.

Shrout, P. E., & Fleiss, J. L. Reliability and case detection. In J. K. Wing, P. Bebbington, & L. N. Robins (Eds.), *What is a case? The problem of definition in psychiatric community surveys*. London: Grant-McIntyre, 1981.

Spitzer, R. L., & Endicott, J. DIAGNO: A computer program for psychiatric diagnosis utilizing the differential diagnostic procedure. *Archives of General Psychiatry*, 1968, *18*, 746–756.

Spitzer, R. L., Endicott, J., Fleiss, J. L., & Cohen, J. The Psychiatric Status Schedule: A technique for evaluating psychopathology and impairment in role functioning. *Archives of General Psychiatry*, 1970, *23*, 41–55.

Spitzer, R. L., Endicott, J., & Robins, E. Research Diagnostic Criteria: Rationale and reliability. *Archives of General Psychiatry*, 1978, *35*, 773–782.

Spitzer, R. L., Fleiss, J. L., Burdock, E. I., & Hardesty, A. S. The Mental Status Schedule: Rationale, reliability and validity. *Comprehensive Psychiatry*, 1964, *5*, 384–395.

Spitzer, R. L., & Williams, J. B. W. Classification of mental disorders and DSM-III. In H. I. Kaplan, A. M. Freedman, & B. J. Sadock (Eds.), *Comprehensive textbook of psychiatry* (3rd ed.). Baltimore: Williams & Wilkins, 1980.

Wing, J. K., Cooper, J. E., & Sartorius, N. *The description and classification of psychiatric symptoms: An instruction manual for the PSE and CATEGO System*. London: Cambridge University Press, 1974.

Wing, J. K., & Giddens, R. G. J. Industrial rehabilitation of male chronic schizophrenics. *Lancet*, 1959, *2*, 505–507.

COMMENTARY

Dr. Gerald L. Klerman*: I hesitate just a bit to disagree with you on what is a very high quality and erudite discussion; however, I think you are a little bit unfair to the DIS. I think you are correct in pointing out the inherent difficulties of any epidemiologic study in detecting a disorder with low frequency. There is, however, one other field study that used a structured interview in a community survey, and that is the Myers–Weissman study. which used an instrument with which I think you are familiar, the SADS, and the RDC. I think a fair comparison would involve the results of that.

Now it is probably true that if you use measures of sensitivity, specificity, and predictive value, any epidemiologic effort, even using laboratory tests, let alone a clinical interview whether conducted by trained clinicians or trained nonclinicians, has an uphill struggle. And I think it is to your credit that you do allude to the recent developments in public-health statistics around sensitivity, specificity, and predictive value, which have only slowly diffused into psychiatry and psychiatric epidemiology.

There is an alternative strategy that the public-health people have used, and that is a two-stage effort. I think Bruce Dohrenwend has recently alluded to this. Given the situation of a disorder with low frequency, the

*Harvard School of Medicine, Harvard School of Public Health, and Massachusetts General Hospital.

strategy is to use a screening technique which is of low cost, and to be willing to tolerate in screening a fair number of false positives, but not being willing to tolerate false negatives. And then in a second stage you go in with more expensive techniques.

This was done, for example, with the tuberculin test as a screen for TB and then X-rays, or the Pap smear as a screen for cervical cancer. Now, we have not done that yet in clinical psychiatry, and I think that until that is done no interview technique, even one as good as the SCID promises to be, is likely to deal with the important problem you raise. I think that to criticize the DIS on those grounds is a bit unfair because those issues are likely to apply to the SCID or any instrument that it takes to detect a disorder with low frequency, because the same problem comes even when there are highly objective laboratory techniques.

Dr. Spitzer: I think you are right. I hope that what I did was not so much criticize the DIS as alert myself and others to the difficulties imposed with using the DIS. But it certainly applies to any assessment procedure.

I think there is perhaps one difference between the DIS and, say, the SADS-L, and that is that the DIS is premised on something that needs to be shown, which is the use of nonclinicians. Therefore, I think perhaps there is a greater burden on using an instrument that is one step removed from a clinical assessment. Perhaps what I am suggesting does raise questions about a single-stage or two-stage procedure, as you mentioned.

Dr. John E. Helzer*: As a co-author of the DIS, I would first like to applaud your talk, and also applaud the development of a variety of interviews to make clinical diagnoses.

In developing the DIS it was never our intention to replace clinicians, and in fact the first interview, which eventually evolved into the DIS, was a clinical interview to make structured diagnoses, much like the SCID promises to be. And that evolved into a nonclinician interview because of the large amount of research that is done by nonclinicians, and primarily also because of the need for this kind of interview in the ECA study, where we would be interviewing many thousands of people repeatedly, and the impracticality of using physician interviewers for that.

Now, I think that much of the DIS does not preclude the evolution, also, into a less structured, perhaps more clinical interview. One of the things that could be done, for example, is to use screenings and cutoffs, as you mentioned, and to use symptom questions that are not fully specified, as they are in the DIS. But one sacrifice of doing that is some degree of sacrifice in the homogeneity of the clinical data. And I think the development of other kinds of interviews is going to give us the opportunity to examine the best,

*Washington University School of Medicine.

most accurate way of collecting clinical data to make diagnoses. And we, in fact, look forward to that kind of comparison.

Dr. Bruce Dohrenwend*: There was a powerful tradition in the field of psychiatric epidemiology that was ignored, and that was the tradition that started with World War II psychiatric screening using psychometrically derived scales, imperfect to begin with, and actuarial procedures.

I wonder if you would care to comment on perhaps why that was left out, especially around such important issues as the applicability of diagnostic instruments developed largely through work with patients, very often educated patients, and the applicability of those instruments to untreated cases in a wide variety of sex, class, ethnic groups, naive subjects, and so on in the general population—the kind of thing that perhaps psychometric techniques with actuarial rationales are particularly useful in attacking.

Dr. Spitzer: Okay, I think what you are asking me is why the SCID—if that is one example of a structured diagnostic interview—has ignored all of this other work.

I guess the answer is because of the shift to looking at specified criteria for specific mental disorders. And the work that you spoke of was mainly concerned with identifying a case and looking at how many items would, in a larger index, be sufficient to indicate that somebody was mentally ill. I mean, that was the Midtown approach, and I guess with the shift in focus in epidemiology to looking at specific mental disorders, that other approach was not incorporated.

Dr. Dohrenwend: I wasn't thinking of that so much as I was thinking of a staged procedure and a multimethod approach, and some opportunity of dealing with that base rate problem by segregating groups within a population, reliably, and different segments of the population where the frequencies of the symptoms are high enough so that you can possibly deal with them.

Dr. Spitzer: Okay, I think what you are really asking about is perhaps the decision in the ECA to go with a structured diagnostic interview. Why did they not consider a two-stage procedure that employed those other assessment procedures? I think that is really what the question is, and I think I am not the right person to ask.

Dr. Helzer: I could make a brief response to that. We have been interested for a long time at Washington University in developing screening interviews that are specifically diagnostically based. One of the problems with that was knowing what universe of symptoms to use and how best to use them. We saw the ECA as an ideal way of gathering symptom data on the general population for all symptoms that are considered psychiatrically relevant and then basing subsequent screening interviews on that large body of data.

---

*College of Physicians and Surgeons, Columbia University.

In fact, that is one of the major reasons that we do not have any cutoffs in the DIS interview. Whether that was the motivation on the part of NIMH I don't know, but that was our own approach to it.

Dr. Robert M. A. Hirschfeld*: A different point altogether. I would like to challenge you on the rationale for comparing the DIS and SCID. It seems to me that the DIS was developed for lay interviewers so that it could be done on a large scale; it is a one-shot interview, so that you cannot go after a lot of other validating information, and so is limited. To me, the logical comparison for you is with the SADS, because the SADS has been the state of the art, has been an attempt to use all of our clinical skills and other kinds of information. I mean, that has been the gold standard on which to base a diagnosis. And now, the one thing that I hear that the SCID has that the SADS doesn't is that it addresses DSM-III rather than the RDC the way the SADS does. And I would like to hear more from you about other innovations: What else have we learned since the development of the SADS I don't know how many years ago, that we can incorporate into an interview like this?

Dr. Spitzer: That is a fair question, and if I had enough time and a different context I would certainly try to indicate to people who were thinking of using a clinical instrument why I think the SCID has some significant innovations over the SADS. It's not just the focus on the DSM-III criteria. It's the whole structure, the fact that the criteria are actually in the instrument, the fact that the judgments are much simpler, only their presence, absence, or question is determined, rather than the scaled judgments in the SADS, which for many users makes it a very arduous procedure.

But I do think it is fair to contrast the SCID and the DIS. For one, the DIS, because it is the only instrument now available that makes DSM-III diagnoses that is being widely used in nonepidemiologic studies. Many people are using this because there is nothing else available as an instrument for clinical research with patients. So I think it is fair to ask questions about its validity.

In addition, there have been questions and there should be questions about any assessment procedure that is used in epidemiologic studies that is one step removed from clinical use. So I think it has been fair to make this comparison. But I was honest when I said that Janet [Williams] and I are proud to have contributed to the development of the DIS, and our friendship with our St. Louis colleagues is one that we care a lot about. That is why I had not only this version but the previous version of this paper reviewed carefully by Lee Robins and John [Helzer]. And I will continue to do that.

Dr. Judith L. Rapoport*: I would like to follow in your great tradition by asking a provocative question. It seems to me that there are really two

*National Institute of Mental Health.

issues you are raising: One is clinicians versus nonclinicians, and the other is a structured interview with or without appropriate probes that have some subjective assessment to them.

I think perhaps one of the most interesting comparisons that you might make is with a few weeks' appropriate training, clinicians versus nonclinicians on the SCID. I ask because we have some interesting data in that regard. We have been looking at the junior version of the DIS, the DIS-C [Diagnostic Interview Schedule—Child Version], administered not by our own clinicians, but by medical students. And these medical students, some of them, have had no psychiatry at all to date, so I consider them, as far as psychiatry goes, nonclinicians.

We have modified the DIS-C to have appropriate probes when there are any positive data. Our numbers are too small to talk about this as appropriate validity data of the stature that you have on these other instruments, but we have a very clear impression that they are doing as well as we would.

Dr. Spitzer: I accept the challenge.

Dr. Hirschfeld: This somewhat follows up on Bruce's [Dohrenwend] comment, and Gerry's [Klerman] remarks were, I think, also referring to it.

It seems to me that the tennis match isn't quite the best analogy. What it seems to me is that an analogy might be struck with what goes on in medicine. There are large screening studies that have been conducted for the prevalence of hypertension in the community, and indeed, individuals are trained to take a blood pressure or two blood pressures, and then individuals are referred to be evaluated by internists or cardiologists for if they really have hypertension, is it really fixed, et cetera.

It seemed that what was very important in the conceptual mode was the development of an instrument to get some idea of the prevalence of conditions that we see clinically in the community, and to have some isomorphism, as it were, between the two domains of discussion. And that is kind of the ground swell or origin from which the DIS grew. Who knows when you really know it is schizophrenia anyway? But the fact is that to get some parallelism between those two seems to be the intellectual background to the development of that.

Of course, they have to be compared, but they are not really fighting with one another, or slapping across the net.

Dr. Spitzer: Your point is well taken. The metaphor of the tennis match comes at the very end of the paper. I told Janet [Williams] that I was going to finish my paper after the discussion here. And she said no, all papers have to be finished before the meeting. So, to do that, I had to finish, and that was the metaphor I finished with.

"THE BOTTOM LINE": INTEGRATING PSYCHOTHERAPY RESEARCH FINDINGS— HOW GOOD IS THE EVIDENCE FOR EFFICACY AND SPECIFICITY?

18

Psychotherapy: Efficacy, Generality, and Specificity

SOL L. GARFIELD
Washington University

As is evident by the topics selected for this meeting, as well as by presentations at other meetings in recent years, the matter of research findings with particular reference to the efficacy of psychotherapy remains a controversial topic. In fact, I have referred elsewhere to the efficacy of psychotherapy as the perennial controversy (Garfield, 1983b). Perhaps more than some other areas, psychotherapy has its true believers and its doubters.

This controversy over the efficacy of psychotherapy has existed for at least the past 30 years and, despite a marked increase in research on psychotherapy, appears to have intensified in recent years. I believe that at least three factors are responsible for this latter occurrence: (1) the matter of third-party payments; (2) the swing from a psychoanalytic to a more biological emphasis in psychiatry; and (3) criticisms of existing research on outcome by behaviorists. The issue, however, is an important one and deserves an adequate analysis and response. The matter is also complex, and I will be able to allude only briefly to some of the problems involved.

THE EFFICACY OF PSYCHOTHERAPY

First, I want to review the conclusions derived from the major reviews of outcome in psychotherapy. Although some critical discussions were published by Obendorf (1943) and by others (Obendorf, Greenacre, & Kubie, 1948) in the 1940s, the first critical appraisal based on empirical studies was that published by Eysenck in 1952. Essentially, according to Eysenck, psychoanalysis was considerably less effective than no therapy and so-called eclectic therapy only slightly less so. Eysenck's critical paper had a considerable impact. It became clear that a need existed to substantiate the claims made for the effectiveness of psychotherapy. Since that time the situation has changed markedly in terms of research, although the controversy remains. A number of important reviews of the literature have also appeared, and I will refer to them and their major conclusions only very briefly as a background for discussion of the issue of efficacy.

Eysenck offered two additional reviews in 1961 and 1966, and reached the same conclusion that he did earlier. In essence, this was that the effectiveness of psychotherapy had yet to be demonstrated. In 1970, Meltzoff and Kornreich reviewed 101 studies, criticized Eysenck for omitting studies favorable to psychotherapy, and concluded that psychotherapy was effective. The following year, Bergin (1971) also was critical of Eysenck on a number of matters, and concluded that the effects of psychotherapy were modestly positive. The most important issue in this instance was that concerning the spontaneous remission rate. Whereas Eysenck offered a spontaneous remission rate of 65–70%, Bergin suggested a rate of about 31% but emphasized that the spontaneous remission rate would differ for the different disorders.

Rachman (1971, 1973), a colleague of Eysenck, tended to agree with Eysenck, and not with Bergin. Except for the behavioral therapies, he found little empirical support for psychotherapy's effectiveness. Luborsky, Singer, and Luborsksy (1975), however, in their review a few years later, concluded "that a high percentage of patients who go through any of these psychotherapies gain from them" (p. 1003), and that all of the therapies have won and should have prizes. Bergin and Lambert's review in 1978 was for the most part consistent with Bergin's (1971) earlier review, except that the spontaneous remission rate was estimated at 43% and admittedly showed considerable variability among the studies evaluated.

The preceding reviews all followed rather conventional styles. The reviewers appraised each study and offered their interpretations of the overall findings. A variant of this has been called the "box-score method," where the reviewer tabulates the results in terms of positive and negative findings. In all of these instances, the reviewer makes subjective judgments about the quality and significance of the studies, decides which studies to include or discard, and offers some sort of conclusion. Obviously, personal bias may enter into such evaluations, and would appear to account in part for the different conclusions secured from the various reviews. In the late 1970s, however, a new and more systematic procedure, meta-analysis, was introduced and applied to various bodies of data including psychotherapy outcome. Surprisingly, however, instead of resolving forever the perennial controversy on the efficacy of psychotherapy, meta-analysis seemingly has led to an increased crescendo in the argument. Because of its importance, let me say a bit about this procedure and the major reports based on it, even though I have no special expertise with regard to the methodology itself.

META-ANALYSIS AND PSYCHOTHERAPY

Meta-analysis is basically a procedure for systematically combining or synthesizing the results of a number of studies dealing with a specific problem. The claimed value for this procedure is that it allows one to analyze studies statistically in a manner comparable to the analysis performed on subjects in an individual study, although studies are usually not selected randomly. In this way, the idiosyncratic, subjective judgments and values of the individual reviewer are apparently minimized.

In essence, once the investigator or reviewer has stated clearly the criteria for inclusion of studies, comparisons of the average difference in outcome between treated and control groups are obtained, and expressed in some standard manner. Thus the data from individual studies can be combined. The degree or extent of change is usually expressed in standard deviation units as an effect size. Smith, Glass, and Miller (1980), in their meta-analytic study of the effects of psychotherapy, expressed the effect size they secured in terms of the mean difference between treated and control subjects divided by the standard deviation of the control subjects. This allows one to go beyond a mere statement of statistical significance and to provide some quantitative estimate of degree of change. The latter, supposedly, indicates more realistically the actual or practical significance of the changes secured.

Other values claimed for meta-analysis include the ability to investigate systematically a number of potentially significant variables that may influence outcome. Such factors as type of disorder, type of therapy, age of patient, length of therapy, and others can be ordered and statistically appraised. For example. Smith *et al.* (1980) found that the "more highly reactive the [outcome] measure, the greater the magnitude of effect" (p. 125). Meta-analysis also "makes obvious the large number of qualitative and often arbitrary decisions that one must make during a research integration" (Strube & Hartmann, 1983, p. 15). There are some other features as well, but this will have to suffice for my purpose here. A description of the procedure and its application to psychotherapy research is contained in the book by Smith *et al.* (1980) and in a special section in the February 1983 issue of the *Journal of Consulting and Clinical Psychology* devoted to meta-analysis and psychotherapy.

It should be mentioned also that meta-analysis is a relatively new procedure, its methods are not perfect, and it has its own statistical-based problems (Fiske, 1983; Strube & Hartmann, 1983). Among these are issues of sampling research studies and the adequacy and accuracy of the data reported in such studies. One should also differentiate between a particular meta-analysis and the method itself. It seems very likely that meta-analysis will be used increasingly in the future and may become the accepted procedure for reviewing the research literature in any specific area.

Our concerns here, however, are not with meta-analysis *per se*, but with the application of this methodology to the appraisal of outcome in psychotherapy, and this means primarily an evaluation of the volume by Smith *et al.* (1980), *The Benefits of Psychotherapy*. In commenting rather briefly on this work, I will touch on both substantive findings and methodological issues.

After publishing a preliminary report based on 375 studies in 1977, Smith and Glass (1977), along with Miller, came out with their final report based on 475 studies of counseling and psychotherapy, both published and unpublished (Smith *et al.*, 1980). Not only was their review of studies the largest ever published, but as you know, their conclusions were among the most positive ever reported. Psychotherapy was judged to be clearly effective, and the obtained effect size of .85 S.D., indicating that 80% of the treated groups exceeded the mean of the control groups, was considered relatively large when compared to studies in other social science areas. The findings of both the preliminary and later reports by Smith and colleagues were eagerly received by many individuals as vindicating their faith in psychotherapy. After all, this was the largest scale and most systematic review ever conducted. On the other hand, a number of criticisms were leveled at the procedures and conclusions of these investigators (Eysenck, 1978; Gallo, 1978; Rachman & Wilson, 1980; Rimland, 1979; Strahan, 1978). I will go into these criticisms shortly. However, before doing so I would like to mention one final review on the effectiveness of psychotherapy, that by Rachman and Wilson (1980).

These reviewers essentially evaluated the effectiveness of several of the best-known forms of psychotherapy. To state matters succinctly, they found no data to support the efficacy of psychoanalysis and limited data to support the view that psychotherapy produces positive results. Behavioral therapies were found to be superior to the other therapies, although the cognitive behavior therapies were considered promising. These authors also were quite critical of the report by Smith and Glass (1977), and specifically mentioned the omission of many well-conducted studies of behavior therapy.

COMMENTS ON THE REVIEWS

Although reported in a very cryptic manner, I have reviewed the principal findings of the major reviews, and to stay within my allotted space, I will offer a few cryptic conclusions. Although the reviews by Eysenck, by Rachman, and by Rachman and Wilson tend to be critical of the effectiveness of psychotherapy and positive with reference to the behavior therapies, all of the other reviewers express more positive evaluations of psychotherapy generally. Nevertheless, although the latter reviews conclude that psychotherapy has been shown to have some degree of efficacy, the extent of efficacy claimed does appear to vary among them. Because the number of studies analyzed by Smith *et al.* (1980) is by far the largest, and their conclusions stated rather unequivocally, their review may be viewed as the most positive. Furthermore, it is important to point out that in the positive reviews the results of the various psychotherapies that have been evaluated have been found to be roughly comparable. However, both individual studies and these reviews of research have been criticized, including the two conclusions just mentioned.

Some of the main criticisms made of many or all of the reviews are that a number of poor studies were included, that the reviewers did not specify clearly the criteria for inclusion or exclusion of studies, that many good studies were excluded, and that mixed samples of subjects were used in terms of categories of disturbance. As a result of such deficiencies, it is believed that the conclusions that can be drawn are limited (Garfield, 1983a). The reviews by Smith and Glass (1977) and Smith *et al.* (1980) have come in for particular criticism, and because of their importance I want next to offer some comments on their reports.

Along with some rather vituperative comments that were offered by some reviewers, there are also some that appear to merit consideration and which should be mentioned. One such criticism is that Smith *et al.* (1980) included studies that varied greatly in quality and yet are treated equally in their meta-analysis. Some were unpublished, some were published, and some were doctoral dissertations. Another criticism was that many of the studies used volunteers or recruited subjects who are not really comparable to clinical samples. The average age of the subjects was about 23 years, and many were college students. Also, certain categories of problems were over-emphasized (e.g., phobias) whereas other common problems such as depression were underemphasized. Finally, many of the therapists were still in training and thus relatively inexperienced.

Smith *et al.* (1980) as well as Glass and Kliegl (1983) offer a number of replies to these criticisms. In brief, they state that there is no reason arbitrarily to discard studies since studies can be categorized in a number of ways and the influence of selected variables can be systematically evaluated. This also reduces the potential bias in selecting and evaluating studies. Thus, the effect size secured from published studies can be compared with unpublished ones, the results of experienced therapists compared with inexperienced ones, and so forth. They offer such comparisons in their book, and in most instances the differences obtained were relatively small.

Although Smith *et al.* (1980) make a reasonably good case in their defense, I would still take issue on some matters. I personally see no need to include obviously inadequate studies and certain selection criteria could be agreed upon among researchers. Other workers, as well, state that minimal requirements for inclusion of studies is desirable before meta-analysis is attempted (Strube & Hartmann, 1983). Clinically relevant samples are also of some importance. Finally, I find it hard to interpret an effect size in clinical terms, and I realize that clinicians and statisticians will disagree on this issue. However, I prefer to know the degree of change in terms of clinical criteria, since patients who improve show a range in their degree of improvement (Garfield, 1980). The type of outcome criteria used is also pertinent here and should be appropriate and relevant to the problems treated.

I should also mention briefly two other reports which attempted partial analyses of the data compiled by Smith *et al.* (1980). Landman and Dawes (1982), for example, attempted to evaluate some of the criticisms made of the Smith and Glass report (1977) by conducting a meta-analysis of 42 selected studies in that report. They identified a set of studies of high methodological quality, they determined the magnitude of placebo effects in those studies with placebo controls, and they examined the influence of statistically non-independent results. In general, their independent analysis upheld the conclusions drawn by Smith and Glass (1977). However, Prioleau, Murdoch, and Brody (1983) did a comparable analysis of 32 studies which used a placebo control, and despite securing the same effect size as Smith *et al.* (1980), interpreted their findings as indicating that psychotherapy was no more effective than a placebo control. Their interpretation, of course, can be challenged but I will not elaborate upon it here (Garfield, 1983a). I mention these two analyses to indicate that criticisms of previous meta-analyses can be evaluated empirically (Fiske, 1983), and also that differing personal interpretations of data secured by means of meta-analysis continue. I don't know that we can ever secure perfect agreement as long as individuals with different value systems interpret bodies of data.

On the basis of existing research, I believe it is fair to say that psychotherapy produces modestly or moderately positive results with certain types of cases, but there is tremendous variability among studies, including the type of control groups used. As stated by the APA Commission on Psychotherapies (1982), "psychotherapy appears efficacious more often than not, but the conditions under which it works are not well understood" (p. vii). Although the lack of differential results for different forms of psychotherapy is critically received by behavioral therapists, I am inclined to accept the finding for what it potentially signifies. Within limits, the general designations used to describe the various therapies lack specific operational meaning and refer to theoretical orientations, or what I have called "brand names" in psychotherapy. Furthermore, they are group findings and they obscure individual variability, which is of great significance. In essence, they perpetuate what Kiesler (1966, 1971) has termed the "uniformity myth." We tend to equate patients, therapists, and treatments, although the reality is otherwise. These comments also suggest related issues pertaining to generality and specificity in psychotherapy, but before I approach these matters I want to add a few final comments pertaining to the efficacy of psychotherapy.

Much of the research on psychotherapy has utilized various samples of subjects that do not necessarily correspond to the majority of patients seen in clinical settings. This matter has been discussed and criticized. Parloff (1982), for example, in commenting on the review by Smith *et al.* (1980), has stated that it is representative of psychotherapy research, but not of psychotherapy in practice. This is at least partially correct. On the other hand, if we disregard these data, we can only fall back on the opinions of psychotherapists or their critics, and in my view this is the greater of two evils. I have yet to encounter a psychotherapist who felt that he or she did not get positive results. The current research is the only research we have, and if necessary, although it is fraught with possible dangers, we can at least make some considered or tentative judgments on that basis. Most of the reviews on outcome in general have been roughly consistent with the findings of Smith *et al.* (1980), although I do not regard the results as being impressive as do Smith and her co-workers and some of the other reviewers.

GENERALITY AND SPECIFICITY: A BRIEF LOOK

The concepts of generality and specificity have not been used in psychotherapy until relatively recently, and they have tended to be used without any precise meaning. Although practically all forms of psychotherapy claim to differ from the others in theoretical rationale and procedures, most of them until recently have been viewed as general therapies, or what I have termed "universal therapies"; that is, they are perceived as "good for whatever ails one." For the most part, they are not specific treatments for specific ailments or disorders. Furthermore, I personally believe that some of the more recent adverse reaction to psychotherapy is a result of psychotherapists' past willingness to attempt to cure every social and behavioral problem.

Different therapies, for the most part, has not meant differences in the sense of specific treatments for different disorders, or even in terms of differential outcomes. The therapies have differed mainly in name and ideology. More recently, however, under the influence of behavior therapy, there has been a greater emphasis on so-called specific therapies for specific disorders, with the greatest success reported in the treatment of phobias. However, supposedly different procedures such as modeling, systematic desensitization, and implosion or flooding have secured comparable results. This may be due, as Marks (1978) suggests, to the common factor of exposure.

In a somewhat similar development, we have a number of different psychotherapies for depression. These include Beck's cognitive therapy (1976), social-skills therapy (Bellack, Hersen, & Himmelhoch, 1981), pleasant-events therapy (Zeiss, Lewinsohn, & Muñoz, 1979), and interpersonal therapy (Weissman, 1979). Some of these therapies are used for other types of problems as well. In this sense, these therapies don't appear to be particularly specific, for such therapists do not necessarily treat only depressives nor do they use a truly different treatment for different types of patients. However, even here, crude and sometimes unreliable categories are employed both diagnostically and therapeutically. The most specific therapy is really arranging a unique program of therapy which is planned for the specific problems of a particular patient. The best example I know of is the treatment arranged by Lang and Melamed (1969) some years ago for a specific patient with chronic ruminative vomiting, and although it was an uncontrolled case study, the results were unequivocally positive and the child's life was saved. Very few therapists appear to operate in quite this way. However, this model of a specific therapy designed for a specific individual appears to be a more truly psychological model than a medical model which emphasizes categories of illness or disturbance. The former may be a more appropriate model for psychotherapy than is an illness model.

Nevertheless, although it is difficult to generalize, it does appear to me that most therapies are rather general therapies since they do not limit themselves to treating only one disorder or one type of patient, and the results of comparative studies show roughly comparable results. Also, because many therapists engage in a variety of activities or behaviors which are not emphasized in their particular approach, I have suggested that at least some common factors are operative in most if not all therapies. These may include a number of factors or variables as I have indicated elsewhere (Garfield, 1980). Among them are such hypothesized variables as suggestion, support, explanations, emotional release, practice, exposure to negative stimuli, encouragement and reinforcement, the relationship in therapy, and the like. Although many therapists tend to view such variables as rather superficial or supportive, I do not. I see them as general, common, and important aspects of all forms of psychotherapy. In a similar manner, in agreement with Frank (1974), I believe patients suffering from a variety of psychological disorders show many common features—demoralization, lack of hope, low self-esteem, and the like. These features are also of some importance, and one should not disregard them in treatment.

It is also likely that in addition to general factors there are also, potentially specific factors for specific problems. Exposure is such a possible specific factor for overcoming various fears. We have as yet made only limited progress in this direction, but we must go beyond the usual view of treatment and problem and consider as well the particular patient and his or her situation. In any event I believe we need to be cognizant of both general and possible specific factors, and a few years ago I suggested that the model

Spearman posited for intelligence might also be a useful model for psychotherapy (Garfield, 1980). We would then hypothesize a general factor (or factors) which would be common to most therapies and important in terms of outcome—the relationship, rapport, motivation, and so on—as well as specific factors for particular kinds of problems and individuals.

Admittedly, we have a long way to go before we can speak more authoritatively about the efficacy, generality, and specificity of psychotherapy. Along with some others, I have advocated more intensive study of that small proportion of cases, perhaps 10–15% or so, that obtain rather marked improvement by means of psychotherapy. Such study might give us some clues as to what variables facilitate significant improvement, and perhaps allow us to select the procedures, the therapist's qualities, or the patient's attributes that appear to be crucial. The present results on outcome, while modestly positive, are not strong enough for us to state categorically that psychotherapy is effective, or even that it is not effective. In fact, as we are all aware, such a global statement is inherently fraught with danger and lacks any kind of scientific precision. Although it appears that psychotherapy is not a truly effective treatment for schizophrenia or related psychotic disorders, I don't think we can make many more generalizations of this type that are really meaningful. Until we are able to secure more definitive research data, the efficacy of psychotherapy will remain a controversial issue.

REFERENCES

APA Commission on Psychotherapies. *Psychotherapy research: Methodological and efficacy issues.* Washington, D.C.: American Psychiatric Association, 1982.

Beck, A. T. *Cognitive therapy and the emotional disorders.* New York: International Universities Press, 1976.

Bellack, A. S., Hersen, M., & Himmelhoch, J. M. Social skills training, pharmacotherapy, and psychotherapy for unipolar depression. *American Journal of Psychiatry*, 1981, *138*, 1562–1566.

Bergin, A. E. The evaluation of therapeutic outcomes. In A. E. Bergin & S. L. Garfield (Eds.), *Handbook of psychotherapy and behavior change.* New York: Wiley, 1971.

Bergin, A. E., & Lambert, M. J. The evaluation of therapeutic outcomes. In S. L. Garfield & A. E. Bergin, (Eds.), *Handbook of psychotherapy and behavior change* (2nd ed.). New York: Wiley, 1978.

Eysenck, H. J. The effects of psychotherapy: An evaluation. *Journal of Consulting Psychology*, 1952, *16*, 319–324.

Eysenck, H. J. The effects of psychotherapy. In H. J. Eysenck (Ed.), *Handbook of abnormal psychology.* New York: Basic Books, 1961.

Eysenck, H. J. *The effects of psychotherapy.* New York: International Science Press, 1966.

Eysenck, H. J. An exercise in mega-silliness. *American Psychologist*, 1978, *33*, 517.

Fiske, D. W. The meta-analytic revolution in outcome research. *Journal of Consulting and Clinical Psychology*, 1983, *51*, 65–70.

Frank, J. D. Psychotherapy: The restoration of morale. *American Journal of Psychiatry*, 1974, *131*, 271–274.

Garfield, S. L. Does psychotherapy work? Yes, no, maybe. *Behavioral and Brain Sciences*, 1983, *6*, 292–293. (a)

Garfield, S. L. Effectiveness of psychotherapy: The perennial controversy. *Professional Psychology: Research and Practice*, 1983, *14*, 35–43. (b)

Garfield, S. L. Does psychotherapy work? Yes, no, maybe. *Behavioral and Brain Sciences*, in press.

Glass, G. V., & Kliegl, R. M. An apology for research integration in the study of psychotherapy. *Journal of Consulting and Clinical Psychology*, 1983, *51*, 28–41.

Kiesler, D. J. Some myths of psychotherapy research and the search for a paradigm. *Psychological Bulletin*, 1966, *65*, 110–136.

Kiesler, D. J. Experimental design in psychotherapy research. In A. E. Bergin & S. L. Garfield (Eds.), *Handbook of psychotherapy and behavior change*. New York: Wiley, 1971.

Landman, J. T., & Dawes, R. M. Psychotherapy outcome: Smith and Glass' conclusions stand up under scrutiny. *American Psychologist*, 1982, *37*, 504–516.

Lang, P. J., & Melamed, B. G. Case report: Avoidance conditioning therapy of an infant with chronic ruminative vomiting. *Journal of Abnormal Psychology*, 1969, *74*, 1–8.

Luborsky, L., Singer, B., & Luborsky, L. Comparative studies of psychotherapies. Is it true that "Everyone has won and all must have prizes"? *Archives of General Psychiatry*, 1975, *32*, 995–1007.

Marks, I. Behavioral psychotherapy of adult neurosis. In S. L. Garfield & A. E. Bergin (Eds.), *Handbook of psychotherapy and behavior change* (2nd ed.). New York: Wiley, 1978.

Meltzoff, J., & Kornreich, M. *Research in psychotherapy*. New York: Atherton, 1970.

Obendorf, C. P. Results of psychoanalytic therapy. *International Journal of Psychoanalysis*, 1943, *24*, 107–114.

Obendorf, C. P., Greenacre, P., & Kubie, L. Symposium on the evaluation of therapeutic results. *International Journal of Psychoanalysis*, 1948, *29*, 7–33.

Parloff, M. B. Psychotherapy research evidence and reimbursement decisions: Bambi meets Godzilla. *American Journal of Psychiatry*, 1982, *139*, 718–727.

Prioleau, L., Murdoch, M., & Brody, N. An analysis of psychotherapy vs. placebo studies. *Behavioral and Brain Sciences*, 1983, *6*, 275–285.

Rachman, S. *The effects of psychotherapy*. Oxford: Pergamon, 1971.

Rachman, S. The effects of psychological treatment. In H. J. Eysenck (Ed.), *Handbook of abnormal psychology*. New York: Basic Books, 1973.

Rachman, S. J., & Wilson, G. T. *The effects of psychological therapy* (2nd ed.). New York: Pergamon, 1980.

Rimland, B. Death knell for psychotherapy? *American Psychologist*, 1979, *34*, 192.

Smith, M. L., & Glass, G. V. Meta-analysis of psychotherapy outcome studies. *American Psychologist*, 1977, *32*, 752–760.

Smith, M. L., Glass, G. V., & Miller, T. I. *The benefits of psychotherapy*. Baltimore: Johns Hopkins University Press, 1980.

Strahan, R. F. Six ways of looking at an elephant. *American Psychologist*, 1978, *33*, 693.

Strube, M. J., & Hartmann, D. P. Meta-analysis: Techniques, applications, and functions. *Journal of Consulting and Clinical Psychology*, 1983, *51*, 14–27.

Weissman, M. M. The psychological treatment of depression: Evidence for the efficacy of psychotherapy alone, in comparison with, and in combination with pharmacotherapy. *Archives of General Psychiatry*, 1979, *36*, 1261–1269.

Zeiss, A. M., Lewinsohn, P. M., & Muñoz, R. F. Nonspecific improvement effects in depression using interpersonal skills training, pleasant activities schedules, or cognitive training. *Journal of Consulting and Clinical Psychology*, 1979, *47*, 427–439.

COMMENTARY

Dr. Robert Rose*: What would you say in answer to the question "How good is the evidence for efficacy?" Would you use the word "fair," and for specificity "poor"?

Dr. Garfield: It's fair to middlin'. Thank you very much. (*Applause.*)

*University of Texas Medical Center, Galveston.

19

Specificity and Strategy in Psychotherapy Research and Practice

DONALD F. KLEIN AND JUDITH GODWIN RABKIN
New York State Psychiatric Institute
and College of Physicians and Surgeons, Columbia University

The following anecdote is told by the senior author.

"My interest in the roots of psychotherapy may stem from an old family tradition since my great-grandfather was a wonder-working rabbi, known from Minsk to Pinsk. His son, also a well-known practitioner of faith healing in the Ukraine, emigrated to New York where during my childhood he lived with my parents. My mother told me that her father had been a faith healer, which piqued my curiosity, so I asked him for details.

"Our communication was marred by linguistic difficulties. Finally, in an attempt to gain clarity, I asked him to tell me about a case. In later life this approach has been generally useful in trying to bring clarity to issues of therapeutic theory and technique. We are, of course, presenting a reconstruction with narrative rather than historical truth.

"Becky was told she was going to marry Shloime, the lout. She started to cry, but my grandfather pointed out that they all cried. She cried for 2 weeks, but this was expectable, even laudable behavior. She then cried for another 2 weeks, and this was considered excessive and somewhat self-indulgent. After 6 weeks of her loudly symptomatic malfunctioning, her distressed parents came to my grandfather for professional help.

"'Bring me her handkerchief,' said the rabbinical authority. 'So they brought me her handkerchief and I said the right prayers over it and told them to place it under her pillow. In the morning, she woke up bright-eyed and cheerful and went forward to her marriage, which was no worse than most marriages.'

"'But,' I inquired, 'Did she know that you had done this?'

"'Of course,' he said, 'It doesn't work otherwise.'

"However, even at an early age I was already pursuing the question of specificity.

"'Zayda, did you have to say the right prayers?'

"'That's what made her better.'

"'But let's say you had not said the right prayers, but she thought that you said the right prayers. What would happen then?'

"'But you have to say the right prayers,' he reiterated. However, for the next several weeks he was seen muttering to himself, 'You have to say the right prayers,' and viewed me with some diminished affection."

Our question remains, "Do you have to say the right prayers?" Furthermore, how would you find out?

DIVERSITY AND COMMONALITY

The number of psychological procedures intended to ameliorate human mental misery is immense. The latest count is up to 250, and includes such exotica as Bioplasmic Therapy, Burn-Out Prevention, Neurotone Therapy, Photo Counseling, Rebirthing, Soap Opera Therapy, Vita-Erg Therapy, and Zaraleya Psychoenergetic Technique (Herink, 1980).

The various therapies differ sharply both theoretically and procedurally. Their enormous variety seems to make it self-evident that they are doing very different things.

With regard to therapeutic process, of apparent importance are both the specific activities of the therapist and those prescribed for the patient. For instance, psychoanalysis is largely identified by the use of the couch, prescription by the therapist of the fundamental rule of free association, and the nondirective, interpretive mode of therapist activity. In contrast, behavior therapy is identified with directive, educational, and supportive behavior by the therapist, with active prescription of such activities as relaxation, systematic construction of anxiety hierarchies, assertiveness training, homework, and exposure *in vivo*. Other therapies are characterized by the direct bodily manipulation of the patient by the therapist, and so on.

Does this diversity reflect different therapeutic mechanisms? Frank (1982) suggests that we should not be looking at what apparently differentiates the therapies, but at what they have in common.

Whether we should look at the differences or the similarities is not an arbitrary, abstract question. We should take guidance from Bertrand Russell's immortal remark, "A difference that makes no difference is no difference."

If various therapies differ in effectiveness, then the search for specificity becomes a scientific necessity. Clearly, if treatment *A* is regularly better than treatment *B*, then treatment *A* is doing something that treatment *B* is not. Finding out what this something is may help us improve our treatments and illuminate the nature of the illness.

DEFINITIONS OF SPECIFICITY AND NONSPECIFICITY

Although the terms specific versus nonspecific can be used descriptively in the sense of unique versus common, the more usual usage relates to theoretical issues of mechanisms of amelioration. "Specific" is defined as that which has a special determining quality. "Special," in turn, is defined as excelling or exceeding in some way that which is usual or common.

Concern about specificity derives from interest in what there is about any particular therapy that makes its effects specially beneficial. Since we explain differences by differences, it makes sense to look at what is manifestly different about the therapies to account for differences in benefits. The specific techniques, which are assumed to be the motor of therapy, generate theories to explain the particular merits of these presumably unique procedures.

Once one has moved to the theoretical level, whether a particular facet of therapy is common or unique no longer suffices to label it specific (i.e., is specifically determining). Further, if Jerome Frank is right, then the common features of the various therapies are actually doing the job. Since he has developed a theory (the antidemoralization theory) to explain the effectiveness of these common features, then they are no longer theoretically nonspecific; they have a special determining quality with a particular relationship to the specific condition of demoralization.

Although the terms specificity and nonspecificity have sunk into the literature, they generate confusion if their descriptive and theoretical meanings are not kept carefully apart.

The whole concept of specificity was an attempt to explain supposed particular therapeutic benefits. One can avoid definitions of either commonality or theoretical importance by simply asking whether any particular aspect of therapy is related to any particular aspect of outcome. How to determine this may be complicated, but the question itself is quite straightforward. This question can be pursued with regard to whether the feature is necessary or sufficient for benefit or, as is more likely, additive in its effect.

The theoretical definition of specificity usually implies that the specific technique is necessary so that the particular outcome simply cannot be accomplished without it (e.g., analysis of the transference). The claim that certain aspects of psychotherapy are sufficient for benefit has been made with regard to abreaction and insight, and more recently for deconditioning. Considering certain aspects of therapy as being either necessary or sufficient allows hard, disconfirming tests. In particular, the claim to sufficiency is common at the very initiation of any therapy's career, but rarely survives much clinical experience.

That a component of psychotherapy may be additive in its effects is compatible with much general thinking about psychosocial process, but clearly is more difficult to evaluate.

COROLLARIES OF THEORIES OF THERAPY

The assumption of specific superior outcome seems a regular feature of all psychotherapies. This is quite understandable insofar as they are persuasive devices. This assumption leads to specific theories of the mechanisms of improvement that have implications for (1) the type of patient suitable for that therapy, (2) the type of person suitable to become a therapist, (3) the particular type of training necessary for the therapist, (4) the relative importance of theoretical understanding, technical skill, and therapist personality in the achievement of benefit, (5) the expected short-term and long-term benefits, and (6) the likelihood of relapse.

Psychoanalytic Theory

A basic tenet of psychoanalysis is that neurotic illness is due to unconscious intrapsychic conflict. Psychotherapy consists of either the dissolution of neurotic defenses, as in psychoanalysis, or the shoring up of such defenses as in all other methods, which are therefore symptom-ameliorating rather than deep in their effects. The corollaries are the following.

Patients suitable for psychoanalysis are neurotics suffering from intrapsychic conflicts. However, this overinclusive initial definition shortly became supplemented by qualifying phrases such as "good ego strength" and "psychological mindedness."

Initially, the personality of the therapist seemed of little importance as long as he or she was successfully psychoanalyzed and had the requisite training. More recently, some analysts feel that the real human qualities of the therapist are prepotent. Nonetheless, psychoanalysis, of all current therapies, puts the heaviest emphasis on theoretical understanding, prolonged training, and technical skill (Strupp, 1977).

With regard to short-term effects, psychoanalysis considers mere symptomatic improvement as due to the effects of positive transference. It is held that this is transient and of little importance. Further, mere symptom improvement is associated with symptomatic shifts because of the unresolved underlying conflicts. Some even claim that rapid symptomatic reduction may result in psychotic exacerbation (Weiss, 1964).

With regard to long-term effects, successful resolution of conflict should obviate relapse.

Behavioral Theory

Behavior therapy, starting with Joseph Wolpe and elaborated by others, also assures therapeutic superiority and makes an immediate leap to specific theories of the mechanism of improvement—in this case reciprocal inhibition of anxiety by pairing relaxation with anxiety responses, using a somewhat

Pavlovian framework. Others emphasize behavior modification by way of operant conditioning. Both branches of behavior therapy have in common the rejection of a belief in a deep, underlying causal conflict and affirm that the symptomatology is the disease. By removing the symptoms by unlearning, one removes the disease. Behavior therapy and psychoanalysis both emphasize their relationship with educational process rather than medical intervention, and both argue that the disorders they treat are primarily at a purely functional level.

What are the theoretical corollaries of behavior therapy?

There is little emphasis in behavior therapy on the type of patient suitable for care. Since symptoms are learned, symptoms can be unlearned, regardless of syndromal embedding. Behavior therapy, like psychoanalysis, considers descriptive diagnosis largely a waste of time, since syndromes are simply convenient categories for discourse, not for guiding treatment.

With regard to the person of the therapist, like psychoanalysis, behavior therapy initially paid little attention. The technique was all-important. Wolpe maintained that patients could just as well be treated by substitute therapists of little training with equivalent effect, as long as they carried out the procedures correctly.

More recently, as with psychoanalysis, there has been progressively greater emphasis upon the personality and interpersonal skills of the therapist.

The degree of training required was initially rather minor, but like psychoanalysis, longer and longer courses of training are now recommended. There is, as yet, no requirement that a therapist be treated by behavior therapy.

Since symptomatic treatment is all that there is, short-term symptomatic benefits are emphasized. Furthermore, since these techniques can be taught, patients should continue to make steady progress and should not relapse. In particular, there should be no displacement effect from symptomatic cure. In fact there should be a generalized improvement in areas other than the presenting problem, as newly learned techniques are applied here also. This is sometimes referred to as a "ripple effect."

Antidemoralization Treatment

According to Frank (1974), it is possible that all psychotherapy modalities, despite apparent wide differences, derive their effectiveness from nonspecific elements which include the following:

    1. Expectation of benefit—improvement accruing from the expectation that by following certain rules and procedures recommended in a relationship with a trusted authority in an identified place of healing,

one will obtain the desired goals. This probably includes an unconscious and irrational hope of a magical cure, the kind of hope that first generated the occupations of faith healer, shaman, priest, and doctor. There is some evidence, however, that maximum expectation of benefit requires congruence between expectations and what actually occurs in therapy. The patient must have at least some idea of what to expect. The expectations are also enhanced by a cohesive explanation (not necessarily true) of why the therapy works; through such an explanation, the terror of the unknown is somehow diminished.

2. New opportunities for learning, both experientially and cognitively. Examples of such learning might be therapist behavior and values that seem worthy of adopting, positive responses from the therapist that counteract early negative reactions from family members, or specific ways of changing sexual or phobic behavior. New learning in therapy includes relief at finding that the therapist (and in group therapy, other patients) is not overwhelmed by whatever bizarre fears and behaviors confesses (a relief similar to that produced by confession in the Catholic Church).

3. Success experiences, such as new insights, behavioral changes, or acknowledgement of responsibility.

4. Decrease in sense of alienation through the relationship itself; acceptance by the therapist counters feelings of unworthiness and contributes to the need for social experience.

5. Emotional arousal.

Although Frank lists many common ingredients in a variety of therapies, he hypothesizes that the core function is to reduce demoralization: a conviction of subjective incompetence associated with distressing symptoms. Demoralization can be secondary to a wide variety of life defeats, including unrewarding or traumatizing life experience, inability to manage one's life because of personality limitations, and psychiatric illness.

What are the corollaries of antidemoralization theory?

The initial impact of psychotherapy is to reduce distress and the level of symptomatic complaint by reduction of demoralization. With more prolonged psychotherapy, the patient can become more socially effective. Frank indicates a possibility that specific techniques may produce benefits over and above the therapy's antidemoralization effects in the area of phobias, sexual disorders, and compulsions. We shall review these data below.

The implication with regard to type of patients suitable for psychotherapy is that apparently anybody is suitable if his or her disability and distress is largely due to demoralization. The more the demoralization is a functionally autonomous residue of a transient life crisis or past emotional disorder, the better the results. Clearly, patients with good premorbid personalities and skills who have suffered a severe disappointment should make the best spontaneous recovery and also respond best to antidemoralization treatment. In this sense, the purpose of psychotherapy is to accelerate natural recovery processes, which is not an insignificant accomplishment. However, if the demoralizing life circumstances are enduring, or the personality limitations that prevent personal effectiveness are immutable, or the demoralization is secondary to a severe, unrelieved, biological illness such as chronic panic disorder or melancholia, then therapy should be useless.

The person of the therapist becomes of paramount importance in this framework. Such characteristics as warmth and empathy are often emphasized. One might think that factors important in prestige suggestion should also play a role.

One implication is that there should be supertherapists who by dint of personality do extraordinarily well across the range of demoralized people. Frank apparently assumes that this is true, and even tentatively suggests that some supertherapists may be telepathic. The converse of this is that certain therapists should be spectacularly poor insofar as they radiate gloom, sabotage forward motion, and substitute intellectualization for positive action.

Type of training is less important in this framework than in either previous model since the various techniques, emphasized by their practitioners, either are superfluous or have a persuasive function that helps establish the patients' faith in the treatment's benefits. Frank (1982) emphasizes, however, that formal training is needed as the basis for the therapist's conviction in his effectiveness.

Most striking about the antidemoralization stand is that the controversy over whether a treatment is deep and etiological or symptomatic is considered irrelevant. Frank's point is that psychotherapy is not even treating the primary problem or illness, but rather a secondary complication. Demoralization may have resulted in functionally autonomous maladaptations, such as escape mechanisms, that complicate the primary problem or illness. Only in the case of the transient life difficulty that has produced a functionally autonomous demoralization, can psychotherapy claim to be actually affecting the entire problem, and here only by accelerating what would occur with time in any case.

Short-term symptomatic improvements should be limited to feelings of helplessness and dysphoria often termed depression. Longer-term improvement should reflect the instigating difficulty.

The demoralization hypothesis has no problem with relapse and recurrence, since it does not claim that therapy treats any primary condition. However, with regard to long-term prognosis, the primary condition, if still active, should be overriding. It is of interest that Frank believes that the benefits of psychotherapy are maintained. This will be reviewed below.

CREDIBILITY OF TREATMENT

It does not follow *a priori* that a form of treatment must be believed in by the patient to make it effective. In fact, Freud specifically denies that the initial faith of the patient in the efficacy of psychoanalysis has any lasting consequence, although it may contribute to short-term symptom relief through positive transference. Siminarly, Wolpe's early descriptions of systematic hierarchical desensitization and reciprocal inhibition sound as if the patient could benefit by passively experiencing the contiguity of the relaxation response with anxiety-provoking stimuli, without believing that this would actually work.

It is the persuasiveness of the antidemoralization hypothesis, as at least a partial explanation for the benefit of psychotherapy, that renders unsatisfactory those psychotherapy studies in which a credible treatment is compared with no treatment. Such designs cannot address the issue of whether the psychotherapy has anything going for it besides its credibility. Credibility is clearly a euphemistic synonym for faith engendering, that allows us to avoid certain negative associations.

THE IMPORTANCE OF SPECIFICITY

Our concern with specificity is not simply an academic preoccupation, but has both practical and heuristic implications.

The clinician, the patient, and the treatment facility must decide which treatments to employ. Since society also pays, the choice of therapy, access to therapy, and qualifications of the therapist become social issues. Data concerning both cost and benefit are clearly required for enlightened individual and social choices, but are largely unavailable (Klein, 1978, 1980).

It is increasingly obvious that our current methods of psychotherapy warrant considerable improvement and that our understanding of mental illness is promising rather than definitive. If some type of therapy shows particular value, this should deepen our understanding of the illness and lead to further therapeutic advances, as has happened with pharmacotherapy. The history of psychiatry indicates that our therapies are not derived from our understanding of psychology and physiology, but rather that the practice of therapy advances our scientific understanding. The scientific study of therapy may be a royal road for progress in both practice and theory.

A core, covert issue in the specificity debate is the uncomfortable realization that if all psychotherapies work about the same, then all of our elaborate psychogenic etiological hypotheses are called into question. Worse, the alternative hypothesis that the root of efficacy for all methods is their common antidemoralization effects implies that such treatments are aimed only at a secondary complication, rather than the underlying problem or illness. In that case, psychogenic etiological theories lose their major persuasive foundation—therapeutic substantiation.

Another consequence of the judgment that nonspecificity is correct is that professional claims by psychotherapists for special deference and large fees, justified by the mastery of a particularly esoteric technique developed during a long period of expensive apprenticeship, or even personal psychoanalysis, cannot be justified. As any sociologist can tell you, there are few groups that willingly give up their privileges or have their self-esteem impaired. It is thus not surprising that the claim for nonspecificity is vigorously resisted by so many clinicians.

It should be noted that we are not stating that, since a motivational interpretation of this resistance can be made, there is no substance to the claim for specificity. That sort of rhetorical device has no place in rational discourse. Its only use is to counter the argument, "If so many respected people believe in something, it must have some truth."

One approach to the current confusion over what works is to adopt an eclectic approach in the name of multidimensionality. Since we don't know whether a patient is suffering from psychological, sociological, educational, intrapersonal, interpersonal, or biological difficulties, we should plainly attend to all these possibilities.

However, in the psychosocial area, the nonspecificity hypothesis holds that simply piling one approach upon another is only useless repetition in new disguises, but at more expense. At least for the biological therapies, we can say with some confidence that for a particular disorder a specific agent is indicated or not. We have yet to attain this level with the vast majority of psychosocial interventions.

Luborsky, Singer, and Luborsky (1975) have suggested that all have won and therefore all must have prizes. Perhaps the lurking fear is that if all have won, none will get government prizes, since how can the government rationally limit its support to any particular set of clients or providers?

COMPARATIVE TREATMENT OUTCOMES

Is the nonspecificity hypothesis supported by scientific studies with regard to treatment outcome? In the past few years, improvements in research design plus the ever expanding number of studies have encouraged leading figures in the field to state with confidence that psychotherapy is demonstrably better than doing nothing for a variety of disorders. These benefits are seen as "reliably superior to those found in comparable groups of patients in the no-treatment or other control conditions" (Parloff, 1982, p. 720). However, the credibility of these controls is not established. Furthermore, the majority assert that all forms of psychotherapy are comparably effective in producing therapeutic benefit (APA Commission, 1982; Frank, 1979; Luborsky *et al.*, 1975; Parloff, 1982; Smith, Glass, & Miller, 1980; Strupp, 1982).

Not all agree with this assessment. Dissenters include Eysenck and others who question if there is any benefit that exceeds the "spontaneous" recovery rates of most of the disorders responsive to psychotherapy.

Eysenck's original critique of psychotherapy research published in 1952 included the estimate that roughly two-thirds of untreated neurotic patients show remission within 2 years of onset. Evidence gathered since then certainly supports the observation that a significant number of patients do get better without formal treatment, a phenomenon also documented by the findings of 20–40% placebo response in drug trials. Nevertheless, spontaneous remission is not a sufficient explanation for the finding of psychotherapeutic efficacy in controlled studies.

With regard to the equivalence of therapies, Bergin (1966) proposed that therapies look similar in outcome because aggregated data are used, lumping together both successes and failures and thereby disguising different patterns of effect. Rachman and Wilson (1980), after appraising the evidence, conclude that the "facts are against" this hypothesis.

The strongest contemporary opposition to the prevailing view of comparability of effect across therapeutic techniques is articulated by Rachman and Wilson (1980). They assert that potential differences between treatments are blurred by the widespread use of "broad, general, qualitative outcome measures of limited range" together with emphasis on psychological problems with a high rate of spontaneous remission.

After a thorough review of behavioral therapy efficacy studies in specific problem areas, Rachman and Wilson conclude that behavior therapy is beneficial in a broad spectrum of problems. Its efficacy is not restricted to treating simple phobias and habit disorders, but applies to virtually all diagnostic categories responsive to any psychotherapy. They assert, in addition, that "specific techniques have been shown to produce significantly greater improvement than others. Patients with phobic and obsessional–compulsive disorders appear more likely to derive benefit from treatment that is performance based than therapy that is strictly verbal or cognitive in nature" (p. 257). They also note that the treatment of sexual disorders has been "enhanced" by the introduction of behavioral methods, although as they themselves point out, the durability of effects in this area remains to be demonstrated.

The term "performance based" seems crucial. A direct *in vivo* approach to symptomatology may produce accelerated benefits in several disorders.

How can antidemoralization theory handle the finding that therapies that emphasize *in vivo* exposure cause more rapid effects than other therapies? One possibility is to assume that such therapies are inherently more persuasive and therefore produce more rapid antidemoralization effects. On the face of it this seems unlikely since *in vivo* therapies have higher dropout rates. Conceivably those who remain in treatment are the true believers. (That *in vivo* exposure may retain the best prognosis patients is a complication we will not further pursue, but one that must be attended to.) To substantiate the hypothesis of superior antidemoralization effects without circularity requires the development of independent antecedent measures of demoralization improvement.

The obvious alternative hypothesis is that the antidemoralization effects of the therapy set the stage for yet other beneficial processes, often conceived of as an extinction of the anxiety response. Alternatively, it could be emphasized that this is a form of reality testing in which patients learn that whatever it was that they were afraid of does not actually occur.

However, even in agoraphobia with unavoidable spontaneous panic attacks, there is some benefit from *in vivo* exposure. How can we explain this?

Patients' escape tendencies are enhanced by the anticipation that not only will they get the intense discomfort of the panic attack, but that they might die or go crazy. We suggest that what is learned in exposure therapy is that the panic attack does not require escape, and that one can sit down and wait for it to go away. Once it is learned that such catastrophic events simply will not happen and that they will live through the panic attack, the patients can unlearn their escape mechanisms. This too is instigated by a more accurate appreciation of reality. Since the escape and avoidance procedures actually disrupted and constricted their lives more than the panic attack did, there is a clear benefit in an achieved stoicism despite maintained anxiety.

The antidemoralization effects of psychotherapy encourage the phobic patient to approach and remain within the feared situation, to make a new evaluation of the realities, to refuse to escape, to decrease anticipatory anxiety, and to unlearn avoidant and escape propensities. Therapies that help the patient translate their decrease in demoralization into courageous action help the patient to unlearn escape tendencies quickly and achieve a stoical tolerance of recurrent distress.

In this sense there is specificity engendered by psychotherapy of phobics, but it is at an entirely different level from the supposed specificity of reciprocal inhibition, operant conditioning, insight into repressed drives, and so forth.

Another aspect of the effectiveness of *in vivo* exposure is that the patient has to hang in and not flee. *In vivo* exposure probably only becomes effective when there is prevention of the escape response, which permits a new evaluation.

Preventing a compulsive ritual results in mounting anxiety, which can be sharply reduced by the ritual act. There seems a nice analogy here if one understands the compulsion as having an escape function. However, what is being escaped from in the obsessive–compulsive is nowhere near as clear as with the spontaneously panicking agoraphobic patient. We also do not understand why the ritual is, at least temporarily, effective. In compulsions, as with phobic avoidance, there may be some instigating intense affective distress that releases the compulsive escape mechanisms. The inciting distress may disappear, leaving to functionally autonomous escape a procedure with a life of its own.

The agoraphobic patient who has ceased to have spontaneous panic attacks may not know this until the information is thrust upon him or her by *in vivo* exposure. Similarly, the compulsive ritualizer may be protecting himself or herself against an internal dysphoric state that is actually in abeyance. Such patients would then respond well to response prevention, whereas other patients for whom the ritual is still required may not benefit from response prevention.

The treatment of erectile dysfunction due to performance anxiety by the Masters–Johnson technique also resembles this paradigm. It is unlikely that performance anxiety directly causes functional impotence. More probably performance anxiety leads to preoccupation with distracting fearful images, which prevents the effective impact of sensual gratification on the involuntary processes of sexual arousal. The Masters–Johnson prohibition against intercourse and prescription of sensate focusing is antidemoralizing, reduces performance anxiety by making the situation a nontrial, and blocks the patient's distraction with fearful imagery by emphasizing the *in vivo*, external, pleasurable focus.

THE ASSESSMENT OF DURABILITY OF EFFECT

Antidemoralization theory relates relapse to the instigating conditions— either internal processes or external events. Enduring improvement, while possible, is not a theoretical necessity. In contrast, behavioral, cognitive, and psychoanalytic theories all claim to remove the basis for symptoms in an enduring way. Relapse, if common, poses a clear challenge to their theoretical stand.

We are interested in seeing whether long-term effects are found for psychotherapy in general, and, if so, whether some treatments have more enduring influence than others. Mash and Terdal (1980) observed, "Discussions of follow-up assessment . . . have shown remarkable consensus on two issues: first, the importance of conducting follow-up evaluations; and second, the lack of adequate information across a wide range of treatments and problems" (p. 102). They cite 12 reviews of behavioral treatment studies to support their position that "the methodological shortcomings of most investigations make it virtually impossible to draw any definitive conclusions regarding the durability of treatment effects over time" (p. 104). Since behavioral research is usually more rigorous than other forms of psychotherapy research, their conclusions suggest that relatively little can be learned from the available literature.

The major methodological problems include sample attrition, use of different measures and/or criteria and/or raters at follow-up from those at treatment termination, and the confounding effects of the variety of events and experiences including additional treatment that occur between treatment end and subsequent assessment. The longer the interval until follow-up, the more pronounced these problems are likely to be. Possibly for these reasons follow-up, when conducted at all, usually is done within 6 months of treatment termination (APA Commission, 1982, p. 72). The major problem is that so little is done at all.

Results from individual long-term follow-up studies (defined as more than 6 months after treatment termination) are inconsistent. These may be actual differences or variations due to methodological flaws. One cannot determine which results are more or less valid.

A more fruitful approach may be to consider generalizations based on aggregated observations, although here also experts arrive at different conclusions. Frank (1982) takes the position that

> follow-up studies seem to show consistently that, whatever the form of therapy, most patients who show initial improvement maintain it. Moreover, when two therapies yield differences in outcome at the close of treatment, with rare exceptions these differences disappear over time, and the closing of the gap seems to depend more on the patients who receive the less successful therapy catching up than on both groups regressing equally toward the mean.

Frank concludes that the main effect of psychotherapy is to accelerate improvement that would have occurred eventually in any case. This finding also implies that the instigating factors do not recur.

Different conclusions are drawn by Mash and Terdal (1980) in their analysis of behavioral therapy. They note a consistent trend showing that, as the length of follow-up increases, the magnitude of treatment effect decreases, as does the amount of difference between techniques observed when treatment terminates. Unlike Frank, they attribute this diminution to a decline in the effect of the initially better treatment, rather than to a catching up of the initially less effective procedures.

Aggregate results from follow-up studies were also assessed by meta-analysis. In their synthesis of nearly 500 psychotherapy outcome studies Smith *et al.* (1980) found that one-third provided some follow-up data, usually within the first 6 months. They found no linear relationship between follow-up time and effective size, and the curvilinear correlation for all studies was only .14. They developed a regression equation for 19 different follow-up times, using a quadratic function of time. Their solution indicated that the estimated average effect of psychotherapy over control conditions is about .90 standard deviation units immediately after therapy, but falls to around .5 units 2 years later. As they say in their summary, "the benefits of psychotherapy are not permanent, but then little is" (p. 183).

Andrews and Harvey (1981) selected a subset of the Smith *et al.* studies, including only those who were "true" patients in the sense of having sought treatment for neuroses, phobias, or emotional–somatic complaints. Eighty-one such studies were identified.

The median duration of therapy was 15 hours. Follow-up results were preesented in tabular form only for the first 9 months after treatment. The authors conclude that "the benefits are stable for many months but decline slowly thereafter at an estimated 0.2 effect size units per annum" (p. 1206). The advantage of treatment dissipated faster for these patients than for the entire sample in the original analysis.

From this selective review of reviews we conclude that no evidence shows that the effects of any variety of psychotherapy are permanent. If anything, the evidence is for progressive decrement.

Certainly, data in this area would be most crucial to those therapies, such as psychoanalysis, that claim success in radical restructuring of the basic personality. The lack of such substantiating data, despite many years of psychoanalytic institutional existence, casts doubt on their remarkable claims. If follow-up showed maintained excellence of result, is there any doubt that we would have heard about it?

In sum, the meager findings indicating loss of therapeutic effect are more congruent with antidemoralization theory than the behavioral or analytic theories.

THERAPIST CHARACTERISTICS AND TREATMENT OUTCOME

Despite the practically universal belief that some therapists are superior, remarkably little empirical support has been produced. Presumably, the personal qualities and experience of the therapist should be crucial.

Investigators have tried for nearly 30 years to identify personality variables that distinguish between more and less competent therapists. As Parloff, Waskow, and Wolfe (1978) point out, the search for "prepotent" therapist characteristics independent of any particular patient relationship assumes that such characteristics are stable and constant for all patients.

Since Holt and Luborsky's 1958 study, considerable vigorous effort has failed to produce substantial results (APA Commission, 1982; Luborsky,

McLellan, Woody, & O'Brien, in press; Meltzoff & Kornreich, 1970). Some investigators differentiated therapists in terms of global scores on standard personality scales; others focused on details as specific as therapist latency of response or postural configurations (Fiske, 1977).

The strategies used have varied. Some, like Holt and Luborsky, first classify therapists as more or less successful and then seek differentiating characteristics. Others select variables considered outcome-relevant based on theoretical assumptions such as warmth, empathy, and genuineness. Parloff *et al.* (1978) note that "the various prescriptions for the ideal psychotherapist have included a litany of virtues more suited perhaps to the most honored biblical figures than to any of their descendants" (p. 235).

A third approach, proposed by Meltzoff and Kornreich but unfortunately never actively pursued, is to identify "supertherapists" who are regarded as masters by their colleagues, and then to describe the "psychotherapeutic personality" associated with consistent, brilliant, clinical successes. (Do they exist?)

One reason for the paucity of findings is the lack of incremental growth; each investigator picks his or her own personality variable or measure while ignoring others' work. Investigators also try to study complex notions like "personality" (APA Commission, 1982). Parloff and colleagues (1978) note that the therapist variables most often studied are "such simplistic global concepts as to cause this field to suffer from possibly terminal vagueness."

Even when many independent investigators have concentrated on an operationally defined, specific dimension in many samples over many years, the results have been disappointing. Dozens of investigators have tried to follow up on Betz and Whitehorn's (1956) distinction between therapists who were particularly successful with schizophrenic patients (A's) and those who were least successful (B's).

Razin (1977) sought out the published and unpublished findings accumulated over 20 years. With enthusiasm and initial sympathy, he reviewed this literature to conclude regretfully that this body of work "reveals only a scant few areas of possible clinical utility. . . . The A–B variable . . . has really not predicted outcome very consistently or very often. . . . The A–B variable is not a powerful predictor of any important process or outcome parameters in real, ongoing therapy" (p. 320). Parloff *et al.* (1978) concur with Razin's assessment.

Today most commentators not only share this pessimistic view of the utility of the A–B variable, but extend it to the whole area of therapist personality variables as predictors of treatment outcome. Sloane, Staples, Cristol, Yorkston, and Whipple (1975) found little published evidence that any standard personality test discriminates successful from unsuccessful therapists. Noting that therapist "personality" and "style" have been repeatedly measured in different terms, they commented acerbically that, "not surprisingly, the findings are seldom replicated, seldom believed, and almost never applied in clinical practice" (p. 41). Frank (1979, 1982) similarly observed that the qualities that account for differences in therapeutic success have remained obscure. Parloff and colleagues (1978) conclude that, "although the view of the general healing qualities of the therapist persists, we know of no studies concerning therapist characteristics conducted independent of the patients . . . or of the therapist's activities within a treatment setting which support this conviction" (p. 235). Strupp (1982) continues to affirm that "the therapist's personality is an important determinant of therapeutic outcome" but regretfully notes that, "real as [therapist characteristics] undoubtedly are, they . . . have eluded quantification. It is becoming increasingly clear that single therapist variables, except perhaps glaring defects in the therapist's personality, are not likely to provide the answers sought" (p. 56).

There seems increasing agreement that continued pursuit of therapist personality variables is an unproductive route to the prediction of treatment outcome. Is it sensible even to try to identify therapist variables in isolation from the type of patient or the circumstances of treatment? Instead of asking what characteristics of therapists lead to better outcome, should we not focus on such issues as "goodness of match" between patient and therapist? Of course, the question then becomes, what are the relevant matching dimensions? Frank (1979) suggests that similarity in level of conceptualization between patient and therapist may be one suitable area of inquiry.

Alternatively, given some minimum level of interpersonal competence, the personality of the therapist may be of little consequence. The antidemoralization effects may be primarily due to the setting and patient expectations. Frank has emphasized the personal qualities of the therapist, but his theory does not require this.

The remarkable unanimity between more recent analytic and behavioral therapists and antidemoralization theorists that the therapist's individuality is of supreme importance is striking—all the more so since there is no evidence for it. We understand this ideological unanimity as rationalizing a residual specificity, if only for the therapist's personality.

THERAPIST EXPERIENCE AND TREATMENT OUTCOME

It would be hard to find a clinician or, for that matter, a patient who would question that greater therapeutic experience contributes to better treatment outcome. Despite the compelling attractiveness of this belief, remarkably little evidence supports it. Since available studies are without exception methodologically flawed, it is also impossible to refute this belief definitively.

We could review all studies that compare groups of therapists who differ in experience. Many possibly relevant studies are rendered uninterpretable by comparison groups with overlapping experience levels, non-random assignment of patients, and contrasts of less and more experienced therapists who also differ systematically on other major variables (e.g., psychiatric residents and senior staff psychologists). Other studies use as their outcome measure only the therapists' ratings so that it is impossible to determine whether therapists' experience leads to change in patients' outcome or changes in therapists' ratings. When such studies are excluded, less than two dozen remain.

Auerbach and Johnson (1977) reviewed 12 studies that compared therapist experience levels. Only five found that experienced therapists achieve better outcomes, and in two of them the only outcome measures were therapist's change ratings and length of treatment. In trying to account for the surprisingly weak findings, these reviewers raise the possibility that the relationship between patient outcome and therapist experience is nonlinear. Severely ill patients may be generally unresponsive whereas basically healthy patients improve with nearly any enthusiastic helper; experience only counts for middling severity. If this interesting conjecture is valid, the linear correlation of outcome and experience across severity levels would mask such a relationship, if it indeed exists. It is a question worth pursuing.

However, Parloff and colleagues (1978) expanded Auerbach and Johnson's review to include more recent studies and end by saying, "our conclusions are even more pessimistic than those of Auerbach and Johnson" (p. 240).

Another approach to the question of therapist experience and treatment outcome is taken by Smith *et al.* (1980) in their meta-analysis. Therapist experience level is noted for each of the 475 studies reviewed. The correlation of therapist experience with treatment effect size for 1,637 outcome measures was exactly (and eerily) 0.00. When therapist experience was studied separately for patients within different diagnostic categories, there was still no predictive utility found for experience.

A major limitation in this data set is the restricted range of experience of therapists. The average experience was only $3\frac{1}{4}$ years, indicating that most were graduate students or residents rather than senior clinicians. While such therapists clearly represent those who participate in research projects, they do not represent the population of practicing clinicians in the community.

In summary, we share the surprise of the other reviewers that even such a presumably sturdy characteristic as therapist experience is not related to treatment outcome, although the limited quality of the evidence precludes the interpretation that no effect exists. However, these negative findings may reinforce the growing conviction that it is fruitless to study therapist variables in isolation from the characteristics of patient and treatment situation.

Alternatively, therapist personality and experience may really not be important variables with regard to outcome. Such a conclusion calls into question those theoretical stands that emphasize careful selection of therapists and meticulous training. Such *a priori* believable positions now require positive evidence for continued credibility.

These findings on experience seem most compatible with the antidemoralization stand.

OVERALL STRATEGY

Given the lack of a secure body of knowledge about psychotherapy effects, how should we try to determine the roots of efficacy? There is a sequence of stages in the evaluation of complex therapies that needs review.

The first question about any therapy is whether it works at all. We can compare our observations with out beliefs concerning the natural course of the untreated illness and conclude that a therapy shows promise. (Some conclude that they have proved their case!) Unfortunately, simply observing cases that get well during treatment is not sufficient because of the fluctuating course of most disorders.

Therefore, this question is usually answered by comparing the outcomes of therapy versus a "no treatment" condition. Given random assignment, adequate assessment methods, and so on, this would control for spontaneous remission, but is not sufficient to prove specific therapeutic action.

Even in evaluating a drug, treatment is a complex reality. The patient not only receives the specific agent, but also a pill, special attention, a medical setting, and so on, all of which may have their own beneficial effects. However, our concern is not with estimating the benefits of these pharmacologically nonspecific variables, but rather with estimating whether a medication has its own specific benefit that can only be attributed to it.

Therefore, patients are randomly divided into comparable groups, one group having the active treatment and the other group (the control group) having every aspect of the treatment, except the active ingredient, in the form of placebo treatment. To test for pharmacological specificity, a no-treatment control group does not suffice since the treatment and control groups differ on multiple confounded variables whose effects cannot be separated.

In psychopharmacology, one progresses from open clinical trials, where the drug effect is assessed against the implicit historical control of past experience, to placebo-controlled, randomized trials. This is a powerful paradigm in the scientific evaluation of therapies.

Psychotherapy studies went through a similar mental evolution. First, anecdotal evidence indicated that psychotherapeutic treatment seemed superior to no treatment at all. After some years, numerous trials compared various psychotherapies to no treatment with frequent reports of superiority. Such trials dominate the literature.

Then the question was raised whether there were specific benefits. It seemed logical to proceed immediately to compare psychotherapy to a psychotherapy placebo. The main difficulty is that the psychotherapy placebo should be, in itself, credible (Kazdin & Wilcoxon, 1976; O'Leary & Borkovec, 1978). Our discussion of the antidemoralization hypothesis indicates the crucial need for this.

THE PSYCHOTHERAPY PLACEBO

Once one stipulates the need for a credible control, there are two alternative approaches. One approach, which has received considerable interest, is the dismantling, deductive approach to placebo construction. Specific aspects of the therapy considered theoretically important, such as training in relaxation or pairing relaxation with anxiety-provoking stimuli, or developing systematic anxiety hierarchies, are deleted from the therapy. Comparison of this dismantled therapy with the full panoply of procedures indicates whether this particular component was necessary or at least has substantial additive value with regard to therapeutic outcome.

Therefore, dismantling has considerable heuristic value. This approach has been largely successful in showing that the elaborate procedures of systematic hierarchic desensitization are superfluous, and that therefore the explanatory theory of reciprocal inhibition is similarly superfluous.

One generally unremarked example of a dismantling approach to a complex psychotherapy is the variable of payment. Early in the history of psychoanalysis, payment was considered an important motivating force that helped the patient to struggle against his or her resistances. Furthermore, it gave the patient a living example of the importance of the reality principle.

That this interpretation of the payment process seems somewhat self-serving was not generally discussed. However, Lorand and Console (1958) published an article concerning their experience with a free psychoanalytic clinic. They indicated that in their informed opinion, the process of analysis seemed in no way affected. Clearly, this was not a proper, controlled study, but it is the basis from which an informed decision could be made as to whether an appropriate comparative study of payment is necessary or desirable.

The issue of payment as an important variable affecting psychotherapeutic efficacy has fallen into the junk heap of history, even without controlled studies (Lorand & Console, 1958). We emphasize that this is quite reasonable. One should not undertake the difficulties and expenses of controlled studies unless the preliminary evidence indicates that there is something there, but that it is not clear-cut.

The dismantling approach has been of major value as a heuristic device. However, to date the dismantling approach has implied nonspecificity since each time a supposedly specific ingredient has been deleted, nothing has happened to efficacy.

The deductive dismantling approach attempts to give a crucial test to a strong theory. However, if our theories are simply not very good, then the concentration of time and effort on attempts to disprove them may well be premature. It may be a superior strategy to realize that the most credible control is simply another credible contrast group, preferably one that seems to differ markedly in its presumptions and techniques.

Insofar as different therapies have different outcomes, then we should search for the differences between therapies that account for differences in outcomes. However, if different therapies have similar outcomes, we are left with three possibilities:

1. All therapies are doing nothing: We are simply seeing the natural, variable course of disease. This hypothesis should already have been discounted by a treatment versus no-treatment trial.

2. Both therapies, although apparently dissimilar, are actually doing the same nonspecific thing, probably antidemoralization.

3. The therapies are actually dissimilar and are doing different things but the net effect is the same.

The last hypothesis, by Russell's criterion, is inherently incredible. If treatments actually differ from each other, it would be an extraordinary coincidence if they produce precisely the same benefits. Different mechanisms should produce a different range of benefits, side effects, and long-term effects.

For instance, in agoraphobia antidepressants primarily blockade panic attacks, which allows a secondary decrease in anticipatory anxiety and avoidant behavior. Behavior therapy probably causes devaluation of the aversive potency of the panic attack which permits a direct instructional prevention of escape. Close attention to the complexities of improvement should reveal entirely different patterns. Marks (1981) also claims that the treatments and benefits of drug and behavior therapy are not identical since he states that behavior therapy has a more enduring effect—though what evidence is available does not support this. Occasionally, analogies are drawn from medicine that radically different therapies, such as digitalis and diuretics or radioactive iodine and thyroid surgery, have similar benefits.

However, these treatments actually have a marked dissimilarity in their range of effects. It is only by a very narrow focus on a particular aspect of outcome that the effects seem similar.

In the grandfather's therapy, a controlled study using the dismantling technique would have been easy to conceive but hard to carry out since no right-thinking faith healer would deprive his clients of his wonder-working interventions. Furthermore, it would be specifically premature, since the appropriate initial study would be to pit faith healers against each other. Each should have different beliefs as to the right prayers, and affirm that the other's methods lacked proper Talmudic authority and not only were ineffective, but were probably prompted by the Devil. In this case, a properly randomized trial of believers who were not swayed by esoteric doctrinal allegiances could establish comparative efficacy. If all proved exactly equivalent, one could argue that all prayers were the right prayers, but would this be the obvious conclusion?

Comparative trials of complex procedures are not a second best; they are the correct initial step. Only if substantial clinical differences are demonstrated should process analyses, or the construction of placebos by a dismantling approach or the construction of new therapies that emphasize apparent specific ingredients be pursued. The apparently scientific demand for a generic psychotherapy placebo is not sound. Any placebo, manufactured *ad hoc*, is open to question with regard to credibility.

Therefore, why get involved with such studies? First, find an outcome difference between real therapies, with real external validity. Then the construction of a theoretically relevant placebo becomes possible and worthwhile, as we shall try to show.

PHOBIA AND THE POSSIBILITY OF A CRUCIAL DISMANTLING STUDY

It is noteworthy that dismantling studies in the area of phobia have shown that various aspects of the systematic desensitization ritual are dispensable. No particular element has proved required for therapeutic activity.

However, by comparing short-term studies of treatments that emphasize *in vivo* exposure versus more office-bound treatment, the belief has grown that *in vivo* exposure is indeed superior. Klein, Zitrin, Woerner, and Ross (1983) compared their group *in vivo* treatment against a historical control of individual psychotherapy. Over a 26-week period they found that *in vivo* exposure did work faster, although it did not benefit any larger proportion of patients in the long run.

Individual office-bound psychotherapy may exert its effect by unsystematic instigation of patient self-exposure. Therefore, in this case there is a strong inference that *in vivo* exposure plays a crucial or even necessary role, in agreement with Rachman and Wilson.

One might study routine systematic hierarchic desensitization associated with varying amounts of *in vivo* exposure. For instance, certain patients could be told that the requirements of the technique were that they have to rest their nerves, and therefore should avoid any real confrontation with the phobic situation. The hope, of course, would be held out that eventually they will come to this, but before a defined period of time this is forbidden, while office-bound therapy is pursued.

Another group might be given a strictly delimited amount of *in vivo* exposure with the explanation that going too far might give them a counter-productive, overly anxious reaction. Yet another group might have an all-out effort at early *in vivo* exposure. The exact methods used are open to discussion, but the overall variation principle is plain. Here dismantling therapy may actually dismantle the benefits, thereby isolating a necessary condition and a specific benefit. The placebo must be tailor-made.

CONCLUSION

The elaborate theoretical constructions that have justified particular thera-peutic practices are premature and have served a primarily persuasive role. There is limited positive evidence indicating any specific value for particular therapists or psychotherapies that exceeds their antidemoralization effects. Claims for superiority must be greeted skeptically. Comparative trials of complex therapies are essential and cannot be avoided, but the insistence on psychotherapy placebos is premature. Such placebos require individual speci-fication derived from factual demonstrations of superior efficacy of certain treatments.

The utility of *in vivo* procedures seems promising and is open to relatively simple studies. We speculate that their specific benefit is due to focused unlearning of escape and avoidance maladaptations. However, un-learning is much more likely to be successful if the primary instigating condition is in remission, as in the case of biological disorder, or the instigating negative life experience has passed over.

REFERENCES

Andrews, G., & Harvey, R. Does psychotherapy benefit neurotic patients? *Archives of General Psychiatry*, 1981, *38*, 1203-1208.

APA Commission on Psychotherapies. *Psychotherapy research: Methodological and efficacy issues.* Washington, D.C.: American Psychiatric Association, 1982.

Auerbach, A., & Johnson, M. Research on the therapist's level of experience. In A. Gurman & A. Razin (Eds.), *Effective psychotherapy*. Oxford: Pergamon, 1977.

Bergin, A. E. Some implications of psychotherapy research for therapeutic practice. *Journal of Abnormal Psychology*, 1966, *71*, 235–246.

Betz, B., & Whitehorn, J. C. The relationship of the therapist to the outcome of therapy in schizophrenia. *Psychiatric Research Reports*, 1956, *5*, 89–105.

Eysenck, H. J. The effects of psychotherapy: An evaluation. *Journal of Consulting Psychology*, 1952, *16*, 319–324.

Fiske, D. W. Methodological issues in research on the psychotherapist. In A. Gurman & A. Razin (Eds.), *Effective psychotherapy*. Oxford: Pergamon, 1977.

Frank, J. D. *Persuasion and healing* (rev. ed.). Baltimore: Johns Hopkins University Press, 1973; New York: Schocken, 1974.

Frank, J. D. The present status of outcome studies. *Journal of Consulting and Clinical Psychology*, 1979, *47*, 310–316.

Frank, J. D. Therapeutic components shared by all psychotherapies. In J. H. Harvey & M. M. Parks (Eds.), *Psychotherapy research and behavior change*. Washington, D.C.: American Psychological Association, 1982.

Herink, R. (Ed.). *The psychotherapy handbook: The A to Z guide to more than 250 different therapies in use today*. New York: New American Library (Meridian), 1980.

Holt, R. R., & Luborsky, L. *Personality patterns of psychiatrists* (Vol. 1). New York: Basic Books, 1958.

Kazdin, A., & Wilcoxon, L. Systematic desensitization and nonspecific treatment effects: A methodological evaluation. *Psychological Bulletin*, 1976, *83*, 729–758.

Klein, D. F. Testimony: Proposals to expand coverage of mental health under Medicare–Medicaid. *Hearing before the Subcommittee of Health Committee on Finance, 98th Congress* (Second Session). Washington D.C.: U.S. Government Printing Office, 1978.

Klein, D. F. *The efficacy and cost effectiveness of psychotherapy*. Background paper #3: Advisory Panel of Psychotherapy, Office of Technology Assessment, Washington, D.C., 1980.

Klein, D. F., Zitrin, C. M., Woerner, M. G., & Ross, D. C. Behavior therapy and supportive therapy: Are there any specific ingredients? *Archives of General Psychiatry*, 1983, *40*, 139–145.

Lorand, S., & Console, W. Therapeutic results in psycho-analytic treatment without fee. *International Journal of Psychoanalysis*, 1958, *39*, 59–65.

Luborsky, L., McLellan, A., Woody, G., & O'Brien, C. Therapist success rates and their determinants. In press.

Luborsky, L., Singer, B., & Luborsky, L. Comparative studies of psychotherapies. *Archives of General Psychiatry*, 1975, *32*, 995–1008.

Marks, I. Behavioral treatment plus drugs in anxiety syndromes. In D. F. Klein & J. G. Rabkin (Eds.), *Anxiety: New research & changing concepts*. New York: Raven Press, 1981.

Mash, E. J., & Terdal, L. J. Follow-up assessments in behavioral therapy. In P. Karoly & J. Steffen (Eds.), *Improving the long-term effects of psychotherapy*. New York: Gardner, 1980.

Meltzoff, J., & Kornreich, M. *Research in psychotherapy*. New York: Atherton, 1970.

O'Leary, K. D., & Borkovec, T. Conceptual, methodological, and ethical problems of placebo groups in psychotherapy research. *American Psychologist*, 1978, *9*, 821–830.

Parloff, M. B. Psychotherapy research evidence and reimbursement decisions: Bambi meets Godzilla. *American Journal of Psychiatry*, 1982, *139*, 718–727.

Parloff, M. B., Waskow, I. E., & Wolfe, B. E. Research on therapist variables in relation to process and outcome. In S. L. Garfield & A. E. Bergin (Eds.), *Handbook of psychotherapy and behavior change: An empirical analysis* (2nd ed.). New York: Wiley, 1978.

Rachman, S. J., & Wilson, G. T. *The effects of psychological therapy* (2nd ed.). New York: Pergamon, 1980.

Razin, A. The A–B variable: Still promising after twenty years? In A. Gurman & A. Razin (Eds.), *Effective psychotherapy.* Oxford: Pergamon, 1977.

Sloane, R. B., Staples, F. R., Cristol, A. H., Yorkston, N. J., & Whipple, K. *Psychotherapy versus behavior therapy.* Cambridge, Mass.: Harvard University Press, 1975.

Smith, M. L., Glass, G. V., & Miller, T. I. *The benefits of psychotherapy.* Baltimore: Johns Hopkins University Press, 1980.

Strupp, H. A reformulation of the dynamics of the therapist's contribution. In A. Gurman & A. Razin (Eds.), *Effective psychotherapy*, Oxford: Pergamon, 1977.

Strupp, H. H. The outcome problem in psychotherapy: Contemporary perspectives. In J. H. Harvey & M. M. Parks (Eds.), *Psychotherapy research and behavior change.* Washington, D.C.: American Psychological Association, 1982.

Weiss, E. *Agoraphobia in the light of ego psychology.* New York: Grune & Stratton, 1964.

COMMENTARY

Dr. Robert M. A. Hirshfeld*: Don, as usual, that was brilliant. It made me think about one thing, and that is that you label credibility as the core, and I wonder about whether you should test that specifically by using the same technique, but done in an *in*-credible or *un*-credible way. You could have very well trained CB therapists who don't believe in it, and you also somehow could indoctrinate your patients or clients so that they expect that it won't work as well.

If it truly works, then—if it is truly a specifically good, efficacious procedure—will it overpower the lack of credibility and work nonetheless?

Dr. Klein: I think that is an important point. There is nothing inherent in the notions of psychotherapy that they should require credibility. That is a testable and falsifiable hypothesis. As a matter of fact, Freud very clearly says in his writings on psychotherapy technique that the patient's belief in the efficacy of psychoanalysis is of little importance except for temporary, positive transferant symptomatic relief. But in terms of the long-term effectiveness of the treatment, it doesn't matter whether the patient believes it or not.

Arthur Shapiro mentioned before that one of the outstanding things about the placebo response, one of the strongest predictors of whether a person will respond positively to a placebo, is whether the placebo is credible for the person. So I think that is a partial answer to your question, though a direct experimental answer, of course, would be better.

Dr. Gerald L. Klerman†: I am troubled by what I thought I detected as an inconsistency between the first half of your brilliant analysis of the bobbe-

*National Institute of Mental Health.

†Harvard School of Medicine, Harvard School of Public Health, and Massachusetts General Hospital.

mysehs, and your own behavior. One might have expected that, confronted with the outcome of your study with Charlotte Zitrin, you would have applied the principle of the first half of your statement and said, "Well, all of the therapies are just giving spontaneous remission or producing faith." But you didn't do that. You invoked a process analysis. You said the common ingredient is exposure *in vivo*. And you did—to your own nonspecific findings of no difference between behavior therapy and supportive, dynamic group therapy—what you said shouldn't be done. You did a process analysis and came up with the hypothesis that the common ingredient was not credibility or faith in the long prayer, but was a specific behavioral mechanism, exposure *in vivo*.

Now I maintain that if you would apply to your own analysis what you said in the first half of your lecture, you wouldn't come up with what you yourself have proposed as a set of studies to test whether or not the common ingredient is not faith or belief, but a specific mechanism, exposure *in vivo*.

Dr. Klein: I think the point that I tried to make is that the credibility and the engendering of faith is necessary, and, for many conditions, helpful. Certainly for generalized demoralization it is helpful. What I am suggesting is that there are certain conditions in which the general antidemoralization of therapy can then allow the use of more specific techniques.

I am struggling with what appears to be a fact. The fact appears to be that the *in vivo* techniques are faster than the ordinary office-bound techniques. You cannot explain that unless you assume that the *in vivo* technique has inherently higher credibility, if you want to stick with credibility as a complete explain-all.

So I am saying "Look, I am stuck with the facts. The facts seem to indicate that there is something more than credibility here. What could that be?" And that is what drives me to do the process analysis, and the process analysis leads me to the idea that it is not the *in vivo* exposure *per se*, it is the *in vivo* exposure combined with response prevention that leads to the decrease in the anticipatory anxiety and the escape behavior.

When I was writing the paper, I went through a sort of similar mental evolution. Initially I was going to say, "Well, the hell with it. Nothing has been shown." And if nothing has been shown, why worry about specificity? But after more thinking about the issue of accelerated effects with *in vivo* exposure and the work of Rachman and Wilson, I think you at least have to pay some attention to specific factors in the phobia area.

Dr. Allen Wilner*: Don, I think that was a really excellent paper. I was especially intrigued with the notion about demoralization, and that psychotherapy might work through influencing demoralization. I would like to see what you think about this testable hypothesis.

*Long Island Jewish Medical Center.

Presumably, subjects in psychotherapy studies will vary in demoralization. Some will be very demoralized, some will be somewhat demoralized, and some, for example, university students in some of the studies mentioned, will be very little demoralized at all. If the main way that psychotherapy works is by reducing demoralization, then if you do a psychotherapy study where you have some patients who are extremely demoralized and others who are very little demoralized, would you expect to see differences in the results?

Dr. Klein: Well, plainly, I think you would. And it is hard to know whether or not there has been anything much in the literature that would speak directly to that point. You could argue two things: You could say that, well, the person is very demoralized, and has the opportunity for showing dramatic gains, where the person who is only slightly demoralized has the opportunity of showing only moderate gains. On the other hand, the person who is very demoralized, although he or she has the opportunity to show dramatic gains, may still end up in a worse place than the person who is only slightly demoralized. So it is a complex situation where I don't think you can make a simple prediction as to how it is going to lay out at the outcome.

There have been reports that one of the things that was most predictive of good effectiveness of treatment was high anxiety levels on the part of the patient. Now demoralization, as defined by Jerome Frank, is a sense of personal ineffectiveness associated with distress of an anxious and depressed nature. It is at least possible that they were treating a nonspecific demoralization there.

Dr. Wilner: Do you know of any scale that might be used to assess demoralization?

Dr. Klein: No, I don't. There is no good scale for demoralization. Bruce Dohrenwend has put together a number of scales which hang together in a highly intercorrelative fashion, which could be conceived of as being demoralization scales because they are so, in a sense, nonspecific. But as Jerome Frank has pointed out, they don't specifically tap the notion of lack of personal efficacy. And I do think that is a crucial notion.

20

Formal Discussion

The Benefits of Meta-Analysis

JACOB COHEN
New York University

Don Klein's charming anecdote reminded me of a Jewish proverb, learned at my mother's knee, that helps define my role here. In the original it goes: "Di skikseh dem rebens kun oich pasken ah sheileh," which crudely translates as: "The rabbi's Gentile serving girl can also answer questions about religious ritual."

And I have some claims, I think, to being a rabbi. I am an ABEPP Diplomate in Clinical Psychology and a Fellow in Division 12 of the psychologists' APA, but these are largely historical. Bob Spitzer didn't ask me to be a discussant here because of my psychotherapeutic prowess or even as a psychotherapy researcher, but rather as a research methodologist—that is, as a helper in research . . . a shikseh.

In this role I want to address the Smith, Glass, and Miller work that has been referred to here and which Bob twisted Sol Garfield's arm enough so that he would talk about it as well.

About the symposium papers, let me quickly say that both in the part of the Garfield paper devoted to the Smith *et al.* work and in the passing reference to it in the Klein and Rabkin paper I found little to quarrel with. In fact, I admired Dr. Garfield's thoughtful critique of that work, and also appreciate and strongly commend to you the current issue of his *Journal of Consulting and Clinical Psychology* which contains a group of invited papers on the Smith *et al.* work. This is a very good way to get entry into this literature if, as I would strongly urge, you want to pursue it and haven't.

I also found that the Klein and Rabkin analysis of specificity and the recommended strategy for dealing with those matters superb.

But I am here to sell meta-analysis.

Now, I think that the Smith, Glass, and Miller work is the most important research in psychotherapy ever published. It summarizes most of the controlled research in psychotherapy that was published up to about 1979, and I don't know whether there is anybody in the audience who doesn't know at least something about it. In case there is, it involved, as has already been mentioned, some 475 studies which incorporated some 1,760 outcome variables. And it was the latter that constituted the unit of analysis.

Now, meta-analysis, a research method that one must attribute primarily to Gene Glass, is a systematic and quantitative procedure for integrating research around some particular topic or issue. As applied to psychotherapy research, what they did was to express outcome as an *effect size*, that is, a standardized measure of the magnitude of the effect, as already described to you. It is simply the difference between a treated and a control group mean on some outcome, divided by the standard deviation for the control group, something which is, by other people, called Cohen's d. It is essentially a difference in means of standardized (z) scores.

The important thing about this is the fact that it makes it possible to describe the size of an outcome in a unit which is a pure number and is thus comparable and commensurate with the sizes of other outcome measures.

Once you have this kind of an outcome-characterizing number, it becomes possible to study how it relates in a meta-analysis involving many researches to other variables: substantive issues, for example, like the school or type of therapy—what Dr. Garfield called the "brand name." Issues like group versus individual therapy. Issues like the duration of therapy. Substantive issues including features of the patients: diagnosis, age, education, sex, whether the patients are volunteers who responded to a notice in the campus newspaper. Also, outcome sizes can be related to characteristics of therapists such as the profession from which they come, the amount of experience they have had, whether or not they were committed to the particular brand of psychotherapy that they were using, etc.

But not only can all these substantive matters be related to therapeutic outcome, but many methodologically relevant factors in research can be so related: for example, whether or not randomization was used; the nature of the outcome measure; its reactivity, a term used by Smith *et al.* to describe the degree of objectivity of the outcome measure. It spans the range from the patient's self-report or the clinician's rating of the patient at the end of therapy, at the most reactive end, to physiological measures, or things like grade-point average, that are not under the patient's immediate control, at the least reactive end.

Also such methodological issues as experimental mortality (dropout rates) can be related to effect size, as well as degree of blindedness of the rater.

So in a meta-analytic inquiry involving many psychotherapy studies it is possible to find out how any of these factors, on the one hand substantive and on the other methodological, relate to the magnitude of the outcome.

Now, from one point of view, you can look upon meta-analysis as a quantitative method for reviewing the literature. But it must be distinguished from other quantitative methods used for this purpose. For example, it is very different from the box-score method which was used for some years. It differs first of all in that once you have defined the subject matter of a research, you are not selective other than to meet those criteria. Thus, for example, in the Smith, Glass, and Miller work, all studies that had one or more groups being given some—one or more forms—of therapy and one or more control groups were included.

The meta-analytic procedure differs from the box-score method also in that the focus is not on significance of results and counting how many were and how many were not (i.e., the box score), but rather on how large each outcome is, and what relates to the size of that outcome.

Significance, however useful it can be in making decisions about the bearing of a single study on some issue, is not very useful when you come to assess many studies. (I will return to this issue.) But it is self-evident, I think, that box-score analyses in which it is noted for example that one study found a significant result in some particular sample and four others didn't, cannot be summarized as offering evidence that the phenomenon doesn't exist without very close attention to such issues as statistical power and other things that you know about.

The Smith, Glass, and Miller findings have already been summarized but I will briefly summarize them once more so you can see how they look from my perspective.

First of all, on the average, psychotherapy is beneficial. The average d-value, the effect size value, they found was .85 of a standard deviation between psychotherapy and control means. Now this is not a familiar unit, but that is a large effect. Long before the Smith, Glass, and Miller work was done, in connection with my work in statistical power analysis, I defined various effect size levels. In my classification an effect size of .2 was operationally defined as small, .5 medium, and .8 large. So .85 is deemed large on the basis of criteria that preceded by about 15 years the findings of the Smith, Glass, and Miller study.

There are other ways you can translate such measures in order to appreciate their magnitude. You can say, for example, that that is equivalent to finding that on the average some 80% of the treated cases exceeded the mean of the outcome for the control cases.

Secondly, on the average, there is little evidence for specificity from the Smith, Glass, and Miller work. That is, specificity of brand name or therapy type. That conclusion may have been somewhat overstated by them; nevertheless, there is little evidence to support any substantial amount of specificity. Indeed, as far as I can gather from the other speakers, that is essentially the conclusion that they drew from their review of that material.

There is little difference as a function of many of the kinds of things that we think matter. Group versus individual, length of treatment, therapist experience, and virtually anything else except for the reactivity of the out-come measure have no demonstrable effect on outcome. Apparently, thera-pist ratings produce larger outcome effects than such variables as grade-point average.

There have been some major criticisms of the Smith, Glass, and Miller work. I would like to address them briefly and add, or emphasize, some of my own.

The first charge, made somewhat inelegantly by Hans Eysenck, came under the rubric of the famous acronym from computer work, GIGO: "garbage in, garbage out." This represented a bitter complaint about the poor quality of some of the studies that were incorporated in the integration.

Stated somewhat more civilly, one gets such reactions from others, including, as we did today, from Dr. Garfield. But this is worth examining somewhat more closely. First of all, if we talk about garbage, it can manifest itself in various ways, as most New Yorkers know.

Poor research design. For example, nonrandomness of assignment of cases to therapy and control groups. Nonblind assessments. High or differ-ential mortality (dropout rates) between treatment and control. So there is that kind of garbage.

And then there is poor outcome measurement garbage like using self-reports or therapist ratings. And then there is "poor subject" garbage, like using student volunteer subjects instead of real patients. Cases with relatively few instances of depression, relatively many of phobia, already mentioned. Poor therapists—that is, relatively inexperienced. And poor therapies, that kind of garbage, like counseling, or someone else's. (*Laughter.*)

Smith, Glass, and Miller argue, first of all, that they deliberately did not exclude researches that otherwise met their criteria because of the likely bias that results when one begins to make judgments of this kind. Now, that is arguable.

But a more telling point they make is that it would be reasonable, *a priori*, to identify certain features of research that make them poor if psychotherapy were an enterprise that was 5 or 10 years old. We could then identify those kinds of problems and screen out studies from further atten-tion on those grounds. But after 50 years of accumulated research, you don't have to decide *a priori* that if you don't have random assignment your effects will be biased. You can find out by tagging each effect-size measure that you found in these many studies with simply the dichotomous issue as to whether it had been obtained from a comparison with randomly assigned control cases or with nonrandom controls. You can easily find out how much it matters. This is merely one example.

Well, if these things are garbage, first of all they found on a measure that they called internal validity, which is a combination of nonrandomness of assignment and either high mortality or differential mortality between experimental and controls, that for 1,760 effect sizes, the correlation between the effect size and internal validity was .03. That was not its p value for significance; that was its value: $r = .03$.

What this means, then, is that if you were to exclude all garbage on that criterion, it wouldn't have mattered at all in terms of the effect sizes that you got.

Take blinding, for example. Everybody knows you shouldn't have people who know what the status of the patient is make judgments. Well, blinding correlates with effect size at $-.01$ in the Smith, Glass, and Miller work.

Take experimental mortality, dropout rate. Well, that correlates in the experimental group at $-.05$ and in the control group at $-.04$.

Garbage? Take short studies. They can't really be doing therapy in a few hours. Well, duration correlates with effect size at $-.05$. Therapist experience correlates with effect size .00. That is, to two places. I don't know about the third; it wasn't reported.

Now to try to meet some of these complaints by means other than simply arguing from the statistical analysis of the Smith material, there have been studies that have already been mentioned in which there was replication or subsampling of the research material of the Smith, Glass, and Miller study.

Landman and Dawes, for example, extracted from the 475 S-G-M studies a sample of 60 studies which contained some 468 outcome measures, and further selected just those instances in which there was randomization in the assignment to treatment and control group. There were 42 such studies. Indeed, they went further. Given the desirability of using placebo controls rather than nontreatment controls (a point that was made by Don in his paper), they studied the subset of studies with placebo controls.

They also investigated the issue of the nonindependence of outcomes. In a review I wrote of the S-G-M work, I complained about the fact that the proper unit should not have been outcomes but rather studies, because outcomes were nonindependent. Well, most people with a statistical eye would have the same reaction. So, in the Landman and Dawes study that issue was also addressed by expressing each study's outcomes in terms of a mean, so that each study counted only once, and the resultant n reflects independent observations.

Well, with all this they found no material differences in the conclusions from their sample of good studies drawn from the same batch of researches that Smith, Glass, and Miller used.

Shapiro and Shapiro, who report (among other places) in the current issue of the *Journal of Consulting and Clinical Psychology*, used *Psychological Abstracts* for the years 1975–1979 to do their own meta-analysis. They selected only "good" studies, as would reasonably be defined. They found

143 such studies in that 5-year period. Only 21 of them, that is, 15% of them, were studies that had been included in the Smith, Glass, and Miller work, since Shapiro and Shapiro came later.

Well, they also found no material difference in the S-G-M conclusions that I summarized.

Now another source of complaint about this work has been—and again, we heard it today—the effect size index that was used. I find it a massive irony that the other social sciences look upon psychology as quantitative. Psychology, for the most part, is not quantitative. That is, in the usual sense of the word it doesn't really deal too often with how big things are, but rather with how significant they are. The game is played with significance chips. *They* are the coin of the realm. They buy things like promotions and funding and publication.

There is nothing that is really quite so highly crafted as t ratios, chi squares, F ratios, and so on. Now, obviously everybody knows that the results of a significance test are a multiplicative function of how big something is and how much evidence there is about it. Unfortunately, what happens is that when you give yourself the three stars of good behavior for a p value that is less than .001, inevitably many (I hope not most) people interpret this to mean that the size of the effect under scrutiny is large. Of course, significance purveyors have no idea of the sizes of their effects. Effect sizes are not reflected in any direct sense by the significance test results. And each zero that precedes the first real digit in a p value adds another "very" to the adjective "significant," *not* the adjective "large."

Sol Garfield doesn't like—finds not clinically very useful—the effect size measures that are used, but it is unavoidable. If you are going to generalize over any area of any diversity, you need to find some kind of common metric, and this is a useful common metric for this purpose. If you can't equate from one clinical study to another the criterial outcomes that would lead you to say that one has had a better effect than the other, then there is no way of integrating anything, unless you are going to restrict yourself to integrating very small areas for which the same criteria have been used. You could perhaps generate such specific common criteria in a narrow symptomatic area, such as phobias. But if your generalization is to cover some ground, you can't do it without a common metric.

Well, I thought that I wouldn't possibly be able to fill 20 minutes, but I should have known better.

Let me quickly offer my critique (and it is not only mine) of the Smith, Glass, and Miller work, and point out to you the fact (also mentioned by Dr. Garfield, but let me emphasize it), that the Smith, Glass, and Miller study was a fair analysis of psychotherapy research, and dealt with representative research in psychotherapy as it appears in public documents (published and unpublished, but publicly available).

But that basis for selection does not, of course, reflect in any accurate way the application of psychotherapy in the clinical context that most of us are familiar with. They summarized studies that dealt with primarily a young, college-educated population, seen in school facilities. Some 46% of their effect sizes came from school settings, in treatment of short duration both in terms of weeks and hours, with therapists of, on the average, 3 years' experience, suggesting that many of them were doctoral candidates. The Shapiros also found that this characterized their sample of studies and objected very violently.

(I am about to wind up. Don't be nervous.)

Let me offer you some incidental benefits of meta-analysis, because this is what I mostly want to say. This holds in psychotherapy research and it holds elsewhere, and is in addition to all the good things that I have already said about meta-analysis. First of all, that kind of approach to data and to an area requires close specification of what it is you are studying, where you are going to get the relevant data, what you will include, what you will not include, and it is all quite public, which means it is replicable. Indeed, in the current issue of the *Journal of Consulting and Clinical Psychology*, in that batch of invited articles, Glass and Kliegl report that there are already some half dozen reanalyses of their data and replications. Now that is something you can do with meta-analytic studies that you can't do otherwise.

Another incidental effect has been that it has uncovered once more how poor our reporting practices are in research. When I did a survey in 1962 of statistical power analysis, I found in one volume of a very respectable journal of the American Psychological Association two studies in which no n was mentioned.

Authors must now ask themselves (and if not authors, certainly journal editors), if a meta-analysis is going to be done in this area, can they use this study? Well, that should make for some difference in the quality of reportage.

Meta-analysis is truly quantitative. It asks how big things are, not whether they are significant. Significance is an important but really a quite secondary issue. Magnitude is what finally counts. And I must say this pleases me no end, because I have been involved in a 20-year crusade to try to get people to say how big things are, not merely to offer me one or more asterisks.

Meta-analysis is heuristic. It serves to make us study what is otherwise assumed. Much of the reaction to the Smith, Glass, Miller work was astonishment. Things that you know often turn out not to be so when you look at enough data.

Meta-analysis is humbling. That is another very good thing about it. It makes researchers, no matter how hard they are working, realize that their work will not definitively settle any issue, but if properly done and properly reported, will be aggregated with other work, and perhaps in that way can have some effect.

Finally, except for the question of the general efficacy of psychotherapy, the meta-analytic findings are mostly negative. That is, they found that very few things were related to effect size. And when we keep that in mind we realize what the implications of negative findings really are. There is plenty of work to be done in this field. One can't conclude positively that there is no specificity from their work. One *can* conclude that specificity has not been demonstrated. What we have now, through meta-analysis, ultimately, is a challenge and a standard for further clinical research.

General Discussion

Dr. Donald F. Klein*: I would like to make a couple of comments on Dr. Cohen's remarks. I think there are two things that bother me about meta-analysis, and I would like to trot them out.

The first thing is the fact that the effect size does not correlate with methodological excellence, and what are we to make of that? I am not interested in randomization, in double blinding, and the various methodological niceties solely because I want an accurate estimate of the effect size. I am interested in doing all these things because I want to be able to allocate the cause of the effect that is determined.

When you have a nonrandom situation, and you've got nonblind measures, and you have all sorts of confounding variables, it may very well be that a bad experiment will end up getting the same effect size as a good experiment. But I can't use the bad experiment because I don't know what it tells me.

So, I submit that putting a bad experiment into a meta-analysis can only do one of two things: Either it will agree with the good analyses, in which case it has told me nothing new, or it will disagree with the good analyses, in which case I will start to tear my hair, and I will simply say "Let's get rid of that stuff because I can't understand it." So I think it is a mistake to put bad analyses into a meta-analysis.

The second point I want to make is the effect-size notion. As a clinician I am offended by the effect size notion. Why should that be? There is a certain amount of sense, of course, to what Dr. Cohen says, that that is one way of covering a lot of ground. But the way you cover a lot of ground is to fly very high. And what you've done is to move to an effect-size notion that is so abstract that anything that can be measured goes on the same metric.

Now, I submit it doesn't make a lot of sense, clinical or otherwise, to have studied a group of schizophrenics and to have studied what happened in their hallucinations, and to have studied a group of phobics and to find

*New York State Psychiatric Institute and College of Physicians and Surgeons, Columbia University.

out what happens to their avoidance behaviors, et cetera, and say the various treatments had a common effect size. It seems to me it just gets us too far away from the sort of things we ought to know about to be able to make sense out of our treatments.

Dr. Jacob Cohen*: The fault is not in the effect-size measure, it is in deciding that you are trying to answer such general questions as "Is therapy effective?" Once you pose the question in those terms, you are implying that there is some common metric on which this issue can be resolved. If you reject the proposition that you can in any way find comparable symptom changes in hallucinations among schizophrenics and with phobias among neurotics, then you have a very simple solution: Study schizophrenics and effects on them separately from those of neurotics. Don't pose the question in more general terms than you are prepared to integrate the data for.

Dr. Klein: I think that is a very fair answer. So let's not do it.

Dr. Cohen: No, no. Do you mean let's not do meta-analysis?

Dr. Klein: Yes.

Dr. Cohen: Well, can't you cast a smaller net over a smaller area?

Dr. Klein: Right, that is what I would like to do.

Dr. Cohen: Well, that is still meta-analysis. You have just defined the area in which you are going to apply it differently. There is no reason in the world why you have to study all psychotherapy at once. But that is the way the problem has been posed.

Dr. Klein: Fine. I am for micro-meta-analysis. (*Laughter.*)

Dr. Cohen: You mean not-quite-so-meta-analysis.

Dr. A. John Rush†: This is for Dr. Klein. One of the arguments you used in discussing specificity, if I understood it, was the issue that certain therapies are used across different disorders with presumed or claimed equivalent or good efficacy. I don't know if that is a valid argument, because if you go back to the analogue of, say, psychopharmacology, where you can use the same drug in apparently different disorders, such as MAO inhibitors, or imipramine in panic or depression, or Tegretol as an antimanic and as an anticonvulsant, I think that sort of skirts the specificity issue. Could you comment on that aspect of your presentation?

Dr. Klein: Are you saying that I said that because a treatment seems to be broadly useful that it must necessarily be a nonspecific treatment?

Dr. Rush: Yes.

Dr. Klein: Well, I don't think I made that precise point. It would certainly seem to me that insofar as these are really different illnesses with different causes and different pathogeneses, if a therapy were broadly useful

*New York University.
†University of Texas Health Science Center.

across them, either it would be tapping into some very common feature, or, as I think is more likely, it would be tapping into some secondary complication, which is common.

Dr. George E. Murphy*: Don [Klein], I want to expand the topic under consideration to this extent. In the comparison studies of cognitive therapy and tricyclic antidepressants, what we have seen are essentially equal outcomes, whether measured by mean change scores or by categorical improvements to a certain level. As I followed your presentation earlier today, which, incidentally, I thought was brilliant, and which I agree with about 100%, it seemed to me that you were giving a considerable amount of weight to the idea that pharmacotherapy is effective.

The question that I really have here is not to argue that if you think it is effective then cognitive therapy must be, too, but rather, the opposite: If pharmacotherapy is no more effective than cognitive therapy, which is only about, perhaps, 60% effective or so, why is it you think that pharmacotherapy, that is, tricyclic antidepressants, are effective? We used an active placebo as a control in our study. We found no difference between that and TCA, and I think there have been other studies like this. Why do you think the tricyclics are effective?

Dr. Klein: I am delighted that you used a placebo in your study because what you have done is demonstrate that the sample you have used is a drug-inappropriate sample by the fact that you showed no drug difference from placebo.

The reason I believe that tricyclics are effective is because there have been a number of very large reviews, including our own in our textbook, which have covered hundreds of studies. We never said that antidepressants are effective. We say the antidepressants are effective for a certain subgroup of depressives, and that, as I said yesterday, it is not difficult to put together a pharmacotherapy study on people who meet depressive criteria, where you will get no pharmacotherapy effect whatsoever. All you have to do is take patients who are primarily hypochondriacal or patients who have a nonmajor depression, or patients who have scored relatively low on the Hamilton scale, and you aren't going to get a tricyclic effect in these patients.

Now, in the studies that have been done reviewing the tricyclic literature, fully one-third of the studies that have been done comparing tricyclics to placebo show no drug effect. Now, two-thirds *do*. So I think I am entitled to the thought that the tricyclics, at least for some people, are effective. But I think we are also entitled to the notion that it is very easy not to get a tricyclic effect, which must mean that it is very easy to slip into a sample where the tricyclics are inappropriate. And I think that is possibly what you have done.

*Washington University School of Medicine.

Dr. Cohen: You should have done a meta-analysis.

Dr. Allen Wilner*: I have a question for Dr. Cohen. You mentioned a whole host of variables that had negligible correlations with effect size. Did Smith, Glass, and Miller find any variables that do correlate with effect size?

Dr. Cohen: I didn't have time to go into that. One of the things that you can do when you have got your data organized this way is you can study simultaneously the effects of many potential influences. You can do path-analytic kinds of things; you can do multiple regression kinds of things. This makes it possible for you to study partial effects or do covariance kinds of analyses.

Now, they started off with a set of 17 potential covariants to use in order to make their comparisons. Out of the 17 only two proved to give correlations larger than .1 with effect size. One was reactivity, which we now all recognize is an important source of variation in outcomes—it had a correlation of .28. And the other was percent male, where the correlation was −.13. The remaining 15 covariants had correlations no larger than .1.

Incidentally, by these means an initial finding in that body of data, with all its clinical unrepresentativeness acknowledged by me, was an initial superiority of behavioral over verbal kinds of therapies that disappeared when they covaried out reactivity. It was simply a matter of the fact that in the cases in which behavioral techniques were used, the studies tended to use highly reactive outcome measures; once that was allowed for, that initial difference disappeared.

Dr. Wilner: One implication of what you are saying is that if you want to get sizable results in psychotherapy research, you should prefer reactive measures and having more women in your study.

Dr. Cohen: Well, there are some people who do that quite systematically, indeed. They know the secret!

Dr. Sol L. Garfield†: I was just going to comment that there are a number of findings in the Smith, Glass, and Miller study that I myself have trouble accepting because they go against my value system, particularly the types of studies in terms of the quality and so on. On the other hand, we always make a point about the experience level of the therapists, which came out as not having any significant impact, which was also found by Art Auerbach in his review of the influence of the therapist in the handbook by Gurman and Razin, if I remember correctly.

I want to elaborate on the point that I made that Jack Cohen didn't agree with me on, and that is the matter of clinical significance—and I don't mean it at an 000 level at all. It is something I have been interested in because the usual significant difference really doesn't mean anything, and if one

*Long Island Jewish Medical Center.
†Washington University.

looks in the reports of many studies, one finds that if you really look at it, only a relatively small number would make changes, let's say, on a rating scale, that are clinically significant, although they may not even come back to a normal level of functioning.

That kind of information I can't get from the effect size. I would be willing to accept the effect size of .85 as being a very large effect size compared to many others in the social sciences, and yet it doesn't give me an operational meaning in terms of symptoms or what have you. I think looking at these studies individually may be required to give it more of an operational meaning. Let me just add, as I mentioned before in my talk, that I don't think there is any question that meta-analysis is going to be the procedure for doing the literature reviews.

Dr. Cohen: When you say a clinically significant difference, I think you mean a large one, or one at least of a certain magnitude. Well, one kind of effect size you could use, if the data were available, would be the percent of cases making a clinically significant change. Now, that is a perfectly reasonable effect-size measure. But I defy you to find it in the literature. That is something you can't integrate, because people rarely report their results in those terms.

Dr. Klein: Jack, you are not reading my papers! (*Laughter.*)

"THE BUCK STOPS HERE": PSYCHOTHERAPY AND PUBLIC POLICY WHEN THE EVIDENCE IS NOT ALL IN

21

Psychotherapy and Public Policy: What Does the Future Hold?

GERALD L. KLERMAN
Harvard Medical School,
Harvard School of Public Health,
and Massachusetts General Hospital

INTRODUCTION

"Policy" refers to the general principles that guide individuals, groups, institutions, and government bodies in decisions regarding their goals, programs, and the allocation of resources. Within that broad definition, the concept of policy could be applied to individuals. We all make decisions about how we allocate scarce resources, particularly our time. In addition to time, our money, attachments, and other resources are limited. We are constantly making decisions about how we choose to live our lives, which in the broadest definition, could be called "policy decisions." However, "policy" more usually refers to those principles that guide formal groups such as hospitals, industrial corporations, and government bodies.

The field of "policy science" or "policy studies" has emerged as a new academic discipline. There are a number of graduate programs in policy, including the Kennedy School of Government at Harvard and similar programs at Stanford and the University of Chicago. The quantitative methodology for policy analysis has derived from economics and statistics. Only recently have these methodologies been applied to issues in mental health, noteworthy being the Weisbrod analysis of the cost–benefit of the Stein–Test Study of chronic mental patients in Madison, Wisconsin, and May's analysis of the follow-up data from his comparative study of psychotherapy versus drugs in the treatment of hospitalized schizophrenics. Applied to psychotherapy, the Congressional Office of Technology Assessment commissioned a report evaluating the possible utility of cost–benefit analysis of psychotherapy.

Policy considerations have only begun to be applied to issues involving psychotherapy. The reason for this is obvious, for until recently psychotherapy was not a sufficiently widely dispersed intervention to warrant public consideration. However, with the tremendous growth of different types of psychotherapy and the range of practitioners, policy considerations increasingly apply as to priorities for research, reimbursement from third-party payments, and nature of training and educational programs for mental health professionals.

In this chapter, I will outline succinctly a public policy position dependent upon the principle of efficacy.

PROPOSED PUBLIC POLICY

The basic principle that guides my views of the public policy issues is that only those health interventions with demonstrated efficacy, safety, and efficiency should be supported financially, programatically, or educationally.

This may seem self-evident; but it is important to recognize that the concern for efficacy is only realistic in this century. Prior to the 20th century, relatively few medical interventions were efficacious. With the advances in biomedical technology and biobehavioral technology, we have increasingly effective, but often costly and even dangerous, technologies.

In principle, the public policy considerations should apply to all health interventions, including drugs, psychotherapy, surgery, radiation, and preventive interventions. However, the only area in which there is a public policy is with regard to drugs. Only after a long period of legislative struggle did Congress pass the Kefauver–Harris Amendments of 1962 which established efficacy as a necessary criteria for the marketing of new drugs. It took the Food and Drug Administration (FDA) 10 years to develop the regulations explicating the criteria for efficacy and to put into place an administrative mechanism for reviewing drugs approved prior to 1962 and for reviewing new drugs.

If we were to adopt a similar policy for psychotherapy, as I strongly advocate, its implementation would require the following ingredients.

1. A public affirmation of this principle, either by legislative statute or by an appropriate announcement of bodies including professional groups and government agencies.

2. A public body to continually review the changing state of knowledge as to efficacy, to identify areas where further research is called for, and to assess the outcome of such research.

3. A research program which would involve available funds to execute the necessary studies, to set priorities, and to set standards for the design and conduct of individual studies.

4. Some mechanism for determining when the body of knowledge with respect to an individual form of psychotherapy is of sufficient validity and certitude that further research is not called for, because the treatment is either effective, ineffective, or too dangerous.

5. Some mechanism to "drive the system" through positive reinforcements (such as reimbursement) or through some form of sanctioning of an adversive negative nature. In the case of drugs, such a system derives from the federal power to regulate interstate commerce in that the pharmaceutical industry is easily regulated since there are only a finite number of firms. In the case of the psychotherapy industry, it would not be feasible to do so even if it were morally justifiable. Therefore some other mechanism is called for—either statements by appropriate public bodies and/or policy with regard to reimbursement.

A number of proposals embodying the above principles and programs were put forward during the second half of the Carter Administration. In 1978–1980, there were proposals put forward in the Congress and the Executive branch. In the Congress, Senator Matsunaga proposed legislation that would have established a National Commission on Mental Health Therapies. This proposal received wide discussion in Washington but was never acted upon because of the change from Democratic to Republican control of the Senate following the election of Mr. Reagan in 1980.

During the same years, a number of proposals were discussed within the Executive branch. Of note were the discussions within the National Center for Health Care Technology to undertake a review of psychotherapy following requests from reimbursement mechanisms (Perry, 1982, in press). Although much of this activity on a federal level has subsided, the basic issues remain unchanged, in my opinion. The basic forces that will propel the system toward adoption of some policy regarding efficacy in psychotherapy as well as other public health interventions and technologies such as surgery and radiation, remain. If anything, the rising cost of health care will contribute toward pressure for more systematic articulation of public policy.

PSYCHOTHERAPY RESEARCH AND PUBLIC POLICY

In any program aimed at implementing a public policy around efficacy, research activities are crucial. The process of generating the relevant evidence required to make judgments about efficacy requires some overall program in policy.

Since World War II, the basic policies governing biomedical and biobehavioral research have been developed by the Public Health Service, particularly through the National Institutes of Health (NIH) and the three institutes in the Alcohol, Drug Abuse, and Mental Health Administration (ADAMHA). Under this policy, the main initiative for designing and executing research projects comes from the researchers in the field, usually in hospitals, clinics, medical centers, and universities. The assumption in this system is that the aggregation of findings from individual studies will accrue such that the health needs of the country will be generated.

For the most part, this program has worked with tremendous success such that American medical research leads the world, particularly in basic research pathophysiology. However, there are a number of areas where there are major gaps between available knowledge and that required for making policy decisions. These areas are toxicology, epidemiology, and therapeutics. In each of these areas, government action has been needed to establish these as priority areas, even though they may not be areas of high prestige and visibility within the scientific community. In the case of environmental health, knowledge of the toxicology of industrial and other compounds is absolutely essential. Similarly, for health planning, information about incidence and prevalence requires ongoing systematic research in epidemiology. The programs of the National Center for Health Statistics and the National Institute of Mental Health (NIMH) Epidemiologic Programs have been developed by federal initiative to fill the gap between knowledge and public policy.

Similar problems exist within therapeutics not only in psychotherapy but in other fields. For example, where drugs are concerned, the profit motive has served to drive research supported by the pharmaceutics industry. There are a number of so-called orphan drugs for which no foreseeable profit is forthcoming and federal activities have been involved. In another area, the cancer-chemotherapy program of the National Cancer Institute (NCI) was developed to encourage the development of the screening of new compounds for the treatment of cancer which were unlikely to be developed by the pharmaceutics industry. The National Heart Institute has developed a number of large-scale trials of diet, exercise, and other interventions aimed at preventing coronary disease or reducing their subsequent disability and mortality. In the field of psychotherapy this gap is even greater. For whatever reasons, the cadre of psychotherapy researchers has been relatively small in psychology, psychiatry, and related fields, and the volume of research undertaken has been inadequate. Dr. Morris Parloff has reviewed this situation in a number of papers and has pointed out the dilemma given the number of treatments and the large number of DSM-III-diagnosable disorders. An inconceivably large research program would be required to generate the evidence for every proposed treatment in every diagnostic category. What is the public to do in this situation?

Some policy is needed which affirms the importance of efficacy research, makes resources available, and develops priorities as to which treatments for which diagnostic categories are of greatest importance. In this respect, the recent elevation to branch status with NIMH of the psychotherapy and behavior change branch is noteworthy, as are the increased funds being made available.

Promotion of research is only one ingredient of the role of government bodies. While most research is supported at the federal level, many of the other activities of government bodies involve state government.

THE ACTIVITIES OF GOVERNMENT BODIES REGARDING PSYCHOTHERAPY

There are five activities which involve governmental responsibility: (1) accreditation of facilities; (2) licensing of professionals; (3) judgments as to safety and efficacy of treatments; (4) use of public monies for funding and reimbursement; and (5) research (discussed in the previous section). It is interesting to note that there are variations as to the role of private and government bodies across these five functions.

Accreditation of facilities, particularly hospitals, is done through a consortium of professional organizations, the Joint Commission on Accreditation of Hospitals (JCAH). This is a joint effort of a number of professional groups, particularly the American Hospital Association, the American Medical Association, the American College of Surgeons, and others which voluntarily banded together a number of decades ago. Their accreditation has close to public legal force since many programs such as Medicare and Medicaid require JCAH accreditation for eligibility for reimbursement.

The licensing of medical professionals has traditionally been the responsibility of state governments. Recently, a large number of states have begun licensing psychologists and there are efforts to expand licensing to include social workers. Licensing as a state function is usually a requirement for certain kinds of eligibility for reimbursement or public funds as well as certain legal procedures such as being eligible for a hospital staff appointment, authority to fill out involuntary commitment papers, and so on.

Certification of a specialist is a function of the professional societies. It is of note that MDs are licensed but that certification of specialists such as surgeons, neurologists, and psychiatrists is done by professional organizations.

Judgments as to safety and efficacy represent an interesting area. As regards drugs, there is a federal agency, the FDA, which is mandated for judgments as to safety and efficacy, deriving its powers from the interstate commerce provisions of the Constitution. Recently Congress expanded the functions of the FDA to include medical devices including diagnostic test procedures and electroconvulsive therapy (ECT) machines. There is no public body mandated by law to make judgments as to the efficacy or safety of psychotherapy or of surgical and radiation procedures. In 1978 Congress did establish the National Center for Health Care Technology as part of the Public Health Service, and mandates that this group make recommendations to the Secretary of Health and Human Services and the Surgeon General as to the current state of knowledge but that these judgments have no legal sanction. The judgments regarding the efficacy of psychotherapy proposed in this report could be done by some federal governmental body such as the FDA and/or the National Center for Health Care Technology. However, it might be more useful to have a voluntary consortium of professional groups as in the precedent that accreditation of hospital and health facilties is provided by the JCAH.

Reimbursement and funding have been a joint public and private responsibility, the public responsibility being shared by the federal government and the states. Some of the current controversy around psychotherapy reimbursement has to do with the rapid expansion of health insurance and the prospects in 1977 for a national health insurance program during the early years of the Carter Administration. Considering the political climate in Washington since the election of Mr. Reagan, it is unlikely that there will be any push for a national health insurance program; the intervening years before such a program is considered again will allow time for more policy discussion. In this respect, it is of note that many Western European countries such as France, Germany, and Austria have extensive programs of national health insurance which provide for reimbursement of psychotherapy services usually only when provided by physicians.

THE EMERGENCE OF PROFESSIONAL INITIATIVES

The current political situation in Washington makes federal initiatives highly unlikely, and it is therefore of interest that a number of professional bodies have undertaken initiatives. The activities of two professional organizations are of particular note. One is the project of the Royal Australian and New Zealand College of Physicians, and the other is the recently created Task Force on Psychiatric Treatment of the American Psychiatric Association. These two activities are of note, because, in my opinion, they represent important steps toward the implementation of public policy emphasizing the criterion of efficacy.

The Royal Australian and New Zealand College of Physicians (RANZCP) a number of years ago began a quality assurance program via a contract with the Australian Ministry of Social Security. In this project, the RANZCP undertook to prepare a series of reports on the available evidence for specific treatments for individual diagnostic categories. The chairman of that project is Dr. Gavin Andrews, and their first report on agoraphobia has appeared. Four features of this report are of note: (1) There was universal agreement as to the importance of efficacy; (2) there was agreement that the most relevant sources of evidence in favor of efficacy was some sort of randomized controlled trials; (3) in the analysis of the available data, meta-analysis as developed by the Smith, Glass, and Miller group was applied by Andrews to the available body of data; (4) very explicit decision-tree recommendations were made regarding diagnosis, management, and treatment of agoraphobia; and (5) agreement was reached between the Australian and New Zealand College of Physicians and the membership and leadership and governmental agency as to the relevance of these recommendations for decisions about reimbursement. It is my understanding from correspondence and discussions with Dr. Andrews that the group plans a series of reports on individual diagnostic groups. (A report on depression is in draft form.)

In parallel with the activities of Australia–New Zealand, the American Psychiatric Association a number of years ago set up a Commission on Psychiatric Treatments during the presidency of Jules Masserman. This commission has been under the chairmanship of Dr. Toksoz Byram Karasu and spent its first 5 years discussing certain general principles of evaluation of efficacy. At one point, the commission proposed the establishment of PTM (Psychiatric Treatment Manual) modeled after the American Psychiatric Association's DSM-III, which would have included detailed recommendations about decisions for treatment, including considerations of age, sex, diagnostic subtype, and so on. In my understanding, the goal was considered immature and too ambitious, and it has been considerably modified. Since Dr. Karasu is on the panel this morning he is in a better position to discuss the evolution of the APA project which he chairs. Currently there is a Task Force on Psychiatric Treatments established by the APA under the chairmanship of Dr. Karasu and three panels have been established, one on schizophrenia, chaired by Dr. Robert Cancro of New York, one on anxiety disorders chaired by Dr. Frankel of Boston and Dr. Orne of Philadelphia, and one on depression chaired by me.[1] The panel I chair has agreed to

---

1. The panel includes Hagop Akiskal, MD, Jules Bemporad, MD, John Davis, MD, William Frosch, MD, George Pollock, MD, A. John Rush, MD, and Myrna Weissman, PhD.

develop a monograph reviewing the state of evidence for specific treatments for subtypes of depression and affective disorder. Among the treatments to be reviewed are drugs and ECT, but also forms of long-term psychotherapy, including psychoanalysis and the newly developed brief therapies, including cognitive, behavioral, interpersonal, and short-term dynamic psychotherapy.

The panel on depression and affective disorders does not intend to come up with specific recommendations for decisions, nor do we plan a decision tree such as that developed by the Australian and New Zealand group. Rather, we intend to review the available evidence. The highest priority, it has been agreed, will be given to randomized controlled trials, but in the absence of such trials other forms of evidence will be noted. Ultimately, these reports will have to be approved by the Board of Trustees of the American Psychiatric Association including the assembly of district branches which represents mainly the practitioners in the field, who we know are concerned about the way in which such recommendations could be used by reimbursement agencies.

CONCLUSIONS

In my opinion, it is long overdue that the principle of efficacy be enunciated as a public policy. This ideally would be a joint effort of federal government agencies and professional associations and the health insurance industry. In the long run, some public body, not necessarily governmental, is required to maintain ongoing evaluation of the quality of evidence and to guide the need for research and the assessment of the outcomes of that research.

Ultimately, as this principle is accepted, it not only will influence decisions as to clinical practice and third-party reimbursement, but should permeate training curricula and peer review of clinical practice.

It is likely that this principle and its policy implications will be debated within the mental health professions and likely be resisted by practitioners and other groups. However, to the extent that psychiatry and other mental health disciplines lay claim to being scientifically based and publicly responsible, the criteria of efficacy will gain increasing recognition.

REFERENCES

Perry, S. The brief life of the National Center for Health Care Technology. *New England Journal of Medicine*, 1982, *307*, 1095–1100.

Perry, S. The National Center for Health Care Technology: Assessment of psychotherapy for policy making. *American Psychologist*, in press.

COMMENTARY

Dr. Robert L. Spitzer*: Yesterday we heard from our distinguished colleagues that there was demonstrated efficacy, although there was not demonstrated specificity for psychotherapy. Now, when you say "efficacy," are you demanding more than we have already seen—are you demanding specificity? If you are not demanding specificity, we have no problem. We have already demonstrated that psychotherapy is efficacious.

The second question is this: Historically, medicine has always had the problem of caring for people who have disorders for which there is no known treatment. Now, what are the public health implications of your policy for those disorders for which perhaps there is no known treatment? Should no public funding be given to their management, or do you make a distinction between management and treatment?

Dr. Klerman: Let me take the second question first; that is relatively easy. Issues of management are themselves subject to studies of an empirical nature. How many visits are needed to manage a diabetic? How many visits are needed to manage a depressive? Five a week? There are qualitative and quantitative issues which are subject to empirical study as to what constitutes management, and which management interventions are effective or cost effective. Ultimately, those are questions of, I think, efficacy, and in principle, at least, some of these are subject to empirical investigation. I would look somewhat askance if someone said that in order to manage a depressive, five sessions a week for 6 years is necessary. I would question whether that is management.

The issue of specificity represents another policy issue. My own view would be to follow the so-called medical model, which would be to ask for evidence not for psychotherapy overall, but for a particular form of psychotherapy in a particular condition. It is like asking if surgery is effective. No one would say that surgery is effective for the common cold, or for acne. You would want to know which surgical procedure for what kind of a peptic ulcer, or what have you.

So specificity to my mind implies some clear designation of the intervention, and some clear designation of the condition. Now, my definition of condition would be very broad. I would want to start, as I think you would, with DSM-III conditions. But I would even be willing to entertain psychotherapy claims for some things such as demoralization or the improvement of the quality of interpersonal relations.

*College of Physicians and Surgeons, Columbia University, and New York State Psychiatric Institute.

Dr. Spitzer: But I don't think you are answering my question. My question is, do you have not only to demonstrate efficacy for the particular disorder of the particular treatment, but to demonstrate that it is better than another treatment?

Dr. Klerman: No. Because, to use again the drug model, in order to get a new drug approved by the FDA you don't have to show that it is better than an available treatment. You have to show that it is better than a control group. So if you wanted to market a new beta-blocking agent, you wouldn't have to show that it is better than propranolol; you would have to show that it was better than a control.

Dr. Spitzer: But doesn't the meta-analysis that we heard indicate that practically all forms of psychotherapy are better than controls?

Dr. Klerman: No. I think if you look at it and you break it down by diagnostic groups—here I would agree with Don Klein—you have to do a separate meta-analysis for schizophrenia and for phobia.

Dr. Spitzer: But Don [Klein] is really asking for specificity as compared to another treatment. I don't think you have really answered that.

Dr. Donald F. Klein*: Okay, let's be more specific. Does the treatment have to be better than placebo?

Dr. Klerman: Yes, but I don't know what the placebo is for psychotherapy.

Let me try again. I don't want to be put in the position of enunciating all the implications of the policy. Just as it took the FDA 10 years to go from the Kefauver–Harris amendments to the explication of what was meant by efficacy in pharmacologic therapy, I think that some general discussion of the type we have had here is called for. I think we have moved from the basic policy to its implementation, and that itself is, I think, a significant step.

Dr. Spitzer: I can understand Gerry's saying that the details of implementation have to be worked out, but I suspect what we are now talking about is really the heart of the matter.

Dr. Klerman: Well, try me again.

Dr. Spitzer: I think the real issue is the one that Don [Klein] says. When you say "efficacious," are you saying efficacious in the sense that for a specific treatment you are demonstrating that there is something above and beyond a credible placebo?

Dr. Klerman: Yes, absolutely.

Dr. Spitzer: Then that is much more than just "efficacious." But okay, then we know what you mean. If that is the case, then we probably don't have the evidence, currently, for any form of psychotherapy, or only minimal evidence. We have, maybe, some evidence for cognitive.

*New York State Psychiatric Institute and College of Physicians and Surgeons, Columbia University.

Dr. Klerman: Well, what do you do in the absence of evidence, which is the title of this symposium?

Dr. Robert Rose*: Gerry, let me, for a moment, expand the scope of the discussion, in terms of definitions of psychotherapy. As you know, the reimbursement policies have, in this country and in many other countries, but certainly in this country, focused with great exclusivity in terms of the propensity of third-party carriers on reimbursing procedures that we do, if you look at the whole scope of medicine.

One of the things we have talked about for many years in psychiatry has been the wish to expand the doctor's role formally as well as informally, in terms of being a care giver and a provider of support. And when we teach this issue to medical students, for example, or residents, especially in other fields, we have emphasized the importance of attending to psychosocial factors that may complicate, if not precipitate, illnesses.

What are your thoughts about that? That is not specifically psychotherapy, unless one would say it is supportive therapy for that grouping of adjustment disorder in DSM-III.

What I am concerned about, I guess, is how do you see us moving to the issue of supporting the education and the clinical care giving of physicians, for example, in listening to and talking to their patients, which is, indeed, a major complaint of the American public, that their doctors don't listen to what is bothering them, which is a little beyond the classical purview of psychotherapy, *per se.*

Dr. Klerman: I would not call that psychotherapy. That might be part of what other people call management. One of the missions that psychiatry has taken upon itself in the 20th century is bringing humanity to the rest of medicine. That is a legitimate mission. I have some hesitation about putting all our eggs in that particular basket, because all we do is end up being nice guys and gals without a technology.

With regard to psychotherapy, though, the claim is made that more is being done than being a nice guy or gal, or being a friend. The claim is made that we have an understanding of the illness on a psychological basis, whether it is Freudian or behaviorist, or interpersonal or gestalt, that guides a set of explicit procedures which will have an outcome in a disorder over and above humane care. And to the extent that we make that claim, I think that is where I am concerned.

Dr. Rose: I agree, and certainly the focus in the meeting today, and the last several days, has been on that. I guess what I am saying or asking for is what kind of evidence of efficacy would you require before you would feel it is appropriate for us systematically to support that issue of humane care in

*University of Texas Medical Center, Galveston.

medicine, of which indeed psychiatry has been the standard bearer for some time.

Dr. Klerman: Well, there is the matter of professional specificity. Social workers claim they can do it as well. Nurses claim that they can do it as well, and there is now emerging a subspecialty called "health psychology" which claims that it can mobilize learning theory and perform those humane functions better than the psychosomaticists. So again, I would say those are matters of empirical outcomes.

Dr. Carl Eisdorfer*: Let me again sharpen this without attempting to belabor it. I think we have set up a sort of two-pole system. Now I'm not sure that you can really do it that easily. I think there is a reasonable body of evidence, and certainly a lot of writing on the notion, that if you explore psychosocial, cultural factors, you will in fact have an impact on treatment and course of illness—the stuff that Kleinman has done. There has been some evidence to demonstrate that that kind of interaction which is not psychotherapy and not just being a nice guy or gal can, in fact, have an outcome. Where would you put that?

Dr. Klerman: Well, I haven't thought that one through. I would personally demand more evidence as to what the outcomes are, and what the interventions are. Then I think there would be a place for some cost–benefit analysis. For example, there is a controlled study in England by the Maudsley group on comparing adding social workers to a group of general practitioners to deal with the psychosocial issues, versus leaving it to the general practitioners. And again, there is some evidence there for efficacy. Now, that is an organizational arrangement. It might well be that the most cost-effective way to deal with the psychosocial aspects of primary care, as the British have it, would be to add one social worker to every five primary care physicians.

That is, I think, a reasonable way. And there is a case where the techniques of so-called policy science, like cost–benefit analysis, would be very *apropos*, which is to determine the most cost-effective way to achieve that particular goal of dealing with the psychosocial, humane aspects. Is it necessary to be a board-certified psychiatrist? One social worker per five general practitioners? A CME course for the receptionist in the clinic? I think that is an open question.

Dr. Herbert J. Schlesinger†: Let me just speak to this last point first, Gerry. Emily [Mumford] just finished a meta-analysis of studies of the use of adjunctive methods of doing psychotherapy—support, emotional education, and that sort of thing—for patients before surgery and following heart attack. It shows that it is enormously effective, reducing hospitalization by a couple of days at a minimum, and reducing complications.

*Albert Einstein College of Medicine and Montefiore Medical Center.
†University of Colorado School of Medicine.

There is a technology for that, too. The question is what kind of support for what kind of people is important. What are the coping styles of the people who receive this support, for instance? Some people do not like to have information thrust upon them. Some need to know everything. So there is a technology, and I think a field for psychiatry and the other health sciences to explore, because I would guess that probably the most important area for psychiatric intervention will be in support of general medical care, particularly as acute disease is done away with and we are all suffering from one form or another of life as a chronic disease.

To go back to the issue of the meta-analysis, aren't we somewhat in the same position now with respect to psychotherapy as coronary artery disease is, where we are not sure if surgical or medical management is called for? Both have evidence of effect. It is not clear which is the better. And for the time being, wouldn't it be best in terms of public policy to allow the field to explore this issue?

Dr. Eugene I. Burdock*: I was very impressed with Gerry's suggestion that there might be a public body of some kind set up, not necessarily governmental, to look into this question. And I thought a good deal of consideration ought to be given to the constitution of this public body in terms of the disciplines included. For example, I didn't hear him mention social work. A great deal of psychotherapy is done by social workers, so certainly they ought to be included.

In view of the discussion since my question came to my mind, we might also want to include some representatives from internal medicine, since these people are at least interested in this problem, even though they may not have a special technology for dealing with it.

Dr. Eisdorfer: If I hear correctly, Gerry's reference to 150,000 psychotherapists by definition includes social workers, but it probably doesn't include medicine, or lay therapists, which would run that figure up to probably a quarter of a million or considerably more than that. That is one of the interesting issues.

Dr. Klerman: I think there are some very interesting precedents for nongovernmental public bodies of a similar nature. There is the Joint Commission on the Accreditation of Hospitals, which performs a very valuable function, although controversial, in court now, challenged as monopolistic and medically dominated. But it is a public body that represents a consortium that serves an important function, and it is not governmental.

The other is the College Entrance Examination Board, which does the SATs, which is another consortium that attempts to bring a technology to bear on a socially important function.

---

*New York University School of Medicine.

22

Psychotherapy Research and Top-Down Policy Analysis

CHARLES A. KIESLER
Carnegie-Mellon University

Research findings and discussions about psychotherapy and its effectiveness have to be placed in the context of overall mental health policy, existing systems of care, population needs, and potential or existing alternative policies.

In this context, the ardor of questioning the effectiveness of psychotherapy may cool. In this report I discuss several policy issues and then relate them to psychotherapy effectiveness. These include national epidemiological estimates of need, the evidence for treatment alternatives to psychotherapy, the place of psychotherapy in systems of care, and outcomes for the patient relative to other national policy issues such as medical costs, productivity, and absenteeism.

Let me say in advance that I believe the evidence for effectiveness and cost-effectiveness of psychotherapy is quite good. In particular, I refer to the meta-analysis of Smith and Glass (1977) of 475 studies of psychotherapy. These analyses and some other follow-up analyses (Landman & Dawes, 1982) indicate that patients undergoing psychotherapy end up with a mental health state that is comparable to the 80th–90th percentile of untreated controls. Leonard Saxe (1980) in a review of the literature carried out for the Office of Technology Assessment (OTA) concludes:

> In summary, OTA finds that psychotherapy is a complex—yet scientifically assessable—set of technologies. It also finds good evidence of psychotherapy's positive effects. Although therapy may not be generalizable to the wide range of problems for which therapy is employed, it suggests that additional research may provide data useful for the development of mental health policy. Given the potential net benefits of psychotherapy, this effort would seem to be justified. (p. 5)

That psychotherapy has some positive effects seems clear. The question of the specificity of the effectiveness of psychotherapy is more open, and has been a topic of a separate session at this meeting. However, there are some important other questions remaining about the effectiveness of psycho-

360

therapy that are especially dovetailed to policy issues. These would include (1) the marginal utility of psychotherapy when added to existing care; (2) the comparative or summative effects of psychotherapy in relation to alternative treatments such as drug therapy; (3) the effects of adding psychotherapy to existing systems of health care, such as health maintenance organizations (HMOs), and the question of integrating psychotherapy in organized systems of care; (4) the breadth of effects of psychotherapy beyond those typically measured in the studies reviewed by Smith and Glass; and (5) the effectiveness of psychotherapy as a tool of national policy.

PSYCHOTHERAPY IN THE CONTEXT OF NATIONAL NEEDS

Assume that psychotherapy is both effective and cost-effective. The question we ask here is the extent to which psychotherapy as a technological tool can be addressed to national needs. Specifically, we ask the question of the matchup between the availability of psychotherapy and the extent to which it might be needed. The results of this comparison are quite startling. Regier, Goldberg, and Taube (1978) estimate that about 15% of the population is in need of mental health services. Let's accept this as a given although it is much more conservative than Dohrenwend, Dohrenwend, Gould, Link, Neugebaur, and Wunsch-Hitzig's (1980) review of the national epidemiological data base.

There currently are approximately 25,000 trained psychiatrists in the United States (Marmor, Scheidemandel, & Kanns, 1975). In addition, Mills, Wellner, and VandenBos (1979) found approximately 25,000 licensed, certified psychologists in the country. Together these two fields offer us a potential base of about 50,000 doctoral-level mental health service providers. Even if we considered that each of these service providers would provide about 30 hours of services per week (a high estimate), and that 90% of all psychologists and psychiatrists would offer such services, this would lead us to a total potential service capability in the United States of approximately 67 million person-hours of mental health services per year. This is only a potential. Psychiatrists and psychologists together now only deliver somewhere between 35 million and 45 million service hours per year.

Fifteen percent of the population amounts to 33 million potential patients to be matched up with the 67 million potential service hours described above. That is, at a maximum, each person needing service could conceivably obtain only 2 hours of service for his or her problem during a year. At the current actual service rate, only about 1 hour a year is available to each person in need.

Some policy implications become clear in this view. However effective psychotherapy is as a tool, its potential as a national policy alternative is severely limited. Phrased a different way, if psychiatrists and psychologists treated their patients with traditional three-times-a-week psychotherapy, the maximum number of hours that they could have available would allow them to treat only 2% of the patients needing services. Given the current number of service providers available and the current national needs, psychotherapy has an obviously limited capacity to handle national problems. One might suggest that people now oriented toward evaluating the effectiveness of psychotherapy might wish to consider also research on policy alternatives, such as alternative modes of treatment; to expand the potential service by subdoctoral service providers and paraprofessionals; to investigate more precisely matchups between therapeutic techniques and specific disorders (the specificity issue); to investigate closely the relative efficacy of various treatment modalities so that effectiveness could be enhanced; and to concentrate on the potential of voluntary organizations, alternative helping groups, self-help techniques, and social networks in ameliorating mental health problems.

This is a good illustration of the potential differences between top-down and bottom-up policy analysis (cf. Kiesler, 1980, 1983). From the bottom up—the more traditional way of looking at mental health policy—we have made continued good progress over the past several decades in enlarging the number of potential service providers available, in enhancing the training of mental health professionals, and in developing a national system of outpatient care that is easily accessible geographically and financially (the Community Mental Health Center [CMHC] system). From the bottom up, it looks as if we have been making good and steady progress—and we have on these dimensions.

The top-down approach to policy analysis involves inspecting the overall national problem, what is done now in the name of mental health (and with what effect relative to what cost), how the problem and current approach match up, and the possible alternative policies in the future. From the top down, the current set of approaches to national mental health problems can never come close to solving the national problem. Psychotherapy as traditionally practiced is too labor-intensive to be a viable solution to overall national problems.

This is not to argue that the top-down policy analysis is the only way to approach such problems. Rather I would argue that the top-down approach has not been used often enough in mental health, and that its utilization illustrates some fairly serious deficiencies in national policy strategy.

DRUG THERAPY

I do not see questions raised in the field about the effectiveness of drug therapy nearly so often or so critically as they are with psychotherapy. However, there is not good evidence that drug therapy is more effective than psychotherapy. Probably the best systematic evidence is that reviewed by Smith, Glass, and Miller (1980), using meta-analytic techniques in the same manner that they applied to psychotherapy research. Smith *et al.* looked at studies in which psychotherapy and drug therapy were used alone and in combination within studies and with random assignment to condition. Their overall meta-analysis of these studies found that psychotherapy with fairly seriously disturbed patients (approximately half of whom were hospitalized) was approximately as effective as drug therapy. In addition, the effects of psychotherapy and drugs did not interact in any way. That is, the effects of psychotherapy and drugs could be predicted completely by simply adding together the effects of psychotherapy and drugs used separately. This is a rather puzzling finding and, I might add, a challenge to our current theoretical understanding of these psychological problems. In addition, some forms of drug therapy have been demonstrated to have some fairly serious long-term negative consequences (American Psychiatric Association [APA], 1980). It is therefore puzzling why drug therapy seems to be touted by often the same people who are criticizing the cost-effectiveness of psychotherapy. If the Smith *et al.* conclusions can hold up in a more detailed and broader network of analysis, then some implications are clear. For example, if drug therapy and psychotherapy are each cost-effective when used alone, then their combination would be even more cost-effective (since the effects are additive, but various costs of each are duplicated when implemented separately).

The Smith *et al.* results also suggest that the quality of research in drug therapy should be elevated to become more relevant to policy analysis. They find so much variation in results across studies in the type of drug, the typicality of place of use, and the type of problem treated that some considerable caution needs to be undertaken. That is, in the future drug therapy studies should use more than one type of drug and more than one type of problem with treatment site varied before confidence is placed in an outcome study regarding policy implementation. At a minimum, people interested in cost-effectiveness of psychotherapy are encouraged to become equally interested in the cost-effectiveness of drug therapy and other treatment alternatives.

BREADTH OF OUTCOME STUDIES

One outcome of psychotherapy that has recently been discussed extensively is that of medical offset—the decrease in the cost of physical health care following mental health care. Although there has been extensive criticism of this network of studies, it seems quite clear that there is some effect of medical offset of psychotherapy. The question really is how much occurs and why and when it occurs. I have suggested elsewhere that the effect of medical offset could as easily be due to the failure of the medical system of delivery of care as to any direct and positive impact of the mental health treatment (Kiesler, 1983). Furthermore, we have not investigated the degree to which these effects occur only in specific treatment sites. All of the original studies reviewed by Jones and Vischi (1980) took place in organized systems of care, such as HMOs. More recently Schlesinger and Mumford (1982) have detected some medical offset in the Federal Employees Health Benefit (FEHB) plan. However, whether any offset of medical utilization routinely occurs in other forms of care, such as private practice, remains to be determined. There is good reason for expecting that it would not generally occur.

More generally these studies illustrate the need for a broader net of outcome variables when looking at the effectiveness of mental health care. The medical offset of patients is only one such variable and it has typically been ignored in previous work on the effectiveness of psychotherapy. As examples, consider as potential outcomes the following: the potential medical offset of other members of the family of a patient undergoing mental health care; various aspects of the school system including staying in school and grades; absenteeism (such as revealed in the Kaiser–Permanente studies); and productivity. Some people have regarded some of these issues as "problems of living." However, I would maintain that such a characterization is to trivialize important national problems with large national costs which mental health care shows some promise of ameliorating. Productivity, for example, is not only an important national problem, but one that is widely discussed in the federal government today. Productivity is obviously closely related to absenteeism and its causes, and the Kaiser–Permanente studies show clear evidence of mental health care's affecting absenteeism. Yet there has been little or no follow-up of this very promising line of potential positive effect of mental health services in general and psychotherapy in particular.

At a different level, this discussion illustrates some of the conceptual difficulties in previous work on the cost-effectiveness of psychotherapy. Only a trivial number of studies of the cost-effectiveness of psychotherapy have included measures of absenteeism, productivity, medical offset, and the like. The narrowness of the scope of the outcome measures in themselves reduces the cost–benefit ratio. Some of these studies suggest that psychotherapy is at least a much more cost-beneficial form of treatment than previously imagined.

THE CONTEXT OF ORGANIZED SYSTEMS OF CARE

The study of the effectiveness of psychotherapy needs to be placed in a context of its potential use. In discussions of national mental health policy we tend to emphasize organized systems of care, incentives for particular kinds of treatment, the context of specific treatments, the funding for alternative programs, and the like. Most studies of psychotherapy are not placed in these policy contexts. For example, does psychotherapy delivered in private practice as fee-for-service under an insurance program have the same outcomes (e.g., absenteeism and medical offset) as does the treatment received in a CMHC under the same insurance program? More generally, consider potential sites of delivery for mental health services: CMHCs; HMOs; private practice; other group practice; emergency rooms; internists' offices. Is "therapy" equally effective in those different sites? Is it the same service? Does the cost-effectiveness vary as a function of the site in which the service is delivered? Do the outcomes vary? A systems analysis would lead us to expect that services delivered in these various sites would not be identical, that they might differ quite dramatically on potential specific outcomes and the breadth of outcome. A purist might not even consider the services delivered at the emergency room or in an internist's office to be psychotherapy in a theoretical sense. However, it is a mental health service and it is an alternative to more traditional forms of therapy in planning for national policy. Clearly, questions of the efficacy of psychotherapy have to be placed in the more general context of issues regarding where it is delivered, with what kinds of problems, by whom, and with what outcome.

Also embedded in this discussion is the general issue of the marginal utility of psychotherapy. Many of the studies of psychotherapy have been carried out in what might be called "environmental isolation." There is little contact of therapists with the rest of the patient's environment and little knowledge of other services that patient might be receiving or could receive. However, in most cases we should take as a given the embedded programs of welfare and health that now exist and for which most people are eligible at some level. In this context, the question is not the effectiveness of psychotherapy taken in isolation but the marginal utility of psychotherapy when added to an existing system of care. A good deal of the policy potential of mental health services rests on the ability of such services to be added on to existing systems of care. Furthermore, the existing system of care which does not include mental health services may be the proper baseline against which to test the marginal utility of such services. The majority of mental health services are now delivered by people who are not qualified to do psychotherapy. The proper policy baseline for considering the effectiveness of psychotherapy is not the absence of therapy but rather how the current overall *de facto* system of care, both formal and informal, would otherwise treat the patient.

My basic message is that the question of the effectiveness of psychotherapy must be placed in the context of policy research and systems research and must be related to issues of national need and marginal utility. It is only in that context that we can discover any solid answers to the question of how (and whether) the country should finance psychotherapy, and whether it is cost-effective as a potential national resource.

REFERENCES

American Psychiatric Association. *Tardive dyskinesia.* Washington, D.C.: Author, 1980.

Dohrenwend, B. P., Dohrenwend, B. S., Gould, M. S., Link, B., Neugebaur, R., & Wunsch-Hitzig, R. *Mental illness in the United States: Epidemiological estimates.* New York: Praeger, 1980.

Jones, K., & Vischi, T. Impact of alcohol, drug abuse, and mental health treatment on medical care utilization: Review of the research literature. *Medical Care,* 1980, *Suppl. 17,* 12.

Kiesler, C. A. Mental health policy as a field of inquiry for psychology. *American Psychologist,* 1980, *35,* 1066–1080.

Kiesler, C. A. Psychology and mental health policy. In M. Hersen, A. E. Kazdin, & A. S. Bellack (Eds.), *The clinical psychology handbook.* New York: Pergamon, 1983.

Landman, J. T., & Dawes, R. M. Psychotherapy outcome: Smith and Glass' conclusions stand up under scrutiny. *American Psychologist,* 1982, *37,* 504–516.

Marmor, J., Scheidemandel, P. L., & Kanns, C. K. *Psychiatrists and their patients.* Washington D.C.: American Psychiatric Association, 1975.

Mills, D. H., Wellner, A. M., & VandenBos, G. R. The National Register Survey: The first comprehensive study of all licensed/certified psychologists. In C. A. Kiesler, N. A. Cummings, & G. R. VandenBos (Eds.), *Psychology and national health insurance: A source book.* Washington, D.C.: American Psychological Association, 1979.

Regier, D. A., Goldberg, I. D., & Taube, C. A. The *de facto* U.S. mental health services system: A public health perspective. *Archives of General Psychiatry,* 1978, *35,* 685–693.

Saxe, L. *The efficacy and cost-effectiveness of psychotherapy* (technical report). Washington D.C.: Office of Technology Assessment, Congress of the United States (GPO stock No. 052-003-00783-5), 1980.

Schlesinger, H. J., & Mumford, E. *Mental health services and medical care utilization in the fee for service system.* Invited paper at the Mental Health Policy Symposium Series, Carnegie-Mellon University, 1982.

Smith, M. L., & Glass, G. V. Meta-analysis of psychotherapy outcome studies. *American Psychologist,* 1977, *32,* 752–760.

Smith, M. L., & Glass, G. V., & Miller, T. I. *The benefits of psychotherapy.* Baltimore: Johns Hopkins University Press, 1980.

COMMENTARY

Dr. Robert Rose*: Dr. Kiesler, I found the analysis you referred to as "top-down" intriguing, and I wonder if you have any information in an analogous

*University of Texas Medical Center, Galveston.

manner about health care in general. As you probably well know, a number of years ago we did a complete 180° turnabout in terms of the production of physicians in this country. We were, for the longest time, operating under the assumption that we were "under-doctored." And then it became clear that it wasn't a question of under-doctoring, it was a question of distribution—both geographic and specialtywise.

If one looks for a moment at the cumulative prevalence of all medical illnesses with the kinds of care requirements that that would indeed indicate, what kind of top-down analysis has been done to kind of say, "Gee, it looks like we have enough people delivering it." Because, by analogy, you say that given a certain prevalence of disorder, the amount of manpower available to take care of that is insufficient.

I wonder if this analysis, applied to the aggregate of all medical problems, would yield the same conclusion in terms of a policy. Do you have any data about that? I would be interested in your perspective.

Dr. Kiesler: There was a National Academy review on the effectiveness of medical treatments that indicated their data are certainly no better than the data on mental health care. Schlesinger and Mumford have done some meta-analyses and summarized some of the literature on the effectiveness of health care. And I will leave that to Herb [Schlesinger] to tell you about it.

I think you would have to say that every attempt to change the system with the incentives you have mentioned has been a dismal failure. And economists, when they discuss economics and public policy, regard health economics as a strange beast that does not follow the economic laws that all the other public policies do. It is a closed system in which cost and demand for services do not match up at all. And there is little or no competition within the system.

Dr. Robert L. Spitzer*: Could you comment on the implications of carrying out Dr. Klerman's suggestion?

Dr. Kiesler: I like his suggestion at one level. At a different level I am concerned with how we would define the terms. But I think it was you who raised the issue that, in one sense, we have already found psychotherapy to be efficacious.

It is clear, if you look at the potential negative or iatrogenic effects of psychotherapy, that we find there are some, at least in aggregate data. A certain proportion of patients—small, thank God—do have a negative outcome of psychotherapy. Does that mean it is not safe? What degree, or what percentage, or what number of patients makes it unsafe?

Dr. Spitzer: I think it is clear from Gerry's [Klerman] response that he meant more than just effectiveness. He did mean specificity over and above,

---

*College of Physicians and Surgeons, Columbia University, and New York State Psychiatric Institute.

say, a placebo, which it seems to me we do not have, or have only in a very modest way for a very small number of treatments.

What would be the implications of, say, a decision that only for cognitive therapy and IPT for depression was there evidence for a modest degree of specificity the other forms of psychotherapy did not have, and therefore public funds could not be used for those?

Dr. Kiesler: Well, I don't agree with that. I think you have to take it more literally; that is, if that sort of thing were applied to medicine, none of us could take aspirin. It is not specific to some particular disorder. The evidence in Smith, Glass, and Miller is overwhelming, I think, about the general effectiveness of psychotherapy. It does not indicate that it is a really powerful technique; but that is quite powerful, given how meta-analyses usually turn out.

So I think you can't differentiate among the psychotherapies. If you only took those two, or any two, you would not be following the data. That is not what the data indicate. There is no more reason to pick those two than any other two, when there are multiple studies, at least.

Dr. Leon Eisenberg*: Your paper, I think, has the enormous value of putting sharply into focus the problems that arise if we take seriously the figures that we are using. You said "assuming for example, 15%," and then there are other studies that would suggest 30%. Well, I don't want to debate the point, but I think we ought to question both figures, which are so enormously large.

Some of the studies that are done seem to find the lifetime prevalence of depression so high that I wonder what we mean by "depression," whether we are talking about anything that corresponds to a clinical condition that is appropriate for a health system. But that is one level of debate.

The other, which bothered me all through yesterday's discussion, and comes up again in the use of meta-analysis, is that we selectively use those results of meta-analysis that suit a particular point. It is very nice for all of us in the mental health professions to say that with this technique, indeed, psychotherapy is efficacious. God be praised! But we don't use the implication that it doesn't make any difference whether or not you know how to do it, at least as reflected by experience, years of training, or whatever. So we continue to talk—and this is all of us, I don't mean this directed at you—of qualified psychotherapists versus others.

If there isn't any evidence for qualified or better-than-marginally-qualified, then one wonders whether indeed, if you did the embedded analysis, you would find that any kind of service, seeing your welfare worker twice a week, or once a week or three times a week, would be just as good as seeing somebody whose title was different, but who provided a human contact. So I

*Children's Hospital Medical Center, Boston.

think that the use of meta-analysis as the base in the paper, and the use of estimates of prevalence based on our present techniques, raise the difficulty without giving us a clear indication of how real it is and whether it ought to be solved.

Now if one turns to the questions that have been posed to you about medical efficacy, there is a rather nice study that Beeson did and published in *Medicine* about 1977 in which he compared the treatments in the first edition of Cecil's *Textbook of Medicine* with those of the current edition, of which he was one of the editors in 1975, I think. He found that, whereas the first edition by today's evidence had 3% of highly efficacious treatment of preventive measures, in the present edition, I think the figure was 20%. And then there was another 30% or 40% of reasonably effective treatments. So if you look at what doctors do of necessity, the best doctors, faced with people in trouble, use lots of treatments that have never been subjected to careful trial, and are based on tradition, usual and customary.

Lord knows what people will say 50 years hence, when they look at today's McDermott and Beeson, or whoever the current editors of Cecil's *Textbook* are.

When the Graduate Medical Education National Advisory Committee attempted to estimate medical needs, they didn't do it on the basis of what was known about efficacious treatment, but used sort of Delphi panels of experts who made the best estimates they could of how many nephrologists you needed, or how many of this or that. Well, that is because we are willing, in the case of general medical care, which has high credibility in the general population, to assume that you ought to have a doctor if you need one or you want one. It is dubious in that case, and it becomes even more difficult in a field like psychotherapy. One of the problems is that we don't have a uniform gold standard that applies across the health fields.

The final point is—and this goes back to Gerry's [Klerman] point as well as yours—the enormous cost of randomized, controlled trials. The problems that come up in replicating the conditions of the randomized, controlled trial (RCT), as you point out, in public practice, make me dubious that we could in fact muster the hundreds of millions of dollars and enormous professional spurts of activity that would be required to go down this street to answer the very important questions we face.

I wonder whether what is needed is some more imaginative approach, and a less costly approach, than an RCT. RCTs are being discussed here as if they were a panacea. It turns out they are a hell of a problem in simpler issues than general medical care. The RCT that was done by the University Diabetes Group just ended in an utter fiasco because people questioned the value of the results and the comparison of oral hypoglycemic agents, and so on, even though that was set up by a consortium, was a multi-university study, and had wise people doing it.

I would just suggest that the notion that the randomized clinical trial is so remarkably effective and reliable a scientific technique that it will answer our questions ought, itself, to be put to question.

Dr. Donald F. Klein*: I think there is a definitional problem. Dr. Kiesler was using the term "specificity" in a fashion that was quite different from the way it had been generally used in the room, as evidenced by his saying that aspirin is not specific because it is used for a variety of different diseases. The term "specific" is used as meaning there is something more than a placebo. Aspirin is clearly something that is more than a placebo for a wide variety of conditions. But it is still a specific agent. So I think that you are continually glossing over the issues of whether psychotherapy, which demonstrably does more than no treatment, is nonetheless doing more than its simple credibility would allow.

I would also like to point out that your discussion about the meta-analysis of pharmacotherapy I think is preposterous. I think the big problem with meta-analysis is that it pushes people into a highly abstract claim. They think they can talk about pharmacotherapy as if it were one thing, or about psychotherapy as one thing, or surgery. It doesn't make any sense. What you need to do sensible meta-analyses is to have a restricted range of conditions with a restricted range of interventions. When you do that, you can get sensible data out of it.

As I said before, what we need is micro-meta-analysis. I will give you an example. Covelli did a very nice meta-analysis of the use of stimulant drugs in hyperkinesis and found enormous effects—very well controlled studies, a homogeneous group, and a sensible range of medication. The Smith, Glass, and Miller study, if you look at the medications used, used everything from antihistamines through phenothiazines through antidepressants. It makes no sense and should not be used.

The reason we are confident that medication works is that we have excellent experimental evidence: randomized, placebo-controlled trials, and that overrides anything that any meta-analysis could possibly tell us. The reason we are concerned about whether psychotherapy works or whether it is specific is that we have no such analogous data.

Dr. Kiesler: Let me make a couple of comments about meta-analysis. To some extent it is like factor analysis in the sense that as they say, "garbage in, garbage out." You are not going to get any more out of a meta-analysis than the quality of the studies in the analysis. In many of the studies of psychotherapy, and in a recent analysis I did of care alternatives to mental hospitalization, people are making a very long-term study with big personal and scientific commitments, and they add lots of measures that they

---

*New York State Psychiatric Institute and College of Physicians and Surgeons, Columbia University.

have no confidence will come out, but it would be interesting if they did, and to some extent they are interesting if they don't. When one does a meta-analysis, one throws all those things in there and sees what comes out. I am surprised that the psychotherapy studies come out as powerfully as they do, given that.

Since meta-analysis is only a tool to aggregate effects across studies and does not say anything about the quality of the studies, one can make the use of meta-analysis much more complicated in a couple of ways in particular. A prior theoretical specification of which things are supposed to be effective and which things are not. or which things are supposed to come out and which things are not, would sharpen a meta-analysis enormously. You can get a good meta-analytic effect with only trivial results coming out and the important theoretical results not being there. Further, even though a good, controlled experiment is the crux of science, I disagree with the gentlemen who said they are too expensive, when we spend $200 billion or $300 billion a year on mental health and health care, and God knows how much in absenteeism and loss of productivity, this work could have an effect on it. What difference does it make whether it costs $100 million? How much went into the scientific work underlying the first moon shot? It is a trivial sum of money given the potential impact on the nation.

But if one does a meta-analysis of some of these studies, you can aggregate and disaggregate studies within a complex network. For example, if there are 27 studies of some particular drug and depression, and 14 studies of another, and so forth, and some of them have random assignment and some of them do not, you can start your meta-analysis with random assignment, and you can sort of aggregate and disaggregate collections of studies, depending on the methodological flaw in the study. Then as long as the results are consistent across aggregations, you have a very powerful conclusion.

So the meta-analysis as it has been practiced, and it has only begun, is the most simpleminded way to use it. The proper way to use it for policy conclusions is to use it as a much more complicated tool.

23

Politics, Practice, and *p* Value in Psychotherapy

TOKSOZ BYRAM KARASU
Albert Einstein College of Medicine
and Montefiore Medical Center

The Washington Post recently ran a headline on its first page: "Psychotherapy Put on Couch by the Government." The Senate Finance Committee proposed an amendment to the Health Care Bill which will extend the mental health benefits until 1984, and after that will limit federal reimbursement to those therapies that have been given a federal seal of approval. These services have to be "safe and effective on the basis of controlled clinical studies which are conducted and evaluated under the general accepted principles of scientific research" (Hilts, 1980), sort of an FDA for psychotherapy. Senators Matsunage and Inouye introduced a bill to establish an 11-member council with broad multidisciplinary representation which will recommend what mental health services should be paid for.

Why is it that such rigid criteria of reimbursement are not applied to the rest of medicine? No one seems to be saying, "Unless you prove the efficacy of the use of steroids in MS or ALS, cytoxan in leukemia, bypass operations in angina, methotrexate in tumors, we'll not pay you." Are we to deny care to cancer patients because the efficacy of present drugs and procedures are not established? Why is mental health singled out? Are we the victimized, innocent bystanders in this sad state of affairs?

I submit to you that we have contributed largely to this present situation by some of our questionable clinical practices, theoretical confusion, research inadequacies, political ineptness, and professional ambivalence. Theoretical differences between Freud and his followers have generated many schools of psychotherapy. In 1975, I surveyed the schools of psychotherapy in New York; there were 52 of them. This proliferation of psychotherapies justifiably raises the question, "What is psychotherapy?" in the public's mind. New therapies are popping up on the average of two per month; most of these are quadriphonic Freuds, using jazzed-up psychoanalysis: There is a Z therapy, based on Zaslow's ticklish theory. The patient is held down by assistants, and tickled until he is exhausted. There is the Soviet electrician, Kirlian, who takes pictures of your energy that extends beyond the skin, with the implication that we may be sending healthy or noxious stimuli to each other by our presence alone. In Aikido, one learns that in feeding pigeons, if you walk toward them, they run away; stay still and they eat out of your hand. In Tibetan meditation, one experiences one-pointed concentration, such as listening to the space between the sounds. Such Eastern mysticism, Americanized by Western technology, gave birth to Biofeedback—"meditation with a machine." When Yogi detachment is adopted by Californized Kantian humanism, one gets Fritz Perl's gestalt prayer.

These new therapies, though, cannot be dismissed just as crazy fashions or peculiar cults, especially by us. We have neglected to explore the very reason for their development, or to understand the changing needs of society, and tried to ignore them by closing our eyes, staying within our own familiar walls. (The religions, incidentally, have erred in the same ways.)

Western man, an empirical man, Lockean and mechanistic, managed to demystify religion, and deromanticized love, sex, and the family. We, the caretakers of the psyche, with our psychodynamic and behavioristic stands, and our emphasis on patients being a product of inner struggles, drives and defenses, learned or unlearned habits, have only compounded their isolation.

Furthermore, therapists have political, economic, and narcissistic battles between them, divided not only along the lines of professional identities, but also on theoretical–ideological lines. Any theory, like any lens, has inherent characteristics that establish boundaries and dimensions of observation. Thus, paradoxically, a theory may be limited at the same time that it is expanded. Likewise, a patient may be understood differently, diagnosed and treated quite differently by one or another clinician; the way you see a patient and interact with him or her depends on your orientation.

Our biases, of course, operate on many levels. If the patient is a YAVIS (young, attractive, verbal, intelligent, and successful), somehow psychotherapy is indicated. But a DOPUR patient (dumb, old, poor, ugly, on relief), even if he or she could manage to get an appointment, will probably leave the office with a prescription or referral to supportive group therapy with someone else.

Despite these biases, the question remains: Is psychotherapy effective? Given the diversity of theoretical and clinical approaches to psychotherapy, the difficulties in describing the nature of psychotherapy as a uniform practice, the range of mental health problems, the variety of settings where psychotherapy is applied, the large number of patient and therapist variables compounded by the interactions between the two, the different outcome measures used by different therapies, and the many methodological problems, the question of the effectiveness of psychotherapy becomes a highly complicated issue. Furthermore, even the sessions of therapists of similar training orientations, beliefs, and value systems do not conform to a uniform practice. In fact, one can say that there are as many therapies as there are therapists.

METHODOLOGICAL ISSUES

Unlike physical illnesses, mental disorders are not usually accompanied by measurable physiological changes. The clinician must depend largely on the patient's or another person's report of symptoms and complaints. Also, the severity of the problem, in part, depends on the individual's reaction and the context in which it occurs. Therefore, as implied, the methodological problems of outcome research are multiple. First is the selection of outcome measures which are appropriate to the goals of the treatment under study. Functional measures of behavioral effects might well be inappropriate to assess dynamic therapy. To overcome this, one recent focus has been the development of measurement procedures that could be utilized across different types of therapies. Here, the use of multiple measures may enhance comparability across studies, or better yet, a "common matrix" may be applied across treatments which are overtly very different. Nonetheless, outcomes have their separate meanings to the patient, the therapist, the family, the community, and the IRS.

A second set of issues pertains to organizing research designs to minimize extraneous factors that might be considered as the cause of treatment effects. A great deal of psychotherapy research has been carried out under laboratory or analogue conditions. These studies may yield rigorous experimental findings, but they have low external validity. The patients are often undergraduate students with some vague and not too severe problems; the therapists are often doctoral students; and the procedures are often theoretically oriented; thus they are not representative of actual practice (Luborsky, Singer, & Luborsksy, 1975). However, to the extent that such data provide support for *in vivo* findings, they are necessary to consider. Since the former refer to ideal rather than actual conditions, they may be regarded as efficacy rather than effectiveness research. Conversely, evaluative studies, although they provide direct information about the actual effectiveness of treatment, often yield equivocal analyses of causality, and must be interpreted in conjunction with the basic research data.

Of course, there are many problems in conducting *in vivo* experimental research: On the one hand, it is difficult to implement with proscribed constraints, especially to create a methodologically sound, ethically acceptable control group. One cannot, obviously, have a double-blind crossover study in psychotherapy. And for "primal scream" research, it has to be double-deaf. In addition, using waiting lists as a "no therapy" group is only applicable to short-term therapies. Even then, the positive expectancy that the patient will soon be helped may be a form of therapy in itself. Similarly, in placebo conditions, merely the "aura" of being in therapy may be therapeutic (Kazdin, 1979).

Because of the problem of not being able to conduct "pure" experimental designs, researchers have attempted quasiexperimental designs. Though a poor substitute, if carefully constituted, it can provide useful information. However, such studies involve complex statistics, and require the collection of much more data than in a "true" experiment. One such common design is referred to as an "intensive design," which may use few subjects but make frequent assessments of them. Most strategically, a clear baseline measure of the patient's functioning is taken with the intent that sudden improvement will be dramatic and closely correlated with the onset of therapy. However, only those therapies which posit observable and rapid behavioral changes can be tested with such a design.

Similarly, in the "return to baseline" design, the patient's functioning is measured during the baseline period and several times during treatment; then the therapy is withdrawn abruptly. It is expected that there will be a return to a lower level of functioning. The process is repeated during the patient's return to therapy (and ultimately the treatment is phased out, but with the hope that therapy gains will be sustained). Allen, Hart, Buell, Harris, and Wolf's (1964) study of a single child, while often cited as exemplary of this technique, utilized only a simple reinforcement therapy. A more complex treatment regime may not be as conducive to such a design.

With a different outcome approach, the "intersubject multiple baseline" design, it is possible to separately treat and assess functioning in different areas of the patient's life. In this way, the treatment is designed to improve one or another aspect of the patient's functioning while the patient's other behaviors are used as a control. Although such a design has the advantage that change can be measured with only one subject, it suffers from the obvious problem that effects may generalize across function areas. Such "ripple effects" may miss the true effects of the therapy.

In summary, given the limitations of the scientific process to develop unambiguous conclusions on the basis of individual research studies, and the diversity of outcomes against which such psychotherapy must be evaluated, methods are required and must be developed to synthesize, aggregate, or integrate the findings of multiple studies.

A final set of methodological problems have therefore to do with the above problem—the synthesis and interpretation of multiple efficacy studies. For example, in literature reviews which encompass several possible research works, it is easy to be selective (for better or for worse). Here, the author makes implicit and explicit choices about which studies to include, which may be overtly or covertly biased. To make this process more scientific, or at least more systematic, a number of procedures have recently been developed and applied to the assessment of psychotherapy outcome literature. These include "box score" analyses (Luborsky *et al.*, 1975) and "meta-analyses" (Smith, Glass, & Miller, 1980).

Box-score analyses systematize the literature review process via a consistent method of categorization and tallying of effects. Here, the authors elucidate their procedures in setting standards and criteria, and explicitly describe their selection of relevant research. However, this approach still does not eliminate the subjectiveness of individual judgment, and does not take into account the strength of findings within particular studies.

Meta-analyses employ a statistical technique for aggregating data and for determining relationships between variables and outcomes. Studies are coded on a set of variables that are to be related to outcome (e.g., the experience of the therapist, setting, quality of the design, etc.), then quantified and correlated with the outcomes. Regardless of particular differences, all such measures must relate in some way to an overall construct of "general well-being." To the extent that all instruments estimate that construct, they are comparable at a general level. In short, the primary task for meta-analysis is to standardize the various measures statistically so that they can be displayed in a common scale, record as many of their characteristics as possible, and then compare the magnitude of therapeutic effect with the characteristics of the instrument. (This magnitude of therapeutic effect— "effect size" (ES)—is the mean difference between the treated and control subjects divided by the standard deviation of the control group.) In this way, the ES permits a quantitative expression of the statements we all make when we speak of "what the literature says." It is like mixing apples and oranges, but then comparing them *not* in terms of their color, shape, or taste, but at a higher level of integration, such as nutritiousness, by using the calorie as a measurement.

THE EFFECTIVENESS ISSUE

Using the same basic data, different researchers have reached different conclusions about psychotherapy effectiveness, with legitimate disagreements among them. For example, Eysenck (1952) reviewed 24 articles in which he compared psychoanalytic to eclectic therapy. After 2 years of treatment, the improvement rates of controls and eclectic therapies were similar (64%), whereas analytical improvement was lower than that of the "no treatment" controls (44%). His findings naturally unleashed an extraordinary reaction. However, when the data have been reexamined, Eysenck's conclusions have been widely subject to criticism: His control group included Denker's (1946) study, for example, in which the so-called "no therapy" group had received the care of GPs and had been given sedatives and other medications. In addition, he had used Landis's (1937) files for mental disability admissions; since these populations were poorly defined, the sample encompassed nonspecific mental illnesses, although the basis of the study was originally for neuroses. Eysenck (1966) updated his review by selectively adding another 11 studies. This time, he found some evidence for the efficacy of behavioral treatment. (Also, it should be noted that he never found psychotherapy to be harmful.) Finally, in 1971, Bergin reanalyzed the original Eysenck data. By eliminating the cases in which individuals left therapy (which Eysenck counted as failure), he found psychoanalytical success in 65% of the cases. Bergin (1971) also reviewed a cross section of 52 outcome studies, which he cross-tabulated in terms of results, and found 22 with positive results, 15 with negative results, and 15 in doubt. He concluded that psychotherapy, on the average, has moderately positive outcomes.

Other recent findings are of note: Meltzoff and Kornreich (1970), who selected their studies on the basis of methodological adequacy (and whose patients were not severely disturbed), found that 80% of the studies had positive results and only 20% had negative or null results. They also found a positive relationship between the research quality and the findings: The better research studies showed the better outcomes.

Luborsky *et al.* (1975) did a box score analysis by using 12 criteria of research quality, graded on a five-point scale (adequacy of sample size, tailoring outcome measures to treatment goals, assignment of comparison groups, etc.). Of 33 well-controlled studies, he found that in 20 studies, psychotherapy was better than no-treatment controls, and that in 13 there was no difference.

Parloff, Waskow, and Wolfe (1978), who organized their review according to the type of mental disorder or disabling condition, found that patients treated with psychosocial treatments showed significantly greater improvement in thought, mood, personality, and behavior than untreated patients, and was most effective for anxiety states, fears, and phobias. Moreover, treatment appeared to have certain distinct limitations (e.g., it was not effective for particular populations, like children), and effectiveness was differentially influenced by the type of therapy and the particular therapist.

Smith and Glass (1977) re-reviewed old papers prior to 1970 that specifically showed the ineffectiveness of psychotherapy, and found them to show its effectiveness. But research is not like wine; it doesn't get better with time.

Finally, Smith *et al.* (1980) did meta-analyses of all available controlled studies of any form of therapy, which represented an integrative approach to 475 disparate research formats. (As noted earlier, each study was coded on a number of dimensions, and their principal dependent measure was a standardized score for the size of the effect or ES, to allow comparison across studies.) Because such studies often included more than one outcome measure, the analyses treated each variable as a separate case (i.e., 1,766 effects size measures). In addition, they coded outcome measures in terms of the type of measure, the instrument, and its reactivity (i.e., susceptibility to social desirability). They found that the difference between average scores in groups receiving psychotherapy and the control group was .85 standard deviation units (ES = .85). This could be translated to indicate that the average person who receives psychotherapy is better off than 80% of the persons who do not. In addition, there was some evidence for "no harmful effects." Differences were found across types of therapies, but these were compounded by patient and therapist variables which were not evenly distributed in each therapy. In fact, their ES may actually have been conservative because they included many influences under treatment (e.g., counseling, placebo, etc.). When these were excluded and the data separately analyzed, the ES was .93. (By comparison, the ES for coronary bypass was .80 with respect to the medical care of angina, and .15 with respect to mortality.)

Although the above findings are considered replicable and reliable (that is, the measure gives the same finding over multiple uses, and provides the same results when used by different researchers), its validity is harder to establish (that is, it is not certain that the measure assesses what it is supposed to measure and that it provides data that is generalized). We do know that the therapies, the patients, the objectives of treatment, and the rigors of the studies were diverse, and that the samples were small (an average of 30 patients in each study). Although the authors say that the results are valid because of the size of the aggregate population (25,000), is it correct to say that the hundreds of small, often poorly controlled studies add up to one large valid study?

Nevertheless, it seems that psychotherapy rests on a reasonable empirical base, although the rigor of scientific research in the field is less than satisfactory. Because of the inherent nature of psychotherapy and the nature of the scientific research process (which often do not appear compatible), answers to questions about psychotherapy will require a sequence of integrative steps and the adaptation of several research technologies. Implicit in this statement is an assumption that psychotherapy represents a researchable intervention. But the technique of psychotherapy is inextricable from the relation between the patient and the therapist. One is thus obliged to ask: Can the rigor of biological research be applicable to the study of human relationships—the therapeutic relationship often likened to that of child and parent, student and teacher, or even friends or lovers? In short, we need to develop research methods applicable to humanistic sciences.

THE DIAGNOSTIC ISSUE

With the above in mind, one of the pressing needs of the 1980s is to establish a comprehensive diagnostic system which will take into account personal qualities and characteristics of patients as people. In this sense, the DSM-III

(1980) classification is a limited instrument. Essentially, it is research-oriented, marked by exclusionary criteria of at least some of its categories. Research diagnostic criteria require that there be a minimum of false-positive diagnoses in order to obtain a homogeneous sample, and to keep any distortion or dilution of statistical data at the lowest level possible. Clinical practice, in contrast, must insist on a minimum of false-negative diagnoses. Therefore, to meet both research and clinical interests, the five axes of the DSM-III is not comprehensive enough.

Recently, I collected what 100 clinicians said they would consider as important dimensions of a patient in diagnoses and treatment planning. There were more than 50 additional dimensions (axes) suggested. Although they may not all be equally relevant in different patients, it demonstrates the complexity of the problem. As patient variables, they are especially important to a researcher. For clinicians, I had earlier proposed a sixth axis to the DSM-III psychodynamic evaluation (Karasu & Skodol, 1980). Unfortunately, the psychodynamic evaluation has rather informal guidelines which lack clarity and preciseness. Therefore:

1. We need to develop a valid and reliable method that would lend itself to the systematic evaluation of psychodynamic dimensions, such as conflicts, object relations, defenses, and so on. These dimensions are equally relevant for evaluation of therapists, because it is quite likely that what is equally important as what the therapist does is *what the therapist is.*

2. We must stop describing psychotherapies by names of saints or charismatic leaders or by their favorite magical maneuvers, and we must define psychotherapy operationally. This operational approach would be limited to an applied science of psychotherapy, and may not be as applicable to the so-called "art" of psychotherapy. The art of psychotherapy is mainly that of the intricate relationship between the patient and the therapist, who is a caring, empathic, accepting, nonjudgmental, optimistic, reliable individual. The art also includes certain nonspecific elements of psychotherapy—suggestion, persuasion, identification, and also certain magical elements, such as the therapeutic setting, containing symbols of healing like one's reputation, office, and title, as well as the multiplicity of silent influences.

3. Finally, we should practice and study this operationally defined psychotherapy as one of the components of the larger therapeutic repertoire. With the advance of pharmacological agents, treatment of psychiatric disorders have drastically changed, as has the role of psychotherapy. The place of psychotherapy in modern psychiatric practice will have to evolve in interface, for example, with pharmacological agents. In short, we need to conceptualize a finer model for psychotherapy and pharmacotherapy.

One step in this direction is seen in the following findings. At the current time, the results of research and clinical practice with combined treatment suggest the following: Psychotherapy and pharmacotherapy are not competitive or inhibitive, but each has differential effects or loci of outcome (drugs have their major manifestations upon symptom formation and affective distress, whereas psychotherapy more directly influences interpersonal relations and social adjustment); each is activated and sustained on a different time schedule (drugs may take effect sooner and be of short-term duration, while psychotherapy results may not reveal themselves until a later point in time, but last longer); and each may best relate to different disorders or their subtypes (drugs for time-limited and autonomous "state" disorders, psychotherapy for long-lasting "trait" disorders).

This ideally noncompeting, noninhibiting, positive synergism of these two modalities, then, may occur through both simultaneous and sequential interactions. They would work in mutual enhancement via the complementarity of their interdigitating effects—timing, aims, and sites of action. Thus, in clinical practice, symptom removal or relief, reduction of anxiety and depression, improvement in attention and control, correction of perceptual disturbances, and so on could be addressed first with the utilization of pharmacological agents. By thus laying the groundwork for the facilitation of accessibility of the patient, they can serve both as prerequisite and continuing conditions for the establishment of a working relationship and ongoing psychotherapeutic intervention.

Increasing refinement of patient subtypes and the progress in both fields (in psychotherapy, the increased specificity and effectiveness; in pharmacotherapy, the open-ended potentials) will fill the pressing gaps. Thus, in the best of all psychopharmacotherapy worlds having cooperative, additive, or even mutually potentiating relationships, the question for psychotherapy of the 1980s is not simply whether psychotherapy is effective, but what is its role (amid the rising repertory of other therapeutic modalities and combinations) in the treatment of a certain specific disorder, in a given individual, with his or her own unique psycho-social-biological characteristics?

REFERENCES

Allen, K. E., Hart, B., Buell, J. S., Harris, F. R., & Wolf, M. M. Effects of school reinforcement on isolate behavior of a nursery school child. *Child Development*, 1964, *35*, 310.

Bergin, A. E. The evaluation of therapeutic outcomes. In A. E. Bergin & S. L. Garfield (Eds.), *Handbook of psychotherapy and behavior change*. New York: Wiley, 1971.

Denker, P. G. Results of treatment of psychoneuroses by the general practitioners. *New York State Journal of Medicine*, 1946, *46*, 2164.

Diagnostic and statistical manual of mental disorders (3rd ed.). Washington, D.C.: American Psychiatric Association, 1980.

Eysenck, H. J. The effects of psychotherapy: An evaluation. *Journal of Consulting Psychology*, 1952, *16*, 319.

Eysenck, H. J. *The effects of psychotherapy.* New York: International Science Press, 1966.

Hilts, P. J. Federal government putting psychotherapy on the couch. *The Washington Post*, September 14, 1980, p. A1.

Karasu, T. B., & Skodol, A. E. VIth axis for DSM-III: Psychodynamic evaluation. *American Journal of Psychiatry*, 1980, *135*, 607.

Kazdin, A. E. Therapy outcome questions requiring control of credibility and treatment-generated expectancies. *Behavior Therapy*, 1979, *10*, 81.

Landis, C. A statistical evaluation of psychotherapeutic methods. In L. E. Hinsie (Ed.), *Concepts and problems of psychotherapy.* New York: Columbia University Press, 1937.

Luborsky, L., Singer, B., & Luborsky, L. Comparative studies of psychotherapies: Is it true that "everybody has won and all must have prizes"? *Archives of General Psychiatry*, 1975, *32*, 995.

Meltzoff, J., & Kornreich, M. *Research in psychotherapy.* New York, Atherton, 1970.

Parloff, M. B., Waskow, I. E., & Wolfe, B. E. Research on therapist variables in relation to process and outcome. In A. E. Bergin & S. L. Garfield (Eds.), *Handbook of psychotherapy and behavior change: An empirical analysis.* New York: Wiley, 1978.

Smith, M. L., & Glass, G. V. Meta-analysis of psychotherapy outcome studies. *American Psychologist*, 1977, *32*, 752.

Smith, M. L., Glass, G. V., & Miller, T. I. *The benefits of psychotherapy.* Baltimore: Johns Hopkins University Press, 1980.

COMMENTARY

Dr. Robert L. Spitzer[*]*:* I found your comment about the relationship between diagnosis and psychotherapy to be an interesting one. I certainly would agree that in the actual practice of psychotherapy, but probably also in the practice of any treatment modality, one goes beyond diagnosis.

But I would dispute your claim that psychotherapy and the choice of patients are really independent of diagnosis. The easiest way to operationalize that is to think of your colleague who considers himself primarily a psychotherapist, and refer to him a patient with progressive senile dementia or schizophrenia or melancholia, and see how he likes that kind of referral. I think he will probably tell you this patient is inappropriate. I think what you are really doing is saying that once the psychotherapist has made sure he or she is not dealing with a serious axis I disorder, for which psychotherapy is now often not considered the treatment of choice, most psychotherapists now concentrate on personality disorder. I would certainly agree that the DSM-III subdivision of the personality disorders is probably pretty irrele-

*College of Physicians and Surgeons, Columbia University, and New York State Psychiatric Institute.

vant, although the borderline notion is certainly one that is not considered irrelevant by many clinicians.

Dr. Karasu: In case it was misunderstood, I meant that one has to go above and beyond the diagnosis, not instead of diagnosis—that diagnosis is a starting point. But then the psychotherapist has to go above and beyond that, and identify other dimensions as well.

Researchers also have to look at those dimensions and have to somehow operationalize those dimensions if they are to study whether coping mechanisms have anything to do with outcome.

Dr. Spitzer: Byram [Karasu], I wonder if you could say something about the Commission—I gather it is no longer a commission as such, but it is now a task force—and what its goals are, and how you see that fitting into Gerry's [Klerman] proposal? Is your work trying to provide that kind of data that could be then operationalized?

Dr. Karasu: Yes, I did not mention it because Gerry already mentioned it and I didn't want to repeat it. Some of you have seen the initial proposal that you have commented on, and that was considered somewhat overambitious and premature. What we initially thought, though the evidence is not in, is what the profession can do. Can we set up the guidelines for what is the treatment of agoraphobia? If your mother has agoraphobia—well, mother is too ambivalent a subject—if your sister has agoraphobia, what treatment would you recommend? And in doing this, we thought that we could pick the best possible people in the field, the experts, and put them together, and tell them, "Look, tell us how you could treat agoraphobia." But after listening to many experts, including Don Klein, Gerry, Bob [Spitzer], and others, we have modified that and taken a rather modest attitude. Instead of defining any kind of decision-tree model of how one can go about treating agoraphobia, the three panels Gerry mentioned will be writing on issues in relation to treatment of that condition, agoraphobia: biological treatment, psychological treatment, and some integration of it and some critique of it. Maybe PTM-I will be the way that ICD-I was, a somewhat primitive beginning. And we are hoping that generations to come will improve on it and may be more specific than we could be right now.

Dr. Spitzer: Are you saying, then, that the original goal, which was to say "here is the evidence for these treatments being effective, and these treatments not being effective," has been modified, and now it is mainly a presentation of the issues, but no longer giving the profession the evidence supporting different treatments?

Dr. Karasu: No. It is expected that the panels will write about evidence of it as well as recommended treatment for a certain condition. But my initial idea was to create a decision tree model. That, it was found, was somewhat premature.

Dr. Spitzer: So the goal is still to say if there is evidence that something is not effective?

Dr. Karasu: That's right.

Dr. Carl Eisdorfer*: Since I think there is reason to believe that probably not more than 10–15% of the aggregate of all psychotherapy in the United States is performed by doctoral-level professionals, the first question is, what has been the relationship between the two APAs, since we are probably fighting in a rate structure of about 1–2% of the aggregate. And secondly, what, if anything, is being done to look outside of the doctoral level of practice of psychotherapy, not that I would presume that there is anything sacred about the doctoral level, but it is a point of departure?

Dr. Karasu: The two APAs have collaborated, I think, quite well in part I of the Commission's task. The many well-known researchers and clinicians from both APAs have contributed to the publication of *Psychotherapy Research*, and I hope you have seen it, if you've not read it, on the efficacy and methodological issues.

Part II of the Commission's work still incorporates a great deal of the work of both APA members and scientists and clinicians. I know that, let's say, in Gerry's task force there are at least two PhDs as members of the panel, but also a large number of individuals will be consulted, MD or PhD and others.

As far as the non-PhD group is concerned, my personal feeling is that people's degrees, MDs and PhDs, have little to do with their quality as psychotherapists. It happens to be that MDs and PhDs, at least some of them, are trained to be psychotherapists. If you look at some of the studies, including the most sophisticated data analyses, there is a clear difference in the patients, and the variability among the treated patient population is quite different from—larger than—the variability in the untreated patient population, indicating that there is something about the person who is doing the treatment.

If I were to invest my money, it would be to look for the people with therapeutic qualities and train them to be clinicians, train them to be therapists. What advantages I see MDs having in the process is the step 1 of the process, that Bob Spitzer commented on. One has to start with a clear diagnosis.

---

*Albert Einstein College of Medicine and Montefiore Medical Center.

24

The Role of Evidence in the Formulation of Public Policy about Psychotherapy

HERBERT J. SCHLESINGER AND EMILY MUMFORD
University of Colorado School of Medicine

The title for Section V, "Psychotherapy and Public Policy When the Evidence Is Not All In," contains some false implications. One is that public policy about health can only be formed when all the evidence is in. Another is that the problem in formulating policy about psychotherapy is the sad state of uncertainty that haunts it. About the first implication: On issues for which all the evidence is in, there is generally no need for policy. Policies, after all, are arbitrary, sometimes rational, but always rationalizable guides to action that emerge somewhere between principles and regulations. They are intended to provide guidance in the absence of certainty. The second implication is also false. There is ample evidence about the effects, effectiveness, and efficiency of psychotherapy, as we will document.

There are other minor implications which for completeness' sake should be pointed out. One is that if all of the facts were in, they would be concordant and point unequivocally in a single direction—toward a truth that would be indisputable, if not self-evident. A little reflection will show that all of the evidence can never be in. There is always the possibility of obtaining more observations, and the likelihood is that all of the observations will not agree. We are accustomed to drawing scientific conclusions from a preponderance of the observations. Even important legal decisions require not absolute certainty, but only proof beyond a reasonable doubt.

There is also another implication in the title, that public policy in regard to mental health service would be governed by the evidence if only it were available. We are encouraged to excuse the inadequacies of certain public policies since the policy makers were probably doing the best they could in the absence of the missing facts. It is dismaying, however, to observe how often public policy is formed without reference to the evidence and sometimes in spite of the evidence. Forming public policy is a different animal from scientific experimentation or legal process. One does not have to be a cynic to recognize that policy and politics are linked by the common Greek root *polis*, and that policies are made by those in power.

It would put the matter too strongly to say that facts are always irrelevant to the formation of public policy. But as all social and behavioral scientists know, facts may not be recognized as such if they conflict with dominant belief systems, particularly when the beliefs are held by groups or individuals with the political power to influence the formation of policy.

Although political forces rather than evidence may well determine the ultimate place of psychotherapy in our health care delivery system, it might be useful nevertheless to summarize the evidence now in hand and estimate the degree to which it would suffice for policy making if policy making were to rely upon evidence.

We will supply evidence in support of several principles or positions important for making public policy about psychotherapy:

1. Health is indivisible. All physical illnesses have emotional and psychological concomitants, and vice versa. Physical and emotional problems covary in the same persons. It is not possible to offer health care of high quality, except in the most trivial instances, while ignoring this principle.

2. Emotional problems can be presented through physical complaints whereas somatic diseases may first be experienced largely through emotional or mental difficulties. Patients often present distress that is largely emotional in origin to internists and general practitioners.[1] Thus, a great deal of mental health care may be sought and given through the general medical care system without being labeled as such. It is not possible to prevent persons from obtaining some kind of care, though not necessarily appropriate care, for emotional problems. It is possible, however, to prevent mental health care from being so labeled on insurance claims forms.

3. Appropriate mental health care should have a favorable impact on physical health as well as emotional health. Providing explicit mental health services may enhance the benefits of medical services by encouraging cooperation with medical advice, and by reducing inappropriate use of medical services to alleviate emotional distress. One should therefore see a subsequent reduction in the use of medical care services.

What is the evidence in support of these positions?

• During the last 50 years there have been more than 60 surveys of psychiatric morbidity among patients seen in general medical settings. These

---

1. Occasionally mental health practitioners may be the first to see patients whose complaints have largely a somatic origin.

surveys report on observations of over 2 million persons and yield incidence rates ranging from 0.5% to 86%, depending on the methods used and the setting. Responsible estimates are that about 30% of patients in general medical settings have identifiable psychiatric disease (Mumford & Schlesinger, 1978).

• Several studies (Lewis & Shanok, 1977; Huntley, 1963; Cooper, Fry, & Kalton, 1969) have reported that in community populations, mild and moderate psychiatric and psychosocial problems are exceeded only by acute respiratory conditions in accounting for daily morbidity.

• During the past 50 years there have been over 20 studies of the incidence of physical disease in psychiatric patients. These studies include over one-half million patients and report an average incidence of 47% of significant physical illness among psychiatric patients. The death rates among such patients tend also to be higher than for control populations (Mumford & Schlesinger, 1978).

• Consider also the repeated worried public health announcements that the most commonly prescribed drugs are the benzodiazopines and more recently cimetidine. While these medications have specific uses for muscle spasm and as an adjunctive agent in cardiac disease or to treat stomach ulcer, the indications are that they are being used largely for their anxiolytic properties or to soothe irritable bowels. It is an additional indication of the extent to which the patients are recognized by general practitioners as having largely emotionally based complaints for which they are treated palliatively.

What happens when specific mental health services are provided? Do they have any impact on persons' general health and utilization of other health care services?

• A meta-analysis of 475 controlled studies of psychotherapy found that the average person treated with psychotherapy surpassed the average control person by approximately .85 standard deviation units across 1,766 outcome variables (Smith, Glass, & Miller, 1980). An analysis of 510 of these outcome indicators with economic including general health implications show differences ranging from .51 to .78 standard deviation units (Schlesinger, Mumford, & Glass, 1980).

• A meta-analysis of 34 studies in which brief psychotherapeutic or educational interventions were used for persons who had recently suffered a heart attack or who were facing surgery showed that these relatively minor interventions produced large effects in terms of speeding recovery, lowering requirements for analgesic and sleeping medication, and shortening hospital stays (Mumford, Schlesinger, & Glass, 1982).

• A review of studies of the effects of psychotherapy on medical utilization showed that the average effect was a reduction in medical utilization between 0% and 20% (Schlesinger *et al.*, 1980; Jones & Vischi, 1979).

• Most of these studies are vulnerable to the challenge that they capitalized on regression effects. Our study of users of mental health and medical services insured by the Blue Cross/Blue Shield Federal Employees Program was designed to minimize regression effects. It dealt with quite sick people whose ages ranged from childhood through elderly. We showed that persons who began outpatient psychotherapy consisting of at least seven visits following the diagnosis of one of four chronic diseases[2] used 66% less medical services during the third year after the diagnosis than a group with the same diseases who did not have psychotherapy. This last finding also implies a dose–response relationship for psychotherapy. The savings in medical utilization following psychotherapy came largely from savings in hospital costs. Persons having outpatient psychotherapy subsequently had fewer hospital admissions and shorter hospital stays. They did not tend to have lower outpatient medical expenditures, implying that they did not substitute mental health visits for medical visits (Schlesinger, Mumford, Glass, Patrick, & Sharfstein, 1983).

The cumulative effect of reviews of the psychiatric and medical morbidity survey literature, the psychotherapy outcome study literature, and cost-offset studies of patients in health maintenance organizations and in fee-for-service practices is that there is ample evidence that (1) psychotherapy in general is effective as a treatment for the conditions for which it is usually undertaken, though evidence on specificity of effects is badly needed. (2) Psychotherapy significantly affects physiological and medical indicators. When used adjunctively for patients with acute or chronic physical diseases, recovery is speeded and costs are reduced. Several mechanisms of effect could be invoked as explanations including improved life-styles, assuming greater responsibility for maintaining one's health, enhanced feelings of hope, and increased self-efficacy. (3) Psychotherapy also can be cost-effective by reducing inappropriate and possibly dangerous use of medical services. (4) Psychotherapy belongs within the health care system.

To return to the issue posed for this section, it is clearly not a matter of how to formulate public policy in the absence of evidence. Rather we should question why the ample evidence that is available is not used for the formation of public policy. This question must be explored from psychological, sociological, and political perspectives. At this point, it is only possible to rule out the assumption that it is a matter of missing evidence.

ACKNOWLEDGMENTS

This work was supported by the National Institute of Mental Health under Grant MH 35194, by the John T. and Catherine D. MacArthur Foundation, and by the Fund for Psychoanalytic Research.

2. Airflow limitation disease, diabetes, ischemic heart disease, or hypertensive heart disease.

REFERENCES

Cooper, B., Fry, J., & Kalton, G. A longitudinal study of psychiatric morbidity in a general practice population. *British Journal of Preventive and Social Medicine*, 1969, *23*(4),

Huntley, R. R. Epidemiology of family practice. *Journal of the American Medical Association*, 1963, *185*(3), 175–178.

Jones, K., & Vischi, T. Impact of alcohol, drug abuse and mental health treatment on medical care utilization: A review of the literature. *Medical Care Supplement*, 1979, *17*, ii–82.

Lewis, D. O., & Shanok, S. S. Medical histories of delinquent and nondelinquent children: An epidemiological study. *American Journal of Psychiatry*, 1977, *134*(9), 1020–1025.

Mumford, E., & Schlesinger, H. J. *A critical review and indexed bibliography of the literature up to 1978 on the effects of psychotherapy on medical utilization*. Report to the National Institute of Mental Health under contract No. 278-77-0049(MH), 1978.

Mumford, E., Schlesinger, H. J., & Glass, G. V. The effects of psychological intervention on recovery from surgery and heart attack: An analysis of the literature. *American Journal of Public Health*, 1982, *72*, 141–151.

Schlesinger, H. J., Mumford, E., & Glass, G. V. Mental health services and medical utilization. In G. VandenBos (Ed.), *Psychotherapy practice, research, policy*. Beverly Hills: Sage, 1980.

Schlesinger, H. J., Mumford, E., Glass, G. V., Patrick, C., & Sharfstein, S. Mental health treatment and medical care utilization in a fee-for-service system: Outpatient mental health treatment following the onset of a chronic disease. *American Journal of Public Health*, 1983, *73*, 422–429.

Smith, M. L., Glass, G. V., & Miller, T. I. *The benefits of psychotherapy*. Baltimore: Johns Hopkins University Press, 1980.

COMMENTARY

Dr. Joseph Zubin*: Let me make one or two comments about Gerry's [Klerman] review of the different kinds of technical advances. We always tend to forget that the first controlled experiment in psychiatry was about 1931 on the focal infection theory, done at the Psychiatric Institute where Henry Carter's focal infection theory said that all mental disorders are due to some kind of foci of infection. As a result, he went in and took out all adenoids and tonsils, and made many a colon into a semicolon, hoping that that way he would reduce the mental disorders in the country. The experiment, of course, pointed out that there was no difference in outcome, only a difference in mortality rate. The operative group died more often.

The thing I wanted to call to your attention was that the American Psychopathological Association has been a rather sensitive index of the market with regard to a variety of psychopathological situations. For example, we were the first to pick up on psychosexual development when it

*University of Pittsburgh School of Medicine.

was still unknown in this country in terms of evaluation. We did the same thing with depression, the same thing with schizophrenia, and the same thing with diagnosis. You can go over the history of the symposia and see that we tend to pick up the thing before it becomes very popular, and then follow it through over the course of the years.

If you do this with the evaluation of psychotherapy, we started out in 1944, during the War, with the first one on evaluation of personality disorders; that one was edited by Bernie Glueck. Then came the Paul Hoch *Study of Failures in Psychiatric Treatment.* And then came the *Evaluation of Psychiatric Treatment* which Hoch and I edited. Then came the Spitzer and Klein *Evaluation of Psychological Therapies.* And now, finally, we have today this meeting.

It turns out that between the first and the second was a 5-year interval; from the second to the third was a 15-year interval; the next was a 12-year interval; the next was a 9-year interval. And I predict if this sequence goes on, there will be 6 years before we have another one, and then 3 years after that we will solve the problem. (*Applause.*)

Dr. Harold I. Lief*: I guess the comment and the question I have should be addressed to Dr. Schlesinger and to a certain extent to Dr. Kiesler. A recent study that was reported by Sharfstein at a meeting of the American College of Psychiatrists a few weeks ago showed that medical utilization goes up sixfold in the year following marital separation. It occurred to me that here is a neat project for research. If we can demonstrate with controlled studies that marital therapy might be effective in salvaging some marriages, one could then compare the medical utilization following separation to that in which separation did not occur. Or, indeed, even failures of marital therapy would provide such data.

But we have the issue of reimbursability, and this is what Dr. Kiesler mentioned. He indicated that our third-party carriers regard this as life enrichment rather than as effective medical therapy. So the whole issue of whether we can conduct appropriate preventive medicine without such reimbursability is the issue. I would like to have both Dr. Schlesinger and Dr. Kiesler comment on that.

Dr. Schlesinger: There has been fairly good documentation that after certain kinds of life crises medical utilization will rise sharply, probably as a function of distress which manifests itself in somatic terms. Bereavement, witnessing an accident, and marital separation are often given as the prototypes for this kind of thing. There has been only a small amount of research done on the topic. One that I know of in Boston has not so far found a preventive effect—that's Simon Budman's work. But I would guess that there is an effect, and good research would find it. And it probably is preventive, but I can't tell you more than my convictions at the moment.

*University of Pennsylvania School of Medicine.

Dr. Gerald L. Klerman*: I think that is a very powerful strategy. Mention was made of the Boston study. Simon Budman is at the Harvard Community Health Plan, and has actually done a randomized trial of a group of people enrolled in that HMO undergoing marital separation, and compared group treatment with a matched control group. The group treated with group therapy reported that they felt better and less distressed. However, they could not, in that particular study, detect an impact on utilization.

That is one study. Myrna Weissman and I are participating with that group in doing a randomized trial of a version of IPT, with offset as one of the outcomes in a group of patients. So I think that particular type of strategy, of picking up people in an HMO with definable circumstances, is an area of great productivity. And I would not be discouraged that one particular trial did not pick up an offset.

Dr. Charles A. Kiesler†: I think also one should add that this research should be encouraged, but there are issues regarding the site of delivery—for example, HMO versus private practice. Also, there is a regional effect in the degree to which these kinds of crises vary. There are many fewer divorces in Pittsburgh than in New York City or Boston, for example. So you would want to see this replicated around the country under different circumstances.

Dr. Carl Eisdorfer§: I think they just leave Pittsburgh to get divorced.

Dr. Mumford: One of the things that might be noted about the Budman study, as I understand it, is that those extra services were truly extra services provided in a context where there was rather generous provision of mental health services generally. I think one of the disadvantages of some of the studies of the cost-offset effects has been that they have been provided in areas where there is already rich provision of services.

I think it is at least possible that if marital therapy or some kind of services had been provided in a setting where there were not already other things that were being offered, and used by those same people, there might have been cost-offset effects.

Dr. Eisdorfer: That is an interesting observation.

Dr. Donald F. Klein‡: I wanted to ask a question of Herb Schlesinger. The idea that providing some human contacts to people in physical distress may be a real help to them in smoothing out their medical course has tremendous face validity; it makes sense. I wonder, though, if in your meta-analysis you address the question of the experience of the therapy provider,

*Harvard Medical School, Harvard School of Public Health, and Massachusetts General Hospital.

†Carnegie–Mellon University.

§Albert Einstein College of Medicine and Montefiore Medical Center.

‡New York State Psychiatric Institute and College of Physicians and Surgeons, Columbia University.

as to whether that affected the effect size? And one of the things that came out of the Smith and Glass meta-analysis, of course, which has been sort of a bone in everybody's throat, is that experience didn't matter. Here, too, one wonders whether what you are reporting is due to some sort of formal psychotherapy with some sort of technical armamentarium, or simply human contact.

Dr. Schlesinger: I wouldn't minimize the importance of human contact. I would hate to be replaced by a computer. I feel a little bit better being replaced by another human being. But to speak to the Smith and Glass analysis, this finding is not a function of the data so much as the quality of the research. That is, the lack of findings that experience matters is not an empirical question yet; it is a methodological issue. Most of these studies were done with very restricted experience ranges. The comparisons were between first- and third-year graduate students, not the kinds of range of experience you would find widely in the field. So the lack of findings is a function of restriction of range. That goes for experience and age, and of course it has to do also with the restriction in the kinds of patients we are treating.

In our own work, the meta-analysis of 34 studies of psychotherapeutic or psychoeducational or psychological interventions in hospitals, we have the capacity to compare who did it. Some of these were done by nurses, some by MDs, some by psychologists, and some by others. We also have the capacity to distinguish those that were done by tape recorders and video cassettes and those done with personal contact.

There are not really enough studies to fractionate that well. Even with 475 studies, Glass found that the sample sizes for homogeneous interventions were not large enough to do that kind of analysis with any precision.

We do find that educational interventions are effective; that is, emotionally based interventions are effective and the two are additive. Those providing both have results better than either alone.

Dr. Klein: I just happened to be reading Lewis Thomas's autobiography in which he has a discussion of that particular question, along with a tribute to nursing, that in his experience as a doctor in complex medical settings, it has been the nurses who have by and large filled the role of keeping the patients' morale up, and making the patients feel looked after. So I think that your study is extremely interesting, but what training you need to provide that sort of help is open to question.

Dr. Schlesinger: Well, doctors have long since given up treatment in favor of letting nurses do it. And nurses are about to give it up so that the aides can do it while they go back to their papers. I don't think it is a question of who ought to be doing the treatment itself.

Our problem here is how to develop new knowledge and the innovative techniques. And that is why I would like these things to remain in the hands of doctoral scientists of whatever persuasion, so that we can carry the field forward, and not settle for the current inadequate level of the art.

Dr. R. Bruce Sloane*: If the average physician's hour in this country costs $120, and probably in Beverly Hills it is a bit more, can you really overlook this in the cost of provision and in the selection? You do not get an hour of a physician's attention unless you can pay for it in some way. And you do not get long treatment unless you can pay for it. And whatever the therapy is, it does lead to a dependency relationship. If you set off to have a time-limited psychotherapy, you may be thwarted. For example, I entered a contract with a patient for 4 months, or 20 interviews, whichever came first, and then we would reconsider. Just before the four months she seriously overdosed. Now, I could say that that is none of my business, which was said earlier in this conference, but it is my business. I have to get up in the middle of the night and I have to go, and I can't easily stop that treatment. So I am costly. And I ask the question, how does one expect to do this?

I mention this because clearly nurses are much underutilized. We may feel that Marks's idea of the behavioral nurse therapist is a crazy British idea, but nurses have the ethos of life and death and yet there are relatively few nurse therapists. So I would say that for my money, the doctor is expensive, whoever she or he is or in whatever discipline.

Dr. James F. Barrett†: There is an area in which psychotherapy is very effective in reducing morbidity in some of the chronic medical diseases, like reducing the effect on families of a depression, and there are some people who probably do it very well. We need to learn from them and to get a little bit away from the discipline approach and back to what sort of interventions by people who have what sorts of skills and in what sorts of patients are helpful. And I guess we are now throwing in a much broader network of outcome indicators which have a lot to do with how people live their lives, as well as the expense of the treatment.

---

*University of Southern California School of Medicine.
†Dartmouth Medical School.

General Discussion

Dr. Joseph Wortis*: Here is a story that deals with a simple method for screening patients who might be suitable for psychoanalytic treatment. The story says you can do things very simply by constructing a house in which the prospective patient enters and finds himself in a room which has only two exits. One says "you loved your mother" and the other says "you hated your mother." The person moves through the proper exit and finds himself in the second room where, again, two doors are labeled, one "you loved your father," the other "you didn't love your father," et cetera, through a series of rooms, until finally you come into a room which has two exits. One says "income above $30,000" and the other says "income below $30,000." If you go through the door that says "below $30,000," you find yourself in the street.

Now, I think for years I have been hoping for a conference of this sort, and it has been a pure delight to be here. But let me remind this audience that, as Alec Guiness says in the lovely movie "Lovesick," in which he impersonates Freud in the best impersonation I have seen, and I have seen the living Freud, "I only intended this to be an experiment. I never wanted it to be an industry." (*Laughter.*)

It takes very little observation to see that the demand for psychotherapeutic service, particularly psychoanalytic treatment, comes from our middle classes, most of whom regard themselves as more or less neurotic. This creates an enormous demand for a service, which is met by the creation of the so-called profession of psychotherapists, although its numbers have been increased by all sorts of professions. (I even saw a sign not long ago off one of the side streets from Fifth Avenue, "Optometrist; Eyes Examined; Psychotherapy.")

As long as this demand exists, the practicing profession of psychotherapists is interested in only one dimension of the problem, and that is the same dimension that any industry is interested in, the dimension of customer satisfaction. Now I haven't heard any reports on evaluation of customer satisfaction in this area, but I would say this would address itself more to the

*State University of New York at Stony Brook.

393

practical needs of the psychotherapists than any of the other evaluative studies that we have heard.

I have the impression that in spite of the welcome aspects of hardheaded research being brought into this field, I say there is such a thing as hyperscience. Not everything is researchable, and not all research leads to incontrovertible conclusions.

As an editor of a research journal, I can say the amount of incontrovertible proof that you find in most research papers is much less than the authors think. There are always new variables, and there are complexities, and particularly in the field of psychotherapy we are dealing with an inordinately complex field.

We do operate, practically, in our daily lives and in the profession, usually on the basis not of proof but of plausibility. If we didn't, we wouldn't get very far. How many of us would take a vacation if we waited for incontrovertible proof that vacations were good for us?

So in practice we operate on the basis of plausibility. When the proposition is suggested that we research whether or not psychotherapy is good for demoralization, reduced to very simple terms, what we are presuming to research is whether somebody ever feels better by having a good talk.

I propose that some propositions are not even worth researching. The proposition of whether psychotherapy can be beneficial can be reduced to its simplest terms of whether talk is very helpful. And that doesn't need to be researched. It is self-evident that talk can be helpful. If you ask helpful to whom and for what, then you might have a research proposition. But the general proposition that talk can sometimes be helpful does not need to be researched.

I close my lengthy remarks with three quotes. The meeting has been long and this is a dwindling audience, so I shall tell you the source of the quotes after I give you the quotes. Quote 1: "We psychoanalysts can describe the path along which a mind moves when it develops a psychosis, but the force that pushes it along this path is hidden from our view. And that force is biochemical. That is where the future of psychiatry lies."

Quote 2: "The future of psychoanalysis will depend more on its use as a research tool than as a method of therapy."

And quote 3, relating to the miracles at the Grotto of Lourdes: "We cannot compete with Lourdes."

The source of these three quotations is Sigmund Freud. And I would say with regard to these three quotes that I have always remained a staunch Freudian.

Dr. Gerald L. Klerman*: I want to respond to Joe's [Wortis] comments

---

*Harvard Medical School, Harvard School of Public Health, and Massachusetts General Hospital.

about Freud and the industry, because I think here is where there are important policy issues. It is exactly because psychotherapy has become an industry that it is increasingly a matter of public policy, and it is because the demand for expenditures has increased faster than other segments of health costs, although psychotherapy is still less than 5%, or even 2%, of the total health dollar. However, the issue of the industry and Freud is as follows: The data that come out of the cost-offset studies that have been reported today indicate that it doesn't take a great deal of long-term therapy in the hands of highly trained people to produce a valuable human and economic effect. Therefore, that kind of evidence is of relatively little value to the highly expensive, highly trained psychoanalysts in their efforts to be covered under national health insurance.

So the group that is most threatened by this kind of discussion are those people, often Freudian, who are most invested in long-term psychotherapy. Now, that is not a trivial group for the following reason. The evidence I have seen from Washington, D.C., is that 90% of the dollar expenditures are accounted for by 10% of the recipients. And it doesn't take much mathematics to realize that one patient in analysis three or four times a week is the equivalent of perhaps 50 people with hypertension being seen even twice a week. So if you look at the actual expenditures in certain systems, the group that is receiving very intensive, long-term treatment may be a statistically small group, but they are accounting for a considerable proportion of the dollars. It is the absence of evidence for the efficacy of that treatment that currently leads many policy makers to cap the psychotherapy benefits.

So, as was pointed out by Herb [Schlesinger], policy is being made, and the current trend in the past 2 years as I have seen it is for most of the insurance companies to cut back on their mental health benefits and to cap costs by putting on a 30-visit or $500-per-year limit—and the group that is most threatened by this are your Freudian colleagues in the long-term psychotherapy industry.

Dr. Charles A. Kiesler*: It has come home to me recently how much nonscientific beliefs and feelings and judgments run our scientific enterprise, that people learn certain things without evidence that then determine what we gather evidence about. I am head of a department that has no clinicians in it. I went around and asked people, "Do you think psychotherapy is effective?" Everybody said no, and very clearly. I said, "Do you think smoking causes lung cancer?" and they all said yes, very clearly. Now, the effect size for the relationship between smoking and lung cancer is about one-fifth the effect size of the positive effects of psychotherapy.

Here is a belief system that is scientifically based. Half of it they should know about. I don't know if they should know the evidence on smoking and

*Carnegie–Mellon University.

cancer, but they should be aware of the evidence of psychotherapy. It is a basic psychological question, and they pretend to be psychologists.

But these belief systems are driving what we ask questions about. They define what is a scientific question and what is not. They define what should be known and what we should aspire to know. And that should not be allowed to happen.

Dr. Robert L. Spitzer*: It seems to me that it is only Gerry [Klerman] who has really presented a challenge, suggesting that things ought to be done differently from the way they currently are. I wonder if I could sharpen the focus of the discussion and ask the panel to respond to this hypothetical scenario.

Let's say that Gerry decides to abandon all the other things he does, to really concentrate on selling this idea, and he goes around the country and for some reason he is able to convince everybody. Maybe one of the ways he does it is to remind them that it took 10 years to actually operationalize the concept of efficacy of drugs. So people are not quite as frightened. And there really is this commission that decides to implement this policy.

Let's say the commission gets together and they realize they have this thorny issue of specificity, and let's say they get Don Klein to give some of his wisdom. And let's say Don convinces them that what really has to be demonstrated is not just general effectiveness, but specificity in terms of demonstrable evidence that the treatment for a particular disorder has effects beyond a creditable placebo.

So they decide that all this meta-analysis is very interesting, but when you really look at studies, there is only that collaborative study of psychotherapy, the results of which just came in, which had a really good design, because there was a placebo group there. And maybe it shows that cognitive therapy has that little advantage.

So cognitive therapy, they decide, is the one therapy it makes sense to have reimbursement for by a professional. Because the cognitive therapy people say not everybody can do it—that you really have to be a professional. And they decide that there is a lot of evidence for the general efficacy of psychotherapeutic contact, but in terms of public policy, you might as well reimburse only those providers who can have some kind of professional status but who will do it for the lowest dollar. So they investigate the area and they find out there is this profession called "mental health aides," in which you get a little bit of training and you can present yourself in a way that is creditable. You are a mental health aide, and all you get paid, assuming inflation is under control, is $6 per hour. So there is no reason to pay $30 or $50 or $120.

---

*College of Physicians and Surgeons, Columbia University, and New York State Psychiatric Institute.

My question to the panel is how would they feel about that policy being carried out?

Dr. Maurice Dongier*: I would like to add a footnote to what Bob said. If we look outside the United States, there are a few countries in the world where those kinds of problems have been not debated, but solved, or policies have been offered. For instance, there has been coverage of psychotherapy in France for about 30 years. There is a social security system covering medicine in general, including psychotherapy, since 1952 or so. In some of the Canadian provinces there has been 100% coverage of medical care, including psychotherapy and including psychoanalysis in a limited fashion, for about 15 years.

Now what happens in these countries is exactly what Dr. Klerman said earlier—that the only coverage is for psychoanalysis and for psychodynamic psychotherapies or whatever other therapy is carried out by a physician. If you try to get cognitive therapy today in Montreal it is not going to be refunded.

Dr. Klerman: The way the French, the Canadians, and the Germans have handled this problem is on a purely economic basis, independent of efficacy. They just say they will only reimburse MD psychotherapists. Since there are fewer MDs because they are so expensive, that is how they have handled the cost containment problem, and they don't want to be bothered by evidence.

Now in Germany they are coming to question that because there has been a tremendous revival of psychoanalysis there, in part because of the very liberal insurance program. But the German GNP quota going to health is up to about 10%, as in this country and Sweden. So the Germans are getting nervous, and there is talk about a legislative commission to review that. But there are no psychologists covered under German reimbursement, and no social workers.

So, as I say, the way that has been handled is not by going to evidence, but by restricting access. And I don't think that is a very rational or equitable approach to policy. But policy is made, and if people are in the insurance world, whether government or otherwise, their main goal is capping costs and expenditures rather than maximizing efficacy or equity.

My view is that the chips should fall where they may. I am much more optimistic than your scenario. I think that even if you demand Don Klein's criteria, and go in for micro-meta-analysis and demand a control group, I think that there will still be a legitimate place for psychotherapy in the kinds of medical conditions that Herb [Schlesinger] has documented: for short-term treatment of depression and for phobia, but not for schizophrenia, and as far as axis II is concerned, since there is no evidence, I don't know.

*McGill University.

Dr. Herbert J. Schlesinger*: Gerry's proposal makes me very anxious, but being an acrophile of a sort, I would like to rise to that challenge. I like the idea, if it would be coupled with ample research funds and a clear set of directions as to how to go about finding the answers. I would love to be part of a group that would determine what is safe and particularly what is effective.

But I think there would be somewhat broader indications. I am not sure that psychotherapy is not indicated in schizophrenia, for instance. At the very least, many schizophrenics I know need help in staying on their medication, and need some help in resocialization after the primary symptoms are dealt with. So I think there could very well be a role for all kinds of psychosocial interventions in all kinds of conditions. But I would like to see clear specificity for what kinds of conditions, by whom, for what length of time or with what rationale, and I would love to be part of the group that takes that up.

Dr. Kiesler: I share some apprehension about this, but if it could be shown that all mental health problems could be handled by $6-an-hour mental health aides, I would support such a policy. I am not a psychotherapist, though, so that answer is easy to give. I am not losing anything by that.

Dr. Robert Rose†: I think it might be worthwhile just to add that we have, for a long time, berated ourselves for not demonstrating sufficient efficacy and specificity. I think it is important for just a moment to step back and look at the whole issue of health care economics, because one of the things that bedevils the health care economist is the fact that everyone knows that health costs have risen an average of 6–7% more than inflation for the last decade, approaching about 9–10% of the GNP in this country. These major costs, by the way, are attributable primarily to what the economists call "inputs per case," which refers to the number of procedures and tests that are done for any given case of whatever kind of illness.

One major problem that has debeviled rational planning in the area has been the difficulty in showing that those rising inputs per case have contributed significantly to reducing morbidity and mortality. So we do more and more health care procedures without a demonstrable increase in benefit.

Dr. Donald F. Klein§: I am a long-term reader of science fiction, so Bob's scenario really came home to me as an interesting fantasy.

I think the major problem with Gerry's suggestion with regard to public bodies is that the public bodies are going to be dominated by guild interests, and the likelihood that any public body is going to come out and say that there is clear evidence that such-and-such a treatment works and such-and-such a treatment does not work is most unlikely.

*University of Colorado School of Medicine.

†University of Texas Medical Center, Galveston.

§New York State Psychiatric Institute and College of Physicians and Surgeons, Columbia University.

I think Byram's [Karasu] experience already gives a little hint of that. It may be that your initial ideas about having a real psychiatric therapy manual were too premature and too ambitious. I think that was not what turned it off, though. I think what turned it off was that people said, "My goodness, that is going to say you can't do something." It was the idea that it would be used as a way of curbing certain types of practice, and nobody wanted to hear that. I don't believe the American Psychiatric Association or the American Psychological Association is going to come up with any such statement.

A wonderful example, I thought, of guild mentality was a brief I have some investment in. There was a Supreme Court brief that went up with regard to the Boston State Hospital case. There was a flurry of *amicus* briefs, and you could have understood what those *amicus* briefs were going to say just by knowing what the organization was. It went very simply. The American Psychiatric Association said we doctors know what we are doing; leave us alone. The American Psychological Association said there is a lot of evidence that drugs are no good for patients, and the patients need protection against the use of those drugs. And the American College of Neuropsychopharmacology said that more research was needed. (*Laughter.*)

Dr. Leon Eisenberg*: I think it illustrates part of the difficulty we are dealing with. There is an enormous difference between what appears to be the case when a therapy is subjected to trial under scientific conditions by research clinicians and what happens when that same methodology is applied in the field.

The trials, for example, on cimetidine in the treatment of peptic ulcer are convincing and impressive, at least as far as symptom suppression is concerned. It doesn't cure it; it comes back. You have to keep on giving it. There are side effects. Still, compared to the other choices, it seems to be a very good therapy.

From the moment that the drug was released on the general market to the present, there has been a use of cimetidine which, by any reasonable calculation, is something like tenfold greater than the number of peptic ulcers we think exist in the population. It is now being used and being paid for for lots of things that were never indicated. I think that is one kind of difficulty.

The second kind of difficulty is that we don't have any requirement in the assessment of therapy for a population medicine approach. That is, there is often the most surprising discrepancy between what you think ought to be the case from a controlled trial of, let's say, an antibiotic in the treatment of an infectious disease, and the inability to demonstrate that overall in the population there is a detectable effect.

There is, for example, from the time isoniazid and streptomycin were first explored in controlled clinical trials in the early 1950s, convincing evidence that they were very effective in the treatment of tuberculosis. On the other hand, several people have done time-trend analysis, which uses what happened when the rates of morbidity and mortality in tuberculosis, at least in Western countries, were declining before any specific therapy was introduced. And then they looked at the changes afterward. The changes that seemed to be attributable to the medication are relatively small compared to the changes that presumably better nutrition, housing, et cetera, account for.

The problem of translating something that is done under fairly controlled conditions into the vicissitudes of the field is, it seems to me, one of the enormous problems we have to face. I think the real problem is what the hell is evidence? When does evidence make you change your mind? And if I may return to the tradition of Don Klein's speech yesterday, I just want to tell one marvelous story, which you ought to hear if you haven't heard it before.

It is the story of a schlemiel in a little town in Shameshul who was not only a schlemiel, but the son of one, the grandson of one, and the great-grandson of one. Not of wonder-working rabbis, but of schlemiels, as far back as the family line could be traced on both sides. There was no doubt about his status. One day he is sitting in his kitchen buttering a piece of rye bread when the bread falls out of his hands and lands butter side up. Now, that never happens to a schlemiel, and he runs through the streets of Shameshul shouting "I am not a schlemiel, I am not a schlemiel!" And everybody gathers. He tells them the story and they are puzzled, because a schlemiel should indeed have the bread land butter side down. Well, there was a great dilemma. They didn't know what to do, so they went to Don Klein's great-grandfather, who was the rabbi in the town, and he thinks about this puzzling question. He pulls on his curls and his forelock and his beard, and he brings down the holy books, wets his thumb, looks through appropriate pages, considers, consults, and finally he says, with great pleasure, "Schlemiel, you are still a schlemiel. Clearly you buttered the wrong side." (*Laughter.*)

Dr. Klerman: I think Don and the others are absolutely right, that vested interests and guild mentality exist. However, I think that a guild should not think that the rest of the world is stopping making decisions. When the health cost percentage of the GNP hits about 8% in most countries, the bells ring. And the main force now that is calling for change is industry. For example, about half of the price differential in making an American automobile as against a Japanese automobile is about $700, owing to health costs. So that one of the main forces, at least in Massachusetts, that is calling for change in reimbursement of all health costs is the insurance pressure that is coming from the industry, which feels that they are having to pay too much in health benefits.

Their value, as I say, is in capping costs. If the guild wants to go on and say, "Well, we don't do anything," they will, in effect, bear the consequence, because the policy makers—as has been pointed out—don't wait for evidence. They are motivated, in the case of the insurance industry, by a need to cap costs. And they don't care whether it is the surgeon's costs or the psychiatrist's costs. And we are more vulnerable for all sorts of reasons. So I think that the guild mentality is very self-destructive.

Dr. Schlesinger: I think what is impressive here is that we have had a range of research findings from a range of research strategies. And one of the advantages of our work is that it is not a controlled experimental design, not in the laboratory, but a naturalistic data base of what people have actually done with medical care and medical dollars. We are using nonreactive measures. The data are already in, and the kinds of findings we are showing that are concordant with the others really add an enormous degree of credibility, since they don't fall prey to the kinds of criticism that can easily be made of laboratory studies.

Dr. Toksoz Byram Karasu*: The scenario that Bob [Spitzer] played, I think, would accentuate the two-class system of care, which we already have anyway. We have people who are paid $6 an hour right now in our clinics doing psychotherapy and other kinds of therapy for the Bronx population. But I know no Manhattan, Wall Street executive who is suffering from anxiety phobia or depression or marital discomfort who is going to worry about how much he pays, or who is reimbursing it. Rich people, basically those making a couple hundred thousand dollars to a couple of million dollars a year, are not going to worry about the public policy. I am worried that the middle class and upper middle class are going to pay from their own pocket and go to psychiatrists even if they charge $150 an hour.

Dr. Spitzer: What's wrong with that?

Dr. Karasu: What you are talking about, the public policy, is going to affect only the poor and underprivileged, and that most likely is not necessarily bad, but that will be the case.

Dr. Carl Eisdorfer*: Let me just add a point from a somewhat different perspective. I think there are three elements that have only just begun to emerge in this discussion. And one, perhaps, has not yet emerged.

I have to live with health policy every day. I have very highly paid people who make it their business to help me avoid the untoward effects of health policy so that we can deliver health care. It is what I call the transduction of health policy into operation, which may or may not be consistent with health policy, but for those of us in positions like mine, tends to be the difference between survival and not survival. And to paraphrase either Ethel Merman or Joe Lewis, "To survive or not to survive? Survival is better."

---

*Albert Einstein College of Medicine and Montefiore Medical Center.

The second element is that data are important in public policy, but I think the public is more important in public policy, and the public may or may not deal with the data. And, in fact, I think the evidence that Charles [Kiesler] gave, given his sophisticated group at Carnegie–Mellon, and other evidence, is that the public tends, by and large, to ignore data. And sometimes they even have the peculiar effect of convincing those people in legislative and executive positions to change public policy.

The third element is that some of the people who are in positions of making policy ignore both the public and the data. To ignore those three elements is, I think, to fail to really grapple with things like reimbursement. Reimbursement may be designed, for example, to stop something, not to support it. Not because the thing that is to be stopped is necessarily bad or lacking in efficacy or anything else, but merely because, as you point out, it is too expensive.

I think that to assume that a careful, meticulous, scientific statement will in fact affect government policy is to ignore the way government policy in fact gets created. And we have a more than ample data base without meta-studies to convince ourselves of that.

I felt I would be remiss if I didn't remind us of reality. I mean, even in psychotherapy we need to reality-test.

Dr. Joseph Zubin*: I am a little astounded by the cavalier manner in which several of the speakers have dismissed psychotherapy for schizophrenia. I don't know what the evidence is for that. It seems to me that even if etiologically you don't believe that there are psychological, psychosocial, intrapersonal factors involved, certainly in the maintenance of the person in the community there is ample reason why we should pay for psychosocial therapy. Furthermore, you know, there are some people for whom neurotropic drugs are poison. So it seems to me this cavalier way of dismissing it is certainly unwarranted.

Dr. Arthur Auerbach†: I think the goal of Gerry's suggestion is to upgrade the quality of psychotherapy and eliminate inefficient therapies. The problem, as has been pointed out, is the enormous difficulty in establishing incontrovertible evidence of the effectiveness of all the therapies that might be considered. I would suggest to you your same goal can be accomplished by some scheme in which reimbursement would depend on participation in research. If you imagine this in some ideal way, any therapy that wants to be reimbursed can get this if it will participate in a logical research program. Perhaps this organization and other organizations could move a little bit in that direction, thus influencing its own guild rigidities by suggesting pilot studies.

Dr. Eisdorfer: Thank you.

---

*University of Pittsburgh School of Medicine.
†University of Pennsylvania.

Name Index

F

G

Subject Index